T0325097

Traditions of Systems Theory

"*Traditions of Systems Theory: Major Figures and Developments* provides a state-of-the-art survey of the increasingly influential and fascinating field of systems theory. It is a highly useful resource for a wide range of disciplines and contributes significantly to bringing together current trends in the sciences and the humanities."—*Hans-Georg Moeller, University College Cork, Ireland*

The term "systems theory" is used to characterize a set of disparate yet related approaches to fields as varied as information theory, cybernetics, biology, sociology, history, literature, and philosophy. What unites each of these traditions of systems theory is a shared focus on general features of systems and their fundamental importance for diverse areas of life. Yet there are considerable differences among these traditions, and each tradition has developed its own methodologies, journals, and forms of analysis. This book explores this terrain and provides an overview of and guide to the traditions of systems theory in their considerable variety.

The book draws attention to the traditions of systems theory in their historical development, especially as related to the humanities and social sciences, and shows how from these traditions various contemporary developments have ensued. It provides a guide for strains of thought that are key to understanding twentieth-century intellectual life in many areas.

Darrell P. Arnold is director of the Institute for World Languages and Cultures and assistant professor of philosophy at St. Thomas University in Miami Gardens, Florida. He has translated numerous books from German, including C. Mantzavinos's *Naturalistic Hermeneutics* and Matthias Vogel's *Media of Reason*. He writes on nineteenth-century German philosophy, contemporary social theory, as well as technology and globalization, with a focus on how these diverse areas relate to the environmental problematic. Darrell is editor-in-chief of the *Humanities and Technology Review*.

Routledge Studies in Library and Information Science

Traditions of Systems Theory

Major Figures and Contemporary
Developments

Edited by Darrell P. Arnold

Routledge
Taylor & Francis Group

NEW YORK AND LONDON

First published 2014
by Routledge
711 Third Avenue, New York, NY 10017

and by Routledge
2 Park Square, Milton Park, Abingdon, Oxon OX14 4RN

*Routledge is an imprint of the Taylor & Francis Group,
an informa business*

Library of Congress Cataloging-in-Publication Data

Traditions of systems theory : major figures and contemporary developments /
    edited by Darrell P. Arnold.
        pages cm. — (Routledge studies in library and information science ; 11)
    Includes bibliographical references and index.
    1. System theory.   2. Cybernetics.   3. Information theory.   I. Arnold,
Darrell (Darrell P.) editor of compilation.
    Q295.T725   2014
    003—dc23
    2013031058

ISBN: 978-0-415-84389-8 (hbk)
ISBN: 978-0-203-75302-6 (ebk)

Typeset in Sabon
by Apex CoVantage, LLC

Contents

Acknowledgements

I am indebted to St. Thomas University for providing a student employee position for editorial assistance in the final weeks of the manuscript presentation, and especially to Dean Scott Zeman for helping to secure that help. Without the assistance, the final tasks in manuscript preparation would have been considerably more difficult. Special thanks, too then, are due to Seyna Yeakey for taking up those tasks, as well as Saron Tutson for her assistance. I would also like to thank Raphael Sassower, Scott Zeman, Rick Wallach, and Sarah Jacob for reading and commenting on earlier versions of the introduction. The work clearly benefited from their comments. Acknowledgements are also due to Robert Drury King for some early editorial assistance and to Ilan Safit for pointing to one redundancy in the text.

Part I

Early Developments and Their Continued Repercussions

Introduction to Part I
Early Developments and Their Continued Repercussions

Darrell P. Arnold

"Systems theory" characterizes a set of disparate yet related approaches to fields as varied as information theory, cybernetics, biology, sociology, history, literature, and philosophy. North Americans often associate it with (1) the general systems theory first developed by Ludwig von Bertalanffy and work by first- and second-order cyberneticians such as Norbert Wiener and Gregory Bateson, as well as the contemporary extensions of such work into ecology, cognitive science, AI, and disciplines as varying as psychology, literature, and media studies, (2) dynamic systems theory, as developed inter alia by Ilya Prigogine, with various developments into chaos and complexity theory, or (3) the world-systems analysis as expounded preeminently by Immanuel Wallerstein. By contrast, Germans and many other Europeans tend to associate it with (4) the work of Niklas Luhmann and his school of sociology. What unites each of these traditions of systems theory (with the exception of perhaps world-system analysis, which focuses more exclusively on economic and political systems) is a shared focus on general features of various systems and their fundamental importance for diverse areas of life. Yet there are considerable differences among these traditions, and each tradition has developed its own methodologies, journals, and forms of analysis.

This book provides an overview of and guide to the traditions of systems theory in their considerable variety. Part one of the book begins with a discussion of the influences of systems thinking on twentieth century thought. This is followed by an article on the early proponents in information theory, a review of cybernetics, and an overview of the Macy Conferences and their impacts; it then treats a group of the main figures in systems theory and second-order cybernetics in areas as diverse as biology, engineering, and earth science and assesses their continued relevance. Part two subsequently examines developments of systems thinking in sociology in the work of Talcott Parsons and Niklas Luhmann, and Immanuel Wallerstein's world systems analysis. Part three provides an introduction to various current developments and uses of systems thinking, including an analysis of the work of systems theory in literature, a proposal to use systems heuristics in the study of digital culture, an overview of one theory of systems ecology, a discussion of Ilya Prigogine and dynamic systems theory, and an exposition of the history and trends of systems thinking in organizational management. The conclusion is an excursus on Gregory Bateson's thought and the continued relevance of cybernetics. It issues a call to cultivate a systems outlook and to live cybernetics.

Short introductions precede each part of the book, discussing the topic of the respective part and outlining the contributions of the authors who write on that topic. The remainder of this introduction serves this function for part one of the book.

THE CHAPTERS FOR PART 1

Chapter 1 of the book provides a general outline of some main developments in systems theory, with a focus on general systems theory and cybernetics—movements to which most of the thinkers in this volume have some relationship (albeit sometimes a distant one). It highlights some of the early impulses of systems theory and evaluates its mixed results. One main point of Chapter 1—which is borne out in the contributions that follow—is that much of the success of systems theory and cybernetics has been because of their influences on developments that continued without them. Because that influence is very significant and often unacknowledged, the history of systems theory can productively be read as a secret history.[1] Still, attention will also be directed to some of the important developments in still-existent forms of systems theory and cybernetics, also a topic of numerous papers in this volume.

In Chapter 2, "The Persistence of Information Theory," Philipp Schweighauser traces the influence of Shannon's and Weaver's communications model into various domains while especially focusing on its value for literary theory. He provides a succinct analysis of Shannon's and Weaver's respective views on noise and of the cybernetic and systems theoretic critical reception of their views. He notes Shannon's own skepticism about applying his communication model beyond the world of communications, and he compares and contrasts Shannon's and Weaver's views with one another and with the work of latter cybernetics and sociological systems theory. Schweighauser concludes by arguing that the work of Shannon and Weaver is worth returning to precisely because it plays up the concept of noise more than the work of cybernetics and systems theory. While cyberneticists and systems theoreticians do critically incorporate the early work of communication theory in important ways, in the end they do not focus on noise but rather on those elements from the noise that can be systemically reordered. In Schweighauser's concluding assessment, in literary theoretic terms, the difference between a Wienerian and a Shannonian conception of art runs parallel to that between the New Critics's "organic unity" doctrine and Theodor Adorno's reflections on the necessary negativity of art. Schweighauser emphasizes the particular value of the latter and argues it has a tendentially greater critical social function than the generally more conservative system theoretic approaches.

In Chapter 3, "Cybernetics: Thinking Through the Technology," Ranulph Glanville offers a general overview of major developments in cybernetics and a catalogue of basic terms needed to understand it. He also offers a counterargument to some of the dominant views in the field. For one, he argues against the broadly accepted view—in part developed under Ludwig von Bertalanffy's sway—that cybernetics is a part of a broader, more theoretical "systems theory." In Bertalanffy's very influential view: "Cybernetics, as the theory of control mechanisms in technology and nature and founded on the concepts of information and feedback, is but a part of a general theory of systems; cybernetic systems are a special case, however important, of systems showing self-regulation."[2] Glanville argues that this is wrongheaded and thinks that an analysis of the ideas will show that cybernetics is in fact the more philosophical of the approaches, and systems theory a rather more applied branch of it. This book does indeed highlight much of the theoretical power of those who identify themselves as cyberneticists, so it offers some support for Glanville's position. Nevertheless, the approach generally taken in this volume is that since systems theory and cybernetics serve more as heuristics than as hard-and-fast research programs, it is in many cases acceptable, as Gordon Pask also thought, to use the terms interchangeably.

Glanville further argues in his chapter that the fundamental characteristic of second-order cybernetics—the inclusion of the observer as part of the system observations—was already existent in first-order cybernetics. Margaret Mead's call for a "cybernetics of cybernetics" entailed precisely such a viewpoint. The trouble was that this perspective was not emphasized, and Wiener's early work set the tone for an understanding of a more technological and less humanistic understanding of cybernetics. While Glanville's careful reading on this point is especially important for a more precise understanding of the history of cybernetics, Glanville, too, still does honor a difference in emphasis between first- and second-order cybernetics. Consequently, in elucidating key terms of cybernetics, he respectively divides his analysis between those concepts dominant in first-order cybernetics (covered in the first part of his chapter) and those dominant in second-order cybernetics (covered in the latter part of the chapter). This chapter—itself written by a key figure in the history of cybernetics—makes important arguments for understanding the history of cybernetics, and it will serve as a helpful reference for a general understanding of some of its basic concepts.

In Chapter 4, "Expanding the Self-Referential Paradox: The Macy Conferences and the Second Wave of Cybernetic Thinking," John Bruni offers an interpretation of how the shift in emphasis in second-order cybernetics gradually occurs in the course of the Macy Conferences and beyond. His article builds on N. Katherine Hayles's view, which he suc-cinctly summarizes, "that the conferences' singular achievement was to create a 'new paradigm' for 'looking at human beings . . . as information-processing entities who are *essentially* similar to intelligent machines,' by routing Claude Shannon's information theory through Warren McCull-och's 'model of neural functioning' and John von Neumann's work in 'biological systems' and then capitalizing on Norbert Wiener's 'vision-ary' talent for disseminating the 'larger implications' of such a paradigm shift."[3] Bruni's argument, however, is that the conferences show this new paradigm only in its "embryonic state." For its development one needs to look at the further work of Norbert Wiener and Heinz von Foerster, as well as at that of members who did not participate in the Macy Confer-ences, such as Humberto Maturana—all of whom emphasize "circular-ity," "reflexivity," and "self-reference." This later work captures the *ethos* of the Macy meetings.

In Chapter 5, "The Hermeneutical System of General Systemology: Bertalanffian and Other Early Contributions to Its Foundations and Development," David Pouvreau provides an introduction to Ludwig von Bertalanffy's general systems theory that shows it to set the groundwork for a systemological hermeneutics. He depicts the perspectivist modalism at work in Bertalanffy and shows how Bertalanffy unites hermeneutical and hypothetical deductive methods, always keenly aware of holism. Pouvreau also evaluates the metaphysical, axiological, and praxeological character of Bertalanffy's work. This very comprehensive overview fully situates Ber-talanffy's thought in reference to his own contemporaries and to impor-tant present work in systemology. Pouvreau concludes that Bertalanffy had implicit elements that were later more clearly developed in critical systems theory, but that theoreticians in that area would still strongly benefit from a renewed look at Bertalanffy's work.

In Chapter 6, "The Ethics of Epistemology: The Work of the Construc-tivist and Cybernetician Heinz von Foerster, From the Vienna Circle to the Cybernetic Circle," Bernhard Pörksen embeds the intellectual biog-raphy of Heinz von Foerster in larger reflections on his constructivism and its implications for von Foerster's ethical perspective. Von Foerster highlights the famous blind spot—that the perceiver inevitably remains blind to the some conditions by which perception constitutes itself—and the selective character of understanding more broadly. Once the inevi-tability of the blind spot is recognized, a certain relativism about one's own views ensues. One may be wrong; one's view is, after all, very lim-ited. This epistemological insight has clear ramifications for ethics, but as Pörksen argues, it does not lead von Foerster to provide a list of moral precepts, but instead to highlight background conditions for ethics—most importantly freedom of choice and the reality of personal responsibility. Among the responsibilities that von Foerster acknowledges is that for the particular blind spots that one has. Yet, unlike Humberto Maturana and Francisco Varela, who increasingly attempt to ground an ethics in the character of Being itself, von Foerster ends with decisionism. We are individuals who have blind spots, who have responsibility for our own blind spots, and who have freedom. But what we are to do in the concrete reality that confronts us remains an utmost personal affair, a matter of individual free choice.

In Chapter 7, "Maturana and Varela: From Autopoiesis to Systems Applications," Bob Mugerauer offers an overview of the work of Humberto Maturana and Francisco Varela. He begins by examining their epistemological and ontological work, which aims to facilitate an understanding of living systems, before discussing certain key ideas in their work more generally and finally contrasting the two thinkers. Maturana and Varela are, of course, best known for introducing a robust version of the idea of autopoiesis; and both retain this throughout their work, although they increasingly move away from the early representationalism that is evident in the work mentioned earlier, "What the Frog's Eye Tells the Frog's Brain," coauthored by Maturana, to views of connectivism and enactivism that have important ramifications for robotics and AI. In Mugerauer's terse formulation, what stands behind it is that "[c]ognition is not a matter of representing a fixed world, but of drawing forth and responding to phenomena through sensorimotor coupling, thereby co-constituting a meaningful world, a world that would not otherwise occur."[4] One key difference between these two thinkers is that while both accept autopoiesis, Varela increasingly moves toward a version paying greater attention to structural couplings. This in part is representative of the increasing sway of Buddhism on his thought. Besides outlining the ideas of both thinkers, Mugerauer underlines their interactions with and influence on and from various areas—evolutionary theory, immunology, and phenomenology, among others. Mugerauer's depiction of the ethical views of Maturana and Varela can be instructively read against the earlier chapter by Pörksen that contrasts von Foerster's ethics with that of Maturana. The remarks that Mugerauer and other authors of this volume note—that both thinkers are skeptical of attempts of sociologists like Luhmann to extend the ideas of autopoiesis into the area of social theory—are necessary for understanding one of the major arguments among contemporary systems theoreticians.

Chapter 8, "Eugene Odum and the Homeostatic Ecosystem: The Resilience of an Idea," is something of an outlier for this book, but an important one given the strong use of systems theory in certain strands of environmental philosophy. The work of Eugene Odum, along with that of his brother, Howard, was fundamental for developments of ecosystems biology. Approaches affected by this work include those like Peter Finke's variety of cultural ecology—outlined in the third part of the book, titled "Evolutionary Cultural Ecology"—as well as work from thinkers such as Fritjof Capra and Donella Meadows.[5] Indeed, something of the later spirit of Odum informs much of the contemporary discussion of sustainability. Eugene Odum situates humans fully in the biological world, accentuating the reciprocal relationships between the human cultural world and other parts of the natural world. In this chapter, Joel Hagen discusses Odum's cybernetic ecosystems model, highlighting the problematic homeostatic concept at the heart of it while fleshing out the conflicts within the earth sciences that ensued between the proponents of such a cybernetic model and more standard Darwinian biologists. Odum was significant in advancing the earth sciences and is important, besides that, for forging links to the broader environmental movement. However, in Hagen's view, Odum made the mistake of not taking his scientific challengers seriously enough. This may of course be a telling moral for some ecosystems thinking today, which is often—perhaps not incorrectly— criticized for having hardened into a form of dogmatism when it might rather benefit from a greater dose of the fallibilist spirit of science. Hagen concludes his chapter by looking at some contemporary attempts that employ the concept of homeostasis but that attempt to avoid Odum's difficulties.

NOTES

1. This idea comes from a conversation with Rick Wallach, the secretary of the Cormac McCarthy Society. While at our favorite North Miami café, the Luna Star, he suggested that work on cybernetics was for the 1950s what Greil Marcus's *Lipstick Traces* was for the latter part of the century; the subtitle of Marcus's great book is, of course, "A Secret History of the Twentieth Century." His book is a whirlwind tour of the cultural history of the twentieth century, from Dada and Surrealism to Punk and Pop Art. It certainly does depict *a* secret history (emphasis on the singular). See Greil Marcus, *Lipstick Traces: A Secret History of the Twentieth Century* (Cambridge, MA: Harvard University Press, 1989). Cybernetics and general systems theory of the midcentury, as should become clear here, are others that are in no way less significant, having a considerable hidden effect on developments in environmental ecology, as well as in cognitive science and robotics. This is not to suggest that they were the only influences but that they have been ones that were vital and not widely enough recognized.
2. Ludwig von Bertalanffy, *General System Theory: Foundations, Development, Applications* (New York: George Braziller, 1969), 17.
3. See p. 78 in this volume.
4. See p. 162 in this volume.
5. See Fritjof Capra, *The Web of Life* (New York: Anchor, 1996); see Donella H. Meadows, *Thinking in Systems: A Primer*, ed. Diana Wright (White River Junction, VT: Chelsea Green, 2008).

REFERENCES

Bertalanffy, Ludwig von. *General System Theory: Foundations, Development, Applications.* New York: George Braziller, 1969.
Capra, Fritjof. *The Web of Life.* New York: Anchor, 1996.
Meadows, Donella H. *Thinking in Systems: A Primer.* Edited by Diana Wright. White River Junction, VT: Chelsea Green, 2008.

1 Systems Theory—A Secret History of the Twentieth Century

Darrell P. Arnold

SYSTEMS THEORY: A MIXED HISTORY

Early systems thinking had lofty aspirations. It saw itself as a research program that could clarify system isomorphisms and beneficially apply the results across disciplinary lines. Bertalanffy, in particular, explicitly expressed an interest in employing such systemics to unify the sciences. As he saw it, "the domain of general systems theory" was concerned with "general aspects, correspondences and isomorphism common to 'systems.'"[1] The knowledge gained from systemic morphology would lead to the unification of science, but not through a reductionist program modeled on physics, as the famous program of Rudolf Carnap and the Vienna circle had attempted.[2] Rather, it would respect differing disciplinary approaches, but highlight the "dynamic interaction" among all areas of reality and the ways in which the varying disciplines were integrated into one megasystem.[3] Though Norbert Wiener, Ross Ashby, and other cyberneticists were more modest regarding aspirations to unify science than Bertalanffy, they clearly enough viewed their variations of communication theory as facilitating the bridging of disciplines, and they consequently applied communication theory to systems—whether natural or social, organic or inorganic. Thus there appeared a hope of linking biology, chemistry, and physics, as well as the social sciences, in a manner admitting greater control over nature.[4]

There were mixed successes in systemic morphology. In general a system was viewed as "a unity or wholeness of some sort that hold [*sic*] its parts together"[5] Such formulations were expounded by many mid-twentieth-century systemists. As Igor V. Blauberg, et al., sum up: a system was viewed by Ludwig von Bertalanffy as "a set of elements standing in interrelations," by W. Ross Ashby as "any set of variable available on the real machine," by Arthur Hall and Robert Fagen as "a set of objects together with relationships between the objects and between their attributes," and by Sankar Sengupta and Russell Ackoff as "a set of activities (functions) that are connected both in time and space by a set of decision-making and behavior-evaluation (that is control) practice."[6] Systems of course were further specified as subject to feedback loops and blind spots, or later as autopoietic, and in various other ways. Still, given the general character of these descriptions, it might come as no great surprise that various earlier thinkers had similar classification schema. Indeed, many systems thinkers preface their books by pointing out some basic similarities between the systems concepts of the twentieth century and those of Kant, Leibniz, Nicholas of Cusa, and others.[7] A few individuals have also noted an uncanny similarity in the level of sophistication in thought about systems that is found in the work of transcendental post-Kantian philosophers.[8] Still, even granting these similarities to early work, there is no denying that systems thinking of the midcentury was more explicit than the work on systems within transcendental philosophy and that it in particular benefited from developments in communication theory.

For all that, though, it did not live up to the aspirations.[9] Systems do not fit as neatly together into a megasystem as Bertalanffy had hoped, and the metaphysical orientations of some versions have proven rather more speculative than scientific.[10] Further, in the end, it also lost out in the fight for public monies, so has hardly continued as a viable research program in the sense of Imre Lakatos.[11] Outside of a pocket of sociological systems theory vital in Europe, still under the sway of Luhmann's students, explicit forms of systems theory today survive more as heuristic approaches to problems than as a full-blown research program. As Raphael Sassower and Nimrod Bar-Am (Chapter 13) note in this volume, such systems heuristics tend to help individuals avoid reductionism and to theoretically maneuver through complex, changing, and interlinked contexts.

Despite that, recent research has highlighted several reasons that mid-twentieth-century systems theory and cybernetics are quite interesting.[12] For one, their thoughts on system interdependencies spurred on ecological thought. Further—and in part connected to this—they played a role in leveling the fundamental distinctions between humans and other animals, on the one hand, and the organic and the inorganic, on the other.[13] Finally, they are interesting given the contours that their observations take on against—and also often in synergetically promoting—a constructivist or constructivist-pragmatist epistemology. These developments lead in numerous directions, about which only some general and simplifying statements can be made here.

The system holism, evident, for example, in the work of Ludwig von Bertalanffy and Gregory Bateson—and connected as this often was with the leveling of the fundamental distinctions between the human and the animal and even between the organic and the inorganic—fostered theoretical reflections on the interrelations between varying systems in the natural world. This influenced the ecology movement, one part of the veiled history being described here. Bateson's own thought on this ends in a mental monism. He and similarly minded systems thinkers emphasize the need for humans to understand themselves as part of an interlinked chain of systems—from cells to individual organisms, to ecosystems, bioregions, geosystems, and so on, and they point to the need for system sustainability. Fritjof Capra is one well-known contemporary figure representing this school of thought. But others include ecological economists and deep ecologists, influenced, for example, by Kenneth Boulding and Donella Meadows.[14] In this volume, work by Joel Hagen (Chapter 8), Nora Bateson and Phillip Guddemi (Chapter 17), and Peter Finke (Chapter 14) indicate some of the trajectories that this form of thought has taken or now takes. It assumes various guises, some materialist, others speculative theological or mystical.[15]

A further development especially pushes the boundaries between the organic and the inorganic but with an emphasis on mechanism. This part of the veiled history paves the way for developments in cognitive science and for radical technical developments of the twentieth century in AI, robotics. These often lead in a contrary direction from those of the eco-strand of systems thinking just characterized and even set the tone for transhumanism, as well as for other less fanciful attempts to technologically enhance human biology with bioengineering innovations.[16]

Besides influencing these two main trajectories of contemporary cultural and intellectual life, systems theory and cybernetics have had considerable further impacts.[17] They have helped to establish the groundwork necessary for developments in complexity theory and dynamic systems theory. They have been influential through Parson's and Luhmann's social systems theory and are now being increasingly productively applied to literature, media, and cultural studies. While some contributions to this book highlight various influences that systems theory and cybernetics have had—unveiling part of the secret history—others show ways in which explicit forms of systems theory and cybernetics do continue and may even be undergoing a renewal.

POSTHUMANIST CONSTRUCTIVISM

One recent contribution of literary, media, and cultural theorists has been in emphasizing how many of the ideas of cybernetics and systems theory have supported main tendencies in posthumanist constructivism. This is evident in recent work by N. Catherine Hayles and Cary Wolfe and is taken up in this volume by Phillip Schweighauser (Chapter 2), Bernhard Pörksen (Chapter 6), and Andrew McMurry (Chapter 12).[18] It is also evident in the work here on Luhmann by Walter Reese-Schäfer (Chapter 10). In general, there is a tendency in the midcentury movement to decenter the anthropocentric focus on reality. This has effects on both epistemology and ontology. Humans are one system among others, with one way of gaining access to the world among others. This view stands behind the 1959 paper "What the Frog's Eye Tells the Frog's Brain," cowritten by Jerome Lettvin, Humberto Maturana, Warren McCulloch, and Walter Pitts—now a classical work in systems cybernetics. Accepting the view that frogs too are systems—engaged in processes of assimilation with the world around them, processing information, patterning reality as they reproduce themselves—the authors explore the mapping of reality by a frog.[19] This of course builds on Jakob von Uexküll's work, though it might instructively also be read as an attempt to provide something akin to Kant's table of categories for frogs.[20] What makes the experience (of frogs) possible—to turn a Kantian phrase—is a patterning that makes them pretty good at simplifying the noise of the complex world around them in a way that facilitates their catching flies. Their patterning serves their purposes as self-reproducing systems.

Implicitly, of course, it is clear that what is generally true of frogs is also true of flies, or fish—or bats. There is a world out there that such systems must live in, that frogs somehow get at, that flies and fish and bats somehow get at. In fact, humans and frogs, and the rest of the animal kingdom, get at this world by simplifying from the enormous complexity in the environment, patterning for certain limited features useful to the respective system. This view—constructed in part on the basis of early work in communication theory, as Schweighauser (Chapter 2) here highlights—squarely aligns with a certain form of constructivism. We don't get at the world directly or fully but only indirectly and incompletely, within the parameters of a particular system, with all that system's limitations. Further, given the recognition that humans are just one of the kinds of animal systems that do this, this immerses us in a certain sort of posthuman worldview. It is decentering to recognize frogs as akin to ourselves and ourselves as akin to frogs. Indeed, the sensibility that this break in the boundaries between the animal and the human world signifies that it is vitally important not only to constructivism but also to one of the main areas of thought influenced by systems thinking—the ecology movement.

CONSTRUCTING SYSTEMS TECHNOLOGIES

But more radical still: the looming question—long answered in the positive by the writing of the previous essay by many cyberneticists—was whether machines might be endowed with similar processing potentials. The spirit of systems thinking and cybernetics looked for potential system similarities even across organic and inorganic lines. And in doing so, they played a vital role in establishing an intellectual climate and worldview that allowed for the radical transformation of technologies.

The all-pervasively important mechanical object of the seventeenth century was the clock. It was the uniquely ubiquitous technology that was endowed with motion but that lacked the soul that Ancients and Medievals had attributed to all objects with motion, including the stars. Yet the clock did not assimilate from the world outside of itself. It did not stand in an interactive relationship with its environment. This fact influenced the classical descriptions of the distinction between mechanical and organic objects. The inorganic—even those wildly constructed inorganic gadgets that could move, clocks—were not interactive with the world around them. Beyond that, they also had no self-organizing principle, like organic systems, and no abilities to learn.

Early cyberneticists in particular envisioned a world of different kinds of objects, objects that react to the world around them the way only animals once had, objects that might learn or even have some capacity for self-maintenance. Indeed, they envisioned a world much more like the one we now inhabit than like the one they did. And in part because of their groundwork, today we walk through a house and the motion detector switches on the light. We hold our hands under the faucet and the water flows. Such "mechanical" (or more precisely, digital) objects are now routinely programmed with simple on-off switches that filter a kind of information from the environment and then react to it. The lessons of early information theory, incorporated and developed as they were in systems theory and cybernetics, have resulted in a new world. And while we already take these developments for granted, such technologies are radically new in history. Early cyberneticists and systems theorists were among the first envisioning such possibilities and making such devices.[21]

They also envisioned and took steps toward building learning machines, and dreamt of the possibility for self-maintaining ones—and indeed steps in these directions have also been taken in the meantime. While lights and faucets do not yet learn, spell programs in some senses appear to. They can anticipate words based on specific language usage in the past. Chess games, available to anyone with a laptop or an iPhone, also are programed to anticipate moves, to operate according to simple algorithms calculating from possibilities after their opponent's earlier moves. This too looks very much like learning. But what of self-repairing, self-maintaining machines? Simple forms of these also exist now—for example, virus programs that regularly check the computer. How much more complex might the self-maintenance and self-generation become? Many systems theoreticians and cyberneticists were positive enough at least to forego foregone negative conclusions.[22]

FORMS OF CONSTRUCTIVISM

Though the constructivism of much of systems theory and cybernetics has been elaborated—and a connection has been made to how this informed some of their engineering projects—a further element of this constructivism is worth pointing out. For systems theory and cybernetics are interesting in reference to constructivist epistemology especially because the proponents of these views were not naysayers of science but rather biologists, engineers, and mathematicians, often very enamored with technologies. This has lent certain forms of system-theoretic constructivist epistemology a unique character—for they have often focused not only on the *social* elements that shape and limit our worldviews but also on the biological ones. Some of these forms of constructivism—evident, for example, in the work of Humberto Maturana and Francisco Varela—emphasize, first, our embodiment, and, second, our sociality. The question of what the frog's eyes tell the frog's brain is closely tied to the question of what the human's eyes tell the human's brain, and what a robot's eyes might be able to tell a robot's brain—first of all with an emphasis on physicality. This is true even though, as Robert Mugerauer (Chapter 7) here shows, the representational epistemology of the early cyberneticists is transformed under the later work of Maturana and Varela progressively into forms of connectivism and enactivism. Still, it is in the context of examining embodiment that many systems theoreticians begin to explore the effect of social constraints.

Of course, there is not one school of systems theory. Nor is there one school of systems-theoretic constructivism. Luhmann's approach, for example, is focused not on our physical embodiment but on the constraints of the respective social system that we work within. It is not entirely a stretch to state that he takes the lesson of "what a frog's eye tells a frog's brain"—the implicit autopoietic view already in the work—and applies it to the economy, law, and the various other social systems. Metaphorically, the questions become: "What does the economist's eye tell the economist's brain?" "What does the lawyer's eye tell the lawyer's brain?" and so on. Frogs may have eyes and brains and physiognomies generally good for catching flies. For their part, economists come to see the world through codes of the economic system, and view trees not as potential refuges for rapidly depleting species but as potential plywood or a possible neighborhood asset for housing developments that can make investors money. And lawyers—at least *qua* lawyers—really are interested in doing more than making money, and operate on the code of the legal and the illegal. Though this is a bit of a loose metaphor, it is not too far afield from what is going on in Luhmann's controversial project, though Luhmann rejects the humanist orientation that might highlight "economists" and "lawyers," or their brains—which might lead to studies more neuroscientific—and he speaks of posthuman economic and legal *systems* instead.

One more point should be made about another form of cybernetic and systems-theoretic constructivism—namely that it is often pragmatic in orientation, or Buddhist instrumentalist. Many of the thinkers outlined here emphasize that ideas are tools that arise out of pragmatic needs for getting around in the world and in fact view practice as serving as the ultimate feedback on the value of the theory. All of this, of course, has great similarities to the ideas of Peirce's "The Fixation of Belief,"[23] or can be seen as embodying the spirit of Karl Popper's critical rationalism.[24] Many cyberneticians, like classical pragmatists and critical rationalists, view our ideas as provisional, limited, subject to the feedback of trial and error. In particular, in this volume, Phillip Guddemi (Chapter 17) mentions such connections to pragmatism, while Ranulph Glanville (Chapter 3) and David Pourveau (Chapter 5) underline them. Raphael Sassower and Nimrod Bar-Am (Chapter 13), for their part, as well as Hagen (Chapter 8), are clear in calls to maintain the spirit of critical rationalism—or if I may, Peircean pragmatism—in system heuristics. While these pragmatic inclinations are important to highlight, Nora Bateson (Chapter 17) does sound a word of caution about the identification of Gregory Bateson's cybernetics with pragmatism insofar as pragmatism—at least in everyday language—is often aligned with an overly tight focus on practicality.

Of course, a lesson of this volume is that systems theories do not form a unified front, and Bateson's theory does differ from that of other cyberneticists. Certainly, many other cyberneticists had a narrower focus on practicality than Bateson did. It is not for naught that cybernetics in popular consciousness is probably most often associated with the postwar striving for technical control. The focus on control is even evident in Wiener's earliest book. Yet there have at the same time been strivings within systems theory and cybernetics for another emphasis. Gregory Bateson's own ideas are reflective of this. He in particular emphasizes a vital role for aesthetic appreciation and underlines the need for a way of viewing the world that ultimately does step back from the engineering spirit and the desire for technical control. Bateson's emphasis on an "ecology of ideas"—which can lead to either sustainable or nonsustainable forms of life—is one of the strands of thought most influential on the environmental movement. Here, paradoxically, a pragmatic interest in planetary survival might well require that we overcome a focus merely on narrowly understood practicality and instead cultivate a form of aesthetic appreciation for a world as formed by complex, shifting systems in interaction with one another.[25] This ecosystemic sentiment is one that Bateson shared with Bertalanffy, who, as Debora Hammond (Chapter 16) and David Pouvreau (Chapter 5) here note, takes issue with the "mechanistic worldview" that appears to characterize much of early cybernetics. He speaks of this worldview as finding "its expression in a civilization which glorifies technology that has led eventually to the catastrophes of our time." Bertalanffy continues, expressive of a hope that is shared by the cyberneticist Bateson, and represented in views in this book in the work of Finke (Chapter 14) and Hammond (Chapter 16): "Possibly the model of the world as a great organization can help to reinforce the sense of reverence for the living which we have almost lost in the last sanguinary decades of human history."[26]

SYSTEMS THEORY DIVERSITY

The quite partial story above is of course simplifying. It attempts to outline some overarching characteristics of quite disparate movements. It leaves out important developments, such as those highlighted by Bettina Mahlert (Chapter 9), Walter Goldfrank (Chapter 10), and Dorothea Olkowski (Chapter 11). Multiple conflicts do arise on the issues highlighted here and along numerous fronts. Some of those conflicts will be evident in the following chapters. Here there are articles depicting posthuman variations of systems theory or systems thinking (Schweighauser, Bruni, McMurry, Reese-Schäfer), along with seemingly more humanist versions (Mahlert, Hammond, Goldfrank), full-throated constructivist views (Pörksen, Mugerauer) and more constructivist pragmatic ones (Pouvreau, Glanville, Bateson, and Guddemi), depictions of new technical emergent understandings (Glanville, Sassower, and Bar-Am), along with a presentation of the view that more cautionary enjoyment of technical developments is appropriate in light of our ecological challenges (Finke, Bateson, and Guddemi). Systems theory has had dramatic effects on various areas of life. It has borne fruit in constructivist epistemology, in AI and robotics, and more generally in digital culture, in the ecology movement, and in chaos and complexity theory, and has been carried forward by proponents of humanism, posthumanism, and transhumanism. It has had varied and multifaceted effects and lives on in varied and multifaceted ways—some secret, some not. Many of them are explored in the chapters that follow.

NOTES

1. Ludwig von Bertalanffy, *General System Theory: Foundations, Development, Applications*, rev. ed. (New York: George Braziller, 1969), xix.
2. See Rudolph Carnap, *The Unity of Science* (New York: Routledge, 2011).
3. For Bertalanffy's explicit statements about a hope of unifying science with general systems theory, see *General System Theory*, 48–49; 86–88. Some such desire does live on in the aspirations of some ecosystems thinkers, but it appears to be more as an ideological political or religious program than as a research program with results supported by science. Here the desire is that all sciences engage in sustainable research. Of course, the difficulty is in figuring out what that might be. Both Wiener and Ashby view communications theory as a key to unifying various sciences. Yet as much as it has had to teach these sciences, it has not been unifying in a strict sense.
4. See the Introduction to Norbert Wiener, *Cybernetics: or Control and Communication in the Animal and the Machine*, 2nd ed. (Cambridge, MA: The MIT Press, 1961), 11. Though Ashby described his goal in his 1956 textbook, *An Introduction to Cybernetics*, his intent being to offer "the framework on which all individual machines may be ordered, related and understood" (qtd, in Pickering, 148), he understood machines to include everything from technical gadgets to the human brain to natural material objects. This ordering, relating, and understanding too was to be done by extending communication theory across disciplines. See Ashby's introduction to *An Introduction to Cybernetics*, 3rd ed. (New York: John Wiley, 1956); see also Andrew Pickering, *The Cybernetic Brain: Sketches of Another Future* (Chicago: University of Chicago Press, 2011), 148.
5. See A. Bahm, "Systems Theory: Hocus Pocus or Holistic Science?" *General Systems* 14 (1969): 175; quoted in I.V. Blauberg, V.N. Sadovski, and E.G. Yudin, *Systems Theory: Philosophical and Methodological Problems* (Moscow: Progress Press, 1977), 269.
6. See Blauberg et al., *Systems Theory*, 126.

7. See Stuart Kauffman, *At Home in the Universe* (New York: Oxford University Press, 1995), 69; Ludwig von Bertalanffy, *General System Theory,* 266.

8. Darrell P. Arnold, "Hegel and Ecologically Oriented Systems Theory," *Journal of Philosophy: A Cross-Disciplinary Inquiry* 7, no. 16 (2011), 53–64; see also Helmut Willke, *Symbolische Systeme* (Weilerwist: Velbrück Wissenschaft, 2005), 8. For some application of Hegelian systems theoretic ideas to issues of global governance, see also Willke, "The Tragedy of the State: Prolegomena to a Theory of the State in Polycentric Society," *Archiv für Rechts und Sozialphilosophie* 72, no. 4 (1986): 455–67.

9. McMurry here points out that it might help us to soften the boundaries; see Ch. 15. For an early criticism of systems theory as a theoretical dead end, see Blauberg et al., *Systems Theory,* 195. For a sober recent assessment of the state of system theory, see *Schlüsselwerke der Systemtheorie,* ed. Dirk Baecker (Wiesbaden: VS Verlag, 2005). For some discussion of the loss of financing to cybernetics, see also Glanville, p. 48 in this volume.

10. See Thomas Berry, *The Great Work* (New York: Random House, 1999).

11. Imre Lakatos, "Falsification and the Methodology of Scientific Research Programmes," in *Criticism and the Growth of Knowledge,* eds. Imre Lakotos and Alan Musgrave (Cambridge: Cambridge University Press, 1970).

12. Ludwig von Bertalanffy, for his part, viewed general systems theory—which he argues should include cybernetics and information theory, among others—as less metaphysical than earlier thought on systems, as constituting a collective research agenda, and as aimed at practical results, linked with what he characterized as "systems technology." See Bertalanffy, *General System Theory,* xx.

13. See Cary Wolfe, *What Is Posthumanism?* (Minneapolis: University of Minnesota Press, 2010).

14. For an overview of Kenneth Boulding, see Debora Hammond, *The Science of Synthesis: Exploring the Social Implications of General Systems Theory* (Boulder: University Press of Colorado, 2003). See Donella Meadows et al., *The Limits to Growth,* 30 year update (White River Junction, VT: Chelsea Green, 2004). For a short overview of Boulding's and Guattari's contrasting ideas on economic sustainability, see Darrell Arnold, "Social Ecology and the Critique of Capitalism: Theories of Sustainability in Kenneth Boulding and Felix Guattari," in vol. 14 of *Sustainable Development and Global Community* eds. George E. Lasker and Kensei Hiwaki (Windsor, ON: IIAS, 2013), 21–26.

15. A speculative, very popular theological strand of such thought is found in Thomas Berry.

16. Transhumanists, in particular, explore the possibilities of using bioengineering to enhance human biology, even taking this to extreme forms of imagining the downloading of consciousness onto a computer chip and imagining individuals eventually attaining physical immortality as techno-cyborgs. Cyberneticists did not develop these ideas, however, and many cyberneticists might share Ranulph Glanville's expressed view that he can hardly imagine that even a brain transplant would not result in "lock-in syndrome." See Glanville, p. 66 in this volume; cybernetics did lay the groundwork for developments of transhumanist thought by pushing the boundaries between the organic and the inorganic.

17. Recent literature on Stewart Brand, a systems theorist and a former editor of the popular *Whole Earth Catalogue,* has also emphasized his simultaneous influence in these countervailing directions. See for example Fred Turner, *From Counterculture to Cyberculture: Stewart Brand, the Whole Earth Network, and the Rise of Digital Utopianism* (Chicago: University of Chicago Press, 2006).

18. See C. Katherine Hayles, *How We Became Posthuman* (Chicago: University of Chicago Press, 1999). See Cary Wolfe, *What Is Posthumanism?*
19. Jerome Lettvin, Humberto Maturana, Warren McCulloch, and Walter Pitts, "What the Frog's Eye Tells the Frog's Brain," *Proceedings of the Institute of Radio Engineers,* 47 (1959): 1940–51.
20. See Jakob von Uexküll, *A Foray into the Worlds of Animals and Humans,* trans. Joseph D. O'Neil (Minneapolis: University of Minnesota Press, 2010).
21. See Pickering for an animated account of many such early developments, focusing on the work of British cyberneticists, in particular Grey Walter, Ross Ashby, Gregory Bateson, R. D. Laing, Stafford Beer, and Gordon Pask. Andrew Pickering, *The Cybernetic Brain.*
22. See Wiener, *Cybernetics,* especially chapter IX, "On Learning and Self-Reproducing Machines," 169–80.
23. Charles S. Peirce, "The Fixation of Belief," in *Charles S. Peirce, Selected Writings,* ed. Philip P. Wiener (New York: Dover, 1966), 91–112.
24. See Karl Popper, *Conjectures and Refutations: The Growth of Scientific Knowledge* (New York: Routledge, 1963).
25. For a view that even more radically questions the constructs of systems, see Felix Guattari, *The Three Ecologies,* trans. Ian Pindar and Paul Sutton (New York: Continuum, 2008). See also Arnold, "Social Ecology and the Critique of Capitalism."
26. Bertalanffy, *General System Theory,* 49.

REFERENCES

Arnold, Darrell P. "Hegel and Ecologically Oriented Systems Theory." *Journal of Philosophy: A Cross-Disciplinary Inquiry* 7 (16) (2011): 53–64.
———. "Social Ecology and the Critique of Capitalism: Theories of Sustainability in Kenneth Boulding and Felix Guattari," vol. 14 in *Sustainable Development and Global Community,* edited by George E. Lasker and Kensei Hiwaki, 21–26. Windsor, ON: IIAS, 2013.
Ashby, W. Ross. *An Introduction to Cybernetics.* 3rd ed. New York: John Wiley, 1956.
Bahm, Archie J. "Systems Theory: Hocus Pocus or Holistic Science?" *General Systems* 14 (1969): 175–77.
Dirk Baecker, ed. *Schlüsselwerke der Systemtheorie.* Wiesbaden: VS Verlag, 2005.
Berry, Thomas. *The Great Work.* New York: Random House, 1999.
Blauberg, I. V., V. N. Sadovski, and E. G. Yudin. *Systems Theory: Philosophical and Methodological Problems.* Moscow: Progress Press, 1977.
Bertalanffy, Ludwig von. *General System Theory: Foundations, Development, Applications.* Rev. ed. New York: George Braziller, 1969.
Carnap, Rudolph. *The Unity of Science.* New York: Routledge, 2011.
Guattari, Felix. *The Three Ecologies.* Translated by Ian Pindar and Paul Sutton. New York: Continuum, 2008.
Hammond, Debora. *The Science of Synthesis: Exploring the Social Implications of General Systems Theory.* Boulder: University Press of Colorado, 2003.
Kauffman, Stuart. *At Home in the Universe.* New York: Oxford University Press, 1995.
Lakatos, Imre. "Falsification and the Methodology of Scientific Research Programmes." In *Criticism and the Growth of Knowledge,* edited by Imre Lakatos and Alan Musgrave, 91–196. Cambridge: Cambridge University Press, 1970.
Lettvin, Jerome, Humberto Maturana, Warren McCulloch, and Walter Pitts. "What the Frog's Eye Tells the Frog's Brain." *Proceedings of the Institute of Radio Engineers* 47 (1959): 1940–51.

Marcus, Greil. *Lipstick Traces: A Secret History of the 20th Century.* Cambridge, MA: Harvard University Press, 1989.

Meadows, Donnella, Dennis Meadows, Jorgen Randers, and the Club of Rome. *The Limits to Growth.* 30 year update. White River Junction, VT: Chelsea Green, 2004).

Peirce, Charles S. "The Fixation of Belief." In *Charles S. Peirce, Selected Writings,* edited by Philip P. Wiener, 91–112. New York: Dover, 1966.

Pickering, Andrew. *The Cybernetic Brain: Sketches of Another Future.* Chicago: University of Chicago Press, 2011.

Popper, Karl. *Conjectures and Refutations: The Growth of Scientific Knowledge.* New York: Routledge, 1963.

Turner, Fred. *From Counterculture to Cyberculture: Stewart Brand, the Whole Earth Network, and the Rise of Digital Utopianism.* Chicago: University of Chicago Press, 2006.

Wiener, Norbert. *Cybernetics: or Control and Communication in the Animal and the Machine.* 2nd ed. Cambridge, MA: The MIT Press, 1961.

Willke, Helmut. *Symbolische Systeme.* Weilerwist: Velbrueck Wissenschaft, 2005.

———. "The Tragedy of the State: Prolegomena to a Theory of the State in Polycentric Society." *Archiv für Rechts-und Sozialphilosophie* 72 (4) (1986): 455–67.

Wolfe, Cary. *What Is Posthumanism?* Minneapolis: University of Minnesota Press, 2010.

2 The Persistence of Information Theory

Philipp Schweighauser

INTRODUCTION

When Claude E. Shannon published "A Mathematical Theory of Communication" in 1948, he could not foresee what enormous impact his findings would have on a wide variety of fields, including engineering, physics, genetics, cryptology, computer science, statistics, economics, psychology, linguistics, philosophy, and aesthetics.[1] Indeed, when he learned of the scope of that impact, he was somewhat less than enthusiastic, warning his readers in "The Bandwagon" that, while "many of the concepts of information theory will prove useful in these other fields, [. . .] the establishing of such applications is not a trivial matter of translating words to a new domain, but rather the slow tedious process of hypothesis and experimental verification."[2] For the author of this essay as well as fellow contributors from the humanities and social sciences, Shannon's caveat has special pertinence. This is so because we get our understanding of information theory less from the highly technical "A Mathematical Theory of Communication" than from Warren Weaver's "Recent Contributions to the Mathematical Theory of Communication" (1949), the now canonical popularization of Shannonian information theory, which was published alongside Shannon's original essay (now renamed "The Mathematical Theory of Communication") in *The Mathematical Theory of Communication* (1949).[3]

Why begin this first essay in a volume entitled *Traditions of Systems Theory* on such a cautionary note? For one, because the strictly technical context in which Shannon developed his theorems impacts their translatability to other fields. Most significantly, it is at least questionable whether his transmission model of machine communication is adequate to describe processes of information exchange taking place within biological and social systems. Accordingly, while Shannonian information theory remains an important touchstone for much contemporary media theory and systems-theoretic varieties of sociology (at least in the German-speaking world), subsequent developments in first-order and second-order cybernetics have abandoned many of the premises of Shannon's model of communication. Finally, in stressing that most contributors to this volume know Shannon via Weaver, I do more than identify a liability. In fact, as I will argue below, Weaver's expository essay opens up new ways of thinking about communication and noise as it reintroduces the semantic considerations Shannon excludes.

INFORMATIONAL ENTROPY

Shannon's model of communication owes its nonhermeneutic scope, i.e., its insistence that the "semantic aspects of communication are irrelevant to the engineering problem," to the institutional context of its genesis.[4] As an engineer employed by Bell Telephone Laboratories, Shannon had little interest in the dynamics of human sense-making. Instead, he worked at increasing the efficiency of telecommunication when he discovered, to his astonishment, that his definition of information corresponded with Ludwig Boltzmann's definition of entropy. This was indeed surprising since entropy is a measure of disorder in a thermodynamic system. Thus, Shannon's finding suggests that chaotic, disordered, entropic messages have greater information value than ordered, negentropic ones. What seems counterintuitive at first makes perfect sense in the context of Shannon's proposal that the amount of information a given message conveys must be calculated in relation to the set of possible messages from which this specific message has been selected. In Weaver's words, "To be sure, this word information in communication theory relates not so much to what you *do* say, as to what you *could* say."[5] For Shannon, information is a purely quantitative measure. The larger the set of possible messages, the higher the sender's freedom of choice in selecting one specific message, the higher the amount of information communicated. This is true irrespective of *what* is being communicated. At the other end of the communication process, the receiver's uncertainty as to what specific message the receiver has selected correlates directly with the sender's freedom of choice: the higher the sender's freedom, the higher the uncertainty the message removed at the receiver's end, the higher the amount of information conveyed. Given this, it seems clear that a message about whose identity the receiver was already relatively certain prior to its arrival contains less information than one that s/he could not have predicted with a high degree of certitude:

> Information is, we must steadily remember, a measure of one's freedom of choice in selecting a message. The greater this freedom of choice, and hence the greater the information, the greater is the uncertainty that the message actually selected is some particular one. Thus greater freedom of choice, greater uncertainty, greater information go hand in hand.[6]

The more possible messages there are, then, the less probable and predictable each specific message is, and the more information each specific message conveys. Conversely, a fully predictable message is redundant and thus devoid of information:

> That information be measured by entropy is, after all, natural when we remember that information, in communication theory, is associated with the amount of freedom of choice we have in constructing messages. Thus for a communication source one can say, just as he would also say it of a thermodynamic ensemble, "This situation is highly organized, it is not characterized by a large degree of randomness or of choice—that is to say, the information (or the entropy) is low."[7]

Let me illustrate Shannon and Weaver's reasoning with an example from the area of human communication. Imagine a situation in which A asks B, "Did you post the letter I gave you?" In an *idealized* speech situation, B's choice of an answer is limited to either "yes" or "no." Consequently, the amount of information conveyed by B's answer is relatively low, for A could have guessed the correct answer with a 50% chance anyway. Another way of saying this is that the probability that B chooses a specific answer is relatively high and that B's answer therefore removes only little uncertainty on the part of A. If, on the other hand, A asks B, "How did you spend the afternoon?" B may choose her answer from a far greater field of possible messages, and her answer removes far more uncertainty on the part of A as to which message out of a set of possible messages B would choose. No matter what answer B chooses, the amount of information conveyed by it is relatively high.

A second factor that determines the entropy of a message is probability. Let us stay with the previous example. When asking the question, "Did you post the letter I gave you?" A will be predisposed to expect one answer from B rather than the other, be it because A possesses knowledge about B's reliability or simply because A has prejudices about her. The two possible answers (yes, no) are therefore not equally probable from A's point of view. Consequently, A's uncertainty concerning B's choice of one of the two messages will not be as high as it would be if the two answers were equally probable, and the amount of information conveyed by the message is correspondingly smaller. A maximally entropic or "informative" message is therefore not only one that has been chosen out of a maximally large set of messages but also one chosen out of a set of messages that are all equally probable:

> In the limiting case where one probability is unity (certainty) and all the others zero (impossibility), then H [entropy] is zero (no uncertainty at all—no freedom of choice—no information). Thus H is largest when the two probabilities are equal (i.e., when one is completely free and unbiased in the choice), and reduces to zero when one's freedom of choice is gone. The situation just described is in fact typical. If there are

many, rather than two, choices, then *H* is largest when the probability
of the various choices are as nearly equal as circumstances permit—
when one has as much freedom as possible in making a choice, being as
little as possible driven toward some certain choices which have more
than their share of probability.[8]

Human language never reaches a state of maximum entropy and is therefore never maximally "informative" in Shannon's sense. This derives from
the fact that the elements human language is composed of (phonemes, mor-
phemes, lexemes, sentences) never occur with equal probability. There are
certain rules that govern the production of human language, and these rules
constrain the freedom of choice on the part of the sender of a message as
well as the uncertainty on the part of the receiver. They increase the probability that certain elements rather than others are chosen by the sender
and therefore decrease the information content of any given message. Let
us return to the above example once more. Take the fourth word in A's
question, "Did you post the letter I gave you?" At the phonetic level, there
are phonotactic rules that govern the sequential arrangement of phonemes
and that constrain, for instance, the choice of possible sounds following the
initial /ð/ in "the." In fact, only vowel sounds could fill this slot. It is such
rules that would make a written sequence of letters such as "Dd u post th
lettr I gv u?" still perfectly understandable for most speakers of English.
Similar rules apply to the sequence of individual words. The probability
that "the" is followed by either a noun or an adjective is much higher than
that of its being followed by a verb or an article. At the level of speech acts,
it is less probable if not inconceivable that A's question is answered with
"12 o'clock" rather than "yes" or "no."

Stochastic processes are processes governed by the laws of probability, and the generation of human language is, mathematically speaking, a
Markoff process, i.e., a "special case of a stochastic process in which the
probabilities depend on the previous events."[9] The probabilities involved
reduce the sender's freedom of choice, reduce the receiver's uncertainty,
make messages more predictable and therefore less "informative." So
while it is true that "the whole purpose of communication is to send messages which are not fully predictable,"[10] i.e., to exchange nonredundant
messages, fully *un*predictable messages are not a possibility in human
communication.

NOISE

Within the framework of Shannonian information theory, fully unpredictable messages are both maximally informative and completely unintelligible. They are *noise,* the direct opposite of redundancy. As indicated, it is,
strictly speaking, impossible to communicate noise. However, in machine

as well as human communication, any perturbation of signal transmission by noise makes messages less predictable. In point of fact, in Shannon's model, noise doesn't only degrade the message sent in that it effects "that the received signal is not necessarily the same as that sent out by the transmitter."[11] Noise, more specifically white noise, is also the most entropic signal and as such conveys the greatest amount of information: "white noise has the maximum possible entropy."[12] Given the engineering context within which Shannon developed his theorems, such a positive valorization of noise comes unexpected. Shannon's research was, after all, geared toward enhancing the performativity of machine communication. In this commercial context, noise is always a force to be reckoned with, but it is by no means a welcome guest. In this scheme, redundancy is necessary precisely because it compensates for the noise that affects all transmissions of information. To return to our example, any distortion of a message like "Dd u post th lettr I gv u?" is more likely to render it unintelligible than a distortion of the message "Did you post the letter I gave you?" because the former message exhibits less redundancy and is for this reason more vulnerable to noise. This has repercussions on the way messages must be coded prior to transmission: "if the source already has a certain redundancy and no attempt is made to eliminate it in matching to the channel, this redundancy will help combat noise."[13]

With Shannon's military metaphor in mind, it comes as little surprise that he and Weaver stop short of giving noise its full due. For them, noise is indeed the most unpredictable signal and as such exhibits the greatest amount of information; yet they characterize the information it communicates as useless:

> Uncertainty which arises by virtue of freedom of choice on the part of the sender is desirable uncertainty. Uncertainty which arises because of errors or because of the influence of noise is undesirable uncertainty. It is thus clear where the joker is in saying that the received signal has more information. Some of this information is spurious and undesirable and has been introduced via the noise. To get the useful information in the received signal we must subtract out this spurious portion.[14]

If one follows Shannon's assertion that "the amount of information received is the degree to which the receiver's uncertainty concerning that event has been diminished,"[15] then noise is responsible for any remaining uncertainty once the signal has arrived at the receiver's end. From an engineering point of view, "[i]f the information source has any residual uncertainty after the signal is known, then this must be undesirable uncertainty due to noise."[16] Shannon calls this "spurious portion" equivocation and defines it as "the average ambiguity of the received signal."[17]

By characterizing noise as "useless" and describing its effects as "undesirable uncertainty," Shannon and Weaver deftly cast out a player in communication processes that they have just defined as that signal which conveys the greatest amount of information. It is as if these two engineers working for a telephone company were not quite prepared to follow their own insights to their radical, counterintuitive end. As we will see, a number of contemporary thinkers, including Michel Serres, Jacques Attali, and William R. Paulson, were much less timid in their creative appropriations of Shannon's reflections on noise. Yet the ground for their work was already laid in *The Mathematical Theory of Communication,* though at least in one respect less in Shannon's contribution to that volume than in Weaver's essay.

In the third and final section of his article ("The Interrelationship of the Three Levels of Communication Problems"), Weaver turns to the semantic questions that neither Shannon nor he ever tired of declaring extraneous to information theory. In Weaver's words, "*information* must not be confused with meaning [. . .]. The semantic aspects of communication are irrelevant to the engineering aspects."[18] This exclusion of meaning-making is integral to the model of communication Shannon proposes:

In oral communication, the information source is the speaker's brain, the transmitter the physical speech apparatus that transforms the message into a coded signal sent over the air; the receiver is the hearer's ear, the destination his or her brain. Given these correspondences, it seems clear that any kind of interpretive activity would take place in either the information source or the destination. Yet Shannon is singularly uninterested in what goes on within these boxes. For him, "there is no ambiguity about what it means for a message to be 'correct'; it means that if the message before it is *encoded* is compared with the message after it is *decoded,* the two will be identical."[19] In this scheme, there is no room for any interpretive activity; what counts is the successful transmission of self-identical information.

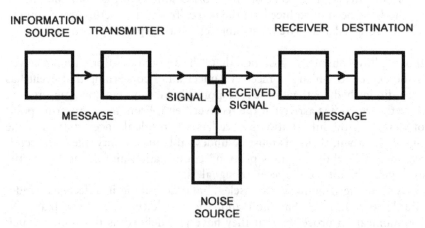

Figure 2.1   (Shannon's communication model)

Yet when Weaver does consider semantics in the final section of his article, he opens up a different avenue of thinking about communication, meaning, and noise:

> One can imagine, as an addition to the diagram, another box labeled "Semantic Receiver" interposed between the engineering receiver (which changes signals to messages) and the destination. This semantic receiver subjects the message to a second decoding, the demand on this one being that it must match the statistical *semantic* characteristics of the message to the statistical semantic capacities of the totality of receivers, or of that subset of receivers which constitute the audience one wishes to affect.[20]

Three years after the publication of "The Intentional Fallacy," Weaver ever so cautiously (and almost certainly unintentionally) joins William K. Wimsatt and Monroe R. Beardsley in moving away from a communication model that declares the sender the sole source of authority and meaning.[21] Moreover, his contention that the semantic receiver's task is to match the message's semantic properties to the receiver's capacity for processing information qualifies his own earlier assertion that the "*semantic problems*" of communication are solely "concerned with the identity, or satisfactorily close approximation, in the interpretation of meaning by the receiver, as compared with the intended meaning of the sender."[22]

Weaver moves even further away from a linear, one-way model of communication when he speculates about the consequences of supplementing Shannon's diagram with yet another box:

> Similarly one can imagine another box in the diagram which, inserted between the information source and the transmitter, would be labeled "semantic noise," the box previously labeled as simply "noise" now being labeled "engineering noise." From this source is imposed into the signal the perturbations or distortions of meaning which are not intended by the source but which inescapably affect the destination. And the problem of semantic decoding must take this semantic noise into account. It is also possible to think of an adjustment of original message so that the sum of message meaning plus semantic noise is equal to the desired total message meaning at the destination.[23]

Weaver's surprising suggestion that distortions of the sender's intended meaning may have to be considered an integral part of the received message rather than an unwanted nuisance not only breaks with communication models that locate all authority in the sender's intention, but also reintroduces the noise expelled by Shannon's categorical distinction between useful and useless information:

Clearly, Weaver's reflections are miles apart from contemporary celebrations of noise as a subversive communicative force and bringer of the new.

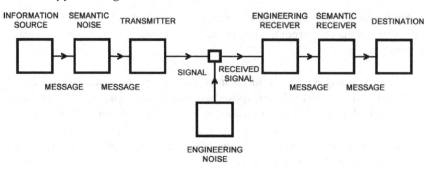

Figure 2.2   (Shannon's communication model with Weaver's proposed additions)

Weaver's model incorporates noise not for its own sake but in order to contain its potentially destructive force. Still, together with Shannon's realization that noise is the signal that conveys the greatest amount of information, Weaver's suggestion that distortions of the sender's intended meaning by "semantic noise" may actually contribute to rather than impair the meaning received at the other end of the communication process forms the basis for more enthusiastic reappraisals of noise in literary and cultural theory since the 1980s.

THE PERSISTENCE OF SHANNONIAN INFORMATION THEORY

That Shannonian information theory should continue to enjoy such currency in a number of contemporary theoretical debates is, however, by no means self-evident. While *The Mathematical Theory of Communication* remains an important reference point for major literary, cultural, and media theorists, including Serres, Attali, Paulson, Friedrich A. Kittler, and N. Katherine Hayles, most communication theorists agree that Shannon's transmission model of communication is too restricted to its technical context to serve as a general theory of communication. A glance at the historical context in which Shannon's seminal article was published shows that the grounds for the latter view were already prepared in the middle of the twentieth century.

"A Mathematical Theory of Communication" was published in issue 27 of the *Bell System Technical Journal* (July/October 1948). Disseminated primarily via *The Mathematical Theory of Communication,* Shannon's bold refunctioning of Boltzmann's definition of thermodynamic entropy, his definition of information as "a measure of one's freedom of choice when one selects a message,"[24] and his decision to divorce the study of data communication from that of sense-making processes had a major impact on a great variety of fields. One legacy of that impact is that Shannon's definition of "information" has even found its way into the *Oxford English*

Dictionary: "As a mathematically defined quantity divorced from any concept of news or meaning [. . .]; spec. one which represents the degree of choice exercised in the selection or formation of one particular symbol, message, etc., out of a number of possible ones, and which is defined logarithmically in terms of the statistical probabilities of occurrence of the symbol or the elements of the message" (sense 2.c). While few laypersons will have heard of Shannon's definition of information, his conceptualization of it as the result of a process of selection provides an important basis for further developments in first- and second-order cybernetics, most prominently Niklas Luhmann's reconceptualization of information as the result of not one but three processes of selection:

> [C]ommunication must be viewed [. . .] as a three-part selection process. [. . .] The standard concept of information elaborated since Claude E. Shannon and Warren Weaver makes it easy to formulate this. According to today's standard interpretation, information is a selection from a (known or unknown) repertoire of possibilities. Without this selectivity of information, no communication process would emerge [. . .]. Furthermore, someone must choose a behavior [i.e., a specific medium] that expresses this communication. That can occur intentionally or unintentionally. What is decisive is the fact that the third selection can base itself on a distinction, namely, the distinction between information and its utterance.[25]

Yet as much as Shannon's pioneering work remains an important reference point for some contemporary sociologists and many media theorists in the German-speaking world, the grounds for a significant shift away from Shannonian information theory were already laid in the year that "A Mathematical Theory of Communication" was published. In 1948, Norbert Wiener's *Cybernetics: or Control and Communication in the Animal and the Machine* was also issued, and even though Wiener near the beginning of the second edition of *The Human Use of Human Beings: Cybernetics and Society* writes that cybernetics grew "from a few ideas shared by Drs. Claude Shannon, Warren Weaver, and myself, into an established region of research,"[26] it was Wiener's cybernetics rather than Shannon's information theory that became the major rallying point halfway through the interdisciplinary Macy conferences (1946–1953). This was decisive, since it was these ten conferences that changed the way we think about communication. While Shannon was a guest at three of the four final meetings and gave talks at two of them, Wiener belonged to its core group for the first seven.[27] Wiener's cybernetics and Shannon's information theory are compatible in several ways, most significantly in their conceptualization of information as the outcome of a process of selection and their disregard for questions of meaning. Indeed, Wiener already in *Cybernetics* explicitly references Shannon's mathematical theory of communication, and Shannon acknowledges that "[c]ommunication theory is heavily indebted to Wiener."[28] But apart from Wiener's equation of information with negentropy rather than entropy (which he inherits from Boltzmann, who observes that more ordered and regular messages are actually less probable than disordered, "noisy" ones), there is an even more decisive difference between the two models.[29] Wiener and his fellow cyberneticians were moving away from Shannon's transmission model of communication to study processes of information exchange, feedback, and self-organization taking place on several distinct levels within complex systems such as computers, the brain, and human communities. As Wiener makes clear, this move away from the engineering context was crucial to the cybernetic program:

> Besides the electrical engineering theory of the transmission of messages, there is a larger field which includes not only the study of language but the study of messages as a means of controlling machinery and society, the development of computing machines and other such automata, certain reflections upon psychology and the nervous system, and a tentative new theory of scientific method. This larger theory of messages is a probabilistic theory [. . .]. Until recently, there was no existing word for this complex of ideas, and in order to embrace the whole field by a single term, I felt constrained to invent one. Hence "Cybernetics," which I derived from the Greek word *kubernētēs*, or "steersman," the same Greek word from which we eventually derive our word "governor."[30]

True, both Wiener's science of communication and control and Gregory Bateson's famous definition of "information" as "a difference which makes a difference"[31] are inconceivable without Shannon's conceptualization of communication in binary terms (which he inherits from Ralph V. L. Hartley's earlier work) as well as Shannon's insight that completely predictable messages are redundant and therefore devoid of information.[32] But Wiener's focus on feedback processes, self-regulation, and learning and Bateson's holistic exploration of open, homeostatic systems are already drifting rapidly away from Shannon's linear, technical model. With the shift of focus to questions of autopoiesis and emergence in second-order cybernetics, the move away from sender-receiver models of communication became ever more decisive.

Indeed, it is not only from the vantage point of an empirically oriented communication studies but also from semiotic and cybernetic perspectives that Shannon's model—which (despite Weaver's modifications to it) considers the transmission of self-identical messages as the touchstone of successful communication—does not seem complex enough to describe communication outside of the model's narrow technical context. Daniel Chandler usefully summarizes objections raised against transmission models: they are based on a transport metaphor that informs commonly used phrases such as "did you get my message?" and "sending information using Bluetooth" but misleadingly conceives of information as "packages" sent from A to B; they accord the receiver an entirely passive role; they mistakenly conceptualize communication as one-way and linear; they wrongly equate content and meaning; they account only for goal-oriented/instrumental communication; they ignore all social and cultural contexts; they cannot account for acts of communication between more than two entities; they deny the temporal dimensions of communicative acts; and they ignore the specific properties and functions of different media.[33] In several senses, then, Shannonian information theory is an imperfect precursor to more sophisticated models of communication.

Yet Shannon's model continues to generate a considerable amount of serious discussion among more theoretically inclined students of media and culture. Why is that so? Chandler suggests that, despite all its deficiencies, Shannon's model has three important advantages: it is simple, generalizable, and quantifiable. Granted, but I believe that it is a fourth feature of Shannon's information theory, one that relates to its generality but is not identical with it, that makes Shannon amenable to more recent media theories. In fact, that feature which made Shannon's model such a continuing success story is precisely one that may be considered its main weakness: its exclusion of semantic considerations (which Weaver only partly qualifies). If, at least in the German-speaking world, the most exciting and influential work in media theory since the 1980s has been produced by scholars intent on developing a technology-centered, postanthropocentric theory of culture, Shannon's technical definition of information comes in handy. Thus, for a theoretical project such as Kittler's, which stages, to translate the title of an early essay collection edited by him, an "exorcism of *Geist* [spirit, mind] from the humanities," Shannon is—pardon the pun—a kindred spirit.[34] Likewise, for Hans Ulrich Gumbrecht and Karl Ludwig Pfeiffer, who stage their various challenges to the hermeneutic tradition's focus on interpretation and meaning under evolving labels such as "materialities of communication," "the nonhermeneutic," and (in Gumbrecht's recent phrasing) "the production of presence" (as opposed to the production of meaning), Shannon's exclusion of questions of meaning is an asset, not a liability.[35] This preference for a technical (some say technicist) understanding of information goes a long way toward explaining why another contender for the title of "founder of information theory" has nowhere near Shannon's currency in current theory debates.

At the eighth Macy conference on March 15–16, 1951, Shannon met Donald M. MacKay, whose contribution to that meeting may have reminded Shannon that the title of his own 1948 article is a misnomer. Since Shannon explicitly excludes all semantic considerations, his "mathematical theory of communication" would more accurately be labeled a "*mathematical theory of data communication*."[36] In the paper MacKay gave at the eighth Macy conference, "In Search of Basic Symbols," and more elaborately in his *Information, Mechanism and Meaning,* he insists that meaning could and should have a place in Shannon's theory but that it was exorcised from it by way of a sleight of hand that neither Shannon nor his followers or critics noticed. Shannon's conviction that the purpose of communication is to transmit messages so that the message received is identical to the message sent is based on the assumption that, apart from distortions introduced by noise, these two messages are basically the same.[37] This assumption, MacKay notes, does not hold ground since the receiver needs to reconstruct the message received against the background of a set of possible messages that may well be different from the set of possible messages from which the sender selected her message. This entails that there is no basic identity between message sent and message received. For the receiver, both the sender's message *and* the set of messages from which s/he chose it are indeterminate, and this double indeterminacy can be reduced only in a negotiation that takes place in social space. MacKay names this negotiation "communication" and adds that meaning comes into play precisely in those moments when we turn our attention to the set of possible messages against which a specific message must be read.[38] In making this argument, MacKay directs our focus on the role of observation in the construction of meaning, thus aligning himself much more closely with classic cybernetic perspectives than Shannon ever does. And yet, though Shannon's transmission model of communication has not stood the test of time, MacKay's contributions have been all but forgotten by today's media theorists. This represents a lacuna in current scholarship that this essay cannot fill. Suffice it to point out that the history of ideas on communication since the mid-twentieth century would have taken a very different turn if it had started from MacKay's observations rather than from Shannon's.

NO ORDER FROM NOISE

So why should humanities scholars continue to engage with Shannonian information theory if its model of communication is flawed and its exclusion of sense-making processes jars with fundamental assumptions most of us have inherited from the hermeneutic tradition? For many of us, it is first and foremost Shannon and Weaver's reflections on noise that have continuing relevance.

In *Noise: The Political Economy of Music* (1977), Jacques Attali, a French cultural theorist, economist, and long-time economic advisor to François Mitterrand, takes direct recourse to Shannon's work to suggest that, in addition to Shannon's conceptualization of noise, a more archaic notion of the term must also be taken into account:

> Information theory uses the concept of noise (or rather, metonymy) in a more general way: noise is the term for a signal that interfered with the

reception of a message by a receiver, even if the interfering signal itself has a meaning for that receiver. Long before it was given this theoretical expression, noise had always been experienced as destruction, disorder, dirt, pollution, an aggression against the code-structuring messages.[39]

Attali stresses both this originary, disruptive, and violent force of noise and its generative potential: "Our science has always desired to monitor, measure, abstract, and castrate meaning, forgetting that life is full of noise and that death alone is silent. [. . .] Nothing essential happens in the absence of noise."[40] Starting from these premises, Attali develops a history of music in which music emerges as "a channelization of noise, and therefore a simulacrum of the sacrifice. It is thus a sublimation, an exacerbation of the imaginary, at the same time as the creation of social order and political integration."[41] What he ultimately calls for is a form of improvisational musical and sounding practices that no longer contain the noise. He calls these practices "composition" and champions their "conquest of the right to make noise, in other words, to create one's own code and work, without advertising its goal in advance."[42] For Attali, composition is prophetic and decidedly political in nature: it "heralds the emergence of a formidable subversion, one leading to a radically new organization never yet theorized."[43]

French philosopher Michel Serres shares Attali's emphasis on the originary and generative force of noise and in his books *Parasite* and *Genesis* proposes especially influential creative rereadings of Shannonian information theory and its cybernetic and systems-theoretic successors.[44] In noise, static, and interference—*bruit parasite* in technical French—Serres finds allies in his sustained philosophical challenge to the exclusionary logic of binary systems of thought. Serres's allegiance to noise is both a positive and a negative one. He rejoices in things being born out of chaos and noise: one of his figures is Aphrodite, this "beautiful goddess," whom he imagines "invisible, standing up, [. . .] born of the chaotic sea, this nautical chaos, the *noise*."[45] Simultaneously, he denounces the violence that inheres in the logic of the excluded third: "Hell is the separation of paradise and Hell, the Devil is the bifurcation between God and the Devil, evil is the crossroads of good and evil, and error is the dualism that only opposes twins."[46] Serres shares Henry Adams's insight that "Chaos was the law of nature, Order was the dream of man,"[47] but, unlike Adams, he is no longer prepared to pay the price to realize dreams of unity and order:[48]

This couple [noise-message] and their relation are set apart by an observer seated within the system. In a way he overvalues the message and undervalues the noise if he belongs to the functioning of the system. He represses the parasites in order to send or receive communications better and to make them circulate in a distinct and workable fashion. This repression is also religious excommunication, political imprisonment, the isolation of the sick, garbage collection, public health, the pasteurization of milk, and so forth, as much as it is repression in the psychoanalytical sense. But it also has to do with a history, the history of science in particular: whoever belongs to the system perceives noises less and represses them more, the more he is a functioning part of the system. He never stops being in the good, the just, the true, the natural, the normal. All dogmatism lives on this division, be it blind or decided.[49]

In Serres's "noisy philosophy," the logic of the parasite informs all systems, and its exclusion always only announces the emergence of another, more powerful parasite. As it does in information theory, noise always remains part of the equation.[50]

With *The Noise of Culture: Literary Texts in a World of Information*, William R. Paulson has written what is still the most sustained reflection on the cultural functions of noise in my own discipline of literary studies.[51] A specialist in eighteenth- and nineteenth-century French literature and culture, Paulson in this monograph considers the changing functions of literature in a "world of information." What value and function do literary texts still have under late capitalism, when readily processable information has become an increasingly desirable commodity? Literature appears to meet none of the requirements of an age that asks for clear, unambiguous, and machine-readable information; it is "a residue of a no longer dominant mode of cultural organization."[52] So what functions can it still perform today? Paulson refuses to give humanistic answers that would stress literature's educational value, its contributions to cultural memory, or its opening up of fictional worlds that allow for vicarious kinds of experience. Instead, he draws on Serres's work, Humberto R. Maturana and Francisco J. Varela's theoretical biology, information theory, systems theory, and Belgian and French formalisms to argue that literature is indeed "the noise of culture":

> Literature is not and will not ever again be at the center of culture, if indeed it ever was. There is no use in either proclaiming or debunking its central position. Literature is the noise of culture, the rich and indeterminate margin into which messages are sent off, never to return the same, in which signals are received not quite like anything emitted.[53]

For Paulson, "noise" designates both formal properties of literary works and their communicative function. Literary noise is internal in the sense that the language of literary texts differs from ordinary, everyday language uses in its aporias, indeterminacies, and ambiguities, and in the complex structural relations between its parts: "Rather than attempting to reduce noise to a minimum, literary communication *assumes* its noise as a constitutive factor of itself."[54] Literary noise is also external in the sense that, due to their linguistic alterity, literary texts cannot be fully assimilated into the communicative and discursive networks that are already in place. It is, then, the literariness of literary works, their internal noise, that enables them to function as a form of cultural perturbation that prompts "new moves in the linguistic and symbolic games that constitute knowledge and society."[55]

In *The Noises of American Literature, 1890–1985: Toward a History of Literary Acoustics,* I embark on an exploration of American literary soundscapes from naturalism to postmodernism.[56] Understanding "noise" both in its everyday sense as the discordant or unwanted sound that literary texts represent and as an information-theoretic notion that helps me conceptualize the communicative and social functions of literature, I develop a history of "literary acoustics" that explores convergences between the representation of noise (noise as an object of literary representation) and its cultural production (literature as a "noisy" form of communication that perturbs the communicative networks that are already in place). As much as the latter line of my argument is inspired by Paulson's work, I do not subscribe to his conclusion that the function of literature today must be understood in the context of "a cognitive community" that "constitutes a kind of self-regulating system, one that continues in its activity by producing differences and then integrating into its organization those differences that it finds acceptable."[57] Here and elsewhere, Paulson draws on systems-theoretic notions of "order from noise" and "self-organization from noise" to argue that the cultural perturbation literature effects is valuable not in itself but because it triggers processes of systemic reorganization that result in new forms of order. In this view of things, literature continues to play an important social role because it facilitates systemic evolution. Literature keeps the system going. This may sound like a harsh indictment of the ultimate political valence of Paulson's theoretical project (which I admire a lot), but it is entirely in line with systems theory's exclusive interest in those forms of environmental disorder and noise that can be reintegrated as systemic order via the "order from noise" principle:

> External influences appear to self-referential systems only as determination for self-determination and thus as information, which changes the internal context of self-determination without eliminating the structural principle that the system must come to terms on its own with everything that ensures that self-determination.[58]

Systems theory is a theory of evolutions rather than revolutions, which is why it has repeatedly been charged with having a conservative political bias.[59] While I refuse to subscribe to such dismissals of systems theory on ideological grounds, I continue to find Shannon and Weaver's description of noise as both a maximally informative and radically unintelligible signal ultimately more helpful than systems-theoretic approaches to describe the communicative and social functions of certain types of literary works.

If Theodor W. Adorno is right in arguing that the social function of highly experimental modernist texts such as Marcel Proust's *À la recherche du temps perdu* (1913–27), Franz Kafka's "In der Strafkolonie" (1919),

Paul Celan's poetry, Samuel Beckett's *Endgame* (1957), and Eugène Ionesco's *Rhinoceros* (1960) depends on their very refusal to conform to the debased and reifying languages of modernity that are the order of the day, then systems-theoretic conceptualizations of "order from noise" and "self-organization from noise" fail to account for the radically unintegrable difference of such texts. I am taking my cue here from Shannon's original essay, where he adduces a classic example of a noisy text with minimal redundancy: "James Joyce's book *Finnegans Wake*," which "enlarges the vocabulary and is alleged to achieve a compression of semantic content."[60] Indeed, Joyce's novel (if that's the word) reinvents the English language to achieve maximum distance from the ways of speaking and writing that we are used to. Witness the beginning of the book's third paragraph:

> the fall (bababadalgharaghtakamminarronnkonnbronntonnerronntu-onnthunntrovarrhounawnskawntoohoohoordenenthurnuk!) of a once wallstrait oldparr is retaled early in bed and later on life down through all christian minstrelsy. The great fall of the offwall entailed at such short notice the pftjschute of Finnegan, erse solid man, that the humptyhillhead of humself promptly sends an unquiring one well to the west in quest of his tumptytumtoes: and the upturnpikepointandplace is at the knock out in the park where oranges have been laid to rust upon the green since devlinsfirst loved livvy.[61]

Joyce scholars have worked exceptionally hard at unraveling the riddles of this supremely difficult book's prose. They have taught us that the seemingly random, hundred-letter sequence of consonants and vowels after "the fall" reproduces the fracas of Adam and Eve's Fall through a rendition of the words "thunder," "noise," and "defecation" in several languages; that "humptyhillhead" and "tumptytumtoes" refer to the somewhat less spectacular fall of Humpty Dumpty; and that "pftjschute" is an ideophonic word that reproduces drunk Tim Finnegan's deadly fall from a ladder.[62] And this scratches only the surface of the multiple historical and linguistic references that Joyce scholars have excavated from this short passage. Yet despite all hermeneutic efforts, *Finnegans Wake* retains its strangeness. In this book, a surplus of noise remains that cannot be reduced to order.

More recent examples of such highly experimental "noisy" texts are Diane Williams's collection of microstories *This Is About the Body, the Mind, the Soul, the World, Time, and Fate* (1990), David Foster Wallace's encyclopedic opus magnum *Infinite Jest* (1996) and his posthumous unfinished novel *The Pale King* (2011), Mary Caponegro's short stories in collections such as *All Fall Down* (2009), and Ben Marcus's ensemble of short experimental prose pieces in *The Age of Wire and String* (1995), as well as his novel *The Flame Alphabet* (2012). The last of these creates a fictional world in which children's speech has become lethal to adults who hear it.

Unlike Joyce, Marcus does not invent new words. Instead, he creates a communicative perturbation by rearranging the words we already know in surprising new ways. Take the following paragraph from the novel's second chapter as an example chosen almost at random:

> When the Esther toxicity was in high flower, when it was no longer viable to endure proximity to our daughter, given the retching, the speech fever, the yellow tide beneath my wife's skin, to say nothing of the bruising around my mouth, that day should have been darker, altogether blackened by fire.[63]

Unlike his fictional children's speech, Marcus's prose does not kill adults; but it leaves us sufficiently unsettled to glimpse something of the existential chasm of the novel's premise, which reverberates down into the hiatus of "fire." In their different ways, texts such as *The Flame Alphabet, The Age of Wire and String, All Fall Down, The Pale King, Infinite Jest,* and *This Is About the Body, the Mind, the Soul, the World, Time, and Fate* do not trigger processes of systemic rejuvenation; instead, they stage an act of communicative refusal. In that, they tap into and rework for our own times a modernist aesthetics of what Adorno calls "negativity":

> Art [. . .] is social not only because of its mode of production, in which the dialectic of the forces and relations of production is concentrated, nor simply because of the social derivation of its thematic material. Much more importantly, art becomes social by its opposition to society, and it occupies this position only as autonomous art. By crystallizing in itself as something unique to itself, rather than complying with existing social norms and qualifying as "socially useful," it criticizes society by merely existing, for which puritans of all stripes condemn it.[64]

In information-theoretic terms, what Adorno calls for is an aesthetics of noise that follows the maxim "Only what does not fit into this world is true."[65] From this perspective, formally experimental and difficult texts can be described as noisy forms of communication whose very hermeticism allows them to retain a critical distance from society. Paradoxically, then, these texts are social in their very asociality and autonomy. Yet this radical and irreducible linguistic alterity falls outside the scope of the systems-theoretic "order from noise" paradigm. And this is precisely why von Foerster, Luhmann, and Paulson are ultimately less important reference points for my own thinking about modernist, postmodernist, and contemporary literature than Shannon and Weaver and their "wilder" successors Attali and Serres.

Shannonian information theory and its progenies have proven more congenial to my own work for yet another reason. To my mind, one fundamental difference between information-theoretic and cybernetic models of communication that I only hinted at above has major consequences for their respective contributions to the study of literature and the arts. Consider Wiener's brief comment on poetry in the second edition of *The Human Use of Human Beings: Cybernetics and Society:*

> Messages are themselves a form of pattern and organization. Indeed, it is possible to treat sets of messages as having an entropy like sets of states of the external world. Just as entropy is a measure of disorganization, the information carried by a set of messages is a measure of organization. In fact, it is possible to interpret the information carried by a message as essentially the negative of its entropy, and the negative logarithm of its probability. That is, the more probable the message, the less information it gives. Clichés, for example, are less illuminating than great poems.[66]

For both Wiener and Shannon, poems (and works of art more generally) are less probable and for that reason more "illuminating" than clichés, but for very different reasons. For Wiener, communication is an activity that enables human beings to set something against the entropic decline of the universe predicted by the second law of thermodynamics: "In control and communication we are always fighting nature's tendency to degrade the organized and to destroy the meaningful; the tendency, as Gibbs has shown us, for entropy to decrease."[67] And artistic creation is, in Wiener's view, the negentropic activity *par excellence* precisely because it is a highly ordered and regular form of human communication. This conception of art is fundamentally different from that favored by critics starting from Shannon's insights. While both views share the premise that art is a special form of human communication, the main difference between them hinges on the question of whether the specificity of art is to be found in an unusually high degree of structural regularity and order or in its opposite, i.e., in the disruption and fragmentation of regular patterns.

In literary-theoretical terms, the difference between a Wienerian and a Shannonian conception of art is that between the New Critics' "organic unity" doctrine and Adorno's reflections on the necessary negativity of art. If we follow Wiener's model, we are, in other words, likely to read modernist literature as T. S. Eliot did in his famous 1923 review of Joyce's *Ulysses:* as "a way of controlling, of ordering, of giving a shape and a significance to the immense panorama of futility and anarchy which is contemporary history."[68] If we follow Shannon's model, we are likely to accede to Adorno's demands for art: "in order to resist the all-powerful system of communication [artworks] must rid themselves of any communicative means that would perhaps make them accessible to the public."[69] Ultimately, then, if we abandon information theory as an imperfect precursor and follow systems theory and its theorization of "order from noise" and "self-organization from noise" instead, we are in danger of losing some of the radicality of the lessons Shannon and Weaver taught us.

NOTES

1. This essay builds and expands on research done for my 2006 monograph *The Noises of American Literature, 1890–1985: Toward a History of Literary Acoustics*. My exposition of the fundamentals of the Shannonian model of communication draws on my entry for "Information Theory" in the *Routledge Companion to Literature and Science*. I would like to thank Ridvan Askin and Andreas Hägler for their useful input on an earlier version of the present essay.

2. Claude Elwood Shannon, "The Bandwagon," *Institute of Radio Engineers Transactions on Information Theory* 2 (1956): 3.

3. In what follows, I am quoting from those versions of Weaver's and Shannon's articles that were published in Claude Elwood Shannon and Warren Weaver, *The Mathematical Theory of Communication* (Chicago: University of Illinois Press, 1963).

4. Warren Weaver, "Recent Contributions to the Mathematical Theory of Communication," in Shannon and Weaver, *The Mathematical Theory of Communication*, 29.

5. Weaver, "Recent Contributions," 8–9.

6. Weaver, "Recent Contributions," 18–19.

7. Weaver, "Recent Contributions," 13.

8. Weaver, "Recent Contributions," 15.

9. Weaver, "Recent Contributions," 11.

10. Jeremy Campbell, *Grammatical Man: Information, Entropy, Language and Life* (London: Allen Lane, 1983), 63.

11. Claude Elwood Shannon, "The Mathematical Theory of Communication," in Shannon and Weaver, *The Mathematical Theory of Communication*, 65.

12. Shannon, "The Mathematical Theory of Communication," 92. In physics, white noise refers to a sound with a very wide frequency range and equal energy (or volume) at every unit of the frequency spectrum. It is called white noise in analogy to white light, which is made up of all the colors of the color spectrum, just as white noise is made up of all the frequencies of the frequency spectrum.

13. Shannon, "The Mathematical Theory of Communication," 75.

14. Weaver, "Recent Contributions," 19.

15. William R. Paulson, *The Noise of Culture: Literary Texts in a World of Information* (Ithaca: Cornell University Press, 1988), 55.

16. Shannon, "The Mathematical Theory of Communication," 75, 99. Shannon adds, "*If the signal and noise are independent and the received signal is the sum of the transmitted signal and the noise then the rate of transmission is [. . .] the entropy of the received signal less the entropy of the noise*" (99).

17. Shannon, "The Mathematical Theory of Communication," 67.

18. Weaver, "Recent Contributions," 8.

19. N. Katherine Hayles, "Information or Noise? Economy of Explanation in Barthes's S/Z and Shannon's Information Theory," in *One Culture: Essays in Science and Literature*, ed. George Levine (Madison: University of Wisconsin Press, 1987), 196.

20. Weaver, "Recent Contributions," 26.

21. William K. Wimsatt and Monroe R. Beardsley, "The Intentional Fallacy," *Sewanee Review* 54, no. 3 (1946): 468–88.
22. Weaver, "Recent Contributions," 4.
23. Weaver, "Recent Contributions," 26.
24. Weaver, Recent Contributions," 9.
25. Niklas Luhmann, *Social Systems*, trans. Eva Knodt (Stanford: Stanford University Press, 1995).
26. Norbert Wiener, *The Human Use of Human Beings: Cybernetics and Society*. (Boston: Houghton Mifflin, 1954), 16.
27. It was at Heinz von Foerster's suggestion that the Macy conferences were titled "Cybernetics: Circular Causal and Feedback Mechanisms in Biological and Social Systems" from the seventh conference in March 1950 onward. Wiener was deeply moved that his peers accepted von Foerster's proposal. See Heinz von Foerster, "Ethics and Second-Order Cybernetics," in *Understanding Understanding: Essays on Cybernetics and Cognition,* ed. Heinz von Foerster (New York: Springer, 2003), 300–01. Ironically, though, the seventh conference was also the last one he attended.
28. Shannon, "The Mathematical Theory of Communication," 85n4.
29. In Wiener's own words, "Just as the amount of information in a system is a measure of its degree of organization, so the entropy of a system is a measure of its degree of disorganization; and the one is simply the negative of the other." Norbert Wiener, *Cybernetics or Control and Communication in the Animal and the Machine,* 2nd ed. (Cambridge: MIT Press, 1961), 11. This view is shared by general systems theorists. As Ludwig von Bertalanffy put it in 1968, "entropy, as we have already heard, is a measure of disorder; hence negative entropy or information is a measure of order or of organization since the latter, compared to distribution at random, is an improbable state." Ludwig von Bertalanffy, *General System Theory: Foundations, Development, Applications* (New York: George Braziller, 1968), 42.
30. Wiener, *The Human Use of Human Beings,* 15.
31. Gregory Bateson, *Steps to an Ecology of Mind* (New York: Ballantine, 1972), 453.
32. Ralph V.L. Hartley, "Transmission of Information," *Bell System Technical Journal* 7 (1928): 535–63.
33. See Chandler's *The Transmission Model of Communication*, Aberystwyth University, http://users.aber.ac.uk/dgc/Documents/short/trans.html (accessed August 28, 2012).
34. The full title of Kittler's essay collection is *Austreibung des Geistes aus dem Geisteswissenschaften: Programme des Poststrukturalismus*. The publication of this volume in 1980 marks a crucial event in German-language literary, cultural, and media studies not only because it was instrumental in introducing (French) poststructuralist thought into Germany but also because it initiated a shift of attention from questions of meaning and interpretation to the materiality of communication.
35. See Gumbrecht's "Materialities / The Nonhermeneutic / Presence: An Anecdotal Account of Epistemological Shifts," in *Production of Presence* (Stanford: Stanford University Press, 2004) for a concise account of the evolution of his (and Pfeiffer's) challenges to the (hermeneutic) culture of sense.
36. Luciano Floridi, "Information," in *The Blackwell Guide to the Philosophy of Computing and Information,* ed. Luciano Floridi (Malden, MA: Blackwell, 2004), 52.
37. Donald M. MacKay, "In Search of Basic Symbols," in *Cybernetics: Circular Causal and Feedback Mechanisms in Biological and Social Systems:*

Transactions of the Eighth Conference, March 15–16, 1952, New York, NY, eds. Heinz von Foerster, Margaret Mead, and Hans Lukas Teuber (New York: Josiah Macy, Jr. Foundation, 1952); Donald M. MacKay, *Information, Mechanism and Meaning* (Cambridge, MA: MIT Press, 1969).

38. My reading of MacKay is informed by Dirk Baecker's account in "Kommunikation als Selektion" in *Schlüsselwerke der Systemtheorie,* ed. Dirk Baecker (Wiesbaden: Verlag für Sozialwissenschaften, 2005).

39. Jacques Attali, *Noise: The Political Economy of Music,* trans. Brian Massumi (Minneapolis: University of Minnesota Press, 1985), 27.

40. Attali, *Noise,* 4.

41. Attali, *Noise,* 26.

42. Attali, *Noise,* 132.

43. Attali, *Noise,* 6.

44. Michael Serres, *The Parasite,* trans. Lawrence R. Schehr (Baltimore: John Hopkins University Press, 1982); Michel Serres, *Genesis,* trans. Geneviève James and James Nielson (Ann Arbor: University of Michigan Press), 1997.

45. Serres, *Genesis,* 25.

46. Serres, *The Parasite,* 20.

47. Henry Adams, *The Education of Henry Adams,* ed. Jean Gooder (London: Penguin, 1995), 427.

48. In the field of literature and science, Henry Adams is best known for the thermodynamic theory of history he developed in *The Education of Henry Adams* (1907/1918) and "A Letter to American Teachers of History" (1910). For a more sustained discussion of Adams and Serres, see my "The Desire for Unity and Its Failure: Re-Reading Henry Adams through Michel Serres," in *Mapping Michel Serres,* ed. Niran Abbas (Ann Arbor: University of Michigan Press, 2005).

49. Serres, *The Parasite,* 68.

50. Serres, *Genesis,* 20.

51. William R. Paulson, *The Noise of Culture: Literary Texts in a World of Information* (Ithaca: Cornell University Press, 1988).

52. Paulson, *The Noise of Culture,* 181.

53. Paulson, *The Noise of Culture,* 180.

54. Paulson, *The Noise of Culture,* 183.

55. Paulson, *The Noise of Culture,* 180.

56. Philipp Schweighauser, *The Noises of American Literature, 1890–1985: Toward a History of Literary Acoustics* (Gainesville: University Press of Florida, 2006).

57. Paulson, *The Noise of Culture,* 157.

58. Niklas Luhmann, *Social Systems,* trans. Eva Knodt (Stanford: Stanford University Press, 1995), 68.

59. Jean-François Lyotard, *The Postmodern Condition: A Report on Knowledge,* trans. Geoff Bennington and Brian Massumi (Minneapolis: University of Minnesota Press, 1984); and Georg Kneer and Armin Nassehi, *Niklas Luhmanns Theorie sozialer Systeme: Eine Einführung* (Munich: Fink, 1993), 186–92.

60. Shannon, "The Mathematical Theory of Communication," 56.

61. James Joyce, *Finnegans Wake* (London: Faber & Faber, 1960), 3.

62. William York Tindall, *A Reader's Guide to Finnegans Wake* (London: Thames and Hudson, 1969), 31–32; Roland McHugh, *Annotations to Finnegans Wake* (Baltimore: Johns Hopkins University Press, 1980), 3; and Joseph Campbell and Henry Morton Robinson, *A Skeleton Key to Finnegans Wake* (Harmondsworth: Penguin, 1980), 15–16.

63. Ben Marcus, *The Flame Alphabet* (New York: Alfred A. Knopf, 2012), 8.
64. Theodor W. Adorno, *Aesthetic Theory*, trans. Robert Hullot-Kentor, eds. Gretel Adorno and Rolf Tiedemann (Minneapolis: University of Minnesota Press, 1997), 225–26.
65. Adorno, *Aesthetic Theory*, 59.
66. Wiener, *The Human Use of Human Beings*, 21.
67. Wiener, *The Human Use of Human Beings*, 17.
68. T.S. Eliot, "Ulysses, Order and Myth," in *Selected Prose of T.S. Eliot*, ed. Frank Kermond (London: Faber and Faber, 1975), 177. Originally published in *The Dial 75*, no 25 (Nov. 1923): 480-483. Cp. Wiener, *The Human Use of Human Beings*, 17.
69. Adorno, *Aesthetic Theory*, 243.

REFERENCES

Adams, Henry. "A Letter to American Teachers of History." In *The Degradation of the American Dogma*, 133–259. New York: Capricorn, 1958.
———. *The Education of Henry Adams*. Edited and with an introduction by Jean Gooder. London: Penguin, 1995. Original edition 1907/1918.
Adorno, Theodor W. *Aesthetic Theory*. Translated and with an introduction by Robert Hullot-Kentor. Edited by Gretel Adorno and Rolf Tiedemann. Minneapolis: University of Minnesota Press, 1997.
Attali, Jacques. *Noise: The Political Economy of Music*. Translated by Brian Massumi. Minneapolis: University of Minnesota Press, 1985.
Baecker, Dirk. "Kommunikation als Selektion: Dirk Baecker über Donald MacKays *Information, Mechanism and Meaning* (1969)." In *Schlüsselwerke der Systemtheorie*, edited by Dirk Baecker, 119–28. Wiesbaden: Verlag für Sozialwissenschaften, 2005.
Bateson, Gregory. *Steps to an Ecology of Mind*. New York: Ballantine, 1972.
Bertalanffy, Ludwig von. *General System Theory: Foundations, Development, Applications*. New York: George Braziller, 1968.
Campbell, Jeremy. *Grammatical Man: Information, Entropy, Language and Life*. London: Allen Lane, 1983.
Campbell, Joseph, and Henry Morton Robinson. *A Skeleton Key to Finnegans Wake*. Harmondsworth: Penguin, 1980.
Chandler, Daniel. *The Transmission Model of Communication*. Aberystwyth University. http://users.aber.ac.uk/dgc/Documents/short/trans.html. Accessed August 28, 2012.
Eliot, T.S. "Ulysses, Order and Myth." *Selected Prose of T.S. Eliot*. Edited by Frank Kermond. London: Faber and Faber, 1975.
Floridi, Luciano. "Information." In *The Blackwell Guide to the Philosophy of Computing and Information*, edited by Luciano Floridi, 40–61. Malden: Blackwell, 2004.
Foerster, Heinz von. "Ethics and Second-Order Cybernetics." In *Understanding Understanding: Essays on Cybernetics and Cognition*, edited by Heinz von Foerster, 287–304. New York: Springer, 2003.
Gumbrecht, Hans Ulrich. "Materialities/The Nonhermeneutic/Presence: An Anecdotal Account of Epistemological Shifts." In *Production of Presence*, 1–20. Stanford: Stanford University Press, 2004.
Hartley, Ralph V. L. "Transmission of Information." *Bell System Technical Journal* 7 (1928): 535–63.

Hayles, N. Katherine. "Information or Noise? Economy of Explanation in Barthes's S/Z and Shannon's Information Theory." In *One Culture: Essays in Science and Literature,* edited by George Levine, 119–42. Madison: University of Wisconsin Press, 1987.

Joyce, James. *Finnegans Wake.* London: Faber & Faber. Original edition 1939, 1960.

Kneer, Georg, and Armin Nassehi. *Niklas Luhmanns Theorie sozialer Systeme: Eine Einführung.* Munich: Fink, 1993.

Luhmann, Niklas. *Social Systems.* Translated by Eva Knodt. Stanford: Stanford University Press, 1995.

Lyotard, Jean-François. *The Postmodern Condition: A Report on Knowledge.* Translated by Geoff Bennington and Brian Massumi. Minneapolis: University of Minnesota Press, 1984.

MacKay, Donald M. *Information, Mechanism and Meaning.* Cambridge, MA: MIT Press, 1969.

MacKay, Donald M. "In Search of Basic Symbols." In *Cybernetics: Circular Causal and Feedback Mechanisms in Biological and Social Systems. Transactions of the Eighth Conference, March 15–16, 1951, New York, N. Y.,* edited by Heinz von Foerster, Margaret Mead, and Hans Lukas Teuber, 181–221. New York: Josiah Macy, Jr. Foundation, 1952.

Marcus, Ben. *The Flame Alphabet.* New York: Alfred A. Knopf, 2012.

McHugh, Roland. *Annotations to Finnegans Wake.* Baltimore: Johns Hopkins University Press, 1980.

Paulson, William R. *The Noise of Culture: Literary Texts in a World of Information.* Ithaca: Cornell University Press, 1988.

Schweighauser, Philipp. "Information Theory." In *Routledge Companion to Literature and Science,* edited by Bruce Clarke and Manuela Rossini, 145–56. New York: Routledge, 2010.

———. "The Desire for Unity and Its Failure: Re-Reading Henry Adams Through Michel Serres." In *Mapping Michel Serres,* edited by Niran Abbas, 136–52. Ann Arbor: University of Michigan Press, 2005.

———. *The Noises of American Literature, 1890–1985: Toward a History of Literary Acoustics.* Gainesville: University Press of Florida, 2006.

Serres, Michel. *The Parasite.* Translated by Lawrence R. Schehr. Baltimore: John Hopkins University Press, 1982.

———. *Genesis.* Translated by Geneviève James and James Nielson. Ann Arbor: University of Michigan Press, 1997.

Shannon, Claude Elwood. "A Mathematical Theory of Communication." *Bell System Technical Journal* 27 (1948): 379–423, 623–56.

———. "The Bandwagon." *Institute of Radio Engineers Transactions on Information Theory* 2 (1956): 3.

———. "The Mathematical Theory of Communication." In *The Mathematical Theory of Communication,* edited by Claude Elwood Shannon and Warren Weaver, 29–125. Chicago: University of Illinois Press, 1963.

Shannon, Claude Elwood and Warren Weaver, eds. *The Mathematical Theory of Communication.* Chicago: University of Illinois Press, 1963.

———. *The Mathematical Theory of Communication.* Chicago: University of Illinois Press, 1963.

Tindall, William York. *A Reader's Guide to Finnegans Wake.* London: Thames and Hudson, 1969.

Weaver, Warren. "Recent Contributions to the Mathematical Theory of Communication." In *The Mathematical Theory of Communication,* edited by Claude Elwood Shannon and Warren Weaver, 1–28. Chicago: University of Illinois Press, 1963.

Wiener, Norbert. *The Human Use of Human Beings: Cybernetics and Society.* Boston: Houghton Mifflin, 1954.

Wiener, Norbert. *Cybernetics: or Control and Communication in the Animal and the Machine.* 2nd ed. Cambridge: MIT Press, 1961.

Wimsatt, William K., and Monroe R. Beardsley. "The Intentional Fallacy." *Sewanee Review* 54 (3) (1946): 468–88.

3   Cybernetics
Thinking Through the Technology

Ranulph Glanville

Cybernetics, in its modern guise, was reborn in 1948 with the publication of Norbert Wiener's book *Cybernetics*.[1] The name was intended to bring focus to "control and communication in the animal and the machine," which was the book's subtitle. In his follow-up, *The Human Use of Human Beings* (Wiener 1950, with a second and much improved edition in 1954), Wiener commented "Until recently, there was no existing word for this complex of ideas and . . . I felt constrained to invent one."[2] He saw the new subject as the outcome of a co-operative process.

These bald statements are an enormous simplification. They are little more than captions, as I indicate by my choice of words. During the Second World War, boundaries across science, and certain aspects of scientific conservatism, were temporarily replaced by an untypical, speculative openness. People took risks, worked across subjects, gave mindspace to the bizarre. Interdisciplinarity was perhaps the great development in working practice.

THE ORIGINS OF CYBERNETICS

Two Sources

Modern cybernetics came out of two sets of meetings that started in World War II and continued thereafter. First, there were dinner parties Wiener held with colleagues at the Massachusetts Institute of Technology (MIT). Wiener had discovered that his colleague, the Mexican neuroscientist Arturo Rosenblueth, and he shared many understandings (particularly of mechanism) across their different fields, hidden by different jargons. Along with others, they met to search for shared understandings, each learning from the advances made in the other's fields.

Second, there were the Josiah Macy Jr. Conferences, chaired by Wiener's MIT colleague, neurophysiologist Warren McCulloch, with the mission to examine what was noted in the MACY Conference title as "Circular Causal and Feedback Mechanisms in Biological and Social Systems." The conferences ran in 1942, and then from 1946 to 1953, generating proceedings (edited by Heinz von Foerster and others) from 1948 to the end (republished by Pias in 2003).[3] There was a glittering list of regular members, including Wiener, who was a member of this group until the 1952 conference. Distinguished guests, such as W. Ross Ashby, were invited for particular conferences.

The Macy conferences had a living system bias, but both groups worked toward creating what Macy participant Margaret Mead[4] later called a common language that allowed people working in different subject areas to better communicate with each other and to find analogies across fields; i.e., general cases developed from particular instances in particular fields, which could be applied to other instances in other fields. Both groups, without favoring behaviorism, were interested in the behavior exhibited by systems.

Two Books

Wiener's two books reflect the difference between the two groups. His first, *Cybernetics,* is grounded in physics and mathematics and is challenging even for a mathematician. Consequently, its readers saw cybernetics as technical and engineering based. *The Human Use of Human Beings* is altogether more philosophical and social, better reflecting the Macy Conference concerns. It is a pity that Wiener published in the sequence he did. The confusion between these two overviews, and the general expectation that cybernetics is a technological subject, has not helped the subject.

Cybernetics and General Systems Theory

The Macy thematic statement uses the word "system." Around the time that cybernetics was reborn (1946), the first article specifically on general systems theory (GST) was published by the biologist Ludwig von Bertalanffy. He claimed to have developed this theory in lectures starting in 1937. Simplistically stated, Bertalanffy's GST was the base that spawned the assorted variety of systems sciences that we have now.[5]

Cyberneticians and systemists have always understood that there was a connection between their two fields. Some see the terms as synonyms. Often it seems the subject that is given precedence is the one in the name of the department where people studied: to systemists, cybernetics is a subset of systems, whereas to cyberneticians, systems is a limited area of cybernetics. People such as Gordon Pask insisted they didn't care what name was used; but Pask stuck to cybernetics. Hopefully these attitudes are changing. What is clear is that GST cannot lay exclusive claim to the word "system."

I introduced modern cybernetics as being "reborn." Cybernetics has a long history, which predates the notion of a systems theory by some considerable time. For instance, Socrates, according to Plato, held that "Cybernetics saves the souls, bodies, and material possessions from the gravest dangers."[6] The name derives from the Greek for helmsman: κυβερ. Socrates used the metaphor of steering a ship 2500 years ago. Greek is also the source of the Latin word *gubernator* (governor). Ampère makes this clear in 1843: "The future science of government should be called *la cybernétique*."[7] He takes his cue from mechanical "governors," such as Watt's, as much as from a notion of a (political) governor. Add to governor and steering the word "regulator," and you have key words of early modern cybernetics.

So is there a substantive difference? Cybernetics seems to be more general, more philosophical, and more abstract than systems theory, which seems full of subdivisions, more pragmatic and more "real world." Perhaps cyberneticians are fascinated by questions whereas systemists like answers. Cybernetics is also essentially concerned with dynamics: Charles François, who compiled and edited the massive *International Encyclopedia of Systems and Cybernetics* (as indispensable as it is unaffordable), characterized cybernetics as the dynamic complement of systems.[8]

Subject and Metasubject

One aspect of cybernetics that needs comment is its status as both subject and metasubject. Like mathematics, cybernetics is a subject used to comment on other subjects, particularly to bring them together by showing common processes and mechanisms. It is also, like mathematics, a subject in its own right. This is a difficult balance, and cybernetics is sometimes expected to fill one role when it is filling the other. Is cybernetics a focused subject or an umbrella-like metasubject? It is both, often (and confusingly) at the same time: there is, as I discuss below, a "cybernetics of cybernetics."

Decline

Modern cybernetics was hailed in its early years as a superscience, but already by 1956, only eight years after the publication of *Cybernetics*, there were problems. One area in which cybernetics was influential was the emerging discipline of computation. Those whose interests were in the uses of general purpose digital computers saw the potential to create an "artificial intelligence" (AI) and believed that this should be the proper subject matter of cybernetics. Others, including the majority of the "founders," saw cybernetics as much broader. The difference reflects the dual aspect of the subject: the AI group saw cybernetics primarily as the subject in itself, while the others saw it as a metasubject. The difference came to a head at a 1956 meeting at Dartmouth College, where AI was formally born. Promising specific and militarily useful outcomes, the AI group gazumped the host subject and its funding at a time when the US military was the major source of research funds in the United States and elsewhere. The fact that few of the promised outcomes were attained seems not to have been noticed, and while AI prospered, cybernetics declined in funding and in recognition. Nor was AI the only cybernetic surrogate: bionics (the engineering emulation and amplification of biological processes) also flourished for a period. Wiener's wish to make sure that there was a balance of power, which involved briefing the Soviets on American developments in the subject, did not help.[9] By the start of the 1970s, cybernetics had largely disappeared from university campuses and more generally worldwide, except as a synonym for control engineering, especially robotics. The enactment by the US Congress of the Mansfield Agreement (1969) (although later relaxed), which prohibited military funding of research lacking direct military application, did not help: technology had won over philosophy.[10] Cyberneticians, with their early claims, which were often wildly ambitious, also contributed to a loss of credibility.

Not the End: Second-Order Cybernetics

But this was not (as some have asserted) the end of cybernetics, even if the subject has since remained low on the horizon. In the 1968 paper already cited, Margaret Mead, one of the original Macy group, addressed the American Society for Cybernetics (ASC), a learned society founded in part as a reaction to the dominance of the computational paradigm of AI, and asked that this new (cybernetic) society consider itself in a cybernetic manner. Her address, called "Cybernetics of Cybernetics," requested consistency: the ASC should behave in a manner reflecting the reflexivity implicit in the approach and knowledge it fostered. Heinz von Foerster, in what is the "official origin" of second-order cybernetics, took Mead's message and applied it to the observer. He talked of a first-order cybernetics of observed systems and a second-order cybernetics of observing systems.[11] In other words, an observer of the system (first-order cybernetics) contrasted with an observer in the system (second-order cybernetics), as I like to put it (Glanville 2005). This is the official origin of second-order cybernetics.

Second-order cybernetics does not preclude first-order cybernetics. Technological cybernetics of control engineering, dealt with in Wiener's first book, survives largely oblivious to and untouched by second-order cybernetics. It remains powerfully effective at what it does. Second-order cybernetics is more philosophical and closer to the concerns of Wiener's second book. It examines what it means when the observer is in the system, normally a scientific taboo. Nevertheless, this issue is important not only for many nonscientific activities but also in many areas of science. Perhaps we might consider this in the following way: science and cybernetics are both concerned with consistency and repeatability, but in science repeatability is valued over consistency whereas in cybernetics this is reversed.

Second-order cybernetics is concerned with the study of circularity wherever it occurs. Consider, for instance, that the observer (sensor/switch) that makes up the "controller" in a thermostatic system has a circular relationship with the rest of the system: this is standard (first-order) cybernetics, which will surprise no one. However, the observer describing this system is also connected to the system in a circular relationship, even if this circularity in his/her observing is rarely noticed (for humans are affected by what we observe: we form, test, and develop concepts). Indeed, we might think of the linearity we presume in most descriptions of observing as a special, limited case of the circular—limited in the sense that we understand the returning (circular, feedback) component as so relatively weak that we don't have to worry about it, undoing the more general circularity so it becomes apparently linear. To treat the observer in both conceptions (first order and second order, linear and circular) in the same way is to invoke consistency.

Opponents argue that second-order cybernetics proposes a solipsistic way of looking at the world: that the inclusion of the observer makes knowledge of systems subjective and open to wishful thinking. Nothing could be further from the case. Second-order cybernetics demands that we test the descriptions we generate (of behaviors) in the way all science is supposed to but sometimes fails to. It simply provides us with an environment in which, and collection of tools with which, to examine systems that incorporate the observer rather than rejecting him/her. It responds to the assertion "Objectivity is a subject's delusion that observing can be done without him," recognizing that the world we inhabit is a world of our experience. Failure by some adherents to live up to these criteria is no basis for rejecting them out of hand any more than the failure of some humans to behave honestly is a reason to reject honesty. Rather than promoting solipsism, second-order cybernetics has a strong relationship with philosophical radical constructivism, which argues that we can neither assert nor (as importantly) deny the existence of a "mind independent reality."[12] However, not all cyberneticians accept second-order cybernetics, or the progression I outline.

Not First-Order, Not Second-Order: Just Cybernetics

The initial theoretical working out of second-order cybernetics as a position occurred roughly between 1968 and 1976. Some feel that cybernetics since then has been waiting for the next great insight. I disagree: I see extensions of the original formulations, and a growing understanding that second-order cybernetics is at least as old as first-order: that the distinction might be dropped.

I see two other developments. The first is that, if one looks back at the early work for which cybernetics was named by Wiener, one sees the observer was often included, although sometimes implicitly rather than explicitly. In my view, the Macy conferences were already implicitly concerned with second-order systems, so cybernetics can be thought to have begun a second-order cybernetics. First-order cybernetics was a simplification that turned into a strategic error. Consider discussions of creativity and intelligence, so important in AI. The current, slow replacing of definitional, algorithmic, outside-view approaches might not have been necessary had the AI pioneers known of the cybernetics of Gregory Bateson,[13] who insisted, in discussing creativity, that when humans use computers (raising the question, is the computer or the human creative/intelligent?), creativity exists not in one or the other but between the human and the computer working in a particular context. This understanding of second-order cybernetics was glossed over in the rush to create a technology that is AI, all the while ignoring an inconsistency between the epistemological stances of the subject itself and that of the observer describing it.

The second reaffirms an understanding of the relationship between theory and practice. Culturally, we have tended to give precedence to theory—as expressed in assertions such as "Don't act until you understand." Yet, as Piaget has shown us, our learning, when we are children, begins with action (practice), from which we develop understanding (theory).[14] Second-order cybernetics sees practice and theory (like action and understanding) as linked in another circularity with precedence given to neither (see diagram below). We can enter the circle of practice/theory (acting/understanding) from either concept, inevitably proceeding to the other and then back to the concept through which we entered. Following Schön, practitioners such as designers have begun to explore, researching in and through their practice, building a body of research that recognizes their practice as equal to theorizing, an approach that is both inspired by second-order cybernetics and deeply antagonistic to the views of more traditional design researchers who look for a more classically "scientific" understanding (and its application) based on linear causality. In this new approach, designers can see what they do (their professional activity) as worthy of research, developing theory from this work rather than being confronted by an alien type of research that simply fails, in its imposition, to recognize what designers do. While not exactly the same, evidence-based research shares this view: we are to value what we experience. Observe and do. An approach to a more cybernetic type of research (in design, through practice) can be found in Glanville and van Schaik, where a doctoral program that particularly values practice is described.[15] We will discuss this in greater detail toward the end of this text.

Many fields have, to use a metaphor, taken from cybernetics, which they have treated as a toolbox, without returning the tools. They have failed to see the stronger coherence existing in the tool set, forgetting its source and history. Nowadays, we find the name "cybernetics" popping up in many guises, usually not well related to the original. We also see "problems" that cybernetics dealt with many years ago reappearing as if new. These problems often reappear in exactly those fields that have taken from cybernetics without giving due credit and without care for coherence and consistency. The current fascinations with self-organization and complexity are but two examples.

Diagram 3.1 The basic model of communication used by Shannon and Weaver. The message is encoded (for instance, speech is converted into a radio signal) and transmitted. Noise (unwanted modifications to the radio signal) enters between transmission and receipt before the resulting, accidentally modified signal is decoded and received as a slight modification of the message.

CYBERNETIC INVESTIGATION

Cybernetics is concerned with behavior. Although Wiener is generally recognized as the father of cybernetics, many believe Ashby's 1956 *Introduction to Cybernetics* is the best general formulation of what it is. Ashby, a psychologist, presented cybernetics through the metaphor of machine with input and output, which became the central metaphor for the investigation of cybernetic systems. A machine should be understood not through an industrial image of cogs and levers, but as a connected suite of mechanisms, specifying predictable, logically consequent, and reliable outcomes of specific actions, revealed as changes in behaviors. As Ashby wrote: "Cybernetics does not ask 'what is this machine?' but 'what does it do?' "[16]

In Ashby's machine, a mechanism connects the in- and outputs causing the input to become the output. Von Foerster divides input/output machines into trivial (predictable machines) and nontrivial (unpredictable machines that learn).[17] On occasion, when we do not know what connects input and output, we use a "Black Box" (a thought experiment devised by the physicist James Clerk Maxwell), which allows us to postulate a mechanism converting a set of inputs into a set of outputs. In my interpretation, we do not know what is inside the Black Box (the Black Box is, itself, a postulate).[18] Any mechanism we propose works while it works: it has viability without actuality. Some confuse the Black Box with the nontrivial machine, but they are essentially different.

Ashby suggests we often face a situation in which we treat what faces us as a Black Box: for instance, when faced with a door handle, a child learns to use it without any idea of what's going on in the mechanism. Ashby speculates that we may treat everything we encounter as a Black Box, including each other.[19] Thus, when faced with a door handle, we do not need to know what happens "inside," but what moving the lever does; and we develop an understanding that allows us a good guess without ever knowing what the hidden mechanism is. The "actual" mechanism doesn't matter: what matters is that we can open and close doors.

Cybernetic investigation uses the metaphor of the machine as a way of explaining behaviors. It also builds machines to behave in such ways. But it still realizes the limits of the machine metaphor, that it is only when the mechanical behavior breaks down that the investigation is teaching us something new, using Foerster's term, that it is nontrivial. The Black Box allows us to imagine a machine that is not only nontrivial, but one for which the notion of triviality has no relevance. The investigator (Ashby's name for the observer) is always present: the system includes him/her. The devices cybernetics has developed for its investigations are in many ways superb models for a modern, skeptical science, based on the notion of explanation by humans.

KEY CONCEPTS

What are cybernetics' key concepts? I have arranged them in four subgroups consisting of error, subtitle, state, and circularity concepts. My choice, and grouping, will not be universally accepted. I have omitted concepts such as self-organization, and also thinkers others might consider of primary importance. Different groupings are possible; and several selected concepts could (and do) appear under more than one heading. As we will see, this is to be expected when we take a position informed by second-order cybernetics.

1) Error Concepts

Probably the best-known "cybernetic" concept, often taken as synonymous with the subject, is "feedback." Feedback provides a way of dealing with something far more ubiquitous: error. Without error, we don't need feedback and may continue to understand the world in the image of Newton's idealized, perfect machine.[20] Cybernetics is distinctive in accepting the ubiquity of error. Newton's model aims for idealized and unchanging perfection, while the cybernetic worldview assumes error is omnipresent. We may reduce it, manage it, alleviate and counteract it, but it persists. It is not an inconvenience that we can get rid of.

In cybernetics, error was initially seen as divergence from a desired path, or a failure to attain some goal point. Early on, Rosenblueth, Wiener, and Bigelow wrote of systems with intentionality: systems that were not simply mechanical but intended to achieve something (for instance, an antiaircraft shell hitting a plane in flight).[21] The introduction of purpose into a system (under the term "teleology") was brave, risking scientific scorn because it betrays a wish to steer the action rather than remain in a neutral state. When examined in this purposive way, failing to hit the plane registered as an error to be measured and corrected. The potential to miss some goal was assumed.

Cybernetics contributed a means of communicating success (or a lack of success) in attaining a goal and an indication of the nature of the miss. The means of communication is a channel passing "feedback" to the actor-agent operating the system, allowing the actor-agent both to recognize there had been an error and to adjust the system so as to reduce this. (Error-reducing feedback is called "negative feedback." Contrastingly, when feedback increases the error, it is called "positive feedback." Probably the best-known example is the rapidly increasing howl that amplifiers can produce.)

A further aspect of purpose is that the system's goal is chosen (by an actor-agent). The operation of the system is through a loop. The behavior of the actor-agent is determined by both the goal (which (s)he usually sets) and the signal (s)he gets back concerning the success of the instigated action. This contrasts with the simple and direct cause and effect normal science gives us.

The system becomes a cybernetic system as a result of the error being reported back: the cybernetic system responds after the event. Cybernetic behavior in a system comes about through continuous testing, checking, acting to change (if necessary), and testing again. This is the circle of that key cybernetic activity, control, which we come to in the next section.

2) Subtitle Concepts

The subtitle of Wiener's book *Cybernetics* is "or Control and Communication in the Animal and the Machine." The subtitle is often taken as a definition, with the phrase "the science of" inserted at the start, but this addition is not in Wiener's original.

The subtitle divides into two parts. The first deals with control and communication, the second with the animal and the machine. The phrase "the animal and the machine" defines the areas in which cybernetics operates, making it specifically both broad and interdisciplinary. Mead, as already noted, saw cybernetics as providing a language, allowing us to cross between disciplines. Cybernetics should provide a way of thinking that allows discussion of both the animal and the machine, a distinction embodied in science as the distinction between biology and mechanics/physics. Error correction (regulation) through feedback is a behavior exhibited by both animals and machines. Descartes's favoring of a mechanical metaphor to explain the living had long been familiar by the 1940s when (for instance) medics discussed the human body in mechanical terms such as "lever."

First-order cybernetics promoted this metaphor (e.g., the brain as computer—for instance, see Arbib and Beer;[22] and although Ashby's re-creation of the biological phenomenon of homeostasis (the ability of a system to return to its normal, stable state in the face of arbitrary perturbations) in a machine—the "homeostat"—might be thought of as the realization of an animal metaphor, Ashby's homeostat was innovatory when introduced.[23] It was another fifteen to twenty years before Humberto Maturana introduced the concept of "autopoiesis" in a paper coauthored with his student Francisco Varela (who formalized the concept mathematically) and his colleague Ricardo Uribe (who created an automaton that simulated autopoietic behavior).[24] I gloss autopoiesis as Maturana's attempt to present life as a process of becoming and remaining alive (in Greek, auto + poiesis translates to self + production), creating a mechanism for the animate and for the autonomy of form that living things generate. This may be interpreted, in hindsight, as a machine using an animal metaphor. The change from the mechanical metaphor for the animal to an animal metaphor for the machine is another way of conceiving the difference between first- and second-order cybernetic.

Maturana continues working in biology and neurology, where he has developed the "Biology of Love." Varela, who died young in 2001, became interested in consciousness, especially embodied consciousness, and was a scientific advisor to the Dalai Lama. The last collaboration between Maturana and Varela was the book *The Tree of Knowledge.*[25]

The concept of autopoiesis has attracted a lot of attention and has been appropriated (against Maturana's wishes) by scholars working in other fields than biology. Probably the most notable is Niklas Luhmann's adoption of the concept in his own work in sociology and communication, for instance in Luhmann's "The Autopoiesis of Social Systems."[26]

The other pairing in Wiener's subtitle directs us to the heart of cybernetics: control and communication. If error is endemic—the aspect of a system's behavior that gives life to cybernetics—control and communication are the concepts that allow a feedback loop to function, to accommodate and alleviate this error.

There can be no control without communication. The controller's wishes impinge on the controlled through some form of communication. Early cybernetics required messages to be sent from one entity to another so the second entity might act in accordance with the wishes of the first. The means of communication was taken to be a channel through which messages were transmitted. This aspect of cybernetics is difficult to separate from Claude Shannon's (Shannon and Weaver 1948) "A Mathematical Theory of Communication" (known popularly though incorrectly as Information Theory), published in 1949. Shannon, Weaver, and Wiener were close and mutually supportive colleagues, although Shannon's publication created a rift.[27] The power of Shannon's understanding is seen in the extraordinary communication and control systems we have today; but there are serious questions about how it helps with human communication, a critical matter for many of the Macy participants and those who have since come to sympathize with them.

Communication is a prerequisite for control; but control is the more important key concept. Yet it is a difficult concept for many people because it suggests restriction and imposition. Cybernetic control aims to facilitate. If we have the goal that a room should maintain a particular temperature, controlling the delivery of heat (in a cold climate) facilitates this wish. If we wish to ski down a slope, being able to act to absorb the unexpected,

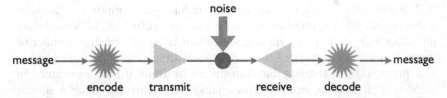

Diagram 3.2 Traditional accounts have an unambiguous relationship between the controller and the controlled. Whenever there is a circular (i.e., cybernetic) system, however, the roles of controller and controlled become less clear. In this case, control exists between the two elements, as shown here in a form of mutual control.

such as irregularities in the physical environment or the sudden appearance of other skiers, is vital. Without this degree of control in our behavior, we would not succeed. In cybernetic terms, for control to be effective, each state that we identify as being one we might have to respond to in the environment (which we call the "variety" of the environment) needs to somehow be mapped into the (controlling) model we have of that environment: i.e., we need at least as much variety in the controlling system as in the system being controlled.

There are systems in which the variety exercised by the controller is (vastly) less than that in the controlled. In these cases, the control is restrictive. One of the worst results is dictatorship. If the controlling system does not have enough variety, it restricts that which is to be controlled. This restrictive form of control is what cybernetics acts against. However, there is a fortunate upside. Consider how the world can be understood as much richer in variety than my brain can ever be. Rather than controlling in a deeply restrictive manner, I may benefit from the variety imbalance by using the variety I do not have as a resource, offering me all sorts of riches I had never imagined![28]

3) State Concepts

We have already mentioned our state concepts. Here we will examine them further.

Let us assume a conventional description of a system as consisting of a number of variables. As determined by some observer, each variable has a number of states the system may attain. The particular state a system is in is, thus, distinct, within the set of states that a variable may take at any moment.

If a state is considered desirable by some observer, it becomes a goal—a preferred state that a system is seen as trying to attain and/or maintain. Some goals are points, like a harbor we sail toward. Others are trajectories, such as a flight path that is followed. Goals are determined by the observer/actor who acts as the actor-agent.

The number of states a system may attain has special importance because it determines what is required so that it may be controlled. W. Ross Ashby introduced the concept of variety, which can be expressed in a number of ways. It measures the states the system may attain, either as a number or as a proportion of the possible states it might attain if not constrained in some way. It is often presented as analogous to entropy, using a similar logarithmic expression. Ashby's argument, expressed in his "Law of Requisite Variety,"[29] is that the controlling system must have at least as much variety as the controlled system: if this condition is not satisfied, some states the system might normally be able to attain will be excluded because the controlling system does not have them, thus restricting performance. Hence the discussion above in the previous section of the role of variety in the two different types of control—facilitative and restrictive. Variety is not, as entropy is, an absolute physical measure. Analysis may be reformulated, and the calculation of the states to be attained and criteria of attainment may alter. A major skill of those interested in big and complex systems is to re-envision a system to be controlled so the requisite variety is reduced. The work of Stafford Beer, the so-called father of management cybernetics, is deeply concerned with variety and variety management, as can be seen in his selected papers.[30]

I used the word "constraint," above. Constraint measures the relation between the variety a configuration might take, and the actual variety it does take. It describes how some of the possible states a system might (in theory) take are not taken up. Often, this provides an advantage: many have experienced paralysis when faced with seemingly limitless variety. Some use constraint to describe what happens when the variety in the controller is less than that needed by the controlled system. I prefer to limit "constraint" to describe a range of possibilities, using "restrict" for variety imbalance.

4) Circularity Concepts

The notion of feedback has already been mentioned several times. Feedback occurs through a channel allowing communication to occur, permitting an actor-agent to decide how successful his/her action has been (did it, and/or does it continue to, attain the goal). Wiener's notion suggested that the energy involved in feedback was tiny compared to that in the "main" action, allowing feedback to be treated as secondary. Hence the actor-agent's action, leading to feedback concerning success in attaining some goal, is understood as the action of the controller. Part of the early cybernetic discussion of control was dominated by the physics of energy, so that which used little energy to control much was taken to be the controller—obvious, perhaps, if you are a physicist, but not so obvious if you are a cybernetician.

If, however, we talk in terms of action and communication rather than of energy, the link between the actor-agent and the objects, trajectories, goals, etc. is circular. The half of the circularity Wiener called feedback is no longer relatively minor (because it is energetically insignificant), but operationally and informationally of equal significance. This matches the conditions as Ashby says, "Cybernetics is the study of the immaterial aspects of systems." Again, using the archetypical cybernetic example, the thermostat, we understand that (in a cold climate) while the switch on the wall controls the provision of heat, the provision of heat controls the switch on the wall. Each element controls the other; each is controlled by the other. The stasis of the system derives from both the (heat) sensor and the (heat) provider elements working together in mutual control and balance to achieve a goal. Cybernetic control is essentially circular: control happens between the elements. It is, in this cybernetic way of looking, impossible to determine which half of the circle is the feedback loop.

We can also interpret control as cause. In a control system, the controller causes the controlled to act as the controller wishes. When control is mutual, each element causes the other to behave in a particular way. The Macy Group's "mission statement" referred to "circular causal and feedback mechanisms." The thermostat operates through a circular mechanism. Thus, we understand from the outset the deep-seated concern of cybernetics with circularity: A controls B and B controls A; the switch controls the heat supply and the heat supply controls the switch. Some behavior in A causes some behavior in B, which causes some (further) behavior in A and so on.

This reconnects us to the cybernetic approach to error. The process of error correction using feedback is one in which the actor-agent controls a (sub)system's behavior, while the system's behavior is used by the actor-agent to determine the next control operation on the (sub)system. As we now understand control, the (sub)system is, in this manner, controlling controls, in this manner, the actor-agent's behavior. Error correction is an unending circular process—for error is endemic and unpredictable.

Cybernetics pursues a behaviorist approach (it observes and tries to account for behaviors), reflected in its mechanical aspect. Through the mechanisms of circularity, the elements, actor-agent and (sub)system, are in some sense changed each cycle around the circle. Thus the behavior of each changes in response to the other. In this sense, the actor-agent's progress around the circle forms a spiral: the circle is like a track, the spiral the experience of circling.

An important note: in a circular system we assume the possibility of similar behavior in each element. Each controls the other; each is controlled by the other. What is possible in one should be possible (in principle) in the other. I have called the notion that, in circular systems, qualities that may be assumed of the one element should, potentially, be assumable of the other "the principle of mutual reciprocity." This is an extension of the Law of Requisite Variety.

We often call a more sophisticated approach to error correction "learning." One way to learn, and we can consider primitive learning, is through error correction. When we think of learning as creating a pattern as we correct errors, extrapolating from a number of specific cases to develop a general understanding through which to modify our behavior, we exhibit learning, and we modify our learned behavior by continuing to test for errors and adapting accordingly, continuing this learning process.

MEAD'S IMPLIED CRITIQUE OF CYBERNETICS: CONSISTENCY

I have recounted how, in her 1968 keynote address to the ASC's first conference, Margaret Mead asked that the ASC learn the lessons of its own subject and apply them to its own functioning and aspirations—both for consistency's sake and to show it valued itself. Foerster provided her with a title, "Cybernetics of Cybernetics."

Mead's intention was managerial: to shape the society to behave cybernetically. She had already noted that the Society for General System Research did not behave systemically. She was concerned that the ASC might become ordinary, traditional, and conventional—in a word, uncybernetic. Foerster (often called the father of second-order cybernetics, but better thought of, in the way that he talked of himself, as its ringmaster) extended Mead's argument in an unexpected way. He took the idea that cybernetics should be self-consistent and applied it to the matter of how cybernetic investigation is carried out.

Here are two moves Foerster made. Please note: these are my explanations, not his. Let me give my accounts of two actions Foerster took. Foerster's first action was to compile a book, the outcome of an elective course taught at the University of Illinois. Also called "Cybernetics of Cybernetics,"[31] it consisted of selected cybernetics texts, illuminated by different cybernetic analyses. The second move was more abstract. In "Cybernetics of Cybernetics" Foerster makes the following differentiation, by now familiar to the reader: first-order cybernetics, the cybernetics of observed systems; second-order cybernetics, the cybernetics of observing systems. I shall attempt to relate this statement to Mead's demand in her keynote address. After all, Mead was the first field anthropologist to work as an active observer, participating with those she studied. She studied as an observing system.[32]

Remember the thermostat. The switch on the wall senses the temperature and "decides" the air is too cold. This action is sensed by the heat provider, which heats the air—which is what the switch senses. When the air is hot enough, the switch ceases to demand heat from the heat provider.

The elements sense each other. "Observe" is a word used in science to indicate sensing. Insofar as control, a key cybernetic activity, depends on sensing, observing is a cybernetic activity. My earlier account of the thermostat insisted each element was controlled by, while also controlling, the other. Substitute the word "observe" for "control," and we have the cybernetics of the observed and of the observing. In first-order cybernetics we consider the behavior of the controlled (observed) element. In second-order cybernetics we consider the controlling (observing). The circularity is of (mutual) observing occurring within the system.

How do we investigate observed and observing in the circularity that is the thermostat? By observing its behaviors. The thermostatic system, itself, has an observer. The thermostat is the observed of another observer's observing. However, in cybernetic systems, control (observation) involves the mutual control (observation) of each element by the other. To be consistent in observing, we must observe our system of interest as we have learned the cybernetic system observes itself. Hence the second-order cybernetics interest in observing, satisfying Mead's demand for consistency: we observe the system as it observes itself. The thermostat and its observer form a circular system. The location of the observer when considered thus changes. Systems can be observed from within and from without: but the view from without forms a new circular system between the (circular) system being observed and the observer (without).

The difference between observing from within and without a system is significant. What may be perfectly stable (continuing as is, without change) when observed from within the system may appear to an outside observer to change: think of how we believe ourselves to be essentially unchanging while to our friends we may seem to have changed a good deal. Cybernetics allows us to understand these differences in viewpoint not as contradictory, but as distinct and often complementary.[33]

Since each observer is understood as different and unique, the observations of each will be different. In the terms that Foerster put this in a conversation with Ernst von Glaserfield: "Objectivity is the delusion that observations could be made without an observer." Second-order cybernetics satisfies Mead's consistency requirement by reformulating the subject so that the investigation of cybernetics occurs in a cybernetic manner.

PHILOSOPHICAL PARALLEL

Second-order cybernetics is more philosophically questioning than the technologically driven first-order cybernetics.[34] In the 1970s, Ernst von Glasersfeld (whose involvement with cybernetics began in the early 1950s) developed a philosophical approach, radical constructivism, that grew out of the work of Piaget and that he related, in title and content, to the philosophies of Vico and Berkeley.[35]

Glasersfeld insisted we live in experience. He argued not that there is no "mind independent reality," but that we cannot know whether there is or is not because we are "wrapped" in experience and our minds do the knowing. For Glasersfeld, knowing is justified through the test of viability rather than of truth: the best we can hope for is that it works, now (this is close to Popper's "Conjectures and Refutations").[36] The knower is always present. Faced with the "undecidable question" of whether there is a mind-independent reality, we may choose (and choose again, differently). There is no "right"—only that which works, under the circumstances and in the particular context. To my mind, we also need an important few whose task is to maintain this undecidability. I count myself among the few.

Thus, Glasersfeld produced an explicit philosophy that comes from the nonexclusion of the knower (observer), creating a parallel with second-order cybernetics. By taking the seven statements of Glasersfeld's "core of radical constructivism" and showing that each is reflected in second-order cybernetics, I demonstrate the close connection between the two.[37] Interestingly, in his seventh core statement, Glasersfeld quotes philosopher Leo Apostel, sounding in 1977 remarkably like Margaret Mead: "A system should always be applied to itself."[38] Glasersfeld understands that radical constructivism cannot be said to be right. It works when and as it works and is but one of the options. And writing about cybernetics, Glasersfeld asserts, "Cybernetics is a way of thinking, not a collection of facts."[39]

WHAT SECOND-ORDER CYBERNETICS CHANGES

Mead's (and Apostel's) requirement suggests that cybernetic investigations should not only report cybernetic behaviors but be executed in a cybernetic manner. A cybernetic investigation of a cybernetic system should be cybernetic in style, based in cybernetic understandings, justifying itself in its own terms. This was not a requirement made of earlier cybernetics![40]

We live with many systems where the observer is inside the system: for instance, Macy's biological and social systems, and in our experience. One way of thinking about social and human sciences, ecology, etc., is to note that throughout their history, they have tried to handle observer inclusion as a problem to be minimized, if not overcome: to construct the system so that the presence of the observer within it, and the interaction between the investigator and the investigated, becomes more like the relationship between observer and observed in Newton's model.[41] Second-order cybernetics takes a different stance, highlighting that the system includes the investigator. It learns how this form of investigation might work and the value of what we might get from the investigation. Characteristically, second-order cybernetics is more interested in learning than in knowledge.

Although many early cybernetic concepts are but slightly affected, second-order cybernetics asks us to reconsider key concepts, for instance, control, communication, and circularity (and concepts associated with them). We will consider each. It also returns us to a more general, philosophical view of cybernetics in keeping with the insights of at least many of the founders, who viewed technological cybernetics as a restricted (but valued) special case. And it leads to a cybernetics in which, using the metaphor of the Black Box, we do not assume we can see inside the box: our explanations are just explanations. Our understanding is based in a lasting and deep ignorance.

1) Control

We have seen how the basic cybernetic activity of control should be considered as circular rather than linear: that is, it is a shared activity within a system. As noted earlier, a control system has two elements: the controller and the controlled, each of which controls the other, so each is controller of the other and controlled by the other.

Ashby's Law of Requisite Variety requires that the controlling element have at least as much variety as the controlled; otherwise the control will not be cybernetic (facilitative) but restrictive. However, in the situation that Ashby apparently did not foresee, when each element is both controller and controlled, the variety of each element must be the same.

This may not be possible. Utilizing the notion of variety and the worldview it espouses, we understand that a group of connected people will have much more variety than one person. Combinatoric differences will be vast, and the only way one could hope to control the group is by massively restricting its variety. Considering ourselves in the universe, it is clear that, as we account for the universe now, there is unimaginably more variety in the universe than in the brain of any of us. This means we are out of control—the universe is unmanageable. The only way we can control the universe is to vastly restrict its variety—to treat it as tiny.

There is an alternative: to give up controlling! Accept the universe as essentially unmanageable. This means at least two things. First, there is a vast source of stuff, potentially new to us, that we can take as a source of personal creativity if we just "keep our eyes open." Second, rather than trying to be in control, we respond to what is on offer to us. We open up our relation to the universe responsively. We learned at the outset that cybernetics is necessarily a responsive approach, so this is a consistent position, modest and humble, familiar to us in several thought systems, for instance Buddhism, which is often characterized as a religion of acceptance and response rather than of proselytization and domination. Buddhist notions of control seem similar to those of second-order cybernetics, too.

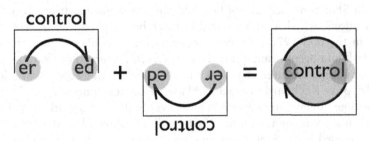

Diagram 3.3

2) Communication

What we all probably treat as the dominant model of communication involves a message encoded, transmitted (distorted), received, and decoded. This is the transmission channel of information theory in Shannon and Weaver's mathematical theory of communication. The point is to get a message from a sender to a recipient without distortion. We assume that the message carries meaning and that the meaning to the receiver is the meaning intended by the transmitter. This is communication by coding.

The moment we assume that the transmitting and receiving observer (actor-agents) are individually different, the transmission of meaning becomes a problem—and the assumptions made in the information theory modeled in Shannon's theory become clear: how could we believe the message has same meaning to transmitter and receiver? We have to test and explore this belief with each other, meaning we cannot assume successful transmission/reception. Code is not given, it's an agreement we arrive at— by negotiation!

If each observer creates his or her own understanding, these understandings are unique to the particular observer/actor and inaccessible to others. How, then, might we communicate? I cannot transmit my meaning to you. I may offer some utterance to which you may give your own meaning. In response, you may make an utterance, and if I find the meaning I generate in response to this close enough to my originally intended meaning, I may believe you "understand" me. Of course, you do not, but your understanding seems to me to "co-ordinate" (as Maturana says) with mine. And if not, I can try again: this is an error-correction action, and either or both of us can take it.

This form of negotiatory communication is familiar: we call it conversation. Conversation is the communication primitive in second-order cybernetics, as it is between humans. Gordon Pask created conversation theory from human conversation to allow students to "teachback" what they had learned in computer-aided learning systems. It has rich consequences. In contrast, a code, such as a fixed meaning of a word, is a *negotiated* agreed restriction.

Conversation is archetypical interaction. Pask's conversation theory is the polar of Shannon's account of how we can communicate. It has very wide ramifications, which Pask explored in three books produced in very short order in the mid-1970s. As Pask accounts for it, conversation is interactive. Pask had been meaningfully concerned with interaction from the early 1950s, building the interactive machines Musicolour and several varieties of Self-Adaptive Keyboard Instructor.[42] Pask's early machines are possibly still the most genuinely interactive machines ever built. Pask's work is, as I have argued in a commentary on his 1961 book, consumed by interaction.[43] In the sense used here, interaction involves an active contribution from both parties, leading, often, to the completely unexpected—as when we find it

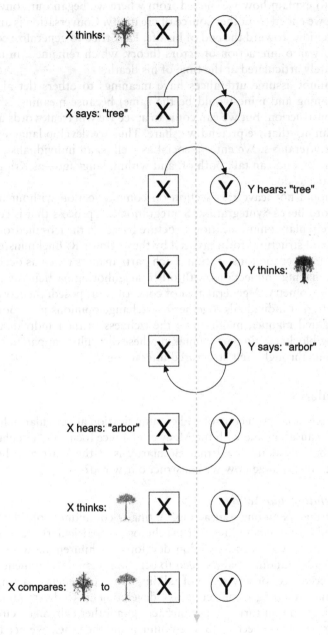

Diagram 3.4 Gordon Pask proposed a type of communication closely modeled on everyday conversation, which allows us to develop personal meanings in parallel with each other and nevertheless to communicate. This diagram shows Pask's structure of conversational exchanges. Depending on the outcome of the final comparison shown, X will determine if Y has understood (constructed a working parallel meaning). If not, X will try again, modifying their earlier attempt.

difficult to explain how we moved from where we began our conversation to where we ended—another source of creativity. Conversation is archetypical interaction. Toward the end of his life, Pask tried to generalize conversation theory into interaction of actors theory, which remained, in my view, inadequately articulated at the time of his death.

We cannot assume utterances have meanings to others (let alone that your meaning and mine would be the same) because meaning is an individual construction. But we can come to agree we will treat words as if they have meanings that we pretend we share. Thus we develop language rather than just utterances. We enter a social as well as an individualist, psychological arena, and can talk both of, and within, language—as Krippendorff would have us do.[44]

We should not leave this section on communication without mentioning Stafford Beer's Syntegration. Syntegration is a process that is contained within a circular communication structure based on the icosahedron, a geometrical and structural form favored by the engineer R. Buckminster Fuller, from whom Beer took inspiration. Each participant is taken as occupying a node and having connections with other, neighboring participants, according to the geometry. A general area of concern is proposed: the icosahedron brings different individuals together to exchange opinions in a coordinated and regulated manner, maintaining the richness of their individuality and dissolving blockages, in part by making these difficulties apparent to all the participants through their structured interactions.[45]

3) Circularity

We have seen that both control and communication are circular in form and circularly causal, in line with the Macy conference focus on "circular causal and feedback systems"; and that circularity is at the heart of cybernetics. How does this change how we construct our world?

Understanding and Acting
Consider understanding and acting. Acting is commonly considered to be predicated on understanding. Yet psychologists (particularly Jean Piaget)[46] working on how conceptualization develops in children show us that, to develop understanding, babies need to act. In human development, if there is any precedence, or any sense of talking about precedence, acting comes before understanding in our cognitive development. Understanding comes from acting, and, in turn, shapes our acting: another cybernetic circularity, and a good one. We need both, each influencing the other. We need to consider the whole rather than a simpler linearization of that whole.

We can understand this relationship when we consider different types of knowledge that may satisfy different aims. I have argued that (second-order) cybernetics and design are complementary.[47] Whereas science constructs knowledge of the world as it is (i.e., understanding), design is interested in changing that world: it wants knowledge for change (acting). The difference is captured in the prepositions "of" and "for."[48] Knowledge for acting leads to new things of which we then gain knowledge. The trick is figuring out how to move from knowledge of what is into effective action, completing another virtuous circle.

Theory and Practice

We may reconceptualize this redrawn relationship between acting and understanding to illuminate the relationship between theory and practice. We have learned to give precedence to theory. But, substituting theory for understanding, practice for acting, we see this relationship also as circular. Giving precedence to understanding/theory brings great dangers of distorting our relationship with our experience. There is a risk rooted in the question of appropriateness that, while it can offer novel options, can equally remove options that properly belong in practice but are absent in the theory. Using examples from Eric Berne's transactional analysis, Graham Barnes shows the danger that patients may be damaged when theory is allowed to dominate practice in psychotherapy.[49] Humans construct patterns to move out of the continuous flow of experience: we create theories derived from our experiences, bringing them together and shaping a world view in a circular act of cybernetic unification. But when we allow pattern to dominate our experience, we can end in conflict and psychological distress.

When we don't pay attention to practice, to what happens in the world of action, we can mislead ourselves greatly. This is what happens all too often when we assume the linear. The circularity of second-order cybernetics helps us guard against this sort of error.

We who often talk of the application need also to be careful of the word "application" (e.g., of theory to practice). Application involves a hierarchical "power play." In conventional cybernetic terms, the application of a theory means the theory is placed over (and hence restrictively controls) practice. This undermines cybernetic circularity. It runs the risk Barnes so clearly demonstrated.[50] Application is an inappropriate concept for the relationship that should hold between practice and theory. This argument means we do not have to accept the priority of that current major driver, utility. Stafford Beer liked to talk of cybernetics as the science of effective action and efficacy: effectiveness is far more valuable and important than efficiency.[51]

Mind and Body

As a final example, consider the great Cartesian duality between mind and body. Think how, in Western culture, we insistently return to the material, requiring that all existence should be subject to that interesting abstract construction, "laws of physics." We talk of mind depending on body, but from a human point of view, the laws of physics are of little interest if we are without mind: hence, Ashby asserts cybernetics is the study of the immaterial aspects of systems. This is not to deny the value of the material, only to insist that it is a necessary primitive condition. On the contrary, we could argue that mind must have precedence over matter: without mind, the existence of the material world is a matter of no concern. James Clerk Maxwell, inventor of the Black Box, described the situation perfectly: "The only laws of matter are those that our minds must fabricate, and the only laws of mind are fabricated for it by matter."[52]

As Bateson insists, there is no schism: mind and body need each other— the ultimate statement of the holistic explanation of experience.[53] For myself, I think of the embodiment of my mind: how I behave is shaped by my body. I cannot imagine that a brain transplant (assuming mind and brain are connected) could result in more than locked-in syndrome.[54]

Mechanisms of Circularity

We can also explore the mechanisms of circularity. Cybernetics has been especially interested in three of these.

Recursion

The concept of recursion matches the concept of circularity. Meaning "to run back," it refers to progression through a circularity: as we go around and around, we return to each point where we were earlier. In effect, we spiral through the circularity and must create our understanding of identity each time we pass over a "same" point. Studies of recursion allow us to better understand how circularity functions. Recursions tend toward fixed points—but, having reached them, they continue to recurse around these fixed points endlessly. Eigenforms (see below) give us good examples.

Reflection and Reflexion

One expression of cybernetic recursiveness is reflection/reflexion, which have a common origin but have developed differing meanings. The centrality of reflection/reflexion in second-order cybernetics was recognized in Frederick Steier's 1991 book *Research and Reflexivity,* including essays by Foerster, Glasersfeld, and Krippendorff.

Reflection entails deep consideration. There is an element, too, of throwing back (in the mirror). In his work *The Reflective Practitioner,* Donald Schön uses both of these meanings.[55] In the 1980s, Schön (who trained as a philosopher and became an educationalist and urban planner committed to a systems view) was concerned that both the way of learning and the knowledge of professional practitioners were ignored and even dismissed by others who believed they owned learning and knowledge. Following a series of studies, he argued that professional practitioners had a way of learning that he called reflection in action: a process of both contemplating and evaluating what they had been doing in their practice and reflecting this back in a circle to create improvement. Schön's work thus places cybernetic circularity, in the form of reflection, at the center of approaches to research, linking theory and practice in a powerful assertion of the viability and centrality of circularity.[56]

Although reflexion is an archaic spelling of reflection, I find it useful to differentiate the two thus: Reflection involves a change in the actor-agent (and is thus clearly in tune with second-order cybernetics), whereas reflexion is more of a systems behavior. An example is the reflexivity theory of George Soros, which Soros developed in economics.[57] Several cyberneticians consider this theory to exemplify second-order cybernetics.[58] Although developed by one of the world's great financiers, it has not found a large audience among economists, who, apparently, still hope to produce a classic, scientific model of economic working, with no room for involving the observer or the actor-agent. It is little wonder the world's finances are in a mess!

Foerster's "Through the Eyes of the Other" (in Steier's book) gives a powerful depiction not only of a circular, reflective (my spelling) process, but also of how the reflective mechanism allows us to build our personal identities through social interaction.[59] Foerster's position is that we learn to understand, even to form ourselves, as we interact with others, seeing ourselves as we understand they see us. The reflexive unit of this process is not the individual, but the interaction between two individuals forming a unit. Reflectivity is thus allied to conversation, creating self-understanding and self-worth: it is indeed central not only to cybernetics but to being human.

Self-Similarity

We may also consider self-similarity (the parts of which a whole is made have similar form to the whole) a variety of circularity and recursion. As a Mandelbrot set reproduces its (fractal) geometry at all levels (scales), so many cybernetic systems do the same. Perhaps best known of these is Beer's 1985 Viable Systems Model, which is intended to provide similar steering and level-jumping resources at all levels of a management system. Beer's model describes a minimum set of criteria for any particular viable system, as well as the recursive nature of viability itself.[60]

Eigenforms

Foerster also pointed us in the direction of eigenforms. An eigenform (from the German "eigen" = self) is a form that, through its own processes, produces and reproduces itself. Eigen processes are thus recursive, and closely related to autopoiesis. Foerster considers them, for instance, as demonstrations of processes that mimic what children do, learning to populate their worlds with what Piaget calls constant objects. Eigen processes lead to a value that, as the process is repeated recursively, remains unchanged. Foerster called these "Eigen Objects."[61]

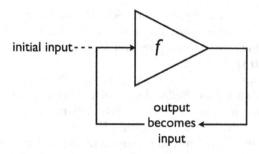

Diagram 3.5 When the function f produces, recursively, an output that converges on and then retains some constant value, it may be called an eigen-function, which operates to produce an Eigen-Object (the whole of the drawing) with an eigen-value. For instance, if the eigen-function is (÷ 2 + 1), the system will quickly stabilize as an Eigen-Object with an eigen-value of 2 (test it) (after Foerster. Although the illustration uses numbers, Foerster did not intend it to be restricted to the numerical.)

Louis Kauffman, whose cybernetic mathematics is a playground of ideas and a constant joy, regularly explores recursion, reflexivity, and eigenforms (along with distinctions, topology, knots, and many other marvels) in a regular column in the journal *Cybernetics and Human Knowing*. In his cybernetic work, he searches for the moments when a mathematical proposition loses its focus, in order to find a new interpretation in the unresolved and paradoxical. However, maybe as important as the work Kauffman produces is the delight he has in doing second-order mathematical cybernetics, for in this he reminds us that cybernetics is something done, a way of acting, not just a study.

Much of Kauffman's thinking derives from George Spencer Brown's *Laws of Form*.[62] This seminal study developed a logic of distinctions, sometimes also called a boundary logic, based on the notion that we bring worlds into being by the act of drawing distinctions, and composing our distinctions together. It can, thus, be seen as a constructivist logic, and it inspired much second-order cybernetic thinking, including my own.

On publication, *Laws of Form* was understood immediately to be of enormous significance. Beer reviewed it for *Nature,* and Foerster (very unconventionally) reviewed it in *The Whole Earth Catalogue,* the 1970s handbook for alternative living and thinking. Foerster used the opening command, "Draw a Distinction," as the abstract of his paper "On Constructing a Reality" (Foerster 1973). Eigen Objects could be said to mimic Piaget's constant objects by constantly distinguishing themselves.

Objects

There is one final cybernetic circular system, introduced because it can be argued it is the primitive second-order cybernetic system. This system is described in the theory of objects, which is founded on both circularity and observing. Second-order cybernetics gives primacy to observing. What sort of organization might be proposed that could be observed differently by each observer and yet taken to be the same thing? The Theory of Objects proposes a self-observing circular system in which observing involves a switch between being observed and observing (Foerster's first- and second-order cybernetic observation), that is, a switch between the roles of the (self-)observed and (self-)observing. These entities are called Objects (Glanville 1975).

The role switch generates both time and empty slots (when an Object is self-observed, it is not self-observing, so another Object could fill the observing slot, observing it). Using temporal synchronicity to establish logical arrangements gives external observers the chance both to enter into observing and to establish relationships between (observations of) Objects—the necessary prerequisite for not only logic but also representation and communication, and hence the whole subject matter of cybernetics.

In the Theory of Objects, the continuing, circular switching between (self-)observing and (self-)observed generates time—by that very act of

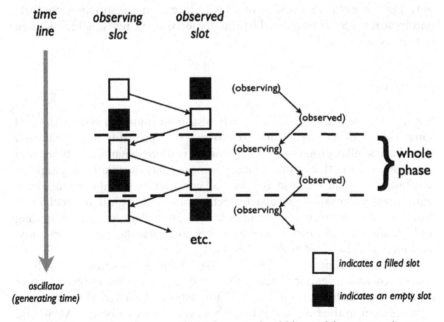

Diagram 3.6 This is a diagram of an Object. It should be read from top to bottom. The "filled" slots are white, the empty black. There is a sequence indicated by the arrows, where a filled (self)observing slot switches to fill a (self-)observed slot and back again to fill a (self-)observing slot, etc., creating a timeline progression. When a (self-)observed slot is empty, another Object may observe through it. In the Theory of Objects, a special formulation is captured to express this.

switching back and forth between the slot for observing and the slot for being observed, each Object being an oscillator, a clock. Switching leaves empty slots. The theory holds that when an Object is self-observed it is not self-observing. The resulting vacant slot may be filled by another Object. Thus, another Object (external observer) than the self may observe that Object. For this to happen, the two Objects must have a degree of synchronicity in order that the empty slot can be filled.

The coming together of two clocks allows an external observation to be made. The coming together in partial synchronicity of several clocks allows logical relationships between the observations of various Objects: the theory proposes, for instance, that if the times of observation by an externally observing Object of two other Objects is exactly the same, there is a logical identity, which may be used either to establish the relationship "same," or to have one of the two Objects "represent" the other. Thus, the basics of observation of one Object by another, and of how we can relate Objects together, is inherent in these structures that the theory names Objects.

Through their structure, Objects allow each of us the freedom to make the meanings we make and the freedom to construct our world as we see fit. Objects are essentially libertarian, providing maximum support for a world full of individual difference rather than assumed and imposed uniformity. For some reason, possibly to do with its extreme abstraction, this preontological (as Scott has called it) foundational work remains little known even in cybernetics.[63]

SUMMARY

We have explored the origins and early history of (modern) cybernetics and some aspects of its relationship to systems. It is probably fair to say that they share similar grounds: that cybernetics is more dynamically based and philosophical and that systems theory is more concerned with the pragmatics of utility. We have considered the way cybernetics moved from inquiring into "circular causal and feedback mechanisms in biological and social systems" to become a technology and how it became divorced from computing and AI, and have examined some of its key concepts—how they work, how they interrelate, and what they offer us.

And we have come full circle, exploring cybernetic consistency (which we contrasted with scientific repeatability) and its expression in second-order cybernetics, which returns us through, for instance, Foerster, Maturana, and Pask (present in the early days) to authors such as Rosenblueth, Mead and Bateson, Ashby, and even Wiener himself, and to the key concepts of (modern) cybernetics: circularity and the inevitability of the observer's presence. We have examined some consequences of thinking within circularity, of how this changes our conception of stability, of goal, of self, of communication and control—without throwing away the benefits of technological, first-order cybernetics—and of some explorations of what circularity means as recursion, reflection/reflexion, and in eigenforms.

We could do worse than to end by requoting Glasersfeld: "Cybernetics is a way of thinking, not a collection of facts."[64] To which I would add: Cybernetics is not just about understanding, but also action: cybernetics is not only to solve problems, but to be lived.

ACKNOWLEDGMENTS

My thanks to the editor and to Roger Harnden, Aartje Hulstein, Lou Kauffman, and Bernard Scott for their help, critical assessment, and input. I, however, gratefully accept responsibility for all errors. After all, I am a cybernetician.

NOTES

1. Norbert Wiener, *Cybernetics* (Cambridge, MA: MIT Press, 1948).
2. Norbert Wiener, *The Human Use of Human Beings: Cybernetics and Society,* rev. 2nd ed. (Boston: Houghton Mifflin Company, 1988), 15.
3. See Claus Pias, ed. *Cybernetics–Kybernetik: The Macy Conferences 1946–1953* (Zürich: Diaphanes, 2003).
4. Margaret Mead, "Cybernetics of Cybernetics," in *Purposive Systems,* eds. Heinz von Foerster et al. (New York: Spartan Books, 1968).
5. Ludwig von Bertalanffy, *General System Theory* (Harmondsworth: Allen Lane, 1971). For a very good (but inevitably flawed) survey of key early thinkers in cybernetics and systems, see Magnus Ramage and Karen Schipp 2009, *Systems Thinkers* (London: Springer, 2009).
6. See Plato's *Gorgias,* 511 c for the origin of the quote. In *Plato in Twelve Volumes,* vol. 3, trans. W. R. M. Lamb (Cambridge, MA: Harvard University Press, 1967).
7. This is found in I. MacCay, *Dictionary of Scientific Quotations* (Philadelphia, PA: IOP, 1991), 3. It is attributed to Ampère, *Essai Sur La Philosophie Des Sciences* (Paris: Chez Bachelier, 1843).
8. Charles François, "The Observer Re-Observed," in *Cybernetics and Systems 2006,* ed. R Trappl (Vienna: Proceedings of the EMCSR, Austrian Society for Cybernetic Studies, 2006).
9. Flo Conway and Jim Siegelman, *Dark Hero of the Information Age: In Search of Norbert Wiener, Father of Cybernetics* (New York: Basic Books, 2004).
10. Stuart Umpleby, "Heinz von Foerster and the Mansfield Amendment," *Cybernetics and Human Knowing* 10, nos. 3–4 (2003): 161–63.
11. Heinz von Foerster et al., *Cybernetics of Cybernetics,* Biological Computer Laboratory (University of Illinois Champaign-Urbana, 1974). Republished 1995.
12. For a comparison of the two, see Ranulph Glanville, "Radical Constructivism = Second Order Cybernetics," *Cybernetics and Human Knowing* 19, no. 4 (2012).

13. Gregory Bateson, "Pathologies of Epistemology," in *Steps to an Ecology of Mind* (New York: Ballentine, 1972), 488.
14. Jean Piaget, *The Child's Construction of Reality* (New York: Basic Books, 1955).
15. See Ranulph Glanville and Leon van Schaik, "Designing Reflections: Reflections on Design" in *Proceedings of the Third Conference, Doctoral Education in Design,* eds. D. Durling and K. Sugiyama (Chiba: Chiba University, 2003).
16. See W. Ross Ashby, *Introduction to Cybernetics* (London: Chapman and Hall, 1956).
17. See, for example, Heinz von Foerster, "On Self-Organising Systems and Their Environments," in *Self-Organising Systems,* eds. M. C. Yovits and S. Cameron (London: Pergamon, 1960), 1–20.
18. See Ranulph Glanville, "Inside Every White Box There Are Two Black Boxes Trying to Get Out," *Behavioural Science* 12, no. 1 (1982): 1–11.
19. W. Ross Ashby, "General Systems Theory as a New Discipline," in *Facets of Systems Science,* ed. George J. Klir (New York: Plenum Press, 1991), 249–57. Originally published in *General Systems* 3 (1958): 1–6.
20. See Gerald M. Weinberg, "The Simplification of Science and the Science of Simplification," in *Facets of Systems Science,* ed. George J. Klir (New York: Plenum Press, 1991), 501–05. Excerpt is from *An Introduction to General Systems Thinking,* silver anniversary ed. (New York: Dorset House, 2001).
21. Arturo Rosenblueth, Norbert Wiener, and Julian Bigelow, "Behavior, Purpose and Teleology," *Philosophy of Science* 10 (1943): 18–24.
22. See Michael B. Arbib, *The Metaphorical Brain* (New York: Wiley Interscience, 1972); Stafford Beer, *Brain of the Firm* (London: Allen Lane The Penguin Press, 1972).
23. See Ashby, *Introduction to Cybernetics.*
24. Francisco Varela, Humberto Maturana, and R. Uribe, "Autopoiesis: The Organization of Living Systems, Its Characterization and a Model," *Biosystems* 5, no. 4 (1974): 187–96.
25. Humberto Maturana and Francisco Varela, *The Tree of Knowledge* (Boston, Shambala, 1987).
26. Niklas Luhmann, "The Autopoiesis of Social Systems," in *Essays on Self-Reference,* Niklas Luhmann, ed., 1–20 (New York: Columbia University Press, 1990).
27. Conway and Siegelman, *Dark Hero of the Information Age: In Search of Norbert Wiener, Father of Cybernetics* (New York: Basic Books, 2004).
28. Ranulph Glanville, "The Value of Being Unmanageable: Variety and Creativity in CyberSpace," in *Netzwerke: Kooperation in Arbeit, Wirtschaft und Verwaltung, Proceedings of the Conference "Global Village '97,"* Vienna, 1997, ed. Hubert Eichmann, Josef Hochgerner, and Franz Nahrada (Vienna: Falter Verlag, 2000).
29. According to Heylighan and Joslyn, writing on the Law of Requisite Variety, this law is the one law in cybernetics and systems sciences that everyone agrees with.
30. Roger Harnden and Allena Leonard, *How Many Grapes Went into the Wine: Stafford Beer on the Art and Science of Holistic Management* (Chichester: Wiley, 1994).
31. Foerster et al., *Cybernetics of Cybernetics,* Biological Computer Laboratory (University of Illinois, Champaign/Urbana, 1974). Reprinted in 1995 in Minneapolis, with Future Systems Inc.

32. See Margaret Mead, *Coming of Age in Samoa: A Psychological Study of Primitive Youth for Western Civilisation* (Harmondsworth: Penguin Books, 1954).
33. See Glanville 1997, "A Ship without a Rudder"
34. See Glasersfeld's "Why I Consider Myself a Cybernetician," *Cybernetics and Human Knowing* 1, no. 1 (1992): 21–25.
35. Ernst Von Glasersfeld, "Aspects of Constructivism: Vico, Berkeley, Piaget," in *Key Works in Radical Constructivism*, ed. Ernst von Glasersfeld (Rotterdam: Sense, 2007).
36. Glasersfeld, "Aspects of Constructivism." Cf. Popper, *Conjectures and Refutations* (London: Routledge and Kegan Paul, 1963).
37. Ranulph Glanville, "Radical Constructivism = Second Order Cybernetics," *Cybernetics and Human Knowing* 19, no. 4 (2012): 27–42.
38. See Bärbel Inhelder, Rolando Garcia, and Jacques Voneche, eds. *Epistémologie Génétique et equilibration: Hommage à Jean Piaget* (Neuchatel: Delachaux et Niestle, 1977), 61.
39. Glasersfeld, "Aspects of Constructivism," 97.
40. For a general survey of second order cybernetics, see Glanville 2002.
41. Weinberg, "The Simplification of Science."
42. Gordon Pask, *An Approach to Cybernetics* (London: Methuen, 1961) and Gordon Pask, "MusiColour," in *The Scientist Speculates*, ed. Iving John Good (London, Heineman: 1962).
43. Ranulph Glanville, "Lerner ist Interaktion: Gordon Pask's *An Approach to Cybernetics*," in *Schlüsselwerke der Systemtheorie*, ed. Dirk Baecker (Wiesbaden, VS Verlag: 2005). Also published as "Gordon Pask's *An Approach to Cybernetics*." In *The Black B∞x*, vol. 2 (Vienna: echoraum/WISDOM, 2013).
44. Klaus Krippendorff, "Cybernetics's Reflexive Turns," *Cybernetics and Human Knowing* 15, 3–4 (2008):173–84.
45. Stafford Beer, *Beyond Dispute: The Invention of Team Syntegrity* (Chichester: Wiley, 1994).
46. Jean Piaget, *The Child's Construction of Reality* (New York: Basic Books, 1955).
47. Ranulph Glanville, "A (Cybernetic) Musing: Design and Cybernetics." *Cybernetics and Human Knowing*, 16, nos. 3–4 (2009): 175–86.
48. Ranulph Glanville, "Certain Propositions concerning Prepositions," in *Cybernetics and Human Knowing* 12 no. 3 (2005): 87–95.
49. Graham Barnes, *Transactional Analysis after Eric Berne: Teachings and Practices of Three Transactional Analysis Schools* (London: Longman, 1978).
50. Graham Barnes, *Psychopathology of Psychotherapy: A Cybernetic Study.* Unpublished PhD Dissertation. (Melbourne: RMIT University, 2002).
51. Roger Harnden and Allenna Leonard, *How Many Grapes Went into the Wine: Stafford Beer on the Art and Science of Holistic Management* (Chichester: Wiley, 1994).
52. This is widely attributed to Maxwell. See James Clerk Maxwell, accessed October 4, 2012, http://quotationsbook.com/quote/22665/.
53. Gregory Bateson, "Metalogue: What Is an Instinct?" In *Steps to an Ecology of Mind* (New York: Ballentine, 1972).
54. See Jean-Dominique Bauby, *The Diving Bell and the Butterfly* (New York: Knopf, 1997).
55. Donald Schön, *The Reflective Practitioner: How Professionals Think in Action* (London: Basic Books, 1983).

56. See Bernard Scott, "Ranulph Glanville's Objekte," in *Cybernetic Circles,* vol. 1 of *The Black Boox,* ed. Ranulph Glanville (Vienna: echoraum/WISDOM, 2012). Originally published in German as "Bernard Scott über Ranulph Glanville's Buch 'Objekte' (1988)" in *Schlüsselwerke der Systemtheorie,* ed. Dirk Baecker (Wiesbaden, VS Verlag, 2005).
57. George Soros, *The Soros Lectures* (New York: Public Affairs Books, 2010).
58. Stuart Umpleby, "Reflexivity in Social Systems: The Theories of George Soros," *Systems Research and Behavioral Science* 24 (2007): 515–22.
59. Heinz von Foerster, "Through the Eyes of the Other," in *Research and Reflexivity,* ed. Frederick Steier (London: Sage, 1991).
60. See Stafford Beer, *Diagnosing the System for Organizations* (Chichester: Wiley, 1985).
61. Heinz von Foerster, "Objects: Tokens For (Eigen-) Behaviours," in *Epistémologie Génétique et equilibration.*
62. George Spencer Brown, *Laws of Form* (London: George Unwin, 1969).
63. See Scott, "Ranulph Glanville's Objekte."
64. Ernst von Glasersfeld, "Declaration of the American Society for Cybernetics," in *Cybernetics and Applied Systems,* ed. Constantin Negoita (New York: Marcel Decker, 1992), 1–5.

REFERENCES

Apostel, Leo. "Le role du sujet dans la connaissance." In *Epistemologie genetique et equilibration,* edited by Bärbel Inhelder, Rolando Garcia and Jacques Voneche. Neuchatel: Delachaux et Niestle, 1977.

Arbib, Michael B. *The Metaphorical Brain.* New York: Wiley Interscience, 1972.

Ashby, W. Ross. *Introduction to Cybernetics.* London: Chapman and Hall, 1956.

———. "General Systems Theory as a New Discipline." Reprinted in *Facets of Systems Science,* edited by George J. Klir, 249–257. New York: Plenum Press, 1991. Originally published in *General Systems* 3 (1958): 1–6.

Barnes, Graham. *Transactional Analysis after Eric Berne: Teachings and Practices of Three Transactional Analysis Schools.* London: Longman, 1978.

———. *Psychopathology of Psychotherapy: A Cybernetic Study.* Unpublished PhD Dissertation. Melbourne: RMIT University, 2002.

Bateson, Gregory. "Metalogue: What Is an Instinct?" In *Steps to an Ecology of Mind.* New York: Ballentine, 1972.

———. "Pathologies of Epistemology." In *Steps to an Ecology of Mind.* New York: Ballentine, 1972.

———. *Steps to an Ecology of Mind.* New York: Ballentine, 1972.

Bauby, Jean-Dominique. *The Diving Bell and the Butterfly.* New York: Knopf, 1997.

Beer, Stafford. (1972). *Brain of the Firm.* London: Allen Lane the Penguin Press, 1972.

———. *Diagnosing the System for Organizations.* Chichester: Wiley, 1985.

———. *Beyond Dispute: The Invention of Team Syntegrity.* Chichester: Wiley, 1994.

Bertalanffy, Ludwig von. *General System Theory.* Harmondsworth: Allen Lane, 1971.

Conway, Flo, and Jim Siegelman. *Dark Hero of the Information Age: In Search of Norbert Wiener, Father of Cybernetics.* New York: Basic Books, 2004.

Foerster, Heinz von. "On Self-Organising Systems and Their Environments." In *Self-Organising Systems,* edited by Marshall C. Yovits and Scott Cameron, 1–20. London: Pergamon, 1960.

———. "On Constructing a Reality." In *Environmental Design Research,* edited by Wolfgang F. E. Preiser. Stroudsberg: Dowden Hutchinson and Ross, 1973.

———. "Objects: Tokens for (Eigen-) Behaviours." In *Epistémologie génétique et equilibration: Hommage à Jean Piaget*, edited by Bärbel Inhelder, Rolando Garcia, and Jacques Voneche. Neuchatel: Delachaux et Niestle, 1977.

———. "Through the Eyes of the Other." In *Research and Reflexivity*, edited by Frederick Steier. London: Sage, 1991.

———, Herbert Brün, and Stephen Sloan. *Cybernetics of Cybernetics*. Minneapolis: Future Systems, 1995. Originally published at Champaign/Urbana, Biological Computer Laboratory, 1974.

François, Charles. *International Encyclopaedia of Systems and Cybernetics*. 4th ed. Munich: KG Saur, 2004.

———. "The Observer Re-observed." In *Cybernetics and Systems*, edited by Robert Trappl, 87–90. Proceedings of the EMCSR, Vienna, Austrian Society for Cybernetic Studies, 2006.

Glanville, R. *A Cybernetic Development of Theories of Epistemology and Observation, with Reference to Space and Time, as Seen in Architecture*. PhD Dissertation. Brunel University, 1975. Main text is published as "The Object of Objects, the Point of Points,—or Something about Things." In Ranulph Glanville, *Cybernetic Circles*, vol. 1 of *The Black B∞x*. Vienna: echoraum/WISDOM, 2012.

———. "Inside Every White Box There Are Two Black Boxes Trying to Get Out." *Behavioural Science* 27, no. 1 (1982): 1–11.

———. "A Ship without a Rudder." In *Problems of Excavating: Cybernetics and Systems*, edited by Ranulph Glanville and Gerard de Zeeuw, 131–142. Southsea: BKS+, 1997.

———. "The Value of Being Unmanageable: Variety and Creativity in CyberSpace." In *Netzwerke: Kooperation in Arbeit, Wirtschaft und Verwaltung: Proceedings of the Conference "Global Village '97,"* *Vienna, 1997*, edited by Hubert Eichmann, Josef Hochgerner, and Franz Nahrada, 27–38. Vienna: Falter Verlag, 2000.

———. "Second Order Cybernetics." In *Encyclopaedia of Life Support Systems*. Oxford: EoLSS Publishers, 2002: net publication at http://www.eolss.net.

———. "A (Cybernetic) Musing: Certain Propositions concerning Prepositions." *Cybernetics and Human Knowing* 12, no. 3 (2005): 87–95.

———. "Lerner ist Interaktion: Gordon Pask's *An Approach to Cybernetics*." In *Schlüsselwerke der Systemtheorie*, edited by Dirk Baecker, 75–94. Wiesbaden: Verlag für Sozialwissenschaften, 2005. Also published as "Gordon Pask's *An Approach to Cybernetics* in Glanville" (2013).

———. "A (Cybernetic) Musing: Design and Cybernetics." *Cybernetics and Human Knowing*, 16, nos. 3–4 (2009): 175–86.

———. "Black Boxes." *Cybernetics and Human Knowing*, 16, nos. 1–2 (2009): 153–167.

———. *Cybernetic Circles*. Vol. 1 of *The Black B∞x*. Edited by Ranulph Glanville. Vienna: echoraum/WISDOM, 2012.

———. "Radical Constructivism = Second Order Cybernetics." *Cybernetics and Human Knowing* 19, no. 4 (2012): 27–42.

———. *Living in Cybernetic Circles*. Vol. 2 of *The Black B∞x*. Vienna: echoraum/WISDOM, 2013.

———, and Leon van Schaik. "Designing Reflections: Reflections on Design." In *Proceedings of the Third Conference, Doctoral Education in Design*, edited by D. Durling and K. Sugiyama, 35–42. Chiba: Chiba University, 2003.

Glasersfeld, Ernst von. "Declaration of the American Society for Cybernetics." In *Cybernetics and Applied Systems*, edited by Constantin Virgil Negoita, 1–5. New York: Marcel Decker, 1992.

———. "Why I Consider Myself a Cybernetician." *Cybernetics and Human Knowing* 1, no. 1 (1992): 21–25.

———. "The Radical Constructivist View of Science." *Foundations of Science*, special issue on "The Impact of Radical Constructivism on Science," edited by A.

Riegler, 2001, vol. 6, no. 1–3: 31–43. Accessed Oct. 1, 2013. http: //www.univie. ac.at/constructivism/pub/fos/pdf/glasersfeld.pdf.

———. "Aspects of Constructivism: Vico, Berkley, Piaget." In *Key Works in Radical Constructivism*, edited by Ernst von Glasersfeld, 91–100. Rotterdam, Sense, 2007.

Harnden, Roger, and Allena Lennard. *How Many Grapes Went into the Wine: Stafford Beer on the Art and Science of Holistic Management*. Chichester: Wiley, 1994.

Heylighen, Francis, and Cliff Joslyn. "The Law of Requisite Variety." Accessed April 11, 2013, written/modified August 31, 2001, created August 1993. http:// pespmc1.vub.ac.be/REQVAR.html.

Inhelder, Bärbel, Rolando Garcia, and Jacques Voneche, eds. *Epistémologie Génétique et equilibration: Hommage à Jean Piaget* (Neuchatel: Delachaux et Niestle, 1977).

Klir, George J. *Facets of Systems Science*. New York: Plenum Press, 1991.

Krippendorff, Klaus. "Cybernetics's Reflexive Turns." *Cybernetics and Human Knowing* 15, nos. 3–4 (2008): 173–84.

Luhmann, Niklas. "The Autopoiesis of Social Systems." In *Essays on Self-Reference*, edited by Niklas Luhmann, 1–20. New York: Columbia University Press, 1990.

MacCay, I. *Dictionary of Scientific Quotations*. Philadelphia, PA: IOP, 1991.

Maturana, Humberto, and Francisco Varela. *The Tree of Knowledge*. Boston: Shambala, 1987.

Maxwell, James Clerk. Accessed October 4, 2012. http://quotationsbook.com/ quote/22665/.

Mead, Margaret. *Coming of Age in Samoa: A Psychological Study of Primitive Youth for Western Civilisation*. Harmondsworth: Penguin Books, 1954.

———. "Cybernetics of Cybernetics." In *Purposive Systems*, edited by von H v. Foerster, J. D. White, L. J. Peterson, and J. K. Russell. New York: Spartan Books, 1968.

Pask, Gordon. *An Approach to Cybernetics*. London: Methuen, 1961.

———. MusiColour, in Good IJ, ed. *The Scientist Speculates*. London: Heineman, 1962.

———. "SAKI: Twenty-Five Years of Adaptive Training into the Microprocessor Era." *International Journal of Man-Machine Studies* 17, no. 1 (1982): 69–74.

Piaget, Jean. *The Child's Construction of Reality*. New York: Basic Books, 1955.

Pias, Claus, ed. *Cybernetics–Kybernetik: The Macy Conferences 1946–1953*. Zürich: Diaphanes, 2003.

Plato. *Plato in Twelve Volumes*. Vol. 3. Translated by W. R. M. Lamb. Cambridge, MA: Harvard University Press, 1967.

Popper, Karl. *Conjectures and Refutations*. London: Routledge and Kegan Paul, 1963.

Ramage, Magnus, and Karen Schipp. *Systems Thinkers*. London: Springer, 2009.

Rosenblueth, Arturo, Norbert Wiener, and Julian Bigelow. "Behavior, Purpose and Teleology." *Philosophy of Science* 10 (1943): 18–24.

Schön, Donald A. *The Reflective Practitioner: How Professionals Think in Action*. London: Basic Books, 1983.

Shannon, Claude E., and Warren Weaver. "A Mathematical Theory of Communication." *The Bell System Technical Journal* 27 (1948): 379–423 and 623–656, July and October.

Scott, Bernard. "Ranulph Glanville's Objekte." In *Cybernetic Circles*, vol. 1 of *The Black Box*, edited by Ranulph Glanville, 63–76. Vienna: echoraum/WISDOM, 2012. Originally published in German as "Bernard Scott über Ranulph Glanville's Buch 'Objekte' (1988)." In *Schlüsselwerke der Systemtheorie*, edited by Dirk Baecker, 325–346. Wiesbaden, VS Verlag, 2005.

Soros, George. *The Soros Lectures*. New York: Public Affairs Books, 2010.

Spencer Brown, George. *Laws of Form*. London: George Unwin, 1969.

Steier, Frederick, ed. *Research and Reflexivity*. London: Sage, 1991.

Umpleby, Stuart. "Reflexivity in Social Systems: The Theories of George Soros." *Systems Research and Behavioral Science*, 24 (2007): 515–22.

———. "Heinz von Foerster and the Mansfield Amendment." *Cybernetics and Human Knowing* 10, nos. 3–4 (2003): 187–90.

Varela, Francisco, Humberto Maturana, and R. Uribe. "Autopoiesis: The Organization of Living Systems, Its Characterization and a Model." *BioSystems* 5, no. 4 (1974): 187–96.

Weinberg, Gerald M. Selections from "The Simplification of Science and the Science of Simplification." In *Facets of Systems Science*, edited by George J. Klir, 501–05. New York: Plenum Press, 1991. Excerpt from Gerald M. Weinberg, *An Introduction to General Systems Theory*. Silver anniversary ed. New York: Dorset, 2001.

Wiener, Norbert. *Cybernetics: or the Control and Communication in the Animal and Machine*. Cambridge MA: MIT Press, 1948.

———. *The Human Use of Human Beings: Cybernetics and Society*. Rev. 2nd ed. Boston: Houghton Mifflin, 1988. Originally published 1954.

4 Expanding the Self-Referential Paradox
The Macy Conferences and the Second Wave of Cybernetic Thinking

John Bruni

According to the American Society for Cybernetics (2012), there is no unified comprehensive account of a far-reaching narrative that takes into account all of the Macy Conferences and what was discussed and accomplished at these meetings. This chapter will thus propose how group dialogues on concepts such as information and feedback allowed the Macy Conferences to act as a catalyst for second-order systems theory, when first-order, steady-state models of homeostasis became supplanted by those of self-reference in observing systems. I will trace how such a development transpired through a conferences-wide interdisciplinary mindset that promoted the idea of reflexivity. According to N. Katherine Hayles, the conferences' singular achievement was to create a "new paradigm" for "looking at human beings . . . as information-processing entities who are *essentially* similar to intelligent machines," by routing Claude Shannon's information theory through Warren McCulloch's "model of neural functioning" and John von Neumann's work in "biological systems" and then capitalizing on Norbert Wiener's "visionary" talent for disseminating the "larger implications" of such a paradigm shift.[1] From this perspective, the most crucial work would achieve its fruition after the end of the Macy conferences. Yet the foundations for such work were, perforce, cast during the discussions at the conferences that epitomize *science in the making* and, as such, warrant our careful attention.

MOVING AWAY FROM THE MIDCENTURY: REFLEXIVE PRESSURES

The ten Macy Conferences took place from 1946 to 1953. These conferences were created by the Josiah Macy Jr. Foundation—as Wendy Leeds-Hurwitz notes, "one of a very few institutions to deliberately encourage multidisciplinary research"[2]—and consisted of "oral, informal" presentations.[3] They featured participation by such luminaries in the fields of informatics and social sciences as McCulloch, Wiener, von Neumann, Shannon, Margaret Mead, and Gregory Bateson. Upon first glimpse, the conferences could be regarded as a product of the Cold-War social atmosphere. As Steve Heims elaborates, in the United States at the midcentury, the sciences—rather than the humanities—held cultural capital, a technocratic optimism, guided by the potential of the social sciences as "human engineering," reigned,[4] and a theory of systems, developed by the eminent sociologist Talcott Parsons, reflected a "conservative view centered on equilibrium, stability, and the continuity of institutions."[5] Centered on the idea of how to model thinking, the conferences were shaped by an interest in human-machine hybrids; these are, as Hayles points out, early versions of cyborgs,[6] joined to a cognitive-behavioral (rather than psychoanalytical) model of psychology that emphasized a scientific approach to knowledge and understanding.

Originally titled "Circular Causality and Feedback Mechanisms in Biological and Social Systems," the conferences were renamed "Cybernetics" (after the Greek word *kybernetes*: pilot, steersman—a term credited to Wiener) on the recommendation of Heinz von Foerster, who joined the group in 1949 and served as secretary of the conference proceedings (American Society for Cybernetics 2012). In particular, von Foerster embodied the multidisciplinary ethos of the conferences with his interests in mathematics, physics, and electrical engineering. The ultimate goal of the meetings, according to Leeds-Hurwitz, was "nothing less than 'the reintegration of science,'"[7] to be brought about by a dialogic, speculative approach "capable of encouraging wide-ranging discussions of overlap between apparently dissimilar fields."[8] Similar to von Foerster, Bateson, an anthropologist, was interested in "illuminating general, transdisciplinary issues."[9] In particular, Bateson's famous dictum that information is a "difference that makes a difference" derived from his work on "initiation rituals" and, to be sure, reflected an interdisciplinary mindset.[10] A collective sense of interdisciplinary consciousness, fostered by the Macy Foundation, thus catalyzed a move away from the monolithic thinking of the Cold-War era and toward a more critical stance of reflexivity. For example, there was a debate, instigated by psychologist Hans-Lukas Teuber, about the publication of conference transcripts.[11] Likewise, Leeds-Hurwitz affirms that there was a tangible awareness that participant conversations were being recorded.[12]

Structurally, we might say, reflexivity was an issue that came into sharp relief, one whose further attention at the conferences was the critical impetus for a viable cybernetic model.[13] Here, we can trace moves both against and toward the second wave. There is, in particular, the (unresolved) debate about information and disembodiment—highlighted by Shannon's choice to define uncertainty in information systems as entropy. By introducing the concept of chaos, or noise, as a formalist criterion for evaluating the performance of such systems, Shannon aligned entropy with information in order to downplay the idea of meaning itself. Supported by Wiener, Shannon insisted that "the 'meaning' of the message is irrelevant," which crucially led to the abstraction of information.[14] Under the byword of Cold-War efficiency, Shannon tried to ramp up the model for information processing by making the formation essentially a mathematical abstraction rather than a more relational (contextual) concept for language processing—eliding both Donald MacKay's model that "recognized the mutual constitution of form and content, message and receiver" and Bateson's definition of information as difference that makes a difference.[15] Although Shannon by no means intended that his model be applied universally, as Hayles observes, "this distinction between signal and noise has a conservative bias that privileges stasis over change."[16] Dynamism, then, critically rests on a contextual (or embodied) foundation. Such a privilege, moreover, arises because science in the making, as Karen Barad argues, is shaped by the social realm, not apart from it.[17] That is, due to Shannon's definition's being more popular with electrical engineers, whose discipline strongly relied on information theory,[18] the steady-state feedback model emerges; this distinct residue of Cold-War thinking extends through the conferences to the connections between disembodied information and early manifestations of the cyborg, one prominent example being "Shannon's electronic rat, a goal-seeking machine that modeled a rat learning a maze."[19]

A similar model, W. Ross Ashby's homeostat, was a machine that, by acting out how organisms, to survive, maintain equilibrium, evinced "the cataclysm of the war" by suggesting the importance of relations between an organism and its environment.[20] From Ashby's homeostat, we move to a discussion about technology and military performance that focused on the image "of an operator sandwiched between a radar-tracking device on one side and an anti-aircraft gun on the other."[21] Rather than to a simplistic picture of the operator as "man in the middle," attention shifted to how the operator was constructed by an observer observing the action (second-order observation). That "psychological complexity was unavoidable" during the proceedings was exacerbated by psychoanalyst Lawrence Kubie, who stressed "the multiply encoded nature of language, which operated at once as an instrument that the speaker could use to communicate and as a reflexive mirror that revealed more than the speaker knew."[22] The subsequent resistance to Kubie's viewpoint (expressed, especially, by McCulloch) suggests that, in the words of Hayles, "The Macy participants were right to feel wary about reflexivity. Its potential was every bit as explosive as they suspected."[23]

POST-CONFERENCE: *OBSERVING SYSTEMS*

Human-machine hybrids, as we will now see, spoke to the increasing complexity of systems that operated not on the basis of equilibrium-seeking (through feedback) but on self-reference. Though it was being challenged by these cyborgs, a return to the traditional liberal humanist Cartesian model of the unified subject (that elevates mind over body), who has the *distinct* privilege of being disembodied, is evident in Shannon's choice to define uncertainty in information systems as entropy.[24] Given that entropy was already a defined term in thermodynamics, it is, certainly, open to question whether Shannon's choice enabled the kinds of thinking necessary for developing cybernetics after the conferences. Jeffery S. Wicken, for one, feels that it adds unnecessary confusion "to affix the same name to different concepts."[25] Conversely, Hayles thinks, "The metaphorical joining of entropy and information . . . allowed complexity to be seen as rich in information rather than deficient in order."[26]

Embracing complexity is key to the (thermodynamic) self-organizing schema that inaugurates second-order systems of observation. While hybridity, defined as a dualistic—rather than singular—self-identity, is largely regarded as the legacy of cybernetics, it does warrant a careful reevaluation. Reading the Macy Conferences as a narrative about the embryonic state of second-order systems thinking achieves precisely this goal. To rightly assess the importance of the Macy Conferences, therefore, requires us to look beyond the conferences to the philosophies of Wiener and von Foerster.

What seems clear, from this vantage point, is that Shannon's choice fits all too well with Wiener's disembodied cybernetics/informatics. In a pivotal moment, Wiener, in *Cybernetics* (1948), hesitates, stopping short of claiming that systems radically destabilize self-identity, that is, they disturb the idea of the corporeal body as a grounding for subjectivity. What Hayles calls "intellectual celibacy" occurs; hence, when Wiener constructs an "analogy" of insect reproduction that depicts pheromones outside of the body acting with hormones inside of the body, for imagining the operation of informational and organizational hierarchies. Hayles suggests that the analogy constructs the body as "a sort of permeable membrane through which hormonal information flows." Yet Wiener retreats from this "disturbing" realization, since it implies that "personal identity and autonomous will are merely illusions that mask the cybernetic reality."[27]

While Bateson further explored reflexivity by organizing a conference in July 1968,[28] it was, arguably, von Foerster's essay collection, *Observing Systems* (1984), that brightly reflected the contribution of the Macy Conferences to systems thinking. As he worked on "the epistemological implications of including the observer as part of the system," von Foerster's schema of second-order observation was enhanced by his inviting Humberto Maturana (notably, not a Macy participant) to speak at a conference at the University of Illinois in 1969.[29] Picking up and going beyond Ashby's emphasis on environment for system self-maintenance, Maturana argued that organisms do not get objective knowledge from their environments— therefore reflexivity is integral to (what now becomes second-order) observation. Maturana's concept that systems are autopoietic, that is, self-maintaining, depends on the self-reference of systems that are both connected to and separate from their environments—a concept that helps von

Foerster to work out, as he so rightly realizes, what is the crucial circularity of self-reference that constitutes the identity of systems, and the final step to second-order systems thinking.[30]

Terms such as "circularity," "reflexivity," and "self-reference" mobilize the second wave; they derive their contextual meaning from the inter-disciplinary *ethos* of the Macy Conferences, where the nascent concept of systems thinking was being viewed from multiple disciplines, thus recharging the idea of observation as something being carried out by *somebody*. Maturana's breaking down of the formalistic register of infor-mation (regarded as being independent from autopoiesis) locates systems autonomy within a second-order definition of closure (that constitutes the system/environment distinction). From the general classification of "intel-ligent machines" promulgated by the Macy Conferences, we move to a more nuanced model of identity that is neither tethered to an essentialist concept of being nor located beyond the autopoietic becomings of com-plex systems. It is, as von Foerster would put it, a second-wave cybernetic world of complex systems where meanings are generated from the para-doxes of self-reference.

NOTES

1. N. Katherine Hayles, *How We Became Posthuman: Virtual Bodies in Cyber-netics, Literature, and Informatics* (Chicago: University of Chicago Press, 1999), 7.
2. Wendy Leeds-Hurwitz, "Crossing Disciplinary Boundaries: The Macy Con-ferences on Cybernetics as a Case Study in Multidisciplinary Communica-tion," *Cybernetica* 37 nos. 3–4 (1994): 360.
3. Leeds-Hurwitz, *Crossing Disciplinary Boundaries*, 361.
4. Steve Joshua Heims, *The Cybernetics Group* (Cambridge, MA: MIT Press, 1991), 2.
5. Heims, *The Cybernetics Group*, 9.
6. Hayles, *How We Became Posthuman*, 63.
7. Leeds-Hurwitz, *Crossing Disciplinary Boundaries*, 354.
8. Leeds-Hurwitz, *Crossing Disciplinary Boundaries*, 357.
9. Heims, *The Cybernetics Group*, 54.
10. Hayles, *How We Became Posthuman*, 51.
11. Hayles, *How We Became Posthuman*, 75.
12. Hayles, *How We Became Posthuman*, 359.
13. Hayles, *How We Became Posthuman*, 73.
14. Heims, *The Cybernetics Group*, 76.
15. Hayles, *How We Became Posthuman*, 56.
16. Hayles, *How We Became Posthuman*, 63.
17. Karen Barad, *Meeting the Universe Halfway: Quantum Physics and the Entanglement of Matter and Meaning* (Durham, NC: Duke University Press, 2007).
18. Hayles, *How We Became Posthuman*, 56.
19. Hayles, *How We Became Posthuman*, 63.
20. Hayles, *How We Became Posthuman*, 66.
21. Hayles, *How We Became Posthuman*, 68.

22. Hayles, *How We Became Posthuman*, 69.
23. Hayles, *How We Became Posthuman*, 70.
24. Hayles, *How We Became Posthuman*, 12–13, 18–19.
25. Jeffrey Wicken, "Thermodynamics, Evolution, and Emergence: Ingredients for a New Synthesis," in *Entropy, Information, and Evolution: New Perspectives on Physical and Biological Evolution*, eds. Bruce H. Weber, David J. Depew, and James D. Smith (Cambridge, MA: MIT Press, 1988), 139–69.
26. N. Katherine Hayles, *Chaos Bound: Orderly Disorder in Contemporary Literature and Science* (Ithaca, NY: Cornell University Press, 1990); and Bruce Clarke, "Systems Theory," in *The Routledge Companion to Literature and Science*, eds. Bruce Clarke and Manuela Rossini (New York: Routledge, 2011), 214–25, 229–30.
27. Hayles, *How We Became Posthuman*, 109; and John Bruni, "The Miseducation of Henry Adams: Fantasies of Race, Citizenship, and Darwinian Dynamos," in *Darwin in Atlantic Cultures: Evolutionary Visions of Race, Gender, and Sexuality*, eds. J. E. Jones and P. B. Sharp (New York: Routledge, 2010), 276–77.
28. Hayles, *How We Became Posthuman*, 75–76.
29. Hayles, *How We Became Posthuman*, 133–34.
30. Bruce Clarke, "Systems Theory," 220–22.

REFERENCES

American Society for Cybernetics. "Summary: The Macy Conferences." http://www.asc-cybernetics.org/foundations/history/MacySummary.htm, 2012.
Barad, Karen. *Meeting the Universe Halfway: Quantum Physics and the Entanglement of Matter and Meaning*. Durham, NC: Duke University Press, 2007.
Bruni, John. "The Miseducation of Henry Adams: Fantasies of Race, Citizenship, and Darwinian Dynamos." In *Darwin in Atlantic Cultures: Evolutionary Visions of Race, Gender, and Sexuality*, edited by J. E. Jones and P. B. Sharp, 260–82. New York: Routledge, 2010.
Clarke, Bruce. "Systems Theory." In *The Routledge Companion to Literature and Science*, edited by Bruce Clark and Manuela Rossini, 214–25. New York: Routledge, 2011.
——— and Manuela Rossini. "Thermodynamics." In *The Routledge Companion to Literature and Science*, edited by Bruce Clark and Manuela Rossini, 226–37. New York: Routledge, 2011.
Hayles, N. Katherine. *Chaos Bound: Orderly Disorder in Contemporary Literature and Science*. Ithica, NY: Cornell University Press, 1990.
———. *How We Became Posthuman: Virtual Bodies in Cybernetics, Literature, and Informatics*. Chicago: University of Chicago Press, 1999.
Heims, Steve Joshua. *The Cybernetics Group*. Cambridge, MA: MIT Press, 1991.
Leeds-Hurwitz, Wendy. "Crossing Disciplinary Boundaries: The Macy Conferences on Cybernetics as a Case Study in Multidisciplinary Communication." *Cybernetica* 37, 3–4 (1994): 349–64.
Wicken, Jeffrey. "Thermodynamics, Evolution, and Emergence: Ingredients for a New Synthesis." In *Entropy, Information, and Evolution: New Perspectives on Physical and Biological Evolution*, edited by Bruce H. Weber, David J. Depew, and James D. Smith, 139–69. Cambridge, MA: MIT Press, 1988.

5 The Hermeneutical System of General Systemology
Bertalanffian and Other Early Contributions to Its Foundations and Development

David Pouvreau

INTRODUCTION

Although the philosopher and biologist L. von Bertalanffy is rightly considered the main founder of "general system theory," a project he formulated for the first time in 1937, his contributions to this project are still not well enough known. It is true that his reflections often remained in a state of outline, imprecise, and scattered. Confusions also arose from the names he gave to his project, and he himself was not satisfied with this. It is neither a philosophical doctrine nor a scientific theory, but instead aimed at becoming a philosophically founded and scientifically fertile system for the interpretation of "reality," able to guide action according to specific values. Inspired by expressions used in 1973 by R. L. Ackoff and J. Kamarýt, I chose to call it the "systemological hermeneutics," or (with M. Drack) "general systemology."[1] The justification for those designations will appear in the present paper, which I have organized around a more sophisticated scheme than the rather crude classification constructed by Bertalanffy himself,[2] the "hermeneutical system of general systemology":

In this scheme, each arrow should be read as "informs." One noteworthy characteristic is the original position of logic, ontology, and methodology at the interface between "basic theoretical systemology" and "philosophical systemology": here the necessity of this position, as consequence of the metatheoretical character of the basic theoretical systemology, will be justified. I claim that the scope of this scheme extends beyond Bertalanffy, because it makes it possible to account for the set of aspects that the architects of general systemology have judged it necessary to insist upon, according to their various sensibilities and foci of interest. It seems to me that this scheme does not betray the inspiration of their works; indeed, it provides an outline of a systematization likely to reveal their complementarity and unity.

My aim here is to point out Bertalanffy's and some other early contributions to the development of this hermeneutical system—along with the contributions to some others, and to make its meaning and coherence intelligible.

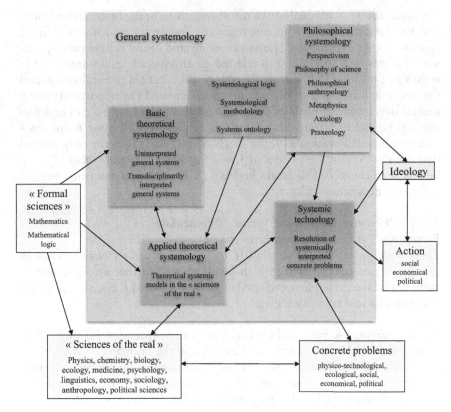

Diagram 5.1

1   THE PHILOSOPHICAL SYSTEMOLOGY

Bertalanffy developed the essential philosophical foundations of general systemology between 1923 and 1949. His later publications clarified them, adapting them to new contexts.

1-1—Principles of Bertalanffy's Philosophical Anthropology

Some elements of Bertalanffy's anthropology were present in his early writings, but he mainly developed it just after the war. It aimed at defining the specificity of man and at justifying the autonomy of human sciences with regard to biology, one task of the latter being nonetheless to account for the prerequisites of the emergence of the "human phenomenon."

1-1-1—Biological Foundations of Human Specificity

From 1940 onward, Bertalanffy pointed to two processes that are supposed to have played a decisive role in this emergence: "progressive cerebralization," with qualitative transformations in the brain architecture; and the "retardation" of human ontogeny (neoteny), which sets it apart from any other anthropoid. Human anatomy and instincts have many primitive features, not specialized in relation to any specific environment. Man is thus in a position of "biological helplessness." But his cerebralization and the abnormal duration of his infantile stage created the opportunity for a mental development that makes a virtue of this "helplessness": in order to survive, he had to "compensate" for this helplessness, opening to his environment and elaborating learning mechanisms. He is thus the only animal that does not retain the pattern of J. von Uexküll's "*Umwelt* theory," since he has been compelled to create his own "*Umwelt*" (environment) beyond biological necessities: culture.[3]

1-1-2—"Creative Cognition" Versus "Immaculate Perception": A Constructivist Framework

Those reflections helped Bertalanffy to justify an early constructivism in essentially neo-criticist style, which he elaborated further after the war in assimilating the principles developed in H. Werner's and J. Piaget's "genetic" psychologies and epistemologies:

> Any organism, man included, is not a mere spectator [of the] world scene [. . .] He is a reactor and an actor in the drama [. . .] It seems to be the most serious shortcoming of classic occidental philosophy, from Plato to Descartes and Kant, to consider man primarily as a spectator (*ens cogitans*), while for biological reasons, he has essentially to be a performer (*ens agens*) in the world he is thrown in.[4]

Bertalanffy reinvested in here the "organismic" scheme of the "primary activity" of the organism, central to his biology (see 2–1-5). His anthropology and theory of knowledge could consequently be firmly rooted in a dismissal of the "copy" theory of cognition and of the "dogma of immaculate perception," which could also draw on K. Lorenz, E. Cassirer, and S.K. Langer. Cognition should be viewed as an internal act: the shaping of objects, which are built up as such in the course of an indefinite objectivization process:

> The principle of the active, psychophysical organism pertains not only to the motoric or "output" part of behavior, but also to "input," to cognitive processes.[5]
>
> Things and mind, objects and subject, are not an ultimate *datum* but rather a *factum*, a shaping of experience within a framework of categories. That the "mind" is not a passive receiver of stimuli, information, *eidola*, sense data (whatever expression you choose) but in a very real sense creates its universes, is not only good Kantian philosophy but a basic insight of modern psychology.[6]

Perception is not a reflection of "real things" (whatever their metaphysical status), and knowledge is not a simple approximation to "truth" or "reality." It is an interaction between knower and known, and thus dependent on a multiplicity of factors [biological, psychological, cultural, linguistic].[7]

1-1-3—Man as a "Symbolic Animal"

The human mind's activity would manifest itself in the creation of symbolic universes, "the primordial fact of anthropogenesis." From 1948 onward, Bertalanffy characterized man as "an animal living in a forest of symbols"— a "symbolic animal," as Cassirer also did:

> Apart from satisfaction of biological needs man shares with animals, man lives in a universe not of things but of symbols [. . .] The objective world around him is *materialization* of symbolic activities [. . .] Man is a symbol-making, symbol-using, symbol-dominated animal throughout.[8]

Bertalanffy insisted on the mediating function of the symbol, the "distanciation" from the "real": between itself and the world of senses, human mind interposes symbolic systems that are like many intermediary universes representing its own requirements and enabling it to organize experience in a significant way, as well as to have a hold on the world:

> In the last analysis, our whole intellectual activity consists in a substitution of signs or symbols for things and in an operation and a calculus with them, not on the things themselves.[9]

Only when symbolism arises does experience become an organized "universe."[10]

The product of this activity would be the construction of a "human universe," independent of the immediate impressions and "un-natural," to which man must incessantly adapt himself and which is the object of an interest "transcending" or even "denying" the vital necessities:

> The universe of man is the world of inner experience [*Erlebniswelt*] organized by symbols.[11]

Hence there is an irreducible duality, inherent in this specific position: man is a "citizen of two worlds," a biological being who "creates, uses, dominates, and is dominated by an upper world, the world of 'symbolic universes' which is usually called 'culture.' "[12]

1-1-4—Origin, Genesis, and Evolutionary Logic of Symbolism

According to Bertalanffy, magic and myth are not primitive stages of thinking doomed to make way for science:[13] human mind objectivizes itself through *every* symbolic form; hence objectivity is not an exclusive characteristic of exact sciences, but a state that can be observed at various levels and in varying expressions. Bertalanffy committed himself to those conceptions as early as 1926, under neo-Kantian influences (H. Vaihinger). He thought that "the mythical feeling is not only a stage prior to scientific knowledge, because scientific thought is itself still bound to myths."[14] And he understood science as a "de-anthropomorphization" process aimed at "getting more and more rid of the [cognitive] moments stemming from the human senses," the representations bound to sensory intuition:

> The scientific mind tends to eliminate the mythical experience from its description of the world [. . .] It tends to replace the mythical picture of things interacting by secret forces by the abstract scheme of a regular succession divested of inner life, but made serviceable for science.[15]

After the war, Bertalanffy integrated anthropological and psychological aspects into those reflections. He thought that mythical thinking and the first languages marked the beginning of a "differentiation between subject and object, reality and symbol" that was "increasingly established" in the course of evolution and through which the representative function of symbols had been "achieved in language, art and science": the "organismic" principle of hierarchization through structural and functional differentiation (see 2–1-5) would apply to psychogenesis as well as to human biological and cultural evolution.[16] Piaget also gave scientific foundations to constructivism, which appealed to Bertalanffy, in showing that categories arise from the operations performed by the child on his environment and that the objectivization process has no end, going on from the sensorimotor level to the representative thinking level through "reflecting abstraction" (the combination of abstractions drawn from the "schemes of action," which is a "construction of operations on other operations"[17]).

1-1-5—*Productivity and Autonomy of Symbolic Universes*
Bertalanffy explained the ability of mind to "de-anthropomorphize" its world view by means of the "productivity" of symbolism, a "magic of the algorithm," which man would only have discovered the existence of when becoming aware of its representative function. The existence of science and technology would be its major expression, and mathematics, its purest incarnation. Isolated symbols remain unproductive, but the situation changes if they are "connected according to pre-established rules" into a system. Their "generativity" arises from the possibility of rule iteration: one gets a "thinking machine," likely to "yield more 'dividends' than the conceptual capital originally invested."[18] In 1948, Bertalanffy connected this idea to the idea of the "autonomy," the "own life" of symbolic systems, i.e.

to Hegel's "objective mind": their productivity would give rise to "immanent logics" of development that justify the study of human organizations
as "supra-individual systems," ruled by laws of their own:

> This is the reason why, by and large and neglecting transitions, we find
> three great realms of levels in the observed world: inanimate nature,
> living systems, and the symbolic universe [. . .], each having its charac-
> teristic immanent laws.[19]

Bertalanffy perceived here a deep significance that constitutes the apex of
his whole anthropology (as well as Cassirer's): human progress should be
viewed from the perspective of a liberation based on the symbolization ability. Language, myth, religion, and arts would be multiple expressions of
this emancipation that culminates in science. And technology, as a material manifestation of symbolism, should be understood as a continuation,
with other means, of an autonomization process that is already typical of
phylogenesis.[20]

1-1-6—The "Tragedy of Culture" According to Bertalanffy
Bertalanffy nonetheless saw a paradox inherent in the human condition
that he had already formulated in his doctoral thesis and discussed again
after the war: the instruments allowing so much human achievements
would also be the ones bringing servitude—a sign of the heritage of Georg
Simmel's theme of the "tragedy of culture": the symbolic function would
be "the basis of the most sublime achievements of man" as well as "the
cause of all his follies." On the one hand, it made possible scientific and
technological triumphs. But on the other, the invention of symbolic universes should also be seen as man's "original sin": man should have to "pay
for his uniqueness." The ability to anticipate future events would be the
source of his grandeur as well as of his anxiety toward the future. And the
autonomy of symbolic universes would imply a trend resulting in the alienation of the individual, of which the wars and neuroses are specific human
consequences. The trend toward the hypostasis of concepts would play an
essential role here; hence the salutary importance of a (neo-criticist) theory
of knowledge.[21]

Bertalanffy located the danger in the ambiguity of symbols outside of
mathematics: the vaguer they are and the more impregnated with feelings,
the more they foster passions and awaken instincts, generating the bloody
course of history. The problem of humanity would therefore consist in taking on the ambiguity of its symbolic creations and of putting them in service of a harmonious development rather than letting them serve destructive
compulsions. Mathematics would hence also have an eminent cultural function, provided their application to human affairs is adequately developed,
i.e. at the service of a systemic perspective.[22]

1-2—Principles of Bertalanffy's Perspectivist Theory of Knowledge

Bertalanffy's anthropology soon became the framework of his theory of knowledge, called "perspectivism" under Nietzsche's and Vaihinger's influences. He mostly worked out this theory between 1926 and 1937 but added new important elements after the war.[23]

1-2-1—Biological and Cultural Relativities of Categories

Its first moment underlined the principle of "dependence" of cognition and knowledge on "biological factors"—called by Bertalanffy the "biological relativity of categories":

> The categories of experience or forms of intuition, to use Kant's terms, are not universal *a priori*, but rather they depend on the psycho-physical organization and physiological conditions of the experiencing animal, man included.[24]

Bertalanffy defended this thesis from 1937 onward. He thus continued a "tradition," initiated by J. Müller and leading to Uexküll, characterized by the attempt to reinterpret the Kantian transcendental esthetics biologically.[25] He joined this form of neo-Kantianism to other forms, also defending (as early as 1924 and under O. Spengler's influence) the thesis of "cultural relativities of categories": the latter would be molded by a specific culture that they in turn also shape. In particular, every scientific theory would be an "expression of its epoch [*Zeitgeist*]."[26] After the war, Bertalanffy could draw on B. L. Whorf's "principle of linguistic relativity," which emphasized the structuring role of language in thinking and explained the difficulty of holism's being able to assert itself in the Western world. This culturalism enabled him to connect the reign of a "mechanistic" thinking to forms of social and political organization that he abhorred (see 1–4-4) and to justify his idea that holistic thinking could assert itself only in the context of a "general intellectual [*geistige*] transformation" pervading the whole culture.[27]

Bertalanffy connected his two "relativity principles," superimposing the second one on the first one. Biological relativity would work only on *perception*, while its cultural homologue would work on *apperception*, the modalities of conceptualization of the world:

> Linguistic, and cultural categories in general, will not change the potentialities of sensory experience. They will, however, change apperception, that is, which features of experienced reality are focused and emphasized, and which are underplayed [. . .] Perception is universally human, determined by man's psycho-physical equipment. Conceptualization is culture-bound because it depends on the symbolic systems we apply [. . .] which are largely determined by linguistic factors.[28]

1-2-2—The Duality of Bertalanffy's Perspectivist Theme

Those relativistic theses were only elements of Bertalanffy's perspectivism. He indeed rejected its reduction to relativism, conventionalism, or utilitarian pragmatism:

> Having indicated the biological and cultural relativity of the categories of experience and cognition, we can on the other hand also indicate its limits. Relativism has often been formulated to express the purely conventional and utilitarian character of knowledge, and with the emotional background of its ultimate futility. We can however easily see that such consequence is not implied.[29]

Bertalanffy regarded Nicholas of Cusa, G.W. Leibniz, W.J. Goethe, and E. Cassirer as the heralds of his perspectivism, which was also influenced by the revolutions in theoretical physics. One of its fundamental ideas was that the knower filters the "real" only in systems of "rigid and separating" symbols, in as many and sometimes antithetical perspectives that enable a conceptual and practical mastery of the "real," but grasp only some of its facets.[30] Another essential idea was that those perspectives nonetheless may in principle have a truth value: the relation of "reality" to science would be homologous to the relation of a building to one of its blueprints; the latter is only a perspective on the former, but a correspondence exists between the "real" and its "stylized" picture, which preserves some of its "traits of order." The human mind would thus be able to restore some structural features of the "real":

> The structure of the real corresponds in view of *some* of its formal traits to the logical structure of our conceptual schemes [. . .] Every science represents a schematized picture of reality in the sense that *some* of its traits of order are put in *univocal* correspondence with a conceptual scheme.[31]

However, the problem still was to explain the reasons for this power: it was out of the question for Bertalanffy to call upon any metaphysical principle of "pre-established harmony."

1-2-3—Perspectivism as Evolutionary and Genetic theory of Knowledge

While keeping his distance from the relativisms in biologicist (Uexküll) and culturalist (Spengler) styles, Bertalanffy rejected G. Fechner's and W. Köhler's theses ("psycho-physical parallelism" and "psycho-physical isomorphism" respectively). But until 1940, he left open the question of the possibility of a correspondence between concept and "reality."

In the first step of his answer, he integrated the work of Lorenz, who had in 1941 interpreted Kantian *a priori* as an *a posteriori* of phylogenesis.

Bertalanffy was then in a position to give an evolutionary foundation to his perspectivism:

> The "*a priori*" forms of intuition and categories are organic functions, based upon corporeal and even machine-like structures of the sense organs and the nervous system, which have evolved as adaptations in the millions of years of evolution. Hence they are fitted to the "real" world [. . . But] it is not required that they fully correspond to the real universe, and even less that they represent it completely. It suffices that a certain degree of isomorphism exists between the experienced and the "real" worlds, so that experience can guide the organism in such way as to preserve its existence.[32]

However, Bertalanffy was not satisfied with this thesis, which did not make it possible to understand *how* this "degree of isomorphism" occurs, nor whether it is *necessary*, nor whether humans have the ability to "de-anthropomorphize" their world view. Moreover, Lorenzian inneism did not make any room for the principle of "creative cognition" to which Bertalanffy gave so much importance. That is why (from 1950 onward) he integrated into his perspectivism the "transactionalism" of J. Dewey and A.H. Bentley, as well as their Piagetian psychological foundations. They gave answers to those questions; and he tried the following combination with Lorenzian thesis: phylogenesis has established the conditions for the possibility of the development of cognitive structures of man in a direction warranting his survival, but those dispositions are actualized in the individual according to a transactional logic of the co-construction of the subject and its objects ruled by psychogenetical principles. This is in position to explain the objectivity of those structures.[33]

1-2-4—Perspectivism as Relationalism

A weakness of Bertalanffy, however, is that he never systematically connected his evolutionary and psychogenetic arguments to the purely philosophical structuralist arguments he developed as early as the end of the 1920s under the influences of those involved in the "de-substantialization" processes of physics, holistic metaphysics (N. Hartmann, A.N. Whitehead), neo-Kantianism (Vaihinger, Cassirer), and neo-positivism (E. Mach).

In a first step, his structuralism promoted a relationalist and constructivist ontology that constitutes the "real" as nomothetic determination of phenomena and subsumes substance and causality under a law of the invariance of phenomenal relations. The action of making relations would be an essential moment of the objectivization process, which would consist not of "finding out connections resulting from the reciprocal action between absolute things" but of "condensing a knowledge of empirical chains in judgments to which a value of object is attributed":[34]

Science has nothing to do with the "internal essence" of things; it exclusively deals with the "laws," the formal relations existing between the "things."[35]

The [natural] law does not belong to the empirical world, but is rather a logical relation between conceptual constructions [. . .] Only constructive thinking builds the laws.[36]

1-2-5—From a "De-Anthropomorphization" Process to "Mathematicist Structuralism"

H. Poincaré once wrote that "freedom is not arbitrariness."[37] It is from this point of view that Bertalanffy (like Cassirer) interpreted perspectivism as a condition of objectivity. As early as 1937, his view of science as a process of "de-anthropomorphization" tended to take the form I am calling a "mathematicist structuralism":

One can see in the theoretical building of modern physics that everything specific to our intuition is progressively eliminated and that only a system of purely mathematical relations is left [. . .] This moment is precisely the proof that it frees itself from our specifically human senses, and this is a token that this system, in its perfect state, does not belong to the human "world" ["*Umwelt*"] anymore, rather having a universal validity.[38]

Bertalanffy insisted on what he called the "convergence of research," i.e. the determination of "universal constants" by independent means. Each of them would be the end of a process in which objectivity is constructed in bringing to light relational invariants constituting the real "substance" of nature, what Cassirer described as the "ultimate stratum of objectivity":[39]

Physical constants cannot be conceived as being simply conventions [. . .]; they represent certain aspects of reality, independent of biological, theoretical or cultural biases.[40]

The only "substance" (i.e. persisting entity) left is certain invariants expressed in highly abstract conservation laws [. . .] In its de-anthropomorphized form, science is a conceptual construct representing certain formal or structural relationships in an unknown X.[41]

Science is interested in the invariant expressing itself in different ways.[42] A. Rapoport may be the one who most efficiently summarized the logic and the major consequence of this "mathematicist" structuralism, defended by Bertalanffy before him:

The only objective descriptions of events and relations are *structural* ones. The language of structure is the language of mathematics.[43]

Any structural description that reaches "all the way" to elements and relations not further analyzable may be identified with "reality" itself [. . .] The philosophical view which declares knowledge to be knowledge of structure underlies the trend in general systems theory that puts mathematical isomorphism at the foundation.[44]

1-2-6—Limits and Dignity of Knowledge

However, even the invariants determined in the course of the objectivization process were considered by Bertalanffy as perspectivist constructions: the "magic of the algorithm" could operate only on the basis of particular perspectives. Hence science could reveal structures only through specific categorical "glasses":

> What traits of reality we grasp in our theoretical system is arbitrary in the epistemological sense, and determined by biological, cultural and probably linguistic factors [. . .] It would be perfectly possible that rational beings of another structure choose quite different traits and aspects of reality for building theoretical systems.[45]

Bertalanffy's structural realism was thus only a moment of his perspectivism, circumscribed by a systemic understanding of "reality." As a matter of fact, his point of view was a neo-criticist idealism, in which every duality between the structures of "mind" and of the "real," reduced to a false problem, vanished in his evolutionary and genetic arguments. He did not conceive the "real" separately from the constructive activity of the knowing subject:

> What reality ultimately is, is no question for science which is only concerned with selected structural aspects of its behavior. Neither is there a gap between reality and our concepts of reality; reality is what we make it for our limited human purposes, and it is inextricably interfused not only with the act of observation but also of conceptualization. The best we can attain is not a copy of reality in knowledge but a projection, as it were, in the coordinates of human categories, of certain of its aspects, being isomorphic with respect to limited and general, formal properties.[46]

Bertalanffy finally synthesized all moments of his perspectivism in this formulation:

> The categories of our experience and thinking appear to be determined by biological as well as cultural factors. Secondly, this human bondage is stripped by a process of progressive de-anthropomorphization of our world picture. Thirdly, even though de-anthropomorphized, knowledge only mirrors certain aspects or facets of reality. However, fourthly, *ex*

omnibus partibus relucet totum, to use Cusa's expression: each such aspect has, though only relative, truth. This, it seems, indicates the limitation as well as the dignity of human knowledge.[47]

1-3—The Perspectivist Philosophy of Scientific Systemology

Perspectivism is the mold of the philosophy of "systems science" through which Bertalanffy justified the legitimacy of that science while defining its nature, objects, and aims.

1-3-1—The Promotion of Theoretical Thinking

He has always castigated the sterility and dangers of a dogmatic empiricism, which overestimates the roles of experimentation and induction, persists in an illusory and superficial "fear of hypotheses," and leads only to the "chaos of facts and opinions":

> It is only when profusion is ordered, organized in a system, ruled by general principles and laws, that a science emerges from a heap of informations.[48]

"Galilean thinking" should be generalized. No science would be able to accomplish its task, the "ordering" and "conceptual mastery of phenomena," without being based on idealizations and abstractions. Bertalanffy identified theoretical science with "nomothetic science," a hypothetic-deductive "science of principles" opposed to a "science of images," where entities like atoms have their place only as heuristic fictions. He made radical distinctions between law ("logical relation between conceptual constructions") and "empirical rule," and between explanation ("logical subsumption of the particular under the general") and description. From 1932 onward, he held the mathematical form for the ideal:

> The goal of science can only be reached when univocally fixed symbols are connected according to univocal rules. Such a system is called mathematics, which is in the last analysis the highest accessible form of rationalization of the real.[49]

Bertalanffy was nonetheless aware of the fact that every genuine mathematization does not operate directly upon the phenomena, but upon a prior representation of them.

He judged the value of a theoretical construction according to four criteria: its ability to give a "unified explanation of a definite factual domain"; the extent of the testable consequences derivable from it and which would have remained unknown without that theoretical construction; its ability to suggest new hypotheses; and its "simplicity," i.e. its ability to explain as many "facts" as possible with a minimum of postulates and free parameters.

Empirical adequacy would be a secondary criterion, subordinated to the previous ones.[50]

1-3-2—Science as a Perspectivist "Art of Omission"

Bertalanffy considered science to be an "array of conceptual schemes" that man "brings into experience" in order to "find his way in the world," a set of "abstractions and stylizations expressing only some traits of order of the real" in "putting them in univocal correspondence with some conceptual schemes which are forever unable to grasp the profusion of phenomena." He defined it as an "art of omission":

> Science is one of those symbolic worlds which man has created for mastering the great enigma of the universe [. . .] It is not concerned with the innermost core of reality. But it is one of the perspectives of reality, representing, by means of interconnected symbols, certain traces of reality, namely, the orderliness in the relations of things. This, however, is sufficient to allow for theoretical as well as practical mastery of nature [. . .] What science can do is to symbolize reality in its way, knowing that it is but a humble way to redraw a few traces of the great blueprint of Creation.[51]

Two aspects would govern this art: "the rather restricted number of conceptual schemes available for the interpretation of reality," a restriction connected to psychobiological and cultural factors, partly explaining that "similar schemes occur in different fields"; and the underdetermination of these schemes with regard to the "real," which implies the need to grasp the latter through complementary constructions.[52]

Like Cassirer, Bertalanffy held all "symbolic forms" for legitimate ways of constituting universes, none of them being in position to pretend to supremacy. The same thing can indeed be constituted as an object according to different points of view; and there is no sense in asking which one is the most fundamental: the value of every statement about this object is relative to the "conceptual framework of reference" leading to its formulation. This pluralism put in perspective the various scientific constructions of the "real" but also the whole set of those constructions with regard to the other "symbolic universes." All forms of scientism were hence rejected; and positivisms were viewed as their "epistemological root."[53]

1-3-3—From Perspectivism to "Modelism": Science as an Art of Interpretation of the "Real"

Bertalanffy was naturally led to what H. Stachowiak has called "modelism," i.e. the idea that there is only knowledge "in models or through models":[54]

> Every science is a model in the broad sense of the word, that is a conceptual structure intended to reflect certain aspects of reality.[55]

Every knowledge only reflects some aspects of the real in more or less relevant models [. . . Here] can be found the limit as well as the fertility of creative scientific thinking. In opposition to the dogmatism of previous eras, one may describe as "perspectivist" this world view, and in that sense, the model represents the essence of every knowledge in general.[56]

He rejected in particular the Kantian hierarchy between "constitutive" and "regulative" judgments, which had been central in the Kantian justification of a "mechanistic" science.[57]

Central in this modelism that Bertalanffy started to develop at the end of the 1920s was what H. Lenk has called the "fundamental principle of interpretativity of every knowledge, perception and action." Bertalanffy judged that "conceptual models are at the basis of any interpretation" of the "real," without which would occur only "a mere enumeration of data." He viewed knowledge as a "projective construction" based upon interpretation schemes fitting the intentions of its creator and therefore having an essentially hermeneutical nature.[58]

Inspired by Goethe's morphology, Bertalanffy understood the theoretical model as an ideal-type. He emphasized the projective trait, the figurative and normative functions of this selective operator to which is delegated the knowledge function, comparing it with a map as well as with "a sort of rape of nature, pressing reality into a Procustean bed and recklessly cutting off what does not fit into its mould."[59] He also emphasized its fictional nature, without renouncing to its explaining power: one operates upon it *as if* it would grasp the essential traits of what it models and *as if* it could be substituted to it. Hence its three "typical moments:"

A theoretical model has a more or less marked fictive character. It cannot be simply drawn from experimental facts, but is a free conceptual construction. And it lays no claim to monopoly.[60]

Bertalanffy rejected the partition between theory, model, and "data" incompatible with his perspectivism. His only distinction was between theoretical models "in a wide sense" and "in a narrow sense," relative to their respective degree of generality and explanatory value:

In the wide sense, every scientific theory can be conceived as a conceptual model. In the narrow sense, a model is an auxiliary construction which illustrates some relations and helps us to work more easily with them.[61]

He simply assimilated "theory" to a model that has been demonstrated, through a procedure of objectivization, to refer to structures independent from its construction.

1-3-4—*From Holistic Logic to "System Laws"*

Bertalanffy reexamined holistic logic in his perspectivist framework, encouraged by a context where it was in vogue in many academic circles while giving rise to nebulous considerations and having strong and dangerous ideological undertones.[62] He wanted to "free the concept of wholeness from pure speculation" and to transform it into an authentic "means of explanation," aiming as early as 1932 at integrating it in the realm of "exact" science:

> Wholeness is neither a metaphysical concept nor a place of formation of wild hypotheses nor an ignorance asylum, but a problem which can and must be grasped with the methods of exact sciences.[63]

Bertalanffy defined a system as "a set of elements standing in interrelation among themselves and with the environment."[64] In 1926, he characterized "integration" as a "sum of elements plus a relationship which keeps them together"[65] and then contested the legitimacy of the "meristic" logics according to which (1) no relationship between elements of an entity can alter their intrinsic properties (i.e. observable in another context); and (2) knowledge of those properties and of their relationships *as inferred on the basis of this knowledge* is necessary and *sufficient* in order to account for the properties of the entity. Bertalanffy defined "system" by opposing these two theses: (1) There can be relationships between elements altering their properties compared to the ones observable in an isolated state. In that sense, elements have "relational" properties. (2) If it is the case, some properties of the entity are "constitutive," i.e. not derivable from the intrinsic properties of its elements and of the relationships inferred on their basis: they depend on their relational properties, and hence are functions of the structure (the set of all their mutual relationships). Their roles lend the entity its systemic nature.

> The meaning of the rather mystical expression according to which "the whole would be more than the sum of its parts" is simply that the constitutive characteristics are not explainable with the characteristics of the parts as known and studied only in isolation. The characteristics of the complex therefore appear as "new," or "emergent," with regard to the ones of the elements. But if one knows the set of the parts gathered in the system and the set of their mutual relationships, then the behavior of the system can be deduced from the behavior of its parts.[66]

Seven years after P. A. Weiss, who coined the expression in 1925, Bertalanffy referred to those "constitutive" characteristics with the expression "system laws" [*Systemgesetze*].[67]

But he was aware of the vicious circle. Since complete knowledge of every part would require knowledge of all their relational properties, knowledge of the whole from its elements and their relationships is presupposed from the beginning. Hence there is, according to Bertalanffy, a "principle of indeterminacy" legitimating two complementary perspectives: one attempt is to undertake a meristic study of the system with the regulative postulate that it will provide significant information; another is to focus on the determination of an "integral law" of the "order of the events" that conditions the interpretation of the partial behaviors (the teleology of which should be identified with their contribution to this order).[68] Bertalanffy conceived these laws as "higher order statistics" involving parameters of a statistical nature subsuming partial processes that underlie the functioning of the system.[69] He regarded this approach as necessary, particularly in view of the fact that the success of meristic procedures depends on conditions that are rarely satisfied in the nonphysical fields (and even in some fields of the physical sciences), where the number of relevant variables and the intensity of their relationships entail a "tremendous complication" incompatible with the "traditional" method of isolation of causal series thanks to "controlled experiment."[70]

1-3-5—"System" as a Perspective: The Constructivist Ontology of Systems

When Bertalanffy referred to some portions of the empirical world as "systems," it was an abuse of language: he saw every system as a conceptual construct derived from specific modes of perception and apperception and from theoretical *a priori* determining its borders, its elements, and their relations. In our environment, as reconstructed in our perception, some relatively stable complexes appear, and a system would be the product of our will to rationally reconstruct their cohesion; at stake was its actual explanatory value:

> An object (in particular a system) is only definable by its cohesion in the wide sense, i.e. by the interactions of its components. In that sense, an ecosystem or a social system is as much "real" as an individual plant, an animal or a human being, and problems like pollution as perturbation of the ecosystem or social problems strikingly show their "reality." However, interactions (more generally interrelations) are never directly seen or perceived: they are conceptual constructs.[71]

Given that a system is a "set of elements standing in interrelations," it is the systemician alone who *constitutes* the things as systems: one should consider systems as "created by the relationships which sustain them,"[72] but in a constructivist spirit. Neither Bertalanffy nor Rapoport held the distinction between "concrete" and "abstract" systems to be relevant:

> I conceive a system as any portion of the world to which an ontological status is *assigned* by a human mind because it is *recognized* as having

a certain cohesion; that is, because it preserves a certain degree of self-identity. Whether it does or not is again a matter of someone's perception [. . .] Whether the features singled out are essential or not is a question to be decided on *a posteriori,* not on *a priori* grounds. The essential features are those that enter a "fruitful" theory [. . .] *Every* system, to my thinking, is an "abstracted" system. Admittedly, there are degrees of abstraction.[73]

Bertalanffy described system as a "guiding idea" or a "paradigm."[74] Hence his postulate according to which "some formal properties apply to every being *as considered as a system*":[75] if one "thing" is grasped through the prism of a systemic model, then the properties of the latter are *ipso facto* applicable to the former, and in this way the "thing" is *transformed* into a *systemic object.* That is why he judged it unnecessary and even impossible to provide any general explicit definition of a "system"; the systemic representation would be "a matter of policy":[76]

The system concept can be defined and developed in different ways, according to the objectives of the research and to the various aspects of the notion one wants to reflect.[77]

This view implies that there is in principle no limit to the systemic constitution of "things." But Bertalanffy also emphasized that most of such constitutions are of "no interest in practice," their legitimacy being won only through their theoretical fertility.[78]

1-3-6—The Isomorphism Concept and the Ontology of "General Systems"

He had in fact understood the intimate reciprocity of the system and model concepts:

"System" is a model of general nature, that is, a conceptual analog of certain rather universal traits of observed entities.[79]

This defined more precisely what he called with Rapoport and Boulding a "general system." This concept reveals two levels of understanding and an interpretation of the "reality" of systemicity in accordance with "mathematicist structuralism." A system is first of all a portion of the phenomenal world as grasped through a theoretical model using systemic concepts. And at a second, metatheoretical level, it is an equivalence class induced by a structural similarity between theoretical models: if two phenomena have relevant models perfectly corresponding to each other in their conceptual structure (isomorphism), there must exist a "general system" that "embodies in abstract form"[80] this correspondence in formalizing the "rather universal traits" detected in that way, and that may in its turn help to construct new specific systemic models. Rapoport and R. Rosen have well summarized the underlying idea:

> The similarity between two phenomena is profound if there exists a *single* underlying theory from which the laws of both phenomena can be deduced.[81]
>
> *Two distinct systems can behave similarly only to the extent that they comprise alternate realizations of a common mathematical or formal structure.* The study of this mathematical structure, through the techniques of mathematics itself, is simultaneously a study of all the realizations of that structure, i.e. of an entire class of analogous but physically distinct systems.[82]

Bertalanffy could therefore talk about a "necessary formal correspondence rooted in the objects themselves as far as they represent systems, whatever their nature," but not in the sense that these objects would share a common "systemic essence" reflected in our models, since they are constructed as systems by the knower: the isomorphisms, partly induced by the limits inherent in our conceptualization modes, would on the other hand also be "grounded in reality," expressing structural invariants that are not accessible outside our cognition but that nonetheless reveal a "reality" that transcends them.[83]

1-3-7—The Perspectivist Interpretation of "Emergence" and "Levels of Organization"

Bertalanffy also applied his perspectivism to the principle of "emergence" and to the concept of "level of organization." He wrote that he "admitted" the former "if it is identified with the appearance of new 'organization relationships'" while being "freed of every metaphysical implication."[84] It was in accordance with his system concept:

> The properties and modes of action of higher levels are not explainable through summation of the properties and modes of action of their only components as studied and known in isolation. But if we know all the components gathered and their mutual relationships, then the higher levels are deductible from their components.[85]

In a discussion of the relevance of the partition of the "real" in various strata of "systemic formations" and of complexity, Bertalanffy most certainly wrote that "the notion of emergence is essentially correct." But it was only in the sense that emergence is an "indispensable maxim of research," which is justified pragmatically as well as ethically.[86]

Instead of basing science on one particular metaphysical interpretation, he instituted a provisional ontological delimitation of various "strata" of the "real," which kept open the explanation problem in each of them. That is why he always judged that the possibility that all biological phenomena are deducible from physic-chemical laws cannot be *a priori* rejected. But also that if one desires that biological complexity does not postpone its actualization in an "inscrutable future," this would necessitate a prior categorical "enlargement" of physic-chemical sciences. And that autonomy of biology has been justified in the meanwhile:

> The integration of new phenomena is accomplished in the form of a synthesis in which originally separated fields merge in a unified domain; and this is not a consequence of a simple application of principles given once for all and of a simple derivation of the higher levels from the lower ones: the latter themselves take on new aspects in this process. This may be interpreted in a realist and in an epistemological sense [. . .] But the realist or metaphysical interpretation fails to take account of the signification of natural science.[87]

It is in 1966 that Bertalanffy has most clearly shed light on his essentially perspectivist understanding of the emergence principle, as well as on his "isomorphism" and "general system" concepts and on the unifying functions he invested them with:

> Whether or not "events" are "irreducible", does not depend on some intrinsic character of these events (which we do not know) but on the categories we apply. Hence, it may well be that events are irreducible in one categorical framework, nevertheless permit a "monistic assumption" in another [. . .] The role of models in science is precisely to present "generalized constructs" unifying concepts that otherwise are "irreducibly different" [. . .] Theoretical "discovery" in science essentially means finding new categories, a new "code" applicable to previously "irreducible" universes of discourse.[88]

1-3-8—*General Systemology as Merging of Hermeneutical and Hypothetic-Deductive Methods*

While diverging from it in some decisive ways, general systemology should be viewed partly as a heritage of Wilhelm Dilthey's hermeneutical conception of human sciences. Dilthey intimately linked "understanding," as method of this hermeneutics generalized beyond the "art of interpretation of written monuments," to the problematic of meaning: "understanding" would always consist in grasping a signification and of reconstructing it from the objectivizations of "spirit." There was here a deep connection with holistic logics, seen by Othmar Anderle and by Bertalanffy after him; understanding a phenomenon indeed consists of grasping how it emerges from other ones and is thus integrated into a whole that gives it a signification:

> To make sense means be integrated to a wider, including relational context [. . .] *"To make sense" must be understood as "to be integrated*

in a structure" [. . .] Pure "elements", single and particular facts, have no "sense" as such [. . .] *One can only talk about sense if and when a domain of objects is ruled by holistic structures.*[89]

Systemology also revisited the opposition between "explanation" and "understanding" through which Dilthey had justified the specificity of hermeneutical method compared to the hypothetic-deductive method that he viewed as specific to "natural sciences": (1) in the "human sciences," the scientist "lives in the object" he is studying; (2) he aims at reconstructing an "interiority" of his objects "through signs exteriorly given by the senses."[90] Bertalanffian perspectivism already rejected this dichotomy in generalizing the idea that the scientist "lives in his object"; and his systemology did not have the "things" as objects, but their systemic study. It had to supply the means of the construction of their systemicity "through signs exteriorly given by the senses," the systemician finding in himself the means to construct in a significant order facts that are in themselves devoid of signification.

But it was also a question of breaking off with the opposition between "hermeneutical" and "hypothetic-deductive" methods, in a perspective later developed by G. Frey:[91] both of them create models representing competing interpretations of a single set of observables, the difference being only that it is easier to decide between those interpretations in the "natural sciences." In opposition to Dilthey, general systemology aimed at helping systemic "understanding" move beyond the domain of intuition; its task was *to merge hermeneutical and hypothetic-deductive methods:*

> The system approach [of the study of man] can be appreciated as an effort to restore meaning (in terms of intuitively grasped understanding of wholes) while adhering to the principles of *disciplined* generalizations and rigorous deduction.[92]

Systemology thus appears as the *matrix of a disciplined systemic interpretation of the "real,"* therefore as a hermeneutics. Bertalanffy described it as "attempting scientific interpretation where previously there was none," and he summarized its spirit with this Schopenhauerian maxim:

> The task is not so much to see what no one has seen yet as to think about what everybody sees in a way that nobody has conceived of it yet.[93]

1-3-9—Scientific Objects and Functions of General Systemology
The rather independent rise of similar holistic approaches and models in different fields led him to see an underlying necessity upon which he based his fundamental postulate:

> There exist *general system laws* which apply to any system of a certain type, irrespective of the particular properties of the system or the elements involved.[94]

Logical homologies follow from general system characters and it is for that reason that formal correspondences arise in the various phenomenal fields.[95]

He "postulated" general systemology in response to the needs of "an epoch turning around an exact science of wholeness and organization,"[96] conceiving it primarily as the metatheoretical framework of a scientific holism. That is, as a "basic science":

> General system theory may be considered a science of "wholeness" or holistic entities which hitherto, that is, under the mechanistic bias, were excluded as unscientific.[97]
>
> We are led to postulate a *new basic scientific discipline* which we call *General System theory*. It is a logico-mathematical field, the subject-matter of which is the formulation and deduction of those principles which are valid for "systems" in general.[98]

He described in the following terms its relationship to the "sciences of the real":

> System theory is *a priori* and independent of its interpretation in terms of empirical phenomena, but is applicable to all empirical realms concerned with systems [. . .] Its fields of application are all levels of science: first, the level of physical; second, of biological; third, of sociological units.[99]

As I will later show, Bertalanffy in fact focused his interest on his "organismic" schemes of interpretation ("primary activity," "flux equilibrium," "hierarchization": see 2–1-5). While rejecting biologicist temptations, he sought to promote them to a level of abstraction such that a biological interpretation of them would appear only as one among other possible ones.[100]

Several scientific functions were then assigned to general systemology:[101]

(1) *heuristic:* opening to science phenomena holding in check meristic modes of thinking.
(2) *taxonomic:* creating "purely logico-structural" definitions and classifications of systems, "devoid of empirical content" and "theoretically fruitful."
(3) *theoretical:* mathematically developing system concepts and "deriving the 'laws', or typical patterns of behavior, for the different classes of systems"; "enlarging the repertoire of conceptual schemes" and laying the ground for theoretical models in the "sciences of the real" that deal with "organized complexity," where theoretical frameworks are missing; and "raising new and well-defined problems" previously held as metaphysical.

(4) *mathematical and nomothetical:* fostering "the mathematization of non-physical realms and their development into exact science" and the determination of specific system laws.

(5) *explanatory:* general systems theories not only are concerned with the *form* of systemic events, but also supply "explanations in principle" of systemic behaviors, which are essentially qualitative in nature; and more specific explanations, possibly quantitative, might be deductible from them through the "introduction of particular conditions."

(6) *regulative:* "facilitating" and "controlling" the "transfers" of conceptual constructs between fields of research; and in this way enabling an "economy" of the scientific work while avoiding "superficial analogies" and supplying criteria for distinctions between systems.

This, then, is the aim of the systems approach: looking into those organismic features of life, behavior, society; taking them seriously and not bypassing or denying them; finding conceptual tools to handle them; developing models to represent them in conceptual constructs; making these models work in the scientific ways of logical deduction, of construction of material analogues, computer simulation and so forth; and so to come to better understanding, explanation, prediction, control of what makes an organism, a psyche, or a society function.[102]

1-3-10—*The Systemological Unity of Scientific Knowledge*

Criticism of meristic science was also a criticism of specialization, the "fragmentation into ever-multiplying disciplines, each with its own inbred vocabulary, methods, foci of interest," leading to "a breakdown of science as an integrated realm" and to a scientific world resembling "an assemblage of walled-in hermits,"[103] a situation threatening to lead to sterility:

History shows that interconnection of different fields and problems is a most important basis of progress. Many of the paramount achievements of science arose on borderlines, and from the synthesis of formerly separated fields.[104]

Another danger would be the "disintegration of education." The training of students would degenerate into areas of disconnected information, obstructing a synthetic vision of their respective disciplines and of the problems deserving to be explored as well as an understanding of each discipline's connections with other disciplines and a conscience attuned to the social impact of science:

The abundance of factual data as well as the intricacy of modern scientific techniques, experimental and theoretical, necessitates utmost specialization. Unavoidable though it is, this specialization involves serious danger for both the education of the scientist and the social function of science.[105]

General systemology aimed at remedying those "dilemmas." By elaborating its concepts and principles in a transdisciplinary language, it was thought, it could foster the integration of specialized disciplines and become the vehicle for a formal unity of science, expressing a compromise between the demands for unity and for respect of the autonomy of each scientific discipline:

> Unity of science is granted, not by a utopian reduction of all sciences to physics and chemistry, but by the structural uniformities of the different levels of reality.[106]

Bertalanffy thus opposed an operational framework for the actual unification of sciences on the basis of systemic isomorphisms, on the one hand, to a physicalism dogmatically laying down a vain horizon, on the other.

1-4—Systemological Metaphysics, Axiology, and Praxeology

Bertalanffy fully integrated metaphysical, axiological, and praxeological features into his systemological project. These are also integral, substantial parts and must not be neglected.

1-4-1—*System Metaphysics and Scientific Systemology*

Among other philosophers, he thought that "metaphysical" questions are in the last analysis the ones to which no answer is given in a definite paradigmatic framework.[107] That science is "de-anthropomorphized" meant for him that it progresses in overcoming the metaphysical characteristics of its concepts and hypotheses. But he did not think that metaphysics is unable to lay claim to its autonomy, nor did he think that it cannot play a fertile role in science, nor that science can do without it. He advanced various reasons for this: (1) Metaphysics is directed at the "essence of things" forsaken by science. Hence only sectarian minds are in position to deny its interest. (2) There is a great value in the methodological use of metaphysical notions as heuristic fictions. (3) Metaphysical *a priori* are necessary for every science.[108]

Bertalanffy always maintained the possibility and the necessity of a reciprocal fertilization between science, mythical thinking, mystical intuition, and metaphysics: each of them could become richer and progress in its own logic while contributing to a "future synthesis." According to him, "two parallel ways" in the study of nature were born in the Renaissance, and he aspired to restore their convergence: the physic-mathematical approach and a mythical thinking "pursuing the pre-Socratic philosophy" which, driven back in the seventeenth century, would since that time have emerged from obscurity only with the *Naturphilosophie.*

He therefore granted its full place to metaphysics in general systemology. After having written in 1932 that "there is no objection to view the universe 'as if' it were a process of organic becoming," in 1968 he called the "view of the world as a great organization" the "natural philosophy" forming the background of systemology. And although he did not himself contribute to it, he defended the legitimacy and the interest, as "inductive metaphysics," of "system metaphysics" like E. Laszló's and A. Koestler's.[109]

1-4-2—*Axiological Features and Purposes of the Systemological Hermeneutics*

Boulding once described general systemology as "a value orientation."[110] Rapoport and Bertalanffy have well expressed the necessity of and the deep justification for this feature:

> The concepts of general system theory put inter-relatedness of things and events at the center of attention. This view is already imbued with ethical and normative commitments [. . .] It provides a nexus between science and ethics, joining what had been rent asunder by the "classical" scientific outlook with its sharp distinction between questions of *what is* and questions of *what ought to be.*[111]
>
> In the discussion of general system theory, it is quite impossible to put aside moral values, because the choice of any portion of reality as a "system" is guided by such values.[112]
>
> If reality is a hierarchy of organized wholes, the image of man will be different from what it is in a world of physical particles governed by chance events as the ultimate and only "true" reality. Rather, the world of symbols, values, social entities and cultures is something very "real"; and its embeddedness in a cosmic order of hierarchies tends to bridge the gulf between C. P. Snow's "two cultures" of science and the humanities, technology and history, natural and social sciences.[113]

The philosophical anthropology and the perspectivism justified the consideration of symbolic universes as autonomous systems and therefore also of the values as "appropriate subjects of scientific inquiry," and the relevance of ethical convictions in the elaboration of the theoretical problematic and concepts.[114]. With one crucial consequence for social sciences, where the "exact" systemic approach would have an "ethical justification":

> The insistence that science is by nature value-free, and that therefore the methodology of the social sciences should be purged of value-determined orientation, reflects a confusion between objectivity (an indispensable requirement of the scientific orientation) and lack of direction (a hindrance in the pursuit of significant knowledge) [. . .]

The social sciences, as they harden, can become both significant and humane. They need not to reject the ideals of rigor and objectivity in order to retain a fundamental value orientation and to serve all of mankind rather than specific power interests.[115]

General systemology was meant to remedy the nihilism induced by the lack of values appropriate to our civilization and fed by reductionism and specialization. Bertalanffy hoped to "restore" with its help what he viewed as the values of the "old culture" (the ones of the humanistic-romantic ideal of *Bildung*),[116] also shared by Rapoport and Boulding: disinterested research and academic freedom, unity of knowledge and the formation of the "whole man," exchange and cooperation at all levels of existence, peace and the infinite respect for life.

Possibly the model of the world as a great organization can help to reenforce the sense of reverence for the living which we have almost lost in the last sanguinary decades of human history.[117]

The mechanistic world view has ushered the world into the unruled domination of physical technology, the mechanization of mankind, and the catastrophic crises of our times. An organismic view may lead to a vaster synthesis and a better adjustment to the problems with which we are confronted—provided that we are aware that such a view also has its limitations.[118]

The systemic view of the world has the most profound ethical implications. For it emphasizes the interdependence of all life on this planet [. . .] System thinking pursued to the full has the most far reaching ethical consequences in politics [. . .] It views struggles for power in the context of the entire global system and from this vantage point sees it as a scandalous dissipation of resources, attention, commitment, and efforts.[119]

1-4-3—*General Systemology as a Praxeological Guide*
In the previous quotations can be perceived that in the eyes of its founders, general systemology was not limited to the status of a tool for the interpretation of the world. It was also meant to transform the latter, more precisely to take on the function of a praxeological guide fulfilling Rapoport's early demand to "integrate knowledge and action":[120]

Science is not an event hanging in the empty space of a pure conceptual development: it is a *factor* as well as an *expression* of the course of history [. . .] In the dreadful crises shaking our time may be left the hope that [general system theory] *will prepare a new step of the development of humanity.*[121]

Bertalanffy was less insistent on this aspect of his project than other general system theorists, and he did not concretely contribute to its actualization.

Especially Boulding, Rapoport, and Mihajlo D. Mesarović did the job, thus contributing to a pacifist activism and to working out global alternatives and solutions to the impasse of a world running a race of destructive growth:

> Modern system theory should be viewed not only as a set of techniques for solving problems arising in conventional frameworks of thought, such as problems of increasingly complex technology, but also as a harbinger of a new outlook, one that is better equipped to cope with the accelerating rate of historical change.[122]
>
> The ever increasing complexity of the world we live in requires that our understanding of this phenomenon be based on a broader theoretical basis. The motivation for an attempt to develop such a theory is therefore both scientific, with the objective of improving our understanding of the natural and social phenomena, and practical (engineering), with the objective to provide better methods for the synthesis and control of complex systems.[123]

1-4-4—General Systemology as Matrix of a "Humanistic Science"

Bertalanffy saw general systemology as the matrix of a "humanization of science." He emphasized this essential humanistic dimension that, according to him, set his project apart from other currents of system research such as cybernetics:

> The humanistic concern of general systems theory marks a difference to mechanistically oriented system theorists speaking solely in terms of mathematics, feedback, and technology and so giving rise to the fear that systems theory is indeed the ultimate step toward the mechanization and devaluation of man and toward technocratic society [. . .] I do not see that the humanistic aspects can be evaded unless general systems theory is limited to a restricted and fractional vision.[124]

One may indeed hold it for a humanistic project in view of at least five of its purposes:

(1) insisting on the uniqueness of the "symbolic animal" and placing him at the center of the scientific interest, hence avoiding any blow to dignity resulting from this specificity;

(2) reintegrating sciences into a dual biological and cultural process while regarding them as imposing expressions of human freedom and creativity, and identifying the causes of their limits and the very causes of their fertility;

(3) unifying knowledge, notably "natural sciences" and "humanities";

(4) restoring an education aimed at the formation of mind and not at the formation of "specialists";

(5) providing the tools for a global conscience, directed to the problems affecting contemporary humanity and searching for solutions to those problems, that respect man instead of reifying him.

One thing very original about this humanism is that it was ultimately based on mathematics: it requires (1), (2), (4), and (5) in order to become effective; and mathematics was necessary for (2), in order to secure the coherence of perspectivism.

1-4-5—*Ideological Backgrounds and Orientations of General Systemology*

General systemology was imbued with ideological schemes, which it promoted back: it rejected an "industrialized and commercialized mass civilization" governed by the military-industrial complex and ruled by utilitarian, materialist, and pseudo-individualist logics that destroy the human in man and in every life in general; it rejected the "drab, idiotic and superficial" life offered by a psychopathogenic and alienating society, where the individual is reduced to a "consumer-robot" and to a "cog" of a "mega-machine," where the social and individual differences are "leveled out in a brave new world of affluent mediocrity," and where individuals in democracy are "degraded" in a "manipulated herd of cattle":

> All my conceptions were "prompted" by the necessity to overcome the positivistic-mechanistic-behavioristic-commercialistic world view which has dominated the first half of the 20th century.[125].

Bertalanffy, who was more readily reactionary than revolutionary, gave no explicit and constructive political alternative. But Boulding, Rapoport, Laszló, and Mesarović strived to sketch out alternatives, militating for the abolition of the "social institution of war" and for the "building of a responsible government at the world level" that would be able to secure a sustainable development—that is, a growth subject to the imperatives of ecological, social, and individual harmony, that would not be "mechanical" and quantitative, but "organic" and qualitative:

> The autonomy and self-fulfillment of individuals are complementary to, not antithetical to, the organization of human life as a viable self-regulating system.[126]
> Integration at the planetary scale does promise at least a breathing spell from the chronic warfare so that stock can be taken of our position, of our chances of survival and, who knows, even perhaps of an existence freed from despair, torment and degradation. This vision [. . .] constitutes the contribution of the system view to the ethical component of contemporary philosophy.[127]

2 THE THEORETICAL SYSTEMOLOGIES

Bertalanffy assigned "system science" to serve the functions previously discussed. It had in fact two theoretical areas, that were to be distinguished: "basic" systemology, which is meta-theoretical and transdisciplinary; and "applied" systemology, at the interface between the latter and the "sciences of the real," dedicated to the systemic modeling of specific phenomena.

2-1—The Basic Theoretical Systemology

I define basic theoretical systemology as the union of the set of general systems and their theorizing, and of the logical (concepts and formalisms) and methodological developments involved in their construction. One should also distinguish two levels in those "canonical" representatives of classes of theoretical systemic models: uninterpreted systems, which are abstract and formalized; and partially interpreted systems, not necessarily formalized but general enough to have transdisciplinary significance (for example: systems opened to matter or information fluxes or growth models).

2-1-1—*Logical and Methodological Aspects*
of the Theorizing of General Systems

One methodological principle was generally shared. They all started with existing systemic representations. They sought to find out their formal structure. They then defined in that way the equivalence classes of systems. They theorized those structures, and established results that may be applied to every model based on them. There existed, however, a divergence between those who already judged it possible to construct axiomatic theories of general systems, deriving the consequences of a body of abstract systemic concepts connected by definite inference rules (Ashby, Mesarović); and those (Bertalanffy, Klir) who, in a typological tradition described as "empirico-intuitive" (or—"inductive"), restricted themselves to the classifying of systemic features common to operational models, in discovering general system concepts, principles, and problems while awaiting additional empirical knowledge and the development of appropriate formal tools.[128] Klir thus defined lists of concepts, characteristics, and specifications of these characteristics that are supposed to be necessary for the construction of general systems, as well as a methodology for such constructions and for the resolution of systemic problems.[129]

Bertalanffy distinguished many alternatives in the modes of systemic description, each time prioritizing their first term: dynamical/static (study of the succession of states/study at constant state); open/closed; deterministic/stochastic; intern-structural/extern-functional (interdependence of state variables/interactions with the environment: "black box"); with continuous/discrete functions. He also noted the great diversity of formal tools and linked their use in the construction of general systems to those alternatives, in particular, sets, graphs, information, games, automata, and dynamical systems theories.[130]

Mesarović and Rosen have thoroughly delved into his conceptions, thinking through the relationship between basic theoretical systemology and the various theories of general systems analogously to the relationship between the mathematical theory of categories and the mathematical theories of structures (algebraic, topological, etc.). They have even seen in this theory of categories, which is an exact treatment of the representation of structural similarities, the appropriate means by which to formalize the general systemological procedure.[131] Each class of similar systems can be interpreted as a category (in the sense of that theory): its objects are the systems in question and its morphisms, their relationships of similarity. A functor F between two classes A and B is then a modeling relationship, establishing a correspondence between their respective systems and similarities: $F(A)$ is a model of A in B and for every system s of A, $F(s)$ is a model of s. Several classes $A_1; \ldots; A_n$ may be functorially related to B (through $F_i{:}A_i \to B$), so that two reciprocal images of B (some $F_i^{-1}(B) \subset A_i$) can be seen as models of each other. One class A may also be functorially related to several classes $B_1; \ldots; B_n$ (through $F_i{:}A \to B_i$) and a system s of A possess several models $F_i(s)$. Hence the task of basic theoretical systemology:

> (1) The analysis of individual systems within a class of related systems; (2) the establishment of functorial relations between such classes of systems (interpreted in terms of modeling or realization), so that a particular mode of analysis within one class may be carried into other classes; (3) the establishment of notions of analogy between systems belonging to different classes, through the sharing of common models. In the process of pursuing this *modus operandi,* we establish a web of inter-relationships between systems belonging to different classes. This web is manifested through the homomorphisms within classes and the functors between classes. And it is this web which is the object of study, and the distinguishing characteristic, of systems research itself.[132]

2-1-2—*The Ambivalent Relationships between General Systemology and "Formal Sciences"*

It appears that the importance of formal sciences for basic theoretical systemology was essential from the ontological, logical, and methodological points of view. The latter had a mediating as well as uncertain place, which has well been summarized by Boulding:

> General Systems Theory is a name which has come into use to describe a level of theoretical model-building which lies somewhere between the highly generalized constructions of pure mathematics and the specific theories of the specialized disciplines.[133]

However, their relationships were ambivalent; R. E. Cavallo has witnessed a "schism":

> A schism exists between those who commit to a reasonable understanding and appreciation of the necessary role that abstraction and mathematics play and those who are more influenced by the often pathetic (and at times potentially dangerous) abuses of this role.[134]

There was an agreement on the difference between a general systems theorist and pure mathematician: the latter is only interested in an abstract order while the former keeps an eye on the empirical meaning of his constructs.[135] But while some, such as Mesarović, identified theoretical systemology with the "branch of applied mathematics" dedicated to systemic modeling, others, such as Bertalanffy, Rapoport and Klir, rejected this reduction, first because the objects of basic theoretical systemology are logical structures of specific models, not phenomena;[136] second, because they saw in an orgy of formalisms—still not proven to be based on the most appropriate logical tools—a risk to narrow the meaning of the systemic concepts:

> It may be preferable, first to have some nonmathematical model with its shortcomings but expressing some previously unnoticed aspect, hoping for future development of a suitable algorithm, than to start with premature mathematical models following known algorithms and, therefore, possibly restricting the field of vision [. . .] The system idea retains its value even where it cannot be mathematically formulated, or remains a "guiding idea."[137]

In his correspondence, Bertalanffy firmly criticized the very sophisticated mathematical general systems models. In fact, he thought that the theoretical systemologies of his time still less needed axiomatic development than a relevant connection to empirical problems:

> There is nowadays a strong trend to axiomatization, to formalization [. . .] But I feel that those developments are going too far, because they do not lead to "discoveries" and, in the end, confuse concepts with things. It is a modern form of scholasticism.[138]

1-2-3—The Example of Lotka-Bertalanffy's "General Kinetics"

But this did not stand in contradiction to his program, inaugurated by formal contributions that, as a matter of fact, aimed only at demonstrating the *possibility* of "theories of general systems." Very influenced between 1932 and 1942 by A. J. Lotka's and V. Volterra's theoretical models of biocenotic systems, he appropriated the former's mathematical and methodological considerations, developed in his 1925 "general kinetics." Namely, that from the general differential system relating n variables $(X_i)_{1\leq i\leq n}$ through n functions $(F_i)_{1\leq i\leq n}$:

$$\frac{dX_i}{dt} = F_i(X_i;...;X_n) \qquad (1 \leq i \leq n) \qquad (1)$$

"a good deal of information of considerable interest can be derived," even "without knowing anything regarding the precise form of the functions," thanks to an "analysis formulated along perfectly general lines which covers every kind of interrelation":[139]

> Although nothing has been said about the nature of the elements or about the functions F_1, F_2, . . . , F_n, i.e. about the relations or interactions within the system, certain general principles can be deduced. We may use our equations (1) in order to show the structural isomorphism in different fields and levels of reality; or, in other words to demonstrate the possibility of a General System theory whose fields of application are to be found in various sciences.[140]

However, (1) was chosen by Bertalanffy only "with an illustrative aim," in order to "highlight some system principles while renouncing full rigor and perfect generality."[141] He agreed with Lotka in judging (1) as a typical formulation of the systemic character but also emphasized the fact that "it is not at all the most general possible" because it abstracts from the history and the spatial and temporal conditions of the system.[142]

Following H. Poincaré and E. Picard, they insisted on the possibility to discuss *a priori* the stationary states of (1) (solutions of $\left(\frac{dX_i}{dt} = 0\right)_{1\leq i\leq n}$). Taking one of them $(C_i)_{1\leq i\leq n}$ as the origin in the phases space, (1) can be rewritten in homologous form with functions $(f_i)_{1\leq i\leq n}$ of the $(x_i = X_i - C_i)_{1\leq i\leq n}$. Bertalanffy emphasized that its integrals can then be described by means of the distance between the "actual" state and the "final" state, a formal version of the "de-anthropomorphized" concept of finality that he had been defending since 1928. If the $(f_i)_{1\leq i\leq n}$ are regular enough, (1) is linearizable in the neighborhood of $(C_i)_{1\leq i\leq n}$ in the form:

$$\frac{dx_i}{dt} = \sum_{j=1}^{n} a_{ij}x_j \qquad (1 \leq i \leq n)$$

The stability of one stationary state depends only on the nature of the eigenvalues of the associated matrix $[a_{ij}]$. For example, exactly ten types of stationary states exist in the case of two variables.[143] These are general system properties, deducible from the relations between variables only. Lotka had moreover demonstrated, while applying them to biocenotic systems, that such abstract analyses may serve to define spectra of conceivable behaviors and to guide the choice of hypotheses and formal structures in systemic modeling. Bertalanffy and Rapoport emphasized after him the methodological value of such *a priori* studies.[144]

Moreover, Lotka and Bertalanffy showed that equations having a wide application spectrum (exponential and logistic "laws" of growth, evolution "laws" of interacting populations) are derivable from simple hypotheses on the $(F_i)_{1 \leq i \leq n}$. Bertalanffy's conclusion must be understood in the context of his perspectivism, in connection with his idea that very few equations can be exactly solved and that there is a natural "compulsion" to use them:

> One may have access to certain natural laws not only on the basis of experimentation, but also in a purely formal-mathematical way [. . .] In that sense, those laws are "*a priori*" and independent of their inter-pretation [. . .] This example may serve to illustrate the existence of a general system theory dealing with the formal properties of systems, of which the real objects may be seen as particular cases. In other words, this example demonstrates the formal uniformity of the world.[145]

2-1-4—The Example of Bertalanffy's "General Open System"

Bertalanffy also adapted Lotka's approach to his own theoretical needs. Since 1932, he had set up as applicable to every biological level the "princi-ple" of the system opened to matter and energies, directed toward or main-tained in a state of "flux equilibrium" (see 2–1–5). From 1940 onward, he tried to demonstrate its very general, transdisciplinary value:

> It is possible to establish certain general principles applicable to open systems, *independently of their specific nature.*[146]

This ambition led him to the study of a formal model of their kinetics. He represented an open system as a set of n components $(C_i)_{1 \leq i \leq n}$ quantified by measures $(Q_i)_{1 \leq i \leq n}$ of a certain variable (concentration, mass, etc.). Using T_i to refer to the transport speed of C_i in a volume element at a definite point of the space and P_i the speed of its production at that point, he obtained the following system of simultaneous partial differential equations:

$$\frac{\partial Q_i}{\partial t} = T_i + P_i \qquad (1 \leq i \leq n) \qquad (2)$$

where the Q_i are *a priori* some functions of the four spatial coordinates, while the T_i and P_i are also functions of the Q_j. He then noted that it is pos-sible to discuss the properties of (2) under certain rather general hypotheses, a possibility that was sufficient for his purpose.

Under the hypothesis that the T_i and P_i are linear in the Q_j, without hav-ing t as explicit argument, Bertalanffy showed that in a stationary state, the composition of the system remains invariant although "reactions" and flux still occur; he further pointed out that the number of elements becoming components of the C_i type by transport and production equals the number of elements "leaving" this type. Another property that he tried to demon-strate the generality of is "equifinality" (the independence of a stationary state of the initial conditions and of the ways taken to reach it), which he,

along with H. Driesch, saw as a typical expression of the holistic functioning of the organism. His aim was to show that openness is in itself a condition of equifinality and makes it possible to deduce it in an "exact" way.
Bertalanffy established two general theorems: the possibility for an open
system to reach a flux equilibrium, characterized by equifinal values of Q_i;
and the impossibility of an equifinality of all those values in a closed system.
Those theorems can also be derived from (1) if its right members are linear
in X_i and have one constant term.[147]

According to Bertalanffy, these analyses had far-reaching consequences,
especially in biology:

> *If* the organism is an open system, then the principles which generally
> apply to systems of this type *must* apply to it—quite independently of
> the nature of the relations and of the processes involving their compo-
> nents, which certainly are tremendously complicated.[148]

The theoretic-systemological procedure was here expressed in the following
series of inferences: (1) the organism, in so far as it is a place of exchanges
with its environment, can *from this point of view* be grasped in the framework of (2); (b) it shares this character with other "concrete" entities,
(2) thus defining an equivalence class: the "general open system"; (c) now,
some properties of (2) are independent of the interpretation of its functions;
(d) therefore, those properties are attributable back to every member of the
equivalence class induced by (2), once interpreted in their specific context;
(e) this is in particular the case with the organism, some characteristics of
which *derive from its membership in this class*.

Bertalanffy's systemology as restricted to open systems was elaborated
after his first presentation of general systemology (1937 in Chicago). In
fact, it appears as a response to a bitter setback he experienced during this
presentation: it then served to spearhead this project, as a means to demonstrate its legitimacy; it enabled him to develop its themes in connection
with specific well-tried models, against the background of the results of his
"organismic" biology.

2-1-5—From "Biological Systemology" to the General Model of Organized System

This biology, mostly elaborated between 1926 and 1937, was a system for
the systemic interpretation of biological "reality," a "biological systemology" that, in its architecture, anticipated in most of its essential characters
the project of general systemology.[149]

It was first of all a theoretical program based upon two interpretation
schemes destined to generate biological models: (1) the "endonom" open
system, self-maintaining "distant from the resting state" in a "flux equilibrium" with conditions fixed in itself. (2) The development through "progressive hierarchization": one "whole," having the strongest self-regulation

capabilities, of which no part is specialized, splits up by "segregation" and "differentiation" into subsystems with specific functions, more or less rigid structures also appearing in this process. This "progressive mechanization" involves a "loss of regulability" and expresses a "disintegrative" trend but accompanies an antagonist "centralization": the subordination of subsystems to "leading parts" that are working at a new type of integration, based upon structures and interactions that were initially missing. The possibility of global transformations in complex systems would then be explainable in reference to a "trigger causality" operating in such a hierarchical structure: there would be an "amplification" of the effect of a variation, affecting a "leading part," the magnitude of which is accorded to the hierarchical level of the latter.

Bertalanffy connected these two schemes in viewing the openness of the organism to be a precondition of the genesis and spontaneous reproduction of its hierarchical order, of its evolution toward more complex structural and functional states ("anamorphosis"). He also connected them in viewing the first one as a "principle" applicable to all hierarchical levels:

> A living organism is a hierarchical order of open systems, maintaining itself on the basis of its systemic conditions through a change of its components.[150]

One consequence of this connection was that it aided in overcoming the opposition between structures and functions, which was the main basis of Bertalanffy's dynamical approach to morphology.

He also associated his biotheoretical program, with a natural philosophy of biology, an "inductive metaphysics" aimed at serving this program as a heuristics, by helping to determine the general signification of its constructions and in facilitating conceptual transfers between biology and other disciplines. It was based on three philosophical schemes of interpretation: (1) The "primacy of wholeness": biological systems cannot be understood merely by the "summation of the modes of behavior of their parts as studied in isolation." (2) The "primacy on the structural-machinist order" of a "dynamical order of the events emerging from the interaction of the forces of the whole system," only "secondarily limited by a progressive mechanization" (a primacy expressed by equifinality and later contrasted by Bertalanffy with cybernetics); (3) the "primacy of activity" on the "reactivity" of the biological system, which interposes its own logic between the environment and its responses to stimuli.[151]

From 1932 onwards, Bertalanffy extended the scope of all those schemes of interpretation to include the associations of organisms. He did it on the basis of a criticism of the concept of "individuality," classically defined by criteria like spatial connectivity that he judged as "very vague, relative and dependent on our human perspective."[152] The only problems would be the existence, or lack thereof, of a "dependence relation" between the elements, and the criteria that are to be chosen in order to make the concept of "higher order integration" operational.[153] His reflection ended with a model of the "organized" (or "organic") system, based on a combination of his theoretical schemes:

> Any organic system is essentially a hierarchical order of processes standing in flux equilibrium, . . . [which] maintains itself through a change of its components on the basis of its system conditions.[154]

He subsumed under this model all biological levels of organization. "Characteristic system properties" like the "mutual dependence of parts and processes," self-regulation or the "trend towards equilibrium states," with distinctions related to the "degrees of centralization," would be working at each of these levels.[155] He thus outlined an architectonics of the biological world, unified in its diversity by an ubiquitous general system, which the "organismic" bio-theory had to elaborate specific interpretations of, as theoretical models of biological entities.

After the war, Bertalanffy continued his generalization strategy: he used (1) in order to deprive his "organized system" model of its biological "coloration." Appropriate conditions imposed on the $(F_i)_{1 \leq i \leq n}$ permitted him to formalize "progressive mechanization" in that way:

$$\lim_{t \to +\infty} \frac{\partial F_i}{\partial X_j} = 0 \qquad \text{for every } i \in [1;n] \text{ and every } j \neq i$$

As for the existence of a "leading part" E_s, he expressed it thanks to rather arbitrary hypotheses (with a restriction to the linear terms of the analytical development) with the inequalities:

$$\left| a_{is} \right| = \left| \frac{\partial F_i}{\partial X_s} \right| >> \left| \frac{\partial F_i}{\partial X_j} \right| = \left| a_{ij} \right| \qquad \text{for every } j \neq s$$

He could therefore also easily formalize the principle of "trigger causality." Although it was still a simple mathematical illustration, Bertalanffy did not hesitate to use the "organized system" model as a major vehicle for his contributions to applied theoretical systemology.

2-2—The Applied Theoretical Systemology

2-2-1—*Between Theories of General Systems and Specific Theoretical Systemic Models*

Applied theoretical systemology occupies a mediating position between basic theoretical systemology and "sciences of the real": it bases itself upon the former in order to represent objects of the latter as systems, and informs basic theoretical systemology in providing its objects. A systemic "model-object" is constructed both through homomorphy to a scientific object (it selects some of its features while preserving their relations) and through isomorphy to a general system (here there is one-to-one correspondence between the elements and their respective relationships); an analysis of the latter provides information that is able to be interpreted at the level of the model-object and that, in connection to knowledge provided by "sciences of the real," makes it possible to specify a construction of this model-object, i.e. a modeling. The result is a systemic model, ready to be empirically tested.[156]

The possible inadequacy of this model may encourage a modification of the specifications involved in the modeling, or the use of another general system, or even a change in the model-object itself.

2-2-2—*The Example of the Construction of the Theoretical Model of Global Animal Growth*

It is in the elaboration, between 1933 and 1941, of his theory of global animal growth that Bertalanffy has best illustrated this procedure. In order to construct his systemic model-object of the growing organism, he took into account only the metabolic exchanges with its environment, from the point of view of a "higher order statistics":

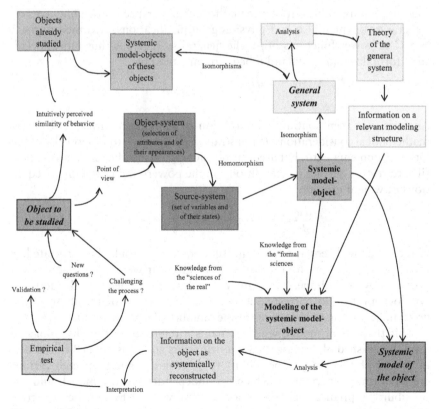

Diagram 5.2

We do not have to study in detail the multiplicity of the assimilation and dissimilation processes; we only need, for a quantitative analysis of growth, to take into account their relationships [. . .] We only need, by abstraction of the individual anabolism and catabolism processes, to introduce expressions signifying in statistical form mean values for the global anabolism and catabolism.[157]

Moreover, this model-object was constructed by isomorphy to the "general open system," under the hypothesis of invariant physiological conditions, first of all in the primitive form:

Mass variation = assimilation – dissimilation (by time unit)

It empirically appears that growth is equifinal and that metabolism rises with mass. The analysis of the general system in differential form hence encouraged a formalization with two positive monotonic-growing functions A and C having the sole mass μ as their argument:

$$\frac{d\mu}{dt} = A(\mu) - C(\mu)$$

The simplest hypothesis from the mathematical perspective (leading to exact integration), which also had physiological justifications, was then to fix A and C as power functions of μ. The general system was thus more specifically formalized (a, c, m, and n being parameters) by

$$\frac{d\mu}{dt} = a\mu^m - c\mu^n$$

Analysis was then continued by a union of biologic-empirical and purely mathematical considerations demonstrating the necessity to suppose $0 < m \leq n$. Other arguments entirely based on physiology of metabolism made it possible to restrict further the conditions on the powers and to obtain the equations of weight growth:

$$\frac{d\mu}{dt} = a\mu^m - c\mu \quad \text{with} \quad \frac{2}{3} \leq m \leq 1$$

"Linear" growth equations of the function $\lambda = \mu^{\frac{1}{3}}$ could be associated, λ referring all the more to a measurable length that weight approaches proportionality to volume. Bertalanffy could then mathematically derive a typology putting in correspondence three ideal types of metabolism and growth, according to the values of the "anabolic" parameter m.

This theoretical model, which remains a reference in the physiology of growth, satisfied all criteria characterizing this status as defined in the Bertalanffian philosophy: the possibility to determine a and c through various corroborating experiments, which are independent of the model, and the possibility to predict phenomena not yet observed; the hypothetic-deductive treatment of the phenomenon under study; and the unification by means of "exact" laws of two domains of physiology hitherto largely separated.

Table 5.1

Metabolic type	Growth type	Examples
Anabolism proportional to surface $m = \dfrac{2}{3}$	Sigmoid weight curves with equifinal stationary state $M = \left(\dfrac{a}{c}\right)^3$; $\mu(t) = \left[M^{\frac{1}{3}} - \left(M^{\frac{1}{3}} - \mu_0^{\frac{1}{3}} \right)e^{-\frac{c}{3}t} \right]^3$ Concave "linear" growth curves with equifinal stationary state $\Lambda = \dfrac{a}{c}$; $\lambda(t) = \Lambda - (\Lambda - \lambda_0)e^{-\frac{c}{3}t}$	Fishes Mammals
Anabolism proportional to weight $m = 1$	Exponential weight and "linear" growth curves. No stationary state: growth is brutally interrupted (metamorphosis, etc.) $\mu(t) = \mu_0 e^{(a-c)t}$; $\lambda(t) = \lambda_0 e^{\frac{a-c}{3}t}$	Insect larvae Helicidae
Intermediary anabolism $\dfrac{2}{3} < m < 1$	Sigmoid weight growth curves with equifinal stationary state $M = \left(\dfrac{a}{c}\right)^{\frac{1}{1-m}}$; $\mu(t)$ $= \left[M^{1-m} - \left(M^{1-m} - \mu_0^{1-m} \right)e^{-(1-m)ct} \right]^{\frac{1}{1-m}}$ Sigmoid "linear" growth curves with equifinal stationary state $\Lambda = \left(\dfrac{a}{c}\right)^{\frac{1}{3(1-m)}}$; $\lambda(t)$ $= \left[\Lambda^{3(1-m)} - \left(\Lambda^{3(1-m)} - \lambda_0^{3(1-m)} \right)e^{-(1-m)ct} \right]^{\frac{1}{3(1-m)}}$	Planorbidae Lymnae

2-2-3—The Example of the Transfer of the Model of Allometric Growth to Social Sciences

Another example of Bertalanffy's systemological approach to modeling is in a work carried out in 1955–56 with the anthropologist R. S. Naroll, which was on the continuity of his biological works. Between 1937 and 1942, Bertalanffy had studied the problem of the relative growth of organs and had demonstrated that one can not only account for the organic form in considering their differential growth (what D'Arcy Thompson had done) but that one can also analyze the latter in terms of relationships between relative growth speeds (i.e. $\dfrac{1}{y}\dfrac{dy}{dt}$ if y is a weight or linear measure of the organ Y). Bertalanffy established the general empirical validity of the "allometric" equation, which, for two organs X and Y, lays down those speeds in a constant ratio α:

$$\frac{1}{y}\frac{dy}{dt} \Big/ \frac{1}{x}\frac{dx}{dt} = \alpha$$

Hence $y = kx^\alpha$, where $k > 0$. In the applicability of this "law" to other biological realms (paleontology, biochemistry of ontogenesis, and physiology of metabolism), he also saw the indication that it is "based upon a general biological relation."[158] His hypothesis was that it is a consequence of a "distribution mechanism," translatable by rewriting the equation in the form: $dy = \alpha \frac{y}{x} dx$: α would be a "distribution constant" expressing the rate of appropriation by Y of the substances assimilated by X. He thus interpreted relative growth as the product of a competition between organs originating in their assimilation capabilities.

Bertalanffy soon went further in making this interpretation and its mathematical expression into a general system of the competition of parts of a system for the appropriation of its resources, showing that, besides that, an "allometric law" can also be derived from (1). It is this general system that he interpreted with Naroll in a sociological context, thus providing an example of the methodological use of an isomorphism.[159] Several synchronic applications of this "law" had recently been made in sociology by G.K. Zipf, R. Vining, and Naroll. The latter showed with Bertalanffy that its application can also be diachronic. Their hypothesis was that a demographic dynamics homologous to the dynamics of relative organic growth exists in each country, based upon a diachronic allometric relation between rural and urban population: α was here interpreted as a measure of the attractiveness of towns. By means of the census, they demonstrated the suitability of such relations, as well as their temporal limits. Discontinuities calling for specific sociohistorical explanations were likely to reveal unobvious demographic consequences of known historical events. In addition to the isomorphism, this thus illustrated an opening to an "exact" treatment of sociological phenomena and its heuristic function.

2-2-4—The Example of Bertalanffy's "Organismic" Psychology and Psychiatry

My third example of a way in which Bertalanffy was able to apply the systemological procedure is in the reorientation of his works, from 1951 onwards, toward psychiatry and psychology: it resulted from the fact that his systemology awoke much interest in those fields, as well as from the fact that in his own discipline molecular biology was being strongly promoted, a development rather unfavorable to his systemic biotheory.

His "organismic" psychiatry and psychology were intimately related to his philosophical anthropology, which fed them while gaining justifications. He grounded them in an interpretation of his "general organized system." They hence promoted an "organismic" model of personality, "essentially dynamic although including structural order, molar though allowing molecular interpretations of the individual processes, and formal though allowing for future material interpretations."[160] Bertalanffy interacted with the gestaltist and humanistic currents; his specific contribution consisted mostly of establishing a continuity with biology and in providing systematic arguments against behaviorist paradigms.

His model was the man as "active personality system": a system opened to his social, cultural, and material environment, which feeds on it in order to structure itself progressively while remaining far from an "equilibrium" state, and which is characterized by a "primary," inner-directed activity, manifest in his creativity, his exploratory pulses, and gaming. This model attributed to culture a "psycho-hygienic" function and identified mental illness, particularly schizophrenia, with a specifically human "perturbation of symbolic functions."

Bertalanffy contrasted it with the "robot model," regarded as "zoomorphic." He saw expressions of the latter model in behaviorism, Freudian psychoanalysis, and cybernetic psychology. He thought that this model failed by focusing on "secondary" regulative mechanisms and reducing man to an automaton, passively responding to the *stimuli* of his environment while seeking release of all tensions, the stability of a homeostatic equilibrium. Bertalanffy fiercely attacked this "pecuniary conception of man," which was dominating a form of psychology that he condemned as a "sterile and pompous scholasticism" dedicated to "provide modern society with techniques for the stultification of mankind." Judging it as essentially "utilitarian," he described it as "an expression and powerful motive of industrialized mass society," serving as a basis for a "behavioral engineering" that worked at manipulating minds. He viewed it as a "menticide" without which the so-called "affluent society" could not survive. While neurosis, delinquency, and "all the symptoms of an ill society" were manifest to an unprecedented degree.[161]

Bertalanffian "organismic" psychiatry and psychology well illustrate the possibility of a theoretical use of a nonmathematical general systems view but also its speculative character (inherent in the use of metaphorical extensions). He was aware of this as well:

> Physics and biophysics deal with open systems which are of course very different from the open systems meant by the psychologist. I nonetheless consider that, as a provisional or reference model, the "open system", with "autonomous activity" and "anamorphosis," is a better starting construction than the "closed system," the "primary reactivity" and the mental organization viewed as an apparatus aimed at maintaining "equilibrium."[162]

3 THE SYSTEMIC TECHNOLOGY

The last field of general systemology I have to discuss, namely systemic technology, will only be very briefly considered here: Bertalanffy did not contribute to its development; he only acknowledged its place in the system and strongly criticized some of its trends.

3-1—Definition and Examples

Systemic technology differs from applied theoretical systemology insofar as it does not aim at theoretical modeling but rather seeks practical solutions to concrete problems, using methods, concepts, tools, models, and perspectives elaborated in the other fields of general systemology. Those complex problems involve a very high number of variables and of relationships between these variables. Therefore resistant to classical meristic-causal approaches, they arise in consequence of the sophisticated physical technology and the substantial economic, social, political, and ecological needs of the contemporary world.

"Operations research," "management sciences," and "systems analysis" were from the 1950s onward the main currents of "soft" systemic technology, directed toward human problems—especially toward the search for optimal solutions to organizational problems. They generally made abundant use of cybernetics, which was also serving "hard" systemic technology, directed toward computer science, robotics, and physical control. A major tool of systemic technology soon became computer simulation: it makes it possible to tackle the complexity of the problems under study while getting around the insuperable difficulties it creates, especially when a mathematical treatment is undertaken. Bertalanffy thought that its epistemological foundation is the possibility to apply formal models to various systems when the components and underlying processes are badly known or unknown.[163] In that respect, one major example of the contribution to a systemic technology is the "world model" of the second report of the "Club of Rome" on the "limits to growth" (1974), directed by Mesarović.[164]

3-2—Humanistic Criticisms of Systemic Technology

In the "Society for General Systems Research" they founded at the end of 1954, Bertalanffy, Rapoport, and Boulding very soon witnessed the rise of scientist and technocratic trends, which they rightly judged incompatible with the humanism of their project: it seemed to them that the contributions of systemic technology to the service of the military-industrial complex, to psychological mass manipulation, to bureaucratic planning, and to an economic optimization concerned only about profitability, threatened to transform the "science of systems" into a "science of domination." On the same wavelength as his friend A. Huxley, Bertalanffy was the first and the most constant voice in the denunciation of this trend:

> We have quite a fair idea what a scientifically controlled world would look like. In the best case, it would look like A. Huxley's *Brave New World,* and in the worst, like Orwell's *1984* [. . .] Just because modern totalitarianism is so terrifically scientific, it makes the absolutism

of former periods appear a dilettantish and comparatively harmless makeshift [. . .] Human society is based upon the achievements of the individual, and is doomed if the individual is made a mere cog in the social machine. This, I believe, is the ultimate precept a theory of organization can give: not a manual for dictators of any denomination more efficiently to subjugate human beings by the scientific application of Iron Laws, but a warning that the Leviathan of organization must not swallow the individual without sealing its own inevitable doom.[165]

CONCLUSION

Although he never systematized it, Bertalanffy developed essential philosophical and scientific elements for the foundation of a coherent systemological hermeneutics, while showing through his own works its potential fecundity. He thus anticipated many later approaches such as "critical systems theory." Their claims to novelty should therefore be put in perspective, and those further developing such views would in any case benefit from a more thorough knowledge of Bertalanffy's views.

NOTES

1. David Pouvreau and Manfred Drack, "On the History of Ludwig von Bertalanffy's 'General Systemology', and on Its Relationship to Cybernetics—1: Elements on the Origins and Genesis of von Bertalanffy's 'General Systemology,'" *International Journal of General Systems* 36, no. 3 (2007); David Pouvreau, *Une histoire de la 'systémologie générale' de Ludwig von Bertalanffy—Généalogie, genèse, actualisation et postérité d'un projet herméneutique,* PhD diss., Paris, E.H.E.S.S., 2013.
2. Ludwig von Bertalanffy, *General System Theory: Foundations, Development, Applications* (New York: Braziller, 1968), xviii–xxiii; see also his "The History and Status of General Systems Theory," in *Trends in General Systems Theory,* ed. George J. Klir (New York: Wiley, 1972), 28–38. His presentation was the following:

Bertalanffy's classification of General System Theory

Systems Philosophy	Systems Science	Systems Technology
Systems epistemology	General systems principles	Physical technology
Systems ontology	Theorizings of general systems	Social, economical
Axiology	Specific theoretical systemic models	and political technology
(theory of values)		

3. Ludwig von Bertalanffy, *Vom Molekül zur Organismenwelt* (Potsdam: Aka-demische Verlagsgesellschaft Athenaion, 1940), 111–18; Bertalanffy, "Das Weltbild der Biologie," in *Weltbild und Menschenbild, III. Internationale Hochschulwochen des österreichischen College in Alpbach,* ed. Simon Moser (Salzburg: Tyrolia, 1948), 263–64; Ludwig von Bertalanffy, *Auf den Pfaden des Lebens—Ein biologisches Skizzenbuch* (Frankfurt: Umschau Verlag, 1951), 209–10; Ludwig von Bertalanffy, "A Biologist Looks at Human Nature," *Scientific Monthly* 82 (1956): 34–37; Bertalanffy, *Robots, Men and Minds* (New York, Braziller, 1967), 19–20.

4. Ludwig von Bertalanffy, "An Essay on the Relativity of Categories," *Philosophy of Science* 22, no. 4 (1955): 256.

5. Bertalanffy, *Robots, Men and Minds,* 92.

6. Bertalanffy, "Mind and Body Re-Examined," *Journal of Humanistic Psychology* 6 (1967): 121, 133.

7. Ludwig von Bertalanffy, "The History and Status of General Systems Theory," in *Trends in General Systems Theory,* ed. George J. Klir (New York: Wiley, 1972), 37–38.

8. Bertalanffy, *Robots, Men and Minds,* 21–22; Bertalanffy, "A Biologist Looks at Human Nature," 37; Ludwig von Bertalanffy, "Some Considerations on Psychobiological Development (Quelques considerations sur le développe-ment psycho-biologique)," paper read at the Study Groups on the Psycho-biological Development of the Child, World Health Organisation, Geneva, WHO/AHP/11 (1956): 18; Bertalanffy, *General System Theory,* 134.

9. Ludwig von Bertalanffy, "Goethes Naturauffassung," *Atlantis* 8 (1949): 362; see also "Das Weltbild der Biologie," 265; Bertalanffy, *Auf den Pfaden des Lebens,* 206; Bertalanaffy, "Philosophy of Science in Scientific Education," *Scientific Monthly* (1953): 239; Bertalanffy, "A Biologist Looks at Human Nature," 38.

10. Ludwig von Bertalanffy, "On the Definition of Symbol," in *Psychology and the Symbol,* ed. Joseph R. Royce (New York: Random House, 1965), 57; see also Bertalanffy, *Robots, Men and Minds,* 32.

11. Bertalanffy, *General System Theory,* 140.

12. Ludwig von Bertalanffy, "The World of Science and the World of Value," *Teachers College Record* 65 (1964): 248; see also Ludwig von Bertalanffy, *Fechner und das Problem der Integrationen höherer Ordnung* (PhD diss., University of Vienna, 1926), 89–95; see also Bertalanffy, *Robots, Men and Minds,* 27.

13. Bertalanffy, "On the Definition of Symbol," 56.

14. Bertalanffy, PhD Dissertation, 10–11; and Ludwig von Bertalanffy, "Vaihingers Lehre von der analogischen Fiktion in ihrer Bedeutung für die Naturphiloso-phie," in *Die Philosophie des Als-Ob und das Leben: Festschrift zu Hans Vaihingers 80. Geburtstag,* ed. August Seidel (Berlin: Reuther & Reichard, 1932), 67.

15. Bertalanffy, *Die Philosophie des Als-Ob,* 68; see also Ludwig von Berta-lanffy, "*Das Gefüge des Lebens*" (Leipzig: Teubner, 1937), 157.

16. Bertalanffy, "On the Definition of Symbol," 56, 62–63.

17. Jean Piaget, *L'épistémologie génétique* (Paris: Presses Universitaires de France, 1970), 19 and esp. 57.

18. Bertalanffy, "Das Weltbild der Biologie," 266; Bertalanffy, *Auf den Pfaden des Lebens,* 4; "A Biologist Looks at Human Nature," 38–39; Bertalanffy, "On the Definition of Symbol," 33.

19. Bertalanffy, *Robots, Men and Minds,* 30; see also Bertalanffy, "Das Weltbild der Biologie," 266; Bertanlanffy, "On the Definition of Symbol," 33.

20. Bertalanffy, *Vom Molekül zur Organismenwelt,* 108–09.

21. Bertalanffy, PhD Dissertation, 91–92; Bertalanffy, "Das Weltbild der Biologie," 265–67; Bertalanffy, *Auf den Pfaden des Lebens*, 206; Bertalanffy, "A Biologist Looks at Human Nature," 38–40; Bertalanffy, "Some Considerations on Psychobiological Development," 15–17; Bertalanffy, *Robots, Men and Minds*, 31–32; Ludwig von Bertalanffy, "General System Theory and Psychiatry—An Overview," *American Psychiatric Association* 176 (1967): 29; Bertalanffy, *General System Theory*, 138.
22. Bertalanffy, "Das Weltbild der Biologie," 266–67; Anatol Rapoport, "Lewis F. Richardson's Mathematical Theory of War," *General Systems* 2 (1957): 90.
23. Especially in Bertalanffy, "An Essay on the Relativity of Categories"; see also Bertalanffy, "Philosophy of Science in Scientific Education"; "Some Considerations on Psychobiological Development" and Bertalanffy, "Mind and Body Re-Examined."
24. Bertalanffy, "An Essay on the Relativity of Categories," 250, and more generally 247–50.
25. Bertalanffy, *Das Gefüge des Lebens*, 154–55.
26. Ludwig von Bertalanffy, "Über die neue Lebensauffassung," *Annalen der Philosophie und philosophischen Kritik* 6 (1927): 252; Ludwig von Bertalanffy, *Kritische Theorie der Formbildung*, Abhandlungen zur theoretischen Biologie, 27 (Berlin: Gebrüder Borntraeger, 1928), 230; Ludwig von Bertalanffy, "Untersuchungen über die Gesetzlichkeit des Wachstums I," *Roux Archiv f. Entwicklungs-Mechanik* (1934): 339; Bertalanffy, *Das Gefüge des Lebens*, 1.
27. Bertalanffy, "Über die neue Lebensauffassung," 229–30; Bertalanffy, *Das Gefüge des Lebens*, 3; Bertalanffy, *General System Theory*, 14.
28. Bertalanffy, "An Essay on the Relativity of Categories," 253–54.
29. Bertalanffy, "An Essay on the Relativity of Categories," 255.
30. Bertalanffy, "Goethes Naturauffassung," esp. 362.
31. Ludwig von Bertalanffy, "Zu einer allgemeinen Systemlehre," *Blätter für deutsche Philosophie* 18, no. 3/4 (unpublished: *B.C.S.S.S. Archives*, Vienna, 1945), 4.
32. Bertalanffy, "An Essay on the Relativity of Categories," 256–57.
33. Bertalanffy, "Some Considerations on Psychobiological Development" and Bertalanffy, *Robots, Men and Minds*, 91–92.
34. Ernst Cassirer, *Substance et fonction* (Paris: Minuit, 1977), 346.
35. Bertalanffy, *Theoretische Biologie*, vol. 1 (Berlin: Gebrüder Borntraeger, 1932), 24.
36. Bertalanffy, *Kritische Theorie der Formbildung*, 91, 94.
37. H. Poincaré, *La science et l'hypothèse* (Paris: Flammarion, 1968), 24, 156–57.
38. Bertalanffy, *Das Gefüge des Lebens*, 156–57.
39. Ernst Cassirer, *La philosophie des formes symboliques III* (Paris: Minuit, 1972), 492, 521.
40. Bertalanffy, "An Essay on the Relativity of Categories," 258.
41. Bertalanffy, *Robots, Men and Minds*, 96, 98.
42. Bertalanffy, "Philosophy of Science in Scientific Education," 236.
43. Anatol Rapoport, "Methodology in the Physical, Biological and Social Sciences," *General Systems* 14 (1969): 185.
44. Anatol Rapoport, "The Uses of Mathematical Isomorphism in GST," in *Trends in General Systems Theory*, ed. George J. Klir (New York: Wiley, 1972), 48–49.
45. Bertalanffy, "An Essay on the Relativity of Categories," 260–62. See also Bertalanffy, *Robots, Men and Minds*, 95–96.

46. Bertalanffy, "Mind and Body Re-Examined," 136.

47. Bertalanffy, "An Essay on the Relativity of Categories," 262.

48. Bertalanffy, *Theoretische Biologie,* vols. 1, 2, 31; see also Bertalanffy, *Kritische Theorie der Formbildung,* 54–55.

49. Ludwig von Bertalanffy, *Das biologische Weltbild—Die Stellung des Lebens in Natur und Wissenschaft* (Bern: Francke AG, 1949), 150–51; see also Bertalanffy, "Über die neue Lebensauffassung," 410; *Kritische Theorie der Formbildung,* 55, 91–95; *Theoretische Biologie,* vol. 1, 22–24, 28–29, 33, 119; Bertalanffy, *Das Gefüge des Lebens,* 15; Ludwig von Bertalanffy, *Theoretische Biologie,* vol. 2 (Berlin: Gebrüder Borntraeger, 1942), 324; Bertalanfffy, "Zu einer allgemeinen Systemlehre" (1945), 4; Bertalanffy, "Goethes Naturauffassung," 359; Ludwig von Bertalanffy, "Theoretical Models in Biology and Psychology," *Journal of Personality* 20 (1951): 24.

50. Bertalanffy, *Kritische Theorie der Formbildung,* 99; *Theoretische Biologie,* vol. 1, 30; Bertalanffy, "Untersuchungen über die Gesetzlichkeit des Wachstums I," 632, 636; Bertalanffy, *Das Gefüge des Lebens,* 105; Ludwig von Bertalanffy, "Basic Concepts in Quantitative Biology of Metabolism," in *Quantitative Biology of Metabolism-First International Symposium,* Helgoländer wissenschaftliche Meeresuntersuchungen 9 (1964): 22.

51. Bertalanffy, "Philosophy of Science in Scientific Education," 239, 236; see also Bertalanffy, *Theoretische Biologie,* vols. 2, 5; Bertalanffy, "Zu einer allgemeinen Systemlehre" (1945), 4.

52. Bertalanffy, "Zu einer allgemeinen Systemlehre" (1945), 4; and Ludwig von Bertalanffy, "Theoretical Models in Biology and Psychology," *Journal of Personality* 20 (1951): 26.

53. Bertalanffy, "Philosophy of Science in Scientific Education," 236; Ludwig von Bertalanffy, "The Psychopathology of Scientism," in *Scientism and Values,* eds. Helmut Schoeck and James W. Wiggins (Princeton: Nostrand, 1960), 202–04.

54. Herbert Stachowiak, "Erkenntnis in Modellen," in *Systemtheorie als Wissenschaftsprogramm,* eds. Hans Lenk and Günter Ropohl (Königstein: Athenäum, 1978), esp. 56.

55. Ludwig von Bertalanffy. "General System Theory—A Critical Review," *General Systems* 7 (1962): 2.

56. Ludwig von Bertalanffy, "Zur Geschichte theoretischer Modelle in der Biologie," *Studium Generale* 18 (1965): 298.

57. Bertalanffy, "Über die neue Lebensauffassung," 253; and "On the Definition of Symbol," 44.

58. Hans Lenk, "Metaphysics, Interpretation, and the Subject," in *The Philosophy of Paul Weiss,* ed. Lewis Edwin Huhn (Chicago: Southern Illinois University, 1995), 57–60.

59. Bertalanffy, *Robots, Men and Minds,* 108; "Basic concepts in quantitative biology of metabolism," 27.

60. Bertalanffy, "Zur Geschichte theoretischer Modelle in der Biologie," 291.

61. Bertalanffy, "Zur Geschichte theoretischer Modelle in der Biologie," 291.

62. David Pouvreau, PhD diss.

63. Bertalanffy, *Das Gefüge des Lebens,* 178; and Bertalanffy, *Vom Molekül zur Organismenwelt,* 119; see also Bertalanffy, PhD diss., 27; Bertalanffy, *Theoretische Biologie,* vols. 1, 6, 29, 90–91.

64. Bertalanffy, "The History and Status of General Systems Theory," 31; Ludwig von Bertalanffy, "Vorläufer und Begründer der Systemtheorie," in *Systemtheorie: Forschung und Information,* ed. Ruprecht Kurzrock, Schriftenreihe der RIAS-Funkuniversität (Berlin: Colloquium Verlag, 1972), 2. His first general definition ("Zu einer allgemeinen Systemlehre" [1945]: 10) was

"a set of interacting elements" but he also defined "interaction" in terms of relations between "elements" ("An Outline of General Systems Theory," *British Journal for the Philosophy of Science* 1 [1950], 143).

65. Bertalanffy, PhD diss., 27.
66. Bertalanffy, "Zu einer allgemeinen Systemlehre" (1945), 5–6; see also *Theoretische Biologie*, vol. 1, 98.
67. Bertalanffy, *Theoretische Biologie*, vol. 1, 98.
68. Bertalanffy, *Theoretische Biologie*, vol. 1, 108–09.
69. Bertalanffy, *Theoretische Biologie*, vol. 1, 105; Bertalanffy, "Untersuchungen über die Gesetzlichkeit des Wachstums I," and Bertalanffy, *Theoretische Biologie*, vol. 2, 232–57.
70. Bertalanffy, *Theoretische Biologie*, vol. 1, 198 and Bertalanffy, *General System Theory*, 19.
71. Bertalanffy, *General System Theory*, xxi–xxii; Bertalanffy, "The History and Status of General Systems Theory," 37.
72. Geoffrey Vickers, "Some Implications of Systems Thinking," *General Systems Bulletin* 8, no. 2 (1978): 10.
73. Anatol Rapoport, "Philosophical Perspectives on *Living Systems*," *Behavioral Science* 25, no. 1 (1980): 62.
74. Bertalanffy, "The History and Status of General Systems Theory," 36.
75. Bertalanffy, *General System Theory*, 19 and, already: Bertalanffy, "Theoretical Models in Biology and Psychology," 341.
76. Bertalanffy, "Theoretical Models in Biology and Psychology," 338.
77. Bertalanffy, *General System Theory*, xiii.
78. Ludwig von Bertalanffy, "Arbeitskreis Biologie," in *Weltbild und Menschenbild, III. Internationale Hochschulwochen des österreichischen College in Alpbach*, ed. Simon Moser (Salzburg: Tyrolia, 1948), 361.
79. Bertalanffy, *General System Theory*, 251 and "The History and Status of General Systems Theory," 31.
80. Kenneth E. Boulding, *The Organizational Revolution* (New York: Harper & Brothers, 1953), xvii.
81. Anatol Rapoport, *Operational Philosophy* (San Francisco: International Society for General Semantics, 1953), 223.
82. Robert Rosen, "Old Trends and New Trends in General Systems Research," *International Journal of General Systems* 5, no. 3. (1979): 177.
83. Bertalanffy, "Zu einer allgemeinen Systemlehre" (1945), 3, 23.
84. Ludwig von Bertalanffy to A. Bendmann, letter, 31 March 1966, in *B.C.S.S.S. Archives*, Vienna.
85. Bertalanffy, *Das biologische Weltbild*, 140.
86. Bertalanffy, "A Biologist Looks at Human Nature," 33 and "Theoretical Models in Biology and Psychology," 343.
87. Bertalanffy, *Das biologische Weltbild*, 141; 145, 151, 162; see already Bertalanffy, *Theoretische Biologie*, vol. 1, 99–100, 112–15.
88. Bertalanffy, "Mind and Body Re-examined," 133–35.
89. Othmar F. Anderle, "Arnold J. Toynbee und die Problematik der geschichtlichen Sinndeutung," *Die Welt als Geschichte* 3 (1960): 144–45, 147. Bertalanffy had this paper and underlined those passages (*B.C.S.S.S. Archives*, Vienna).
90. Wilhelm Dilthey, *La naissance de l'herméneutique*, in *Œuvres* 7 (Paris: Cerf, 1995), 292. Originally published 1900.
91. Gerhard Frey, "Hermeneutische und hypothetisch-deduktive Methode," *Zeitschrift für allgemeine Wissenschaftstheorie* 1, no 1 (1970). Bertalanffy knew this paper: it can be found in his personal library (*B.C.S.S.S. Archives*, Vienna).

92. Anatol Rapoport, "Foreword," in *Modern Systems Research for the Behavioral Scientist,* Walter Buckley (Chicago: Aldine, 1968), xxii.
93. Qtd. in Bertalanffy, *Das biologische Weltbild,* 15; see also Bertalanffy, *General System Theory,* 14.
94. Bertalanffy, "An Outline of General System Theory," 138.
95. Bertalanffy, *Das biologische Weltbild,* 186–87. See also *Auf den Pfaden des Lebens,* 244.
96. Bertalanffy, "Goethes Naturauffassung," 360.
97. Bertalanffy, *Robots, Men and Minds,* 70.
98. Bertalanffy, "Das Weltbild der Biologie," 272; "Zu einer allgemeinen Systemlehre," *Biologia Generalis* 195 (1949): 114; *Das biologische Weltbild,* 185; "An Outline of General System Theory," 139.
99. Bertalanffy, "Theoretical Models in Biology and Psychology," 304.
100. Bertalanffy, *Das biologische Weltbild,* 12, 176; Bertalanffy, "An Outline of General System Theory," 165.
101. Bertalanffy, "Zu einer allgemeinen Systemlehre" (1945), 22–23; Bertalanffy, "Zu einer allgemeinen Systemlehre" (1949): 125–27; Bertalanffy, "An Outline of General System Theory," 139–42; Bertalanffy, "Theoretical Models in Biology and Psychology," 304, 307, 339; Ludwig von Bertalanffy, "General System Theory," *Main Currents in Modern Thought* 11 (1955): 75; Bertalanffy, *Robots, Men and Minds,* 80; Bertalanffy, "General System Theory and Psychiatry," 35–36; Rapoport, "The Uses of Mathematical Isomorphism," 44–45; Anatol Rapoport, "The Search for Simplicity," in *The Relevance of General Systems Theory,* ed. Ervin Laszló (New York: Braziller, 1972), 28.
102. Bertalanffy, "General System Theory and Psychiatry," 36.
103. Rapoport, "The Uses of Mathematical Isomorphism," 43; Bertalanffy, "Philosophy of Science in Scientific Education," 233 and "General System Theory," 75; Kenneth E. Boulding, "General Systems Theory: The Skeleton of Science," *General Systems* 1 (1956): 12.
104. Bertalanffy, "Philosophy of Science in Scientific Education," 233.
105. Bertalanffy, "Philosophy of Science in Scientific Education," 233.
106. Bertalanffy, "An Outline of General System Theory," 164.
107. Bertalanffy, "Vaihingers Lehre von der analogischen Fiktion," 70–73; Herbert Stachowiak, "Erkenntnis in Modellen," in Hans Lenk and Günter Ropohl, *Systemtheorie als Wissenschaftsprogramm* (Königstein: Athenäum, 1978), 58.
108. Bertalanffy, "Vaihingers Lehre von der analogischen Fiktion," 70–71.
109. Bertalanffy, *General System Theory,* 29, 212–14 on Koestler; Bertalanffy, "The Quest for Systems Philosophy," *Metaphilosophy* 3, no. 2 (1972) and "Foreword," *Introduction to Systems Philosophy,* ed. E. Laszló (New York: Gordon & Breach, 1972) on Laszló.
110. Kenneth E. Boulding, "General Systems as an Integrating Force in the Social Sciences," in *Unity Through Diversity,* eds. William Gray and Nicholas D. Rizzo (New York: Gordon and Breach, 1973), 951.
111. Anatol Rapoport, "Review of E. Laszló: *The System Approach of the World Order,*" *General Systems* 19 (1974), 247.
112. Anatol Rapoport, *Allgemeine Systemtheorie* (Darmstadt: Darmstädter Blätter, 1988), 36. Originally published 1986.
113. Bertalanffy, *General System Theory,* xxii–xxiii and "The History and Status of General Systems Theory," 38.
114. Kenneth E. Boulding, *The Image* (University of Michigan Press, 1956), 174; Rapoport, "Lewis F. Richardson's Mathematical Theory of War."
115. Rapoport, "Methodology in the Physical, Biological and Social Sciences," 182, 185; see also Rapoport, *Modern Systems Research for the Behavioral Scientist,* xxii and "Allgemeine Systemtheorie," 8, 35.

116. Bertalanffy, "The World of Science and the World of Value," 497–98; Bertalanffy, *Robots, Men and Minds,* 116.
117. Bertalanffy, "General System Theory," 81.
118. Bertalanffy, "Theoretical Models in Biology and Psychology," 311.
119. Rapoport, "General Systems Theory: A Bridge between Two Cultures," 15–16.
120. Rapoport, *Operational Philosophy:* "Integrating Knowledge and Action" was the subtitle of the book and one of its major themes.
121. Bertalanffy, *Auf den Pfaden des Lebens,* 224, 245.
122. Anatol Rapoport, "Modern Systems Theory—An Outlook for Coping with Change," *General Systems* 15 (1970), 25.
123. Mihajlo D. Mesarović, "Preface," in *Views on General Systems Theory,* ed. Mihajlo D. Mesarović (New York: John Wiley, 1964), xiii.
124. Bertalanffy, *General System Theory,* xxii–xxiii and "The History and Status of General Systems Theory," 38.
125. Bertalanffy, "Mind and Body Re-examined," 132; see also Bertalanffy, "The Psychopathology of Scientism," 214–15; Bertalanffy, "The World of Science and the World of Value," 497–507; Bertalanffy, "Zur Geschichte theoretischer Modelle in der Biologie," 296; *Robots, Men and Minds,* 11–14; Bertalanffy, "Vorläufer und Begründer der Systemtheorie," 13.
126. Rapoport, "Review of E. Laszló," 249.
127. Anatol Rapoport, "General Systems Theory: A Bridge between Two Cultures," in *General Systems Theorizing—An Assessment and Prospects for the Future,* Proceedings of the annual North American meeting, Society for General Systems Research, ed. J. D. White (1976): 16. See also Boulding, "General Systems as an Integrating Force in the Social Sciences," 965–66; Mihajlo D. Mesarović and Eduard Pestel, *Menschheit am Wendepunkt* (Stuttgart: Deutsche Verlags-Anstalt, 1974), esp. 8–27.
128. Bertalanffy, "General System Theory—A Critical Review," 4–7; William Ross Ashby, "General Systems Theory as a New Discipline," *General Systems* 3 (1958): 2; Mihajlo D. Mesarović, "Systems Theory and Biology—View of a Theoretician," in *Systems Theory and Biology,* ed. Mihajlo D. Mesarović (Berlin: Springer, 1968), 60; Mihajlo D. Mesarović and Yasuhiko Takahara, *General Systems Theory: Mathematical Foundations* (New York, Academic Press, 1975), x, 6; George J. Klir, *An Approach to General Systems Theory* (New York: Van Norstrand Reinhold, 1969), viii, 274.
129. Klir, *An Approach to General Systems Theory,* esp. 40–61.
130. Bertalanffy, *General System Theory,* 252–56; Bertalanffy, "The History and Status of General Systems Theory," 30–34 and "Vorläufer und Begründer der Systemtheorie," 12; Rapoport, "The Uses of Mathematical Isomorphism," 49.
131. Mesarović and Takahara, *General Systems Theory;* Robert Rosen, "Biology and Systems Research: An Overview," in *Applied General Systems Research,* ed. George J. Klir (New York: Plenium, 1978), esp. 499–500.
132. Rosen, "Biology and Systems Research," 500–02.
133. Boulding, "Some Considerations on Psychobiological Development," 11.
134. Roger E. Cavallo, *Systems Research Movement: Characteristics, Accomplishments, and Current Developments,* Special issue of *General Systems Bulletin* 9, no. 3 (1979): 30.
135. Bertalanffy, "An Outline of General System Theory," 142; Bertalanffy, "Theoretical Models in Biology and Psychology," 339–342; Bertalanffy, "General System Theory," 76; Mesarović, "Systems Theory and Biology," 64.
136. Rapoport, "The Uses of Mathematical Isomorphism in GST," 56–57.
137. Bertalanffy, *General System Theory,* 24–25.

132   *David Pouvreau*

138. Ludwig von Bertalanffy A. Locker, letter, 11 April 1969; see also the manuscript of a letter to George J. Klir (1972), in *B.C.S.S.S. Archives,* Vienna.
139. Alfred J. Lotka, *Elements of Physical Biology* (Baltimore: William and Wilkins, 1925), 57.
140. Bertalanffy, "An Outline of General System Theory," 144; see also Bertalanffy, *Theoretische Biologie,* vol. 2, 324; Bertalanffy, "Zu einer allgemeinen Systemlehre" (1945): 7 and "Zu einer allgemeinen Systemlehre" (1949): 116.
141. Bertalanffy, "Zu einer allgemeinen Systemlehre" (1945): 5; Bertalanffy, "Zu einer allgemeinen Systemlehre" (1949): 115; see also Bertalanffy, "An Outline of General System Theory," 143.
142. Bertalanffy, "Zu einer allgemeinen Systemlehre" (1945): 6–7; see also Bertalanffy, "Goethes Naturauffassung," 115–16.
143. Lotka, *Elements of Physical Biology,* 146–48.
144. Anatol Rapoport, "Open Linear Systems with Positive Steady States," *Bulletin of Mathematical Biophysics* 14 (1952).
145. Bertalanffy, "Zu einer allgemeinen Systemlehre" (1945): 11.
146. Bertalanffy, "Der Organismus als physikalisches System betrachtet," 522, 52; Bertalanffy, *Theoretische Biologie,* vol. 2, 28.
147. Bertalanffy, *Theoretische Biologie,* vol. 2, 30–33; see also Anatol Rapoport, "Open Linear Systems with Positive Steady States" and "Mathematical General System Theory," in *Unity through Diversity,* eds. William Gray and Nicholas D. Rizzo (New York: Gordon & Breach, 1973), 441–43.
148. Bertalanffy, "Der Organismus als physikalisches System betrachtet," *Die Naturwissenschaften* 28 (1940): 528 and *Theoretische Biologie,* vol. 2, 41–42.
149. Pouvreau, PhD diss.
150. Bertalanffy, *Das biologische Weltbild,* 124.
151. Bertalanffy, *Das Gefüge des Lebens,* 133–34.
152. Bertalanffy, *Theoretische Biologie,* vol. 1, 274; see also *Das Gefüge des Lebens,* 57.
153. Bertalanffy, PhD diss., 52.
154. Bertalanffy, *Das biologische Weltbild,* 124; see already Bertalanffy, *Theoretische Biologie,* vol. 1, 275.
155. Bertalanffy, *Das Gefüge des Lebens,* 27–28; *Vom Molekül zur Organismenwelt,* 72; *Theoretische Biologie,* vol. 2, 321 and *Das biologische Weltbild,* 59.
156. Mesarović, "Systems Theory and Biology," 61–72; Klir, *An Approach to General Systems Theory,* 95; Robert A. Orchard, "On an Approach to General Systems Theory," in *Trends in General Systems Theory,* ed. George J. Klir (New York: Wiley, 1972), 210–12; Jean Louis Le Moigne, *La théorie du système général—Théorie de la modélisation* (Paris: Presses Universitaires de France, 1977), 48–58; for details, see Pouvreau, "Une histoire de la 'systémologie générale,'" 940–43.
157. Bertalanffy, "Untersuchungen über die Gesetzlichkeit des Wachstums I," 622.
158. Bertalanffy, *Das Gefüge des Lebens,* 94; *Theoretische Biologie,* vol. 2, 285.
159. Ludwig von Bertalanffy and Raoul S. Naroll, "The Principle of Allometry in Biology and the Social Sciences," *General Systems* 1 (1956).
160. Bertalanffy, "Theoretical Models in Biology and Psychology," 36.
161. Bertalanffy, "Theoretical Models in Biology and Psychology," 31–32; Bertalanffy, "Some Considerations on Psychobiological Development," 7–8, 14–19; Bertalanffy, *Robots, Men and Minds,* 6–18; Bertalanffy, "General System Theory and Psychiatry."
162. Bertalanffy, "Some Considerations on Psychobiological Development," 9.
163. Ludwig von Bertalanffy, "Biologie und Weltbild," in *Wohin führt die Biologie?,* ed. Michael Lohman (Munich: Carl Hanser, 1970), 24.

164. Mesarović and Pestel, *Menschheit am Wendepunkt.*
165. Bertalanffy, "General System Theory," 82.

REFERENCES

Anderle, Othmar F. "Arnold J. Toynbee und die Problematik der geschichtlichen Sinndeutung." *Die Welt als Geschichte* 3 (1960), 143–156.

Ashby, William Ross. "General Systems Theory as a New Discipline." *General Systems* 3 (1958), 1–6.

Bertalanffy, Ludwig von. *Fechner und das Problem der Integrationen höherer Ordnung.* PhD diss., University of Vienna, 1926.

———. "Über die neue Lebensauffassung." *Annalen der Philosophie und philosophischen Kritik* 6 (1927), 250–264.

———. *Kritische Theorie der Formbildung.* Special issue, *Abhandlungen zur theoretischen Biologie* 27. Berlin: Gebrüder Borntraeger, 1928.

———. "Vaihingers Lehre von der analogischen Fiktion in ihrer Bedeutung für die Naturphilosophie." In *Die Philosophie des Als-Ob und das Leben: Festschrift zu Hans Vaihingers 80. Geburtstag,* edited by August Seidel. Berlin: Reuther & Reichard, 1932, 82–91.

———. *Theoretische Biologie—Band I.* Berlin: Gebrüder Borntraeger, 1932.

———. "Untersuchungen über die Gesetzlichkeit des Wachstums I." *Roux Archiv f. Entwicklungs-Mechanik* 131 (1934), 613–652.

———. *Das Gefüge des Lebens.* Leipzig: Teubner, 1937.

———. *Vom Molekül zur Organismenwelt.* Potsdam: Akademische Verlagsgesellschaft Athenaion, 1940.

———. "Der Organismus als physikalisches System betrachtet." *Die Naturwissenschaften* 28 (1940), 521–531.

———. *Theoretische Biologie.* Vol. 2. Berlin: Gebrüder Borntraeger, 1942.

———. "Zu einer allgemeinen Systemlehre." *Blätter für deutsche Philosophie* 18, nos. 3–4. Unpublished: *B.C.S.S.S. Archives,* Vienna, 1945.

———. "Das Weltbild der Biologie." In *Weltbild und Menschenbild, III: Internationale Hochschulwochen des österreichischen College in Alpbach,* edited by Simon Moser. Salzburg: Tyrolia, 1948, 251–274.

———. "Arbeitskreis Biologie." In *Weltbild und Menschenbild, III: Internationale Hochschulwochen des österreichischen College in Alpbach,* edited by Simon Moser. Salzburg: Tyrolia, 1948, 355–357.

———. "Zu einer allgemeinen Systemlehre." *Biologia Generalis* 195 (1949), 114–129.

———. "Goethes Naturauffassung." *Atlantis* 8 (1949), 357–363.

———. *Das biologische Weltbild—Die Stellung des Lebens in Natur und Wissenschaft.* Bern: Francke AG, 1949.

———. "An Outline of General Systems Theory." *British Journal for the Philosophy of Science* 1, no. 2 (1950), 134–165.

———. "General System Theory: A New Approach to Unity of Science." *Human Biology* 23 (1951), 302–312, 336–345, 346–361.

———. "Theoretical Models in Biology and Psychology." *Journal of Personality* 20 (1951), 24–38.

———. *Auf den Pfaden des Lebens—Ein biologisches Skizzenbuch.* Frankfurt: Umschau, 1951.

———. "Philosophy of Science in Scientific Education." *Scientific Monthly* 77 (1953), 233–239.

———. "General Systems Theory." *Main Currents in Modern Thought* 11 (1955), 75–83.

———. "An Essay on the Relativity of Categories." *Philosophy of Science* 225 (1955), 243–263.

———. "A Biologist Looks at Human Nature." *Scientific Monthly* 82 (1956), 33–41.

———. "Some Considerations on Psychobiological Development" (Quelques considerations sur le développement psycho-biologique). Paper read at the Study Groups on the Psychobiological Development of the Child, World Health Organisation, Geneva, WHO/AHP/11, 1956, 1–22.

———. "The Psychopathology of Scientism." In *Scientism and Values,* edited by Helmut Schoeck and James W. Wiggins. Princeton: Nostrand, 1960, 202–218.

———. "General System Theory—A Critical Review." *General Systems* 7 (1962), 1–20.

———. "The World of Science and the World of Value." *Teachers College Record* 65 (1964), 496–507.

———. "Basic concepts in quantitative biology of metabolism." *Quantitative Biology of Metabolism-First International Symposium,* Helgoländer wissenschaftliche Meeresuntersuchungen 9 (1964), 5–37.

———. "On the Definition of Symbol." In *Psychology and the Symbol,* edited by Joseph R. Royce. New York: Random House, 1965, 26–72.

———. "Zur Geschichte theoretischer Modelle in der Biologie." *Studium Generale* 18 (1965), 290–298.

———. "Mind and Body Re-Examined." *Journal of Humanistic Psychology* 6 (1966), 113–138.

———. *Robots, Men and Minds.* New York: Braziller, 1967.

———. "General System Theory and Psychiatry—An Overview." *American Psychiatric Association* 176 (1967), 33–46.

———. *General System Theory: Foundations, Development, Applications.* New York: Braziller. 1968.

———. "Symbolismus und Anthropogenese." In *Handgebrauch und Verständigung bei Affen und Frühmenschen, Symposium der Werner-Reimers-Stiftung für anthropogenetische Forschung,* edited by Bernhard Rensch. Bern: Huber, 1968, 131–148.

———. "Biologie und Weltbild." In *Wohin führt die Biologie?,* edited by Michael Lohman. Munich: Carl Hanser, 1970, 13–31.

———. "The History and Status of General Systems Theory." In *Trends in General Systems Theory,* edited by George J. Klir. New York: Wiley, 1972, 21–41.

———. "Vorläufer und Begründer der Systemtheorie." In *Systemtheorie: Forschung und Information,* edited by Ruprecht Kurzrock. Schriftenreihe der RIAS-Funkuniversität. Berlin: Colloquium Verlag, 1972, 17–27.

———. "The Quest for Systems Philosophy." *Metaphilosophy* 3, no. 2 (1972), 142–145.

———. "Foreword." In *Introduction to Systems Philosophy,* edited by Ervin Laszló. New York: Gordon & Breach, 1972.

———, and Raoul S. Naroll. "The Principle of Allometry in Biology and the Social Sciences." *General Systems* 1 (1956), 76–89.

Boulding, Kenneth E. *The Organizational Revolution.* New York: Harper & Brothers, 1953.

———. *The Image.* Ann Arbor: University of Michigan Press, 1956.

———. "General Systems Theory: The Skeleton of Science." *General Systems* 1 (1956), 11–17.

———. "General Systems as an Integrating Force in the Social Sciences." In *Unity through Diversity*, edited by William Gray and Nicholas D. Rizzo. New York: Gordon & Breach, 1973, 951–966.

Cassirer, Ernst. *Substance et fonction*. Paris: Minuit, 1977. Originally published 1910.

———. *La philosophie des formes symboliques III*. Paris: Minuit, 1972. Originally published 1929.

Cavallo, Roger E. *Systems Research Movement: Characteristics, Accomplishments, and Current Developments*. Special issue of *General Systems Bulletin* 9, no. 3 (1979).

Dilthey, Wilhelm. *La naissance de l'herméneutique*. In *Œuvres 7*. Paris: Cerf, 1995. Originally published 1900.

Frey, Gerhard. "Hermeneutische und hypothetisch-deduktive Methode." *Zeitschrift für allgemeine Wissenschaftstheorie* 1, no. 1 (1970), 24–40.

Klir, George J. *An Approach to General Systems Theory*. New York: Van Norstrand Reinhold, 1969.

Le Moigne, Jean Louis. *La théorie du système général—Théorie de la modélisation*. Paris: Presses Universitaires de France, 1977.

Lenk, Hans. "Metaphysics, Interpretation, and the Subject." In *The Philosophy of Paul Weiss*, edited by Lewis Edwin Huhn. Peru, IL: Open Court, 1995, 55–63.

Lotka, Alfred J. *Elements of Physical Biology*. Baltimore: William & Wilkins, 1925.

Mesarović, Mihajlo D. "Preface." In *Views on General Systems Theory*, edited by Mihajlo D. Mesarović. New York: John Wiley, 1964, xiii–xvi.

———. "Systems Theory and Biology—View of a Theoretician." In *Systems Theory and Biology*, edited by Mihajlo D. Mesarović. New York: Springer, 1968, 59–87.

———, and Eduard Pestel. *Menschheit am Wendepunkt*. Stuttgart: Deutsche Verlags-Anstalt, 1974.

———, and Yasuhiko Takahara. *General Systems Theory: Mathematical Foundations*. New York: Academic Press, 1975.

Orchard, Robert A. "On an Approach to General Systems Theory." In *Trends in General Systems Theory*, edited by George J. Klir. New York: Wiley, 1972, 205–250.

Piaget, Jean. *L'épistémologie génétique*. Paris: Presses Universitaires de France, 1970.

Poincaré, Henri. *La science et l'hypothèse*. Paris: Flammarion, 1968. Originally published 1902.

Pouvreau, David. *Une histoire de la 'systémologie générale' de Ludwig von Bertalanffy—Généalogie, genèse, actualisation et postérité d'un projet herméneutique*. Doctoral thesis, Paris, E.H.E.S.S., 2013.

Pouvreau, David, and Manfred Drack. "On the History of Ludwig von Bertalanffy's 'General Systemology', and on Its Relationship to Cybernetics—Part 1: Elements on the Origins and Genesis of von Bertalanffy's 'General Systemology.'" *International Journal of General Systems* 36, no. 3 (2007), 281–337.

Rapoport, Anatol. "Open Linear Systems with Positive Steady States." *Bulletin of Mathematical Biophysics* 14 (1952): 171-83.

———. *Operational Philosophy*. San Francisco: International Society for General Semantics, 1953.

———. "Lewis F. Richardson's Mathematical Theory of War." *General Systems* 2 (1957): 55–91.

———. "Foreword." In *Modern Systems Research for the Behavioral Scientist*, edited by Walter Buckley. Chicago: Aldine, 1968, xiii–xxii.

———. "Methodology in the Physical, Biological and Social Sciences." *General Systems* 14 (1969), 179–186.

———. "Modern Systems Theory—An Outlook for Coping with Change." *General Systems* 15, 1970, 15–26.

———. "The Uses of Mathematical Isomorphism in GST." In *Trends in General Systems Theory*, edited by George J. Klir. New York: Wiley, 1972, 42–77.

———. "The Search for Simplicity." In *The Relevance of General Systems Theory*, edited by Ervin Laszlo. New York: Braziller, 1972, 13–30.

———. "Mathematical General System Theory." In *Unity through Diversity*, edited by William Gray and Nicholas D. Rizzo. New York: Gordon & Breach, 1973, 437–460.

———. "Review of Laszló E.: *The System Approach of the World Order*." *General Systems* 19 (1974), 247–250.

———. "General Systems Theory: A Bridge between Two Cultures." In *General Systems Theorizing—An Assessment and Prospects for the Future*, Proceedings of the annual North American meeting, Society for General Systems Research, edited by J.D. White, 1976, 9–16.

———. "Philosophical Perspectives on *Living Systems*." *Behavioral Science* 25, no. 1 (1980): 56-64.

———. *Allgemeine Systemtheorie*. Darmstadt: Darmstädter Blätter, 1988. Originally published 1986.

Rosen, Robert. "Biology and Systems Research: An Overview." In *Applied General Systems Research,* edited by George J. Klir. New York: Plenium, 1978, 489–510.

———. "Old Trends and New Trends in General Systems Research." *International Journal of General Systems* 5, no. 3 (1979), 173–184.

Stachowiak, Herbert. "Erkenntnis in Modellen." In *Systemtheorie als Wissenschaftsprogramm*, edited by Hans Lenk and Günter Ropohl. Königstein: Athenäum, 1978, 50–64.

Vickers, Geoffrey. "Some Implications of Systems Thinking." *General Systems Bulletin* 8, no. 2 (1978), 9–14.

6 The Ethics of Epistemology[1]
The Work of the Constructivist and Cyberneticist Heinz Von Foerster, from the Vienna Circle to the Cybernetic Circle[2]

Bernhard Pörksen

When anyone asked Heinz von Foerster, whom people described as the "Socrates of cybernetics," whether he considered his work or himself constructivist, as a rule he answered with a joke. The constructivist label appeared to him to be unsuitable—a key concept for a taxonomy that would tend to divert one's attention from an examination of his work and provide an occasion for narrow academic disputes between realists, relativists, and solipsists. Perhaps one could call him a "curiositylogist"; in any case, he was Viennese. The latter really cannot be denied. He was born in Vienna; he simply had to accept that label. Perhaps this reference to his own origins in the Vienna of the turn of the century and the reference generally to his own biography in fact provides a decisive key for understanding and classifying the work of the cybernetician Heinz von Foerster and for deciphering the principles of his inter- and transdisciplinary epistemology. As various biographical sketches note, he was raised in Vienna at the turn of the century in a world of artists and creative minds.[3] His great-grandfather, an architect, provided Vienna with its urbanistic identity. His grandmother, Marie Lang, was among the first representatives of the women's movement in central Europe. Already as a youth he had come into contact with the Bohemians of the city. After taking his high school exams, when he began to study physics in Vienna, he came into the Vienna Circle. This experience, which made it possible to combine diverse worlds of thought and perception into a stimulating panopticum, was again manifest here, in the salons of the von Foerster's home. Heinz von Foerster's own reflections have only a little in common with the views of the Vienna Circle, which on the eve of an outbreak of bloody irrationalism promoted clarity of thought and decisively rejected metaphysically contaminated argumentation. The later views of Foerster have nothing more to do with the ideas of the logician Rudolf Carnap, who thought there was something like unshakable connections between symbols and the world, knowledge and reality. But as a student he became acquainted with this form of thought, and it accompanied him his entire life, providing a measure of his own intellectual position: it can be transcribed with the terms *inter- and transdisciplinarity* and means in the last analysis the ability to perceive the internal validity of diverse paradigms, methodologies, methods, and models, the ability to view perceptible differences primarily as enriching, and the ability then to emphasize the connections (and not primarily the differences) in discussions in transdisciplinary cooperation with other thinkers.

However, before Heinz von Foerster was able to develop his own work, the Second World War broke out. After completing his studies, he first worked as a physicist in Cologne and then finally returned to Vienna. Because his family and his Jewish grandfather were well known, he fled to Berlin, where he survived undiscovered and unknown in the power center of National Socialism, the Reich's capital. He again found work as a physicist, engaged in basic research, and managed his way back to Vienna after the war, where he was employed as a technician of a telephone company and—in the meantime also as a journalist—led the culture and science editorial department for an American broadcaster, *Rot Weiß Rot*. Simultaneously, between two careers, he wrote his first book, *Das Gedächtnis: Eine quantenphysikalische Untersuchung* [Memory: A Quantam-Physical Study],[4] which drew the attention of the early American cyberneticists. He was invited to visit. Although his English was initially not strong, he gave presentations on his theory of memory and from one moment to the next was taken into a circle of scientists who, in the 1950s, on the invitation of the Josiah Macy Foundation, met for what became known as the Macy Conferences.[5] He was made secretary and editor of the Macy Conference Proceedings. Norbert Wiener, John von Neumann, Gregory Bateson and Margaret Mead, Warren McCulloch and Walter Pitts—all of them and a good dozen other researchers formed a group of interdisciplinary working enthusiasts who might be characterized as the *Cybernetic Circle*. Under the umbrella of the Macy Foundation, people spoke about topics that in the broadest sense were to be characterized as cybernetic. Issues included the construction of sensory prosthetics, teleological mechanisms and circular causality, and more fundamentally, the mode of operation of living beings. The work of Warren McCulloch and Walter Pitts, "A Logical Calculus of the Ideas Immanent in Nervous Activity" (1943), which dealt with the impulse receptivity and response of neurons, allowed a logical-technical formalization of neurological activity.[6] And because the brain consists of neurons that are connected to one another over synapses and axons, it was thought that a possibility for a logical-technical reconstruction of the brain had been discovered. The computer metaphor, which describes people as information processing systems, thinking as data processing, the brain as a powerful parallel computer, and memory as storage, has its origin here. At this time there was already spirited talk of the construction of an "artificial brain."

Heinz von Foerster, who remained friends with the members of the Macy meetings and whose research remained connected to theirs, finally developed an epistemology that is characterized as *second-order cybernetics*. Its core idea consists in appealing to the fundamental principle of cybernetics (the idea of circularity or of circular causality) and thinking it through deeply. The starting point is the apparently innocent question: What does one need to understand a brain? The answer: a brain. The theory, which from this vantage appears to be necessary, becomes circular. It must meet the demand to describe itself. The strict separation between a subject and an object, which first-order cybernetics is based on, disappears. The observer and the observed appear in second-order cybernetics inextricably interwoven. And this epistemological position fundamentally discredits a concept that is central to efforts to achieve scientific apperception: it is the concept of truth, which can only be understood against the presupposition of an observer-independent world, such that a correspondence between the mind and the object can be achieved (*adaequatio intellectus et rei*). With second-order cybernetics comes the obligation to be conscious of one's own idiosyncrasies and blind spots, to link objects to oneself, and to understand them seriously as one's own product.

After an interlude at the University of Illinois as head of the Electronic Tube Laboratory, Heinz von Foerster managed again to set off for new horizons. At the Massachusetts Institute of Technology he became familiar with the issues of neurobiology, studied physiology with Arturo Rosenblueth in Mexico City, and in 1957, again at the University of Illinois, founded the biological computer laboratory (BCL), which moved to the center of cognitive-science innovations.[7] In the inspired atmosphere of the BCL, philosophers and electrical engineers, biologists, anthropologists and mathematicians, artists and logicians discussed epistemological questions from the perspectives of the natural and human sciences. They addressed laws of calculation in humans and machines and analyzed the logical and methodological problems that knowledge of knowledge and observation of observers inextricably involves. The mathematician Lars Löfgren worked here on concepts of logic, affirming rather than rejecting the self-referential character of utterances, which, according to Aristotelian logic, are to be dismissed as meaningless. Löfgren called it "autologic." The neurobiologist Humberto R. Maturana published his important article, a foundational document of constructivism entitled "Biology of Cognition," first of all as a research report of the BCL.[8] The still-young researcher Francisco J. Varela found a forum here for his interest in theoretical biology. Gordon Pask established here the basis for his communication theory. Ross Ashby gave lectures on cybernetics. And an Israeli dancer taught forms of movement, whose knowledge was to be used for the construction of purposive, moving machines. The likely first parallel computer was built at this institute. Heinz von Foerster acquired the necessary external funding from the Office of Naval Research and the Air Force Office of Scientific Research and published central works on the concept of self-organization that are still discussed today and organized conferences under the title "Principles of Self-Organization" (1960), which Friedrich von Hayek, Ludwig von Bertalanffy and Anatol Rapoport, among others, participated in. He also defended a five-page-long student doctorate against the objections of the university establishment. In the years following this, however, a series of outstanding scientists departed; the external financing became increasingly difficult to find. And when a law was passed in 1968 (the Mansfield Amendment) that prohibited money providers of the military from supporting projects that did not have clear military uses, the Computer Laboratory, whose existence was entirely linked to the commitment of Heinz von Foerster, was closed at the beginning of the 1970s when von Foester retired. After his retirement— initially under the influence of the family therapist Paul Watzlawick (Palo Alto), and then influenced by the decisive publication program of the media theorist Siegfried J. Schmidt (Siegen, Münster) and the diverse reference to the works of Heinz von Foerster in the work of the system theoretician Niklas Luhmann (Bielefeld)—he became well known among a broader group of intellectuals. His books were published in rapid sequence with respected German publishers. And he spoke until late in his life to a steadily growing circle of therapists, sociologists, media theorists, communications researchers, and educators and began decisively to formulate and hone the ethical, moral, and social relevance of his views. Beyond this—and certainly aided by his increasing popularity—he cultivated an extraordinarily unconventional writing and presentation style, intellectually vibrant and creative, combining poetic-philosophical aphorisms and mathematical formalism in his work with reference to the work of neurobiologists, logicians, anthropologists, and philosophers.

THE CONNECTION BETWEEN EPISTEMOLOGY AND ETHICS AS A KEY QUESTION

It is the connection between epistemology and ethics, point of view and insight that inspired Heinz von Foerster—presumably also because of personal biographical experiences—and that he later consistently worked out.[9] Put differently, in the form of a key question: Should one accept his views, what consequences follow from the epistemological perspective that in cognition (*Erkennen*) people are inevitably prejudiced? What follows from the assumption that the observer—who in principle is never entirely transparent, is analytically indeterminate and thus fundamentally autonomous— cannot be separated from knowing process? Or in renewed short shrift: What does epistemology (constructivism and second-order cybernetics) imply for ethics? In order to pursue the question, I have chosen—inevitably highly selectively—three points of emphasis: first, the blind spot, the central illustrative example of Heinz von Foerster, will be presented. It serves as the starting point for the observer's creative self-irritation. This will be followed by a look into his observer-relative ethical conception, which assumes the autonomy of the individual. Finally, the differentiation between trivial and nontrivial machines will be presented, which comprehends the core attribute of autonomy differently still and can be understood as the basis for a groundwork of a constructivist-cybernetic anthropology.

THE PARABLE OF THE BLIND SPOT

Within the book *Understanding Understanding*,[10] the reader is asked to participate in a small experiment that Heinz von Foerster presented time and again, and in varying contexts. As a part of the experiment, one is challenged to take ahold of the first illustration of the book, which presents a black star and a black spot. The star is to remain fixed, the left eye closed, and one is to move the paper back and forth along the visual axis until the black point is invisible. If the star is intensively enough fixed, the black spot remains gone, even if one moves the sheet of paper parallel to itself to the right or the left or higher or lower. The physiological explanation for this phenomenon of suddenly not seeing what is so obviously present is that the black spot at this specific distance meets an area of the retina that lack rods and cones because the optical nerve leaves the eye here.[11] The assumption is that, if photoreceptors do not exist in a certain part of the eye, then one must go through the world with a visual gap of a certain size. But this is certainly not the case. The field of vision appears to us to be closed, so long as we do not engage in experiments with our ability to see and in this way discover the blind spot to begin with.

"We do not see"—thus runs the paradoxically graceful formulation of Heinz von Foerster for this phenomenon "that we do not see."[12] There is no gap, because our cognitive systems provides for balance and constructs an experience of continuous space. The construction of the world and one's own knowledge appear to be commensurable, comprehensive, and closed off to alternatives. People are not aware of their own role in constructing this world, but they can become aware of this should they so desire. This seeing of the not seeing as well as the discussion of not seeing of the not seeing thus is transformed into a provocation, which, in light of the everyday experiential evidence, can only be staved off with great difficulty and once again shaken. One begins to perceive the blind spot as one's own blind spot, even outside of the experimentally prepared settings—in looking into paradigms and dogmas, in examining confrontations with prejudices and ideologies, in analyzing conformity, group behavior, and the mechanisms

Diagram 6.1 The experiment with the blind spot.[1]
Foerster, *Wissen und Gewissen*, 26.

of manipulations, in reflecting on one's own flaws and mistakes. And it becomes clear that even the seeing of not seeing and the knowledge of bias does not result in a recognition of the world precisely as it is, but one can recognize that it is not possible without a blind spot, that in the act of perceiving, every perception ignores, indeed must ignore, the conditions by which it constitutes itself.[13]

ETHICS OF THE SECOND ORDER: THE RESPONSIBILITY OF THE OBSERVER

This teaching parable draws attention to the inevitable biases and the blind spots of an observer who approaches an object of description that is alleged to be independent of him. At issue is the constructive character of perception and the basic necessity to continually relativize one's own certainties, to rescind the validity claims through perspectivist breaks and relating issues back to the observer. And with the goal of a new candor, it provides an impulse to systematically study the blindness of one's own and others, as well as the fundamental phenomenon of blindness as related to the blindness of one's own and others. This experiment in particular concisely reveals a central interest of Heinz von Foerster: the irritation of the observer, of the knower, who then—once productively unsettled—encounters the ethical-moral responsibility for his view of things and his inevitably existing blind spots. However, it is more than doubtful that the Socratic-maieutic oriented cybernetician and constructivist in fact worked out a constructivist ethics that operates with concrete behavioral rules and substantially proves what ought to be desired.[14] A closer examination indicates that this is obviously not the case. His credit consists rather in having embedded epistemological-ethical reflection into a framework following strictly linked lines of argumentation that make ethical behavior—irrespective of their concrete form—justifiable. The constructivist ethics of Heinz von Foerster that can be distilled from the book *Wissen und Gewissen* is actually an *ethics of making ethics possible*[15] or an ethics of the second order, an observation of a form of argumentation in the area of ethics that, for its part, occurs with ethical intentions. This type of observation lists the central presuppositions of ethical-moral behavior and is worked out according to the principle of the most vigilant possible avoidance of problems. Accordingly, the relevant preconditions and premises of ethical-moral action appear to be: the assumption that individuals possess freedom of choice; the emphasis and recognition of personal responsibility, which must be allowed every individual; the specific link between epistemology and ethics, which is not comprehended as a strict causal and deductive relationship ("position A determines . . ."). Possible conceptual mistakes that would bring the whole concept into contradiction with constructivist premises are: the recourse to justifications that [one considers] necessarily valid; a moral self-righteousness; attempts to force one's own ethical conception on others; the specification of moral-ethical orientations and proposals for reflection into substantive prescriptions, laws, imperatives.

When it comes to ethical issues, the book *Wissen und Gewissen* and Heinz von Foerster's entire ouvre can be read from a dual perspective: for one, as a description of a transcendental ethics; for another, as an attempt to provide an implicit warning of the abyss of good intentions, which does not or does not want to recognize its own power structure. The main question is: How is a (second-order) ethics constructed that clarifies and embodies, with all of the ramification of the argumentation, its own proclaimed goal—the emphasis of freedom of choice, the recognition of responsibility, the avoidance of force—and refers back to the centerpiece of constructivist thinking, the observer? From such a perspective all starting points are contingent, but one can coherently begin this line of argumentation with a sentence from Heinz von Foerster. "Objectivity," in his view, "is a subject's delusion that observing can be done without him. Invoking objectivity is abrogating responsibility, hence its popularity."[16] This type of formulation presumes that there is a connection between epistemology and ethics to be more specifically determined. More precisely stated: the ideal of objectivity is negated for epistemological reasons and criticized in light of ethical-moral considerations. The structurally based principle of such considerations is the contrast between an observer-independent and an observer-dependent conception of knowledge, which here however is given a turn toward an ethics of responsibility. Heinz von Foerster declares:

> *Reality, objectivity, ontology.* These are all static notions that can be used by people to separate themselves from the world. They can be used as a justification for your own indifference by saying that there is nothing you can do about it, since it is always a matter of an immutable existence that is rigid and timeless. [. . .] This means that you can contrast two fundamentally different positions. The attitude of uninvolved observers contrasts with the attitude of people who empathize and are involved and who see themselves as part of the world. Their basic assumption is, "Whatever I do will change the world." They are connected to the world and its fate and are responsible for their action.[17]

Herewith, a further, new contradiction comes into play: the question is not about objectivity or subjectivity, but about the fundamental issue of whether one's own epistemological partisanship can be used to view oneself as separate from the world, to [allow one to] slip into the role of the distanced (and not participating) observer, who depersonalizes his observation through recourse to the objective perception of what is disclosed (*Gegebenen*).

One can question whether and how the emphasis on one's own responsibility—strictly in the logic of constructivist thinking—can be justified. Some authors have at least rhetorically suggested the possibility of an ultimate justification. Peter M. Hejl—also as a constructivist—orients himself explicitly on the mode of the deduction from facts (what is) to values (what should be) in this, or rather in his, case: from the reality, which is declared to be constructed, to the ethical conceptions, which are conceded to be constructed. He maintains [that there is] a deductive relationship between epistemological assumptions and ethical postulates and thus consciously resorts to an approach to justification that is discussed in philosophy as the *naturalistic fallacy*. The criticism of opponents of this form of justification is that the deduction of norms from descriptive statements is often granted under recourse knowledge from the natural sciences, which is assigned with particular dignity.[18] That means that the content that Peter M. Hejl deals with in his project is constructivist; however, the form of argumentation that maintains a clear separation between ethics and epistemology is better suited to the tradition of realism and is probably oriented on the model of positive law, and thus results in an identification between law and morality that is problematic in another respect.[19] In the work of Humberto R. Maturana and Francisco J. Varela one also occasionally finds the jargon of irrevocability and the rhetoric of necessary responsibility, which, in my view, presents a break with the character of constructivist argumentation; the form and message are ajar. So, at the end of the *Tree of Knowledge,* one finds:

> *The cognition of cognition obliges.* Knowledge obliges us to take an attitude of constant vigilance towards the temptation of certainty. It obliges us to see that our certainties are not proofs of truth, that the world as seen by everyone is not *the* world but *a* world that we bring forth together with the others. It obliges us to see that the world will only change when we change our ways of living. (emphasis in original)[20]

In short: this is about an ethics "that we cannot evade."[21] Clearly under the influence of Buddhism, Francisco J. Varela in the end radicalizes his views in metaphysical directions and ultimately sees ethical-moral behavior as ontologically justified. In his book *Ethical Know-How,* he agreeingly appeals to the assumption that "the authentic care is immanent in the foundation of all Being and can be unfolded to full flowering by sustained ethical education."[22] This is very clearly a proclamation of an ultimate foundation; ethical action is here moved in the direction of the fulfillment of a duty that is immanent to Being.[23]

In contrast, Heinz von Foerster firmly maintains that when he makes a choice in favor of responsibility and the attitude of the participating observer, he cannot deduce this from his epistemological understanding or, further still, from the ground of Being. His deliberations on ethics are reflections inspired by epistemology, but they are *not* a consequence of a linear causal immediacy, resulting from the premises of the epistemology. "For if it were a consequence it would be a necessity. I assert however: it is not a necessity. It is an attitude that we can select from amongst all possible other attitudes."[24] This means: when it comes to question of the relationship between epistemology and ethics, Heinz von Foerster accepts a *relational-logic agnosticism*,[25] which allows only the validity of the decisive choice of the individual; this kind of attitude is obviously inspired by epistemology, but it does not imply any necessary link between epistemological understanding and ethical-moral behavioral duties that can be spelled out in detail.

In order to clearly indicate the possibility of the choice and the inevitability of free choice, in the book *Wissen und Gewissen* he develops the difference between *decidable and undecidable questions* and develops an argumentative structure that is equally interlaced with logical rigor and the display of individual leeway.[26] The question of one's own ethical-moral preference is considered undecidable in principle and is connected with the appeal of an individual and thus is a decision for which one alone is responsible. Heinz von Foerster:

> A decidable question is always decided within a framework that determines the possible and right answer from the outset. Its decidablity is guaranteed by certain rules and formalisms, although they have to be accepted. Syllogisms, syntax, and arithmetic are all examples of these types of formalisms. Within the framework of a logical-mathematcal network you get from one junction (the question or the problem) to the next junction (the answer or the solution). This is what makes the question of whether or not the number 2546 can be divided by 2 so easy to answer within seconds, since we all know that the numbers that have a final digit that is even can be divided by 2. (Foerster and Pörksen 2002: 148)

Undecidable questions, by contrast, touch on the core area of metaphysics; they are concerned with the origin of the universe, the existence of God, etc. and must in principle be considered undecidable; the question of whether knowledge is dependent on or independent of observers is in this sense also in principle undecidable, with a truth status that can neither be proven nor disproven. One is called to make a choice. In general:

> Only those questions that are in principle undecidable, *we* can decide. [. . .] Why? Simply because the decidable questions are already decided by the choice of the framework in which they are asked, and by the choice of the rules used to connect what we label "the question" with what we take for an "answer." In some cases it may go fast, in others it may take a long, long time. But ultimately we arrive after a long sequence of compelling logical steps at an irrefutable answer; a definite "yes," or a definite "no." But we are under no compulsion, not even under that logic, when we decide on in principle undecidable questions. There is no external necessity that forces us to answer such

questions one way or another. We are free! The complement to necessity is not chance, it is choice! *We can choose who we wish to become
when we have decided upon an in principle undecidable question.* That
is the good news, as American journalists would say, now comes the
bad news. With this freedom of choice we are now responsible for the
choice we make.[27]

If one decides upon an undecidable question (whereby essentially even the
question of whether a given question is undecidable is already undecidable),[28] then one chooses a view of things that, because of the topics treated
and the lack of ability to verify the presuppositions, can never really be
conclusively clarified. Deciding upon an undecidable question clarifies one's
own responsibility; it ends the possibility of delegating this responsibility:

> You decide to view the objects, the world, and your fellow human beings
> in a certain way and to act accordingly. You become responsible for the
> decision that you made and that no one else can take away from you.[29]

If one follows this line of argumentation, the ethical-moral decision can
only be legitimized by a single authority: the individual, with a choice
among simultaneously postulated possibilities for which he or she alone is
responsible.

The entire plan hereby acquires the character of a suspended construction that combines relativist epistemology and ethical-moral security in an
individual decision. This sabotages an ethics that is formulated with clear
awareness of its inevitable relativity: with the decision one determines—
responsible for oneself—which alternatives are closed off, and one creates
an unambiguousness necessary for action; however, one does so fully aware
of its nonrescindable contingency. The problem of justification is solved in
that the fundament of ethics itself is an ethical-moral decision. One relin-
quishes external authorities (nature, God, law, lawfulness, a telos of history, etc.); the constructivist postulate (plurality of realities, autonomy of
the individual, the impossibility of an ultimate justification, the rejection of
the terrorism of truth), and the possible "correlates of such assumptions"
(tolerance, recognition of responsibility and autonomy, etc.) can no longer
be forced into logically deductive relationship.[30] If one decides in favor of an
ethical-moral intention, they are at best *"orders of investigation, postulates
of reflection, or obligations of observation of the second order* [. . .], which
may in the given situation in question serve as a framework of finding a
decision by the morally acting agents."[31]

It is central that this framework of decision making is not substantively
filled by commands and restrictions.[32] In view of this, a consistent, well-
thought-out, concrete second-order ethics must appear diffuse, precisely
because the developed form is left to the individual. The *problem of con-
veyance* is also to be posed carefully. What has been realized as right and

correct cannot be propagated in the mode of certainty and with missionary zeal and furor because this would immediately provoke a rhetorical self-contradiction.[33] In this context, both Heinz von Foerster and Humberto R. Maturana have suggested differentiating between ethics and morality, also to characterize differing styles of mediation. They consider the moral to offer an occasion for authoritarian appeal, the sermon, the prescription; it is announced in the mode of an imperative. In Humberto Maturana, that means, for instance:

> The moralists stand for the adherence to rules, which they consider as the external reference lending authority to their statements and strange ideas. They lack awareness of their own responsibility. People acting as moralists do not see their fellow human beings because they are completely occupied by the upholding of rules and imperatives. They know with certainty what has to be done and how everybody else has to behave. People acting ethically, on the contrary, perceive others, consider them important, and see them. It is, of course, possible that persons argue like moralists but act in an ethical way. It is imaginable that persons are moralists without being ethical, or that they are generally held to be immoral while, in fact, acting ethically. In each of these cases, the possibility of ethics and of being touched arises only when the other human being is seen as a legitimate other, and when the possible consequences of one's actions for that other's well-being are reflected.[34]

One is only in command of one's own actions. And ethical action deserving of the name cannot follow from fear of punishment, as reactions to commands. The concern is the "I should" and not "You shall!"[35] Ethics must thus—this is the key concept of Heinz von Foerster developed in the book *Wissen und Gewissen*—remain *implicit*; it should be interwoven in the action of the individual in order to avoid the standing of an explicit precept.[36] It seems a bit paradoxical, against this background, that Heinz von Foerster himself formulates an ethical imperative in the middle of *Wissen und Gewissen*:[37] Act always so as to increase the number of choices.[38] Of course, such a formulation fits, on the one hand, to the idea of a second-order ethics; on the other hand, it does not fit after all. It appears fitting that the increase in possibilities inevitably increases the number of alternatives of thoughts and actions, and thus that it is a formal criterion to increase the degree of freedom and thereby maximize the chances for decisions for which one is personally responsible. However, presenting this in the form of an imperative appears unfitting because the idea of the imperative (if not the content of this requirement) at the very least has misleading connotations that are opposed to reflections for which one is personally responsible. Heinz von Foerster was aware of this and once conceded that in formulating his imperative he did not choose his words very carefully and could give people the impression that he also wanted to "order people around."[39]

Only in the realm of one's personal actions can one determine when ethics remains implicit and when it is transformed into an explicit morality and might turn into a strategy for subjugation. Here one cannot avoid one's own reflection, the decisions about the in principle undecidable, which the observer cannot shake and delegate to other authorities of authorization. That means: an argumentational logic is offered and a justified unjustifiability, the means and ends, ethical reflection and practice—inextricably linked with one another. One has the choice and is then responsible for it, and following this logic, must confront one's own freedom.

THE FORMAL ANTHROPOLOGY OF HEINZ VON FOERSTER: THE NONTRIVIALITY OF THE OBSERVER

The emphasis on freedom of choice shows clearly that Heinz von Foerster underlines a specific view of man. However, Foerster more thoroughly worked out this view—and illustrated it with an analogy that (at least for readers socialized in the social sciences and humanities) is surprising and, if anything, seemingly out of place. He differentiates (first of all in reference to the broadly understood machine concept of Alan Turing) between trivial and nontrivial machines. A *machine* in this view is a formal concept. It is not necessarily referring to "an assembly of cogwheels, buttons and levers, or chips, discs, and connectors," but to abstract entities with well-defined functional characteristics, which of course very well are able to assume the form of a classical machine.[40] In order to more clearly define a trivial machine, one must first of all differentiate between a cause or an input and a rule of transformation, which transforms the cause into an effect or the input into an output (see diagram 6.2).

According to Heinz von Foerster,

> You need to imagine a group of events that we can denote with A, B, C, D and with the numbers 1, 2, 3, 4. In the case of a trivial machine, we will see that there is a regular relationship between these events. That means that following a predetermined rule, the machine takes a stimulus, a cause, or an input and produces a corresponding response, effect,

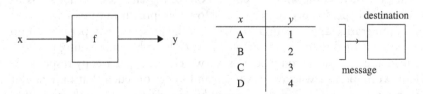

Diagram 6.2   The trivial machine provides predictable results.

or output, reliably and flawlessly. For example, you give the machine an A and it outputs a 1. Give it a B, and it will output event 2.[41]

In a trivial machine there is an unchanging existent, a continually reliable relationship between the input and output, cause and effect, stimulation and reaction; inner states, which one, if anything, assumes in this opaque enduring entity, remain unchanged. The trivial machine is synthetically determined, independent from the past, analytically determinable, and predictable. Should the expected effect begin to fail to occur after all, then one can—in alignment with the model of the immanent logic of the research on defects—diagnose the cause of the defective output production and repair the machine so that it returns to predictable behavior. The repairing process, with the goal of reestablishing computability and ensuring predictability, can be referred to within the framework of the descriptive language chosen here as *trivialization*. Heinz von Foerster notes:

> While our pre-occupation with the trivialization of our environment may be in one domain useful and constructive, in another domain it is useless and destructive. Trivialization is a dangerous panacea when man applies it to himself. Consider, for instance, the way our system of education is set up. The student enters school as an unpredictable "nontrivial machine." We don't know what answer he will give to a question. However, should he succeed in this system the answers he gives to our questions must be known. They are the "right" answers [. . .] Tests are devices to establish a measure of trivialization. A perfect score in a test is indicative of perfect trivialization: the student is completely predictable and thus can be admitted into society. He will cause neither any surprises nor any trouble.[42]

Nontrivial machines, by contrast, also transform the rules according to which the transformations occur—and thus thereby neutralize the linkage between cause and effect that is thought to be secured. Once again, one can mark a group of events or inputs formally with the letters A, B, C, and D and distinguish these from a group of possible results (again, for example: 1, 2, 3, and 4). "Again," according to Heinz von Foerster,

> a simple experiment can be performed. For instance, you might input the letter A, and the machine will output the number 1. Then you repeat the procedure, and this time the number 4 is output. You input an A again, and a 1 is output, but when you input an A again this time it outputs another result.[43]

The explanation for the incalculability of a nontrivial machine is that it is able to change internal states, whose rule-bound attributes are inaccessible to the observer.[44] Nontrivial machines always also interact with their own states. They process the input in recursive loops to a potentially continually changing, perhaps even an entirely missing, outcome (see diagram 6.3). The respective output value y is not only dependent on the input value x but it is also on the internal state z, in which the machine finds itself at [a given] moment. If z were constant and continually unchanging, the predictability of y would be no problem. However, because this isn't the case and the internal states of the machine shift in dependence upon x as well as z, new internal states continually emerge, making it impossible for the observer to differentiate the rule of transformation. The result: it is not possible to prognosticize the output value. Also it can be shown that one cannot determine the operative characteristics in a finite series of experiments. All that can be culled from the (still unpredictable) relationship between input and output, cause and effect of apparent laws is speculation, and it will be repudiated by continually varying results. Because internal dynamics of the changes in the states inevitably remain hidden from the observer, the transformation rules cannot be determined from the perspectives that are accessible to him. In short: a nontrivial machine breaches the basic need for certainty, calculability, transparence, and control; it is synthetically determined, path dependent, analytically indeterminable, and unpredictable.

Characteristic of these considerations, Heinz von Foerster pleaded to interpret human beings as nontrivial machines, in order, partially through this decision, to defend them from more or less unworthy attempts at trivialization. From a perspective like this, people are transformed into *creatures of chance or possibility*; they are not stimulus-response machines that, with certain knowledge, can be always forced, with the right input, to yield the expected output. The indeterminate character of man is the determinate; the principle unpredictability of his behavior is one of the central characteristics of his normalcy. His "nature" is not a stock of content that can be fixed.

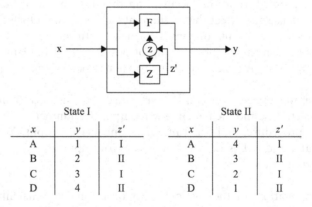

	State I				State II		
x	*y*	*z'*		*x*	*y*	*z'*
A	1	I		A	4	I
B	2	II		B	3	II
C	3	I		C	2	I
D	4	II		D	1	II

Diagram 6.3 The nontrivial machine has an internal state that continually changes in dependency on x and earlier internal states.

What is going on internally, how his internal states are transformed and continually newly constituted, dependent on external influences and past experiences, existing views and moods, must be viewed as intransparent. Attempts at trivialization would be fatal.

RECEPTION AND EFFECT: PRESCRIPTIONS AND ANTIDOTES

Such an attempt to keep one theoretical architecture open in all directions, as well as the decisive interest in unpredictability, which is in principle conceded, make one thing clear: The work of Heinz von Foerster cannot be interpreted as a trivial educational platform that presupposes certain views; in this respect, he at the same time lacks a direct formulaic, or prescriptive, relevance. His tendentially indirect uses consist in the fact that he makes available a reservoir of new perspectives and possibilities for observation, which have provided for furor in varying disciplines and areas of application. Numerous Festschriften, diverse films, and a special edition of the journal *Cybernetics & Human Knowing* that was published after his death on October 2, 2002 (along with diverse articles in German language newspapers of high quality) are documents to an intensive reception.[45] The Heinz von Foerster Society (Vienna) oversees research work and regularly coordinates international conferences, often in cooperation with the *American Society for Cybernetics*, which is also tending to the legacy of its earlier member. The extensive intellectual legacy is largely in the possession of the University of Vienna. In journals such as *Constructivist Foundations,* Heinz von Foerster is still viewed as an innovator and his name is still often found as a header; he is cited as a researcher in the theory of self-organization, as a founder of second-order cybernetics, and as a constructivist epistemologist and ethicist. Some books (partially written with his cooperation) have further popularized his postulates and parables, above all in the German-speaking world.[46] The most important articles from *Wissen und Gewissen* were once again published in 2003 under the title *Understanding Understanding: Essays on Cybernetics and Cognition.* His views have been and continue to be widely discussed, for example, on psychotherapy, education, organizational consulting, and social work. These are all disciplines and areas of application that in one way or another deal *with changes in human beings* through communication, that is that take up the question of how attempts at external steering can be transformed internally into propositions for self-steering that are in fact applied.[47] The representatives of these disciplines wrestle with the problem of how human autonomous observers, with personalities, in some way can be purposively influenced and can change their constructions of reality, that is with how one somehow launches potentially obstinate systems on their own goals. As has been shown, as a rule, Heinz von Foerster's constructivism is operative at two levels in the disciplines that are concerned with human change: At the *level of critique,*

Foerster's thoughts provide a basis for criticizing trivial steering concepts and for rejecting them as insufficient. The belief in a linear-directive possibility for influence is unmasked as erroneous, often with reference to the noted differentiation between trivial and nontrivial machines.[48] At the level of the *general conceptual orientation* and of the *view of human anthropology* and *the educational program* it appears—in accord with the Foerster reading provided—that the respect for the autonomy of the other is justifiable. This corresponds, then, ideally, with a new sensibility for surprises and unpredictable effects, as well as with sources that appear to be extremely marginal, the butterfly effect.[49]

Certainly, thought through consistently, this type of antidote cannot be allowed to become a formulaic prescription or to become an arrogantly championed metaprescription; the shock of dogma cannot be turned into a new dogma. Rather, it is important, following the Socratic cybernetician Heinz von Foerster, to retain a moment of doubt and precisely not the ultimately determinable. It is important to be skeptical of certainty, continually in search of the different, of new possibilities for thought, to be fascinated and in a curious way inspired by the world, which is in principle opaque.

NOTES

1. Translated by Darrell P. Arnold, PhD.
2. This article draws on the author's previous publications and texts on Heinz von Foerster.
3. Heinz von Foerster, *Der Anfang von Himmel und Erde hat keinen Namen: Eine Selbsterschaffung in 7 Tagen,* eds. Albert Müller and Karl H. Müller (Vienna: Döcker, 1997); Heinz von Foerster and Bernhard Pörksen, *Wahrheit ist die Erfindung eines Lügners: Gespräche für Skeptiker* (Heidelberg: Carl-Auer-Systeme, 1998); Heinz von Foerster and Monika Bröcker, *Teil der Welt: Fraktale einer Ethik. Ein Drama in drei Akten* (Heidelberg: Carl-Auer-Systeme, 2002).
4. Heinz von Foerster, *Das Gedächtnis: Eine quantenphysikalische Untersuchung* (Vienna: Franz Deuticke, 1948).
5. Steve Joshua Heims, *The Cybernetics Group* (Cambridge, MA: MIT Press, 1991).
6. For more on this work, see Foerster and Pörksen, *Wahrheit ist die Erfindung eines Lügners,* 105ff.
7. Albert Müller, "A Brief History of the BCL: Heinz von Foerster and the Biological Computer Laboratory," in *An Unfinished Revolution? Heinz von Foerster and the Biological Computer Laboratory (BCL), 1958–1976,* eds. Albert Müller and Karl H. Müller (Vienna: edition echoraum, 2007), 277–302; Albert Müller, "The End of the Biological Computer Laboratory," in the same text, 303–21.
8. Humberto R. Maturana, *Biology of Cognition: Biological Computer Laboratory Research Report BCL 9.0* (Urbana, IL: University of Illinois, 1970).
9. Here one can only speculate, but presumably it is anything but arbitrary that precisely the founders of constructivism continually reflected on the connection between epistemology and ethics and the consequences of the terrorism

of truth. They all suffered under dictators and were confronted with dogmatically held realities. Lacking the necessary "Arian proof" in Berlin at the time of National Socialism, Heinz von Foerster had to elude the monitoring attempts for that by employing a stall tactic. Ernst von Glasersfeld left Vienna when the National Socialists came to power; Paul Watzlawick continually indicated how much the NS regime shocked him. Francisco Varea fled—after the death of Salvador Allende and the power grab of the Pinochet rebels—to Costa Rica. Humberto R. Maturan remained in Chile, also in order to study the dangers of ideology-caused blindness. Such a revealing personal historical as well as scientific background of course says nothing about the plausibility of their respective reflections. However, it does indicate a strong connection between theory formation and personal biography.

10. Heinz von Foerster, *Wissen und Gewissen: Versuch einer Brücke,* eds. Siegfried J. Schmidt (Frankfurt am Main: Suhrkamp, 1993).
11. Heinz von Foerster, *Understanding Understanding: Essays on Cybernetics and Cognition* (New York: Springer, 2003), 212.
12. This prompts two metaphors: Perceiving is doing, and If I don't see I am blind, I am blind; but if I see I am blind, I see; see Foerster, *Understanding Understanding,* 213.
13. Norbert Bolz, *Weltkommunikation* (Munich: Fink, 2001), 17.
14. Lutz Kramaschki, "Wie universalistisch kann die Moralphilosophie diskutieren? Hinweise aus radikalkonstruktivistischer Sicht," in *Konstruktivismus und Ethik: DELFIN 1995,* eds. Gebhard Rusch and Siegfried J. Schmidt (Frankfurt am Main: Suhrkamp, 1995), 266.
15. [Translator's note: The German term is the "Ethik der Ethik-Ermoeglichung."] This term is drawn from Lutz Kramaschki, "Wie universalistisch kann die Moralphilosophie diskutieren? Hinweise aus radikalkonstruktivistischer Sicht," in *Konstruktivismus und Ethik: DELFIN 1995,* eds. Gebhard Rusch and Siegfried J. Schmidt (Frankfurt am Main: Suhrkamp, 1995), 262f.
16. Heinz von Foerster and Bernhard Pörksen, *Understanding Systems: Conversations on Epistemology and Ethics* (New York: Plenum, 2002), 148.
17. Heinz von Foerster and Bernhard Pörksen, *Undstanding Systems,* 151f.
18. For the constituting principles of the argumentation, see, for example, Peter M. Hejl, "Ethik, Konstruktivismus und gesellschaftliche Selbstregelung," in *Konstruktivismus und Ethik: DELFIN,* eds. Gebhard Rusch and Siegfried J. Schmidt (Frankfurt am Main: Suhrkamp, 1995), 46, 52f.; for a discussion of the obvious objection that this is a form of the naturalistic fallacy, see 49ff.
19. Siegfied J. Schmidt, *Faszination: Medien—Kultur—Wissenschaft in der Mediengesellschaft* (Weilerswist: Velbrück Wissenschaft, 2000), 66.
20. Humberto R. Maturana and Francisco J. Varela, *Tree of Knowledge* (Boston: Shambhala, 1998), 245.
21. Maturana and Varela, *Tree of Knowledge,* 245.
22. Francisco J. Varela, *Ethical Know-How: Action, Wisdom, and Cognition* (Stanford: Stanford University Press, 1999), 77.
23. For more on the dispute about this question, see Varela's discussions with Pörksen in *The Certainty of Uncertainty—Dialogues Introducing Constructivism* (Exeter: Imprint Academic, 2004), 85ff.
24. Foerster and Bröcker, *Teil der Welt,* 64.
25. This concept is drawn from Konrad Ott, "Zum Verhältnis von Radikalem Konstruktivismus und Ethik," in *Konstruktivismus und Ethik,* eds. Gebhard Rusch and Siegfried J. Schmidt (Frankfurt am Main: Suhrkamp, 1995), 296.
26. Foerster, *Understanding Understanding,* 291ff.
27. Foerster, *Understanding Understanding,* 293.

28. Von Foerster notes: "I would even go so far as to say that the question is undecidable as to whether an experiment can be found that unequivocally determines if a question is undecidable or not. The problem of undecidability cannot even be decided on the level of the second order." (Foerster and Pörksen, *Understanding Systems*, 155).

29. Foerster and Pörksen, *Understanding Systems: Conversations on Epistemology and Ethics* (New York: Plenum, 2002), 155.

30. Schmidt, *Medien—Kultur—Wissenschaft in der Mediengesellschaft*, 65.

31. Schmidt, *Medien*, 65.

32. This void or gap in content is also a characteristic of liberal democracies or open societies in general. They form the frame, metaphorically speaking, but not the concrete picture, whose concrete layout and form is not to be predetermined.

33. In the case of the logical self-contradiction, utterances are logically incompatible. ("The truth is that there is no ultimate truth.") With the idea of the rhetorical self-contradiction I mean, by contrast, the way that the diction that is chosen does not fit to the utterance. One approaches an authority and a demand for finality and ultimate certainty that one, if remaining faithful to the self-formulated premises, cannot lift. The possibility of an ultimate justification and objective statement is suggested already by the use of the stylistic device—and simultaneously disputes it at the level of content, using a diction, a jargon of irrevocability, that does not harmonize with the self-proclaimed basic assumption. This really ought to inspire different, more open, and, above all, observer-connected forms of presentation and speech.

34. Maturana and Pörksen, *From Being to Doing: The Origins of the Biology of Cognition* (Heidelberg: Carl-Auer-Systeme, 2004), 207f.

35. Foerster, *Understanding Understanding*, 290f. Here Heinz von Foerster draws on Ludwig Wittgenstein, whose interpretation he paraphrases as follows: "Wenn ein ethisches Gesetz der Form 'Du sollst' aufgestellt wird, dann ist der erste Gedanke: 'Und was dann, wenn ich es nicht tue?' Es ist aber klar, dass die Ethik nichts mit Strafe und Lohn im gewöhnlichen Sinne zu tun hat. Also muss diese Frage nach den Folgen einer Handlung belanglos sein. (Nichtsdestoweniger) muss es eine Art von ethischem Lohn und ethischer Strafe geben: *diese müssen in der Handlung selbst liegen.*" Cited in Heinz von Foerster, *Wissen und Gewissen: Versuch einer Brücke*, ed. Siegfried J. Schmidt (Frankfurt am Main: Suhrkamp, 1993), 347 (emphasis in the original).

36. Foerster, *Understanding Understanding*, 290f.

37. One can show that Foerster—first of all, a cybernetician and bio-epistemologist, later a cybernetically inspired ethnician—continued to more consistently work out his ethical conclusions over the course of time. The ethical imperative first appears in his early articles, the relativization of the demand for unconditionality later. His later books (Foerster, *Der Anfang vom Himmel*; Foerster and Pörksen, *Wahrheit ist die Erfindug eines Lugners*; Foerster and Broeckner, *Teil der Welt*) portray the history of his thought and show, as a whole, a progressive radicalization of his skeptical position; the recourse to an epistemological justification of autonomy and ethics disappears while the freedom of choice is emphasized.

38. Foerster, *Understanding Understanding*, 227.

39. Foerster and Pörksen, *Understanding Systems*, 37.

40. Foerster, *Understanding Understanding*, 357. Of course the concept of the machine that Foerster (with his specific meaning) uses provokes criticism. The objection is that the discussion of a machine already suggests calculability and clarity. The machine metaphor suggests that every aspect of the entity under discussion can be unriddled. However, in principle the issue is

the opposition between triviality and nontriviality (Foerster and Pörksen, *Wahrheit ist die Erfindung des Luegners,* 59).
41. Foerster and Pörksen, *Understanding Systems,* 54.
42. Foerster, *Understanding Understanding,* 208f.
43. Foerster and Pörksen, *Understanding Systems,* 56.
44. Simon, Fritz B. *Unterschiede, die Unterschiede machen: Klinische Epistemologie: Grundlage einer systemischen Psychiatrie und Psychosomatik: Mit einem Geleitwort von Helm Stierlin,* 3rd ed. (Frankfurt am Main: Suhrkamp, 1999), 45.
45. For an exemplary case, see Peter Krieg and Paul Watzlawick, eds., *Das Auge des Betrachters: Beiträge zum Konstruktivismus.* Heidelberg: Carl-Auer-Systeme, 2002.
46. See Lynn Segal, *Das 18: Kamel oder Die Welt als Erfindung: Zum Konstruktivismus Heinz von Foersters* (Munich: Piper, 1988); Foerster, *Der Anfang von Himmel und Erde hat keinen Namen: Eine Selbsterschaffung in 7 Tagen,* eds. Albert Müller and Karl H. Müller (Vienna: Döcker, 1997); Foerster and Pörksen, *Wahrheit ist die Erfindugn des Lugners;* Foerster and Broecker, *Teil der Welt;* Pörksen, *Die Gewissheit der Gewissheit,* esp. the article "In jedem Augenblick kann ich entscheiden, wer ich bin."
47. An initial overview of the essential impulse in this area is offered in Foerster and Pörksen, *Understanding Systems,* 65ff.
48. The goal is by no means, as Niklas Luhmann assumes in his discussion of the difference between triviality and nontriviality, above all to propagate the "opposing model of education for unreliability, for surprising creativity, to the production of nonsense" (Niklas Luhmann, *Das Erziehungssystem der Gesellschaft,* ed. Dieter Lenzen [Frankfurt am Main: Suhrkamp, 2002], 78); this would "not only have little chance of being realized, but it would contradict the justified interest of society in predictability" (79). It appears central rather to work to "end the [sense of] rivalry in the concept of transformation" that is the conceptual focus of the process of human change. (Baecker here cites Rudolf Wimmer, "Wider den Veränderungsoptimismus: Zu den Möglichkeiten und Grenzen einer radikalen Transformation von Organisationen," *Soziale Systeme 5,* no. 1 [1999]: 169).
49. Theodor M. Bardmann, "Der zweite Doppelpunkt: Systemtheoretische und gesellschaftstheoretische Anmerkungen zur politischen Steuerung," in *Irritation als Plan: Konstruktivistische Einredungen,* eds. Theodor M. Bardmann, Heinz J. Kersting, H. Christoph Vogel, and Bernd Woltmann (Aachen: Kersting, 1991), 29.

REFERENCES

Bardmann, Theodor M. "Der zweite Doppelpunkt: Systemtheoretische und gesellschaftstheoretische Anmerkungen zur politischen Steuerung." In *Irritation als Plan: Konstruktivistische Einredungen,* edited by Theodor M. Bardmann, Heinz J. Kersting, H. Christoph Vogel, and Bernd Woltmann, 10–31. Aachen: Kersting, 1991.
Bolz, Norbert. *Weltkommunikation.* Munich: Fink, 2001.
Foerster, Heinz von. "Das Gedächtnis." In *Eine quantenphysikalische Untersuchung.* Vienna: Franz Deuticke, 1948.
———. *Wissen und Gewissen: Versuch einer Brücke,* edited by Siegfried J. Schmidt. Frankfurt am Main: Suhrkamp, 1993.
———. *Der Anfang von Himmel und Erde hat keinen Namen: Eine Selbsterschaffung in 7 Tagen,* edited by Albert Müller and Karl H. Müller. Vienna: Döcker, 1997.

———. *Understanding Understanding: Essays on Cybernetics and Cognition.* New York: Springer, 2003.

Foerster, Heinz von, and Bernhard Pörksen. *Understanding Systems: Conversations on Epistemology and Ethics.* New York: Springer, 2002.

———. *Wahrheit ist die Erfindung eines Lügners: Gespräche für Skeptiker.* Heidelberg: Carl-Auer-Systeme, 1998.

Foerster, Heinz von, and Monika Bröcker. *Teil der Welt: Fraktale einer Ethik. Ein Drama in drei Akten.* Heidelberg: Carl-Auer-Systeme, 2002.

Heims, Steve J. *The Cybernetics Group.* Cambridge: MIT Press, 1991.

Hejl, Peter M. "Ethik, Konstruktivismus und gesellschaftliche Selbstregelung." In *Konstruktivismus und Ethik: DELFIN 1995,* edited by Gebhard Rusch and Siegfried J. Schmidt, 28–121. Frankfurt am Main: Suhrkamp, 1995.

Kramaschki, Lutz. "Wie universalistisch kann die Moralphilosophie diskutieren? Hinweise aus radikalkonstruktivistischer Sicht." In *Konstruktivismus und Ethik: DELFIN 1995,* edited by Gebhard Rusch and Siegfried J. Schmidt, 249–75. Frankfurt am Main: Suhrkamp, 1995.

Krieg, Peter, and Paul Watzlawick, eds. *Das Auge des Betrachters: Beiträge zum Konstruktivismus.* Heidelberg: Carl-Auer-Systeme, 2002.

Luhmann, Niklas. *Das Erziehungssystem der Gesellschaft,* edited by Dieter Lenzen. Frankfurt am Main: Suhrkamp, 2002.

Maturana, Humberto R. "Biology of Cognition." *Biological Computer Laboratory Research Report BCL 9.0.* Urbana, IL: University of Illinois, 1970.

Maturana, Humberto R., and Francisco J. Varela. *The Tree of Knowledge: The Biological Roots of Human Understanding.* Translated by Robert Paolucci. Boston: Shambhala, 1998.

Maturana, Humberto R., and Bernhard Pörksen. *From Being to Doing: The Origins of the Biology of Cognition.* Heidelberg: Carl-Auer-Systeme, 2004.

McCulloch, Warren, and Walter Pitts. "A Logical Calculus of the Ideas Immanent in Nervous Activity." *Bulletin of Mathematical Biophysics* 5 (1943): 115–33.

Müller, Albert. "A Brief History of the BCL: Heinz von Foerster and the Biological Computer Laboratory." In *An Unfinished Revolution? Heinz von Foerster and the Biological Computer Laboratory (BCL), 1958–1976,* edited by Albert Müller and Karl H. Müller, 277–302. Vienna: edition echoraum, 2007.

———. "The End of the Biological Computer Laboratory." In *An Unfinished Revolution? Heinz von Foerster and the Biological Computer Laboratory (BCL), 1958–1976,* edited by Albert Müller and Karl H. Müller, 303–21. Vienna: edition echoraum, 2007.

Pörksen, Bernhard. *The Certainty of Uncertainty—Dialogues Introducing Constructivism.* Exeter: Imprint Academic, 2004.

———. *Die Gewissheit der Ungewissheit: Gespräche zum Konstruktivismus.* Heidelberg: Carl-Auer-Systeme, 2002.

———. " 'In jedem Augenblick kann ich entscheiden, wer ich bin.' Heinz von Foerster über den Beobachter, das dialogische Leben und eine konstruktivistische Philosophie des Unterscheidens." In *Die Gewissheit der Ungewissheit: Gespräche zum Konstruktivismus,* edited by Bernhard Pörksen, 19–45. Heidelberg: Carl-Auer-Systeme, 2002.

Ott, Konrad. "Zum Verhältnis von Radikalem Konstruktivismus und Ethik." In *Konstruktivismus und Ethik: DELFIN 1995,* edited by Gebhard Rusch and Siegfried J. Schmidt, 280–320. Frankfurt am Main: Suhrkamp, 1995.

Schmidt, Siegfried J. *Kalte Faszination: Medien—Kultur—Wissenschaft in der Mediengesellschaft.* Weilerswist: Velbrück Wissenschaft, 2000.

Segal, Lynn. *Das 18. Kamel oder Die Welt als Erfindung: Zum Konstruktivismus Heinz von Foersters.* Munich: Piper, 1988.

Simon, Fritz B. *Unterschiede, die Unterschiede machen. Klinische Epistemologie: Grundlage einer systemischen Psychiatrie und Psychosomatik.* 3rd ed. Foreword by Helm Stierlin. Frankfurt am Main: Suhrkamp, 1999.

Varela, Francisco J. *Ethical Know-How: Action, Wisdom, and Cognition.* Stanford: Stanford University Press, 1999.

Wimmer, Rudolf. "Wider den Veränderungsoptimismus. Zu den Möglichkeiten und Grenzen einer radikalen Transformation von Organisationen." *Soziale Systeme* 5, no. 1 (1999): 159–80.

7   Maturana and Varela
From Autopoiesis to Systems Applications

Bob Mugerauer

Humberto Maturana (1928–) and Francisco Varela (1946–2001) have made a major contribution to systems theory by empirically and theoretically defining, describing, and interpreting living systems as autopoietic. Additionally, they have substantially developed dynamic systems perspectives on biology of cognition, perception and action, immunology, neurophenomenology, ethics, and pedagogy.

EPISTEMOLOGY AND ONTOLOGY

Maturana and Varela explicitly work out the epistemological and ontological foundations necessary to understand living systems. In a strong phenomenology that breaks with the received view of scientific objectivity, they contend that we need to distinguish a) the phenomena as they appear to the perspective of the observer (our only possible position) from b) the system's own phenomena as they occur in the unitary perspective of the organism centripetally, within itself. In regard to closed neuronal networks (organisms), the latter perspective is the phenomenal domain of the "changing states of activity of the nervous system as a whole" and the former is that of the history of causes of the change of states.[1]

Only observers distinguish living beings such as cells from their physical surroundings by specifying their "inside" separated by a membrane from their "outside," and then proceed to generate concepts such as organization, structure, and internal/external causality to account for law-like physical and chemical transactions. We can think of the relation of the two domains in terms of a box that contains another box within it. The inner box is the realm of the organism and its operative environment, wherein the organism proceeds through changing states in the course of living, directly engaged with what is an environment *for* that organism.[2] Here we have the living system's world as defined by its structural constitution, which brings forth what is relevant to the particular living system at that moment.[3]

In contrast, the containing box outside the box of the organism is the realm of the observer who distinguishes the entity from its physical surroundings as they appear to us (as the environment *of* the organism) and enter into our communications, that is, into our observations and descriptions with which we try to explain the causes for the change of states (of the closed neuronal network itself):[4]

> The distinction between internal and external causes of change of state can be made only by an observer who beholds the organism as a unity and defines its inside and outside by specifying boundaries.[5]

It should be noted that even in "Autopoiesis: The Organization of the Living" Maturana and Varela modified their strong initial position on the differences between the two domains in that they ceased insisting that we (observers) could say nothing of the living system's world in itself. Instead they later allowed that we could at least make the general characterization as just summarized above. If one were too rigid in dealing with the basic point, since observers only are able to see (or attempt to see) how things in the external environmental cause changes of states, all that would appear would be elements or processes in the organism's surroundings producing the organism's components and organization (allopoietics) rather than the organisms producing their own (autopoietics).

CORE IDEAS

Autopoiesis

Living systems are fundamentally the process(es) of self-constituting a homeostatic identity.[6] Not only are organisms formally autonomous as are other types of complex systems, but further they are autopoietic (strongly self-constituting) insofar as they operate through a system of processes that produce and maintain the very components and dynamic network that they are. In this uniquely strong self-organization of the living there is a reciprocal causality between local components and the global properties of the entity.[7]

Organizational Closure and Structural Coupling

Conscious that we can speak only of what appears to us, Maturana and Varela contend that, as observers, in regard to the organism in the context *of* its environment, we discern two further domains (which together would provide the substantive content of the outside-containing box in the metaphor used above): the organism's internal, invariant organization and the variable structure connecting it to its environment. They posit that the core reality of the organism lies in the paradoxical, reciprocal relationship of closed organization and open structural coupling: "the living system must distinguish itself from its environment and at the same time maintain its coupling."[8]

Insofar as an entity can appear to an observer, it must be perceived as having a distinct identity against the background of what surrounds it. Here the term "organizational" names the features that characterize an entity as the kind of entity it is. (Maturana and Varela use the example of a table as an entity with a top and legs, which is a different organization than a chair with legs and a seat.) "Closure"—which is not a physical concept—specifies that such a defining pattern remains unchanged (the table remains a table, not becoming a chair).[9] Thus, "the organization of an organism is itself invariant"; "its internal regulation maintains the pattern definitive of the kind of organism it is";[10] and "The defining element of living units is a certain organization independent of structure, the material that embodies it" (as a table can be made of wood, steel, plastic or have one, three, or four legs, each with different processes of production).[11]

At the same time, the organism is not cut off from its environment. Quite the opposite; it can maintain its organization only by way of continuously open dynamic interactions with its surroundings. That is, a living system's physical-chemical constitution is in flux and exchange with its environment.[12] Maturana and Varela use the term "structural" to refer to these variable physical-chemical components and processes.

Further, the continuity of the living system is possible because "a structurally plastic system in an environment with recurrent perturbations" will produce a continued selection of the system's structure.[13] Hence the history of a living system is a story of structural coupling: "if we can consider the system's environment also as a structurally plastic system, then the system and the environment will have an interlocked history of structural transformations, selecting each other's trajectories."[14]

First- and Second-Order Systems

Maturana and Varela take cells to be the first order autopoietic systems. They manifest and maintain their unity via membranes, while those same membranes facilitate the physic-chemical flows necessary to maintain life. Multicellular organisms such as animals, understood as whole organisms with full, strong self-constituting capacity, are second-order systems. Maturana insists that as distinct from such genuine autopoietic organisms, other multicellular systems are colonies only.[15]

It is with second-order autopoietic systems that we can appreciate more adequately the sense in which organisms are cognitive. On the one hand, cognition is a dimension of "structural coupling, that is, the operational link with the environment allowing for its continuity as an individual entity"; on the other, it is an interpretive dimension in which a physical interaction acquires a "surplus of significance due to the perspective provided by the global action of the organism."[16]

Enaction and Antirepresentational Cognition

The sensiomotor coupling that occurs through our movement, cognition, and perception constructs, over time, regularities.[17] The continuously reciprocal codetermination of the structural plasticity of both the organism and its environment builds up a history of structural coupling that both learns from variations and constructs invariances, which appear, for example, as phenomenal size- and color-constancy. In short, cognition, perception, and memory cannot be separated from an organism's embodied action.

The primary finding for this new orientation came from Maturana's early work in neurobiology of vision, for instance with frogs' visual cortex and color vision of birds and mammals, which focused on developing cognition as a biological phenomenon (related to the Macy Conferences' dealing with cybernetics and circular causality, and also congruent with the work of Heinz von Foerster in its focus on the observer and reflexivity).[18] In "What the Frog's Eye Tells the Frog's Brain," J. Y. Lettvin, Maturana, W. S. McCulloch, and W. H. Pitts reported the empirical findings of the ways in which the frog's retina could not be mapped directly onto, thus convincingly indicating that the organism constructs its world (a finding parallel to von Uexküll's ideas concerning the *Umwelt*, complete with the latter's parallel problems with the primacy of organisms' "bubbles" that nonetheless had to correlate with "webs").[19] Unfolding the implications of this research Maturana, Varela, and colleagues developed two dimensions that have proven to be especially influential: *antirepresentational cognition* and *enaction*.

The mode in which organisms constitute their world, eliciting what is relevant for them from an environment's total possible affordances, obviously entails that cognition cannot be a matter of finding a set of fixed features or "the meaning" of things in an "objective" world. For example, Maturana and Varela in *Tree of Knowledge* (1987), then Varela, Evan Thompson, and Eleanor Rosch in *The Embodied Mind* (1993), systematically provided a critique of and alternative to the received representational views, especially as they have dominated cognitive research, computing, and information theory.[20] They argue that cognitivism is inadequate in its fundamental dimensions because it proceeds from the assumption that cognition is mental representation and an action with or manipulation of symbols to solve problems (as famously developed by Simon and Minsky); hence its practical appeal and application in computing, information theory, and robotics. But, given the evidence that our embodied consciousness brings forth a meaningful world in the course of movement and engagement in life, representational theory is not only inadequate but also misleading in that it depends on and perpetuates the subject-object dualism as well as an untenable account of the relation of representations to the world supposedly represented (congruent with more than thirty years of postmodern and poststructuralist attacks on representation).[21]

As discussed in this chapter, the approach labeled connectivism/self-organization is a significant advance over cognitivism in that the former holds cognition to be a matter of the emergence of global states or properties in a network of simple components, arguing that "representation consists in the correspondence between such an emergent global state and the properties of the world; it is not a function of particular symbols."[22] The successful working out of connectivist dimensions of natural-biological processes has been a large part of the understanding of complex, self-organizing systems. Yet, despite its importance, their contributions to it, and the large role it continues to play in their own theories, finally Maturana, Varela, and colleagues contend that even connectivism/self-organization is finally not adequate because it remains representational and because we cannot separate cognition, perception, and action. Hence their further move to enactivism, which holds that we literally enact a meaningful world as we elicit and interact with what is relevant in our environment, primarily through the generative circularity between movement and cognition and perception (the idea also is found in Bateson). Cognition is not a matter of representing a fixed world but of drawing forth and responding to phenomena through sensorimotor coupling, thereby coconstituting a meaningful world, a world that would not otherwise occur.[23] The theory has implications for robotics, artificial intelligence, and computer-based information systems.[24]

DIFFERENCES BETWEEN MATURANA AND VARELA; OUTSTANDING ISSUES

There have been differences between Maturana, the senior figure of the two, and Varela from the start. For example, in the early *Autopoiesis and Cognition* (written in1980, presenting work from the early 1970s), they could not agree on how to give the account that would situate the new ideas and their import, so Maturana wrote it himself. Differences continue to appear in the later *Tree of Knowledge,* where both authors appear as drawn characters with boxed ideas clearly attributable to one or the other (though there are some that they share). Or, in *The Embodied Mind* (done with other colleagues Thompson and Rosch), his own "Making it Concrete" (from 1992), and in agreement with his colleague Zeleny (from 1980), Varela appears "open to fusing autopoiesis with dynamic self-organization systems, seeing organisms as engaged in rapid responses to change, a position seeing them as more open and flexible than an overemphasis on homeostasis would allow."[25]

Maturana initially developed autopoiesis in terms of homeostasis. Throughout his career, he continued to hold that the core characteristic of autopoiesis is the living system's maintaining self-identity and organizational closure. Varela certainly agrees with this central tenet but places less stress on autopoiesis throughout the development of his thinking. Further, in dealing with autopoiesis Varela's dominant interest lies with the organism's open-ended interactions with its environment and embodied movement to understand how perception is constituted through (recursive) perceptually guided actions that occur as self-reflexive cycles. Though in agreement about autopoiesis then, Maturana holds to organizational closure as the most critical dimension, while for Varela it is the complementary structural coupling.

Third-Order Systems

From first-order autopoietic processes there emerge composite systems, most importantly second-order, multicellular entities and organisms that are autopoietic entities in their own right. Further, Maturana and Varela agree that for humans, linguistic coupling generates not only the network of what we see as belonging to an individual consciousness but moves us to the next higher level. That is, it produces the autonomous cultural-ecological units in which we are both participants and components. Of course, we are part of social-ecological aggregates, with shared traditions and biological structures. From our world of shared regularities there emerge the collective interactions of a social tradition, leading to the further critical issue of whether the third-level animal or human systems that emerge out of second-order systems are autopoietic.

Integral to their definition and description is Maturana and Varela's contention that autopoietic systems have as a criteria of distinction a topological boundary, and that the processes they define occur "in a physical-like space, actual or simulated on a computer"[26] wherein they self-produce and maintain the very components and processes that they are.[27] Consequently, they hold that systems such as animal societies or human linguistic-cultural institutions can be considered autonomous in regard to each other as centripetal structures that are formally coherent and internally consistent (cf. structuralism and poststructuralism) but, failing to meet either of these two central criteria, are not themselves autopoietic (but instances of coupling among independent autopoietic entities generating a higher-order system).

Accordingly, both Maturana and Varela disagree with Niklas Luhmann's view that society is produced by "autopoietic," autonomous communication subsystems of law, economy, science, education, or religion, holding that it rests on the substantial category mistake of confounding autonomy with the autopoiesis of the living. Maturana, particularly, strenuously objected to the unwarranted overextension of the concept of autopoiesis by Erich Jantsch and Luhmann, protesting their "using the concept out of the proper context of application" and eliminating individuals (crucial for democracy) from the social order.[28]

Virtual Systems, Artificial Intelligence, and Robots

Given that one of the central criteria for autopoiesis is that the processes that the system defines occur, as just noted, "in a physical-like space, actual or simulated on a computer," a major area of debate and research concerns virtual systems, artificial intelligence, and robots. Not only is this a tangled debate overall, but in addition to disagreeing on some points, Maturana and Varela have changed their minds from time to time on this issue. Clearly physical-like space can be simulated on a computer, and was done early on by Varela, Maturana, and Uribe,[29] and again by Varela, for instance in "On Organic Closure and Structural Coupling" to explore a system of "tessellation autonoma," simulating autopoietic dynamics, especially the way boundaries maintain themselves and break down.[30] At the least, systems in complexity theory generally, of which living systems would be a subset, would be virtual autonomous agents with closure in a formal-mathematical sense. It would seem, however, that they would fail to meet the other central criteria in that these systems appear to be allopoietic, that is, they produce something other than their own components and organization.

Maturana and Varela not only modify their positions and apparently endorse several versions of a resolution but they (not to mention others who use the terms) also do not use "autopoietic" and "living systems" in a stable manner. As Mingers points out, Maturana and Varela have held that their models were not only autonomous but also autopoietic insofar as they "establish a dynamic with self-defined boundaries producing its own components."[31] Their initial position, with the strong, double criteria noted above for third-order systems, led to the conclusion that physical biological entities or computer systems could be autopoietic. Here, as the wording above indicates, Maturana agreed that either physical or virtual space could be acceptably classified as autopoietic. At the same time, a limitation was imposed in order to be clear and coherent in light of the fact that part of the reason for defining "autopoietic" as they did was to define the living: thus only those autopoietic systems in physical space would be considered living, while autopoietic systems in virtual space would not be.[32] But, clearly there is confusion or contradiction at the core, at least between common sense experience and the expectation of what "living" phenomena are like. In later work, Maturana said that they originally intended to provide a non-common sense definition, but they set this aside in order to be accepted as making sense: he indeed was willing to consider virtual autopoietic systems living.[33] A third position has been held, at least at times, by Varela—namely that autopoiesis was to mean to refer only to physical, living systems, not virtual ones—or, the other way around, only physical living systems should be called "autopoietic" (thus not agreeing with the two-part definition given above in the section on third-order systems).[34] Quite a range of views!

To take a slightly different focus, and bearing in mind that up to the early 1980s they both considered that artificial systems could become autopoietic unities, their differing emphasis on language and cognition naturally surfaced in regard to issues of cognitive science and artificial life. As discussed above, Maturana consistently stressed the stability of homeostasis and Varela the dynamic interactions of structural coupling. As commentators have noted, a shift begins to appear in 1980–81 when, on the one hand, Varela strongly agrees with Maturana in opposing the idea that social systems produce their components in any way close to the way cells and animals do.[35] On the other hand, in the same essay, Varela also articulated a greater openness to "symbolic or systems-theoretic explanation" that would recognize a fuller role of "more abstract ideas that help to construct systems at a higher level of generality."[36] He would extend his position further to consider information and coding flow as a possibly complementary mode of description for autopoiesis, though still insisting that symbolic description is not a substitute for the operational description of autopoiesis.[37] In 1992, with Bourgine, considering robots and artificial intelligence, Varela continued to explore how autonomous agents, defined in terms of formal closure in an algebraic sense, operate in a domain with applications at all scales, from cells to societies. Open to the virtual, he says that "the passage to cognition occurs at the level of a behavioral entity, and not as in the basic cellular self, as a spatially bounded entity" or in terms of the "constitution of a cognitive agent via the nervous system."[38] This position is consistent with the view elaborated in *Tree of Knowledge* where the first- and second-order systems occur within the horizon of third-level social order, though the latter is only autonomous but not autopoietic.

Of course, though they are the authors of autopoietic theory, Maturana and Varela neither direct the range of empirical and theoretical investigations nor have the authority to settle the debates. Perhaps the strongest advocate of an alternative view is, as treated above, Luhmann, who extensively adopted and expanded the concept of autopoiesis in relation to social systems. He has written at length arguing that society is produced by communication subsystems such as law, economics, science, education, and religion that not only may be closed, autonomous sub-systems (with which Varela agrees), but are actually autopoietic. Luhmann's argument is that the communications that social systems use are recursively produced and reproduced by a network of communications and cannot exist outside such a network; accordingly, such communications would be a particular mode of autopoietic reproduction.[39]

Ethics—Beyond Autopoiesis

Both Maturana and Varela spent substantial effort in working out the social-ethical implications of their work beyond any technical concern for the tight definition of autopoiesis. Remaining in Chile during the difficult and dangerous years of the Pinochet regime when many colleagues and students fled, Maturana developed dynamic systems theory in areas of ethics, psychotherapy, and education. As noted above, one of the reasons why Maturana protested against Luhmann and Jantsch's extension of the concept of autopoiesis beyond second-order living systems to focus on autonomous, artificial institutional communication systems is that they dealt with the development of social order without focusing on the critical role of humans.[40] Even more strongly, Maturana contended that they effectively eliminated individuals, thus undercutting democracy—a manifestation of his social theory's complex position regarding the "liberal subject,"[41] which indeed was important in the face of the oppressive regime under which he lived. In this body of work he focused on action insofar as it is embedded in networks of social relations and on the pedagogy of listening, as granting others a space of legitimate presence. He strove to reconnect science and ethics via the concept of structural coupling, especially by rejecting the often dominant scientific ideas of objective distance and separation. In *From Being to Doing: The Origins of the Biology of Cognition,* he considers how political power struggles, insofar as they constitute an autonomous system, incorporate—actually dominate—others. He stresses how the fact that we bring forth a world with our acts of understanding and awareness can give rise to the feeling of responsibility for what we are doing. As all of us bring forth a world, both as individual consciousnesses and as members of specific linguistic-cultural groups, a space of common reflection opens up, a sphere of cooperation. Hence it is not only important but fully legitimate to critique totalitarianism/imperialism, which forces the view of one group on the highly diverse range of others, rather than respecting the latters' autonomously generated worldviews.

Since for his core theory cognition, perception, and action operate by recursive cospecification, emotions in fact are dispositions for action. Thus Maturana can and does call for mindful action—reflective responsibility—that results in care for someone else. In short: "love is the prime emotion that makes ethical behavior possible"[42] and from which mutual trust and respect can emerge. Though beyond the scope of this chapter, his work on therapy and pedagogy includes cofounding, with Ximena Dávila Yánez, the Matristic Institute for the teaching of the biology of cognition and the biology of love, in which emphasis on individualism, listening skills, and the multitude of worlds open to humans biologically would lead to respecting others' views while also being able to take responsible, reflective action to oppose them.[43] His influence in psychotherapy has been especially strong in the area of family, as initially spread by Paul Dell and journals such as *Family Therapy Networker* in the early 1980s.

For his part, Varela works out two especially important ethical-social insights that follow from autopoiesis. In light of the functioning of the entrained cycle of cognition, perception, and action, where for example what we perceive is recursively constituted precisely through perceptually guided actions, ethics would not consist of abstract theories or rules that we then apply in specific cases (as is one of the shortcomings characteristic of many major ethical theories such as deontology). Rather, it would be a matter of ethical know-how, a practical, experientially gained understanding and ability (more akin to Aristotle's *phronesis*). For Varela, this means that in the history of structural coupling in the lived situations of our recurrent microworlds, we acquire the resources for appropriate action. In our own experiences we generally become conscious of and respond to the needs of a particular situations; specifically, we do [can] in fact learn "concern and appropriate action for the welfare of others" (know how). In this regard Varela elaborates details of this view with the teachings of the Confucian master Meng-tzu (Mencius) on human capacities. In the course of our lives, the regularities of our embodied consciousness and action (which play across the constant flow of unique experiences) generate a large number of dispositions. At the level of interactions with other persons, these include compassion—the capacity for authentic caring.[44]

To highlight another of their interesting differences, in contrast with Maturana, in Varela's ethical theory he replaces the traditional Western idea of the substantial, basically fixed subject with a) the autopoietic view that in our situated embodiment we have a flow of processes, coconstituting our experiences of coherent life in our relatively constant worlds, and with b) the idea of "no self," which he pursues by developing the connections between his thought and Buddhist traditions of mindfulness and nondualism, especially by comparing the Madhyamika views of Naajuna with Merleau-Ponty.[45] These varieties of Buddhism, he believes, appear to hold insights into how we have the impression of self-continuity while in fact there is no self: the sense of continuity is, in fact, a series of iterations, or microidentities that occur as "readiness to action" in the lived context of recurrent microworlds (that arise and subside in a succession of shifting patterns). Hence dispositions for compassion can emerge in the course of our lives in the midst of others.

AUTOPOIETIC APPLICATIONS, DEVELOPMENTS, AND INFLUENCES

The core dimensions and findings of autopoiesis provide a rich basis for the elaboration of specific scientific issues. This is especially true of the implications of their view on the limitations of the observer, the emphasis on whole organisms (second-order living systems), and the recurrent, centripetal self-production and maintenance of organizational pattern and processes. Here we find a wide range of investigations, which Maturana and Varela usually carry out with a variety—indeed a large number—of other colleagues rather than just with each other.

Emphasis on the Organism, Development, Evolution, and Natural Drift

The core emphasis on first- and second-order living systems, especially the latter where the whole organism is seen to display the most magnificent dynamic of organizational closure and structural coupling, leads to

Maturana and Varela having powerful insights that do not agree with the dominant, received positions.

In regard to evolution, Maturana and Varela have argued that, given the priority of autopoiesis and autonomy in understanding living systems, self-constitution and maintenance are the features of primary importance. It follows that self-reproduction is not intrinsic to the definition of the living— a perhaps unsettling idea. After the primary autopoiesis, reproduction follows as a "complexification": "Reproduction requires the existence of a unity to be reproduced, and it is necessarily secondary to the establishment of such a unity."[46] The autopoietic emphasis on the organism counters the neo-Darwinian overemphasis on populations, thus playing an important role in the larger movement, which includes developmental systems theory (DST) and dialectical biology in contesting the neo-Darwinian shift from the individual to species.[47] Parallel to this disagreement about the macroscale, the same sort of opposition against the current overemphasis on the gene occurs at the microscale.[48] As is pointed out repeatedly with too little avail to both professional scientists and the general public, DNA operates only within a cell's metabolism and that, in turn, only within the organism as a unity. Further, it is not simply genes or DNA that are reproduced, but the whole organism with its full autopoietic capacity—which is what makes living systems what they are and enables life to continue (otherwise we would have just inert material elements).[49] The importance of the "processes in which the structures are formed and the constraints that delimit possibilities for change" are often overlooked in attempts to explain evolution.[50] However, evolutionary change critically depends on "functioning developmental systems, ecologically embedded genomes."[51] Indeed, growth and developmental studies have assumed increased importance in accounting for how an organism "maintains a unity" at all times, a unity in its fullness, not in exhibiting a transformation from incomplete to complete, while undergoing dynamic, discontinuous change.[52] Current research and reassessments in developmental systems theory (DST), constructivist interactionism, emergence, and coevolution are elaborating an epigenetic position (versus the performatist view wherein development is understood to "be performed by genes") that clarifies the interactive dynamic among organisms and their environments.[53] Not only humans but organisms at all scales modify and are modified by their environments in ways that are far more complex than are accounted for in dominant neo-Darwinian genetic-environment modeling.[54] "In general, the morphology, physiology, metabolism, and behavior, i.e., the phenotype of an organism at any moment in its life is a product of both the genes transmitted from the parents and the environment in which development has occurred up until that moment."[55]

Empirical and theoretical analyses of organism-engineered environments further show that a higher-order self-organizing system (beyond autopoietic cells and individual organisms) unfolds when the environments selected as relevant, produced, or modified influence the development of offspring, for example in the cases of oviparous insects or with the nurturing that occurs in nests and dens. Such niche construction provides "a bonafide inheritance system" that shapes future populations.[56] "The point here is that as embryological landscapes and genetic networks become more familiar, the most powerful explanatory accounts will appeal increasingly to the intrinsic self-organizing properties of such networks" that emerge in the course of the "mutual enfoldment of life and world."[57]

If organisms primarily live through processes of autopoiesis, both organization and the adaptation that comes via structural coupling are what are most importantly conserved, not only in the lifetime of the organism, but over time and reproduction if the living are to remain living.[58] Since the autopoiesis of the individual cells of a multicellular system is subordinate to the organism's autopoiesis and thus to a second-order system, neither the micro—the genetic—nor the macro—the species—is at the heart of evolution, any more than it is in development.[59] Instead, the global character of whole organisms is the key factor. Maturana and Varela introduce the term "natural drift" to characterize the evolutionary process: over the course of an organism's life the structural couplings are highly variable, so naturally there will be dynamic changes in the organism. This means that conserving that coupling over continuous generations will result in a history of changes that are transformative but not teleological—since they are based on what turns out to continue, at each moment, to be relevant to the organism.[60] Hence we arrive back at evolution but with a fresh interpretation.

Immunology

Maturana and Varela devoted substantial energy, working with many others, to elaborate the nervous and immune networks as rich, distributed, autonomous cognitive systems. In specific application to immunology, Varela continued to be a key figure in developing the Autonomous Network Theory (ANT) that has opposed the dominant Clonal Selection Theory (CST) paradigm of self/nonself-differentiation and the application of ideas of linear causality.[61] The most active revisionary pursuit of "such an ambitious theoretical and experimental program" has been by the Paris School (Antonio Coutinho, John Stewart, Francisco Varela, Nelson Vaz, and colleagues).[62]

Scientific debates have centrally involved evidence and interpretation in regard to autoimmunity and, congruently, concerning recognition and reaction to the self and to foreign antigens. The complex of phenomena is usually referred to as the AI (Auto-Immune) Network. Because their early work already rejected (and replaced) the received metaphysical and scientific view in which subjects and objects, inside and outside are posited as fundamental categorical phenomena and the objective observer is unquestioned as the source of knowledge, it became clear that a new approach to immunology was possible.[63] With organizational closure and structural plasticity, autopoietic theory could overcome the failure of the reigning system to account for what was taken to be "immunological tolerance to autocomponents." Since we apparently do not react to self-antigens, it was assumed they must be eliminated very early in life; but further observations found that autoantigens are normal in newborns and adults. This means that immune responses against "the self" are constantly going on. These responses had been taken to be among the ways in which the organism recognizes itself, an idea certainly limited by what now appears to be an overly simple idea of causality.

With autopoiesis, a change came not through novel experiment and evidence but at the fundamental level of an interpretation that provided an alternative explanation, shifting the viewpoint from an antigen-centered to an organism-centered one. The "central distinction would not be self/nonself, but a question of what can/cannot interact with immunological structure" so that the task would not be to attempt to define a fixed identity but to discern the difference between what is operatively intelligible and what occurs as nonsense/noise.[64] Here rather than being viewed as reacting "from the inside to what intrudes from the outside," the immune system is understood as an autonomous unit seeking homeostasis by restoring its balanced centripetal processes. Along with the nervous network, also an autonomous system, the immune system generates and operates as a freely distributed connectivity within the whole organism.[65]

Cognitive Science and Naturalizing Neurophenomenology

There are two areas especially worth noting in regard to the broader development and influence of autopoietic epistemology and ontology in relation to cognitive science: first-person approaches to consciousness and naturalizing phenomenology. These occur within and significantly contribute to the larger contemporary movements to appreciate consciousness as embodied, to overcome the erroneous metaphysical dualism of mind and body/subject and object, to replace the correlated inadequate theories of knowledge and communication as representational, and to appreciate situated knowledge.

Maturana and Varela's insistence that observers can only observe, describe, and try to understand the phenomena that appear to them of course rejects the classic scientific view that objective, distanced, disinterested knowledge is possible, much less the only valid knowledge. Part of the heritage and approach of the received view is that while a detached objective, second-party view is requisite, the supposedly contrary of "subjective" experience (as in a self's direct experiences) is rejected as of no significance for science; hence the interesting current work to elaborate the character of first-person dimensions of consciousness, including both their theoretical and pragmatic operationalization, so as to produce scientifically acceptable methodologies and corresponding formalization.[66]

A central tangled technical issue involves naturalizing phenomenology. The phenomenological character of Maturana and Varela's work on autopoiesis promises to avoid undesirable, even untenable, dichotomies of traditional research and reductionism; yet, at the same time, there are significant complications and contradictions.[67] To simplify, natural science and much philosophy wants to explain the world in unproblematic material terms without recourse to "extra-natural" phenomena or events, whether vitalistic or of any other sort.[68] Though not used consistently, "naturalism" is the term connoting the belief that 1) there foundationally and finally are only natural processes in reality and that 2) these are all that would count as providing acceptable explanatory knowledge.

Phenomenology has been at the forefront in actively resisting naturalism, viewing it as founded on untenable dualisms and as being unjustifiably reductivist. First, phenomenology argues that a materialist solution continues rather than eliminates the untenable matter-spirit, or body-mind dualism, in fact still operating with it but simply translating it into natural-material terms. Second, most phenomenologists follow the lead of the founder, Edmund Husserl, who aimed to refute naturalizing science because, he insisted, there are dimensions of phenomena for which purely materialist explanations cannot account. Heidegger, Scheler, and Merleau-Ponty pointed to the richer "meaning dimension" of phenomena that constitutes our primary realm of prereflective experience—the life world. This includes things such as experiences of being at home, moods such as boredom that orient our interpretations of the world before we reflectively or "rationally" think (in the ordinary sense), emotions as discernments of value and guides to action, or the very givenness of the phenomena as given at all. To this Maturana would add, for example, the encounter between two people.[69] Acknowledging the existence and need to interpret the realm of such "living experience of meaning and value," it is argued, clearly precludes reductivism, that is the acceptance of only physicochemical processes and the belief not only that all more complex phenomena can be reduced to such causal sequences among the basic components but also that there finally is no other meaning than these material-energetic events.

Phenomenology contends that both the problematic dualisms and reductivism can be avoided by holistic accounts that provide multilevel accounts of meaning that do not need to deny the fundamental character of the physical dimension of the world (many phenomenologists have broken with Husserl on the grounds that he remained within the mind-spirit dualism, simply moving in the opposite direction from naturalism by translating the natural into terms of the mental—the transcendental—finally in a form of idealism in his later work.) Specifically, many of the major phenomenologists, such as Heidegger and Merleau-Ponty, whose work turns out to be especially compatible with complexity theory and autopoiesis, often cited or even incorporated into the latter two, remain tensed with naturalism and seek a way to avoid the dualisms.[70]

The work of Maturana and Varela of course, as noted, does not include any "extra-natural" processes. They also participate in the mathematical exploration of complex dynamic systems, and thus are mainline figures and in agreement with other complexity thinkers such as Ilya Prigogine, Stuart Kauffman, and Harold Morowitz, as well as thousands of researchers who study what can be done by way of computer simulation of networks or the differential systems of physics, geology, etc.

It would seem that autopoiesis—and perhaps complexity theory generally—might satisfy all the demands of an adequate nonnaturalist theory. In one dimension, autopoiesis posits that all processes are generated from "the bottom up," from physical-chemical events, to living autopoietic processes, to the emergence beyond first- and second-order living systems of complex third-order linguistic-social life and to knowledge and ethical action (even love). No mysterious "extra-natural" forces or events are called for in these explanations. In another dimension autopoiesis both recognizes and gives an account of two complementary features. First, it explains how hierarchically organized lower level local phenomena—the biochemical elements within the cell, the cell within the organism, even organisms within their specific cultures—are constrained by the global properties of the higher-level network. This constraint of the subelements by the whole dynamic system often is seen as the best operative definition of a scientific "law." Second, it recognizes that the first- and second-order autopoietic units generate societies and meanings that themselves are not autopoietic: organisms are not only biophysical phenomena, but further bring forth realms of significance that amount to experientially meaningful and valued worlds. Thus, these latter spheres are acknowledged as higher-level emergent phenomena without reducing them to the material-energetic processes that lie even below first-order systems—since the higher dimensions are open and not deterministically set and since the lower levels are to some extent governed by the higher, nonmaterial meanings in the reciprocal causality of continuously recursive feedback loops.[71] A multilevel theory of meaning and explanation would avoid reductionism without in the least ignoring the generative power of the material foundation.[72] This might basically resolve the dilemmas if we could simply leave off here.

But mind-numbing complications set in, especially involving phenomenologists who want to naturalize the approach and because of the nonunivocal, even equivocal, meaning of the term "naturalize." In yet another twist, though Varela is exemplary in attempting a "middle" way in regard to both autopoietic theory and legitimized phenomenology, at times he embraces a materialism via a reorientation of Husserl's phenomenology and disagrees with Husserl's foundational view and mainstream antinaturalism. In the early *Principles of Biological Autonomy* he asserts that "our approach will be mechanistic," employing only physical forces and principles. He takes this as more or less the same as cybernetics and systems theory in general;[73] especially in Chapter 16, "Epistemology Naturalized," he aligns himself with Piaget and Bateson.[74] Similarly, in a late project, he coedited *Naturalizing Phenomenology*, a book that comprehensively covers all the major positions.[75] Some of the contributors—including Varela—make the argument that legitimate versions of phenomenology can overcome Husserl's position and reservations "to yield a new, naturalized interpretation of Husserlian phenomenology" and even of "the transcendental life-world" because current sophisticated mathematics and "scientific progress have made Husserl's position [on the limitations of these two disciplines] largely obsolete," since naturalism could be modified to fit with the "categories of a phenomenological ontology" and given that parts of Husserl's own work might provide "a legitimate way of understanding 'naturalization'" in "psychology and in the other natural sciences."[76]

More widely, some figures self-identifying as neurophenomenologists or cognitive phenomenologists combine and reject various arguments and evidence from Husserl and Merleau-Ponty and modulate the equivocal senses of "naturalize." Evan Thompson advocates for a "naturalism of neurophenomenology" (which he takes to be a correlate with Varela's view in his 1997 paper, "The Naturalization of Phenomenology as the Transcendence of Nature"):[77] "The naturalization of phenomenology as the transcendence of nature: searching for generative mutual constraints"[78] that would "pass from the natural attitude of the scientist to the transcendental phenomenological attitude" of philosophy proper by means of a "transcendental level of analysis" that could "integrate the orders of matter, life, and mind."[79] Shaun Gallagher and Dan Zahavi consider "a phenomenologically enlightened experimental science" that would proceed by "front-loading" phenomenological insights into experimental design, thus "informing the way experiments are set up," with the subsequent and reflexive intention to "test and attempt to corroborate the description" provided by phenomenology.[80]

The deeper question is not only whether one sides with Husserl's antinaturalism but whether phenomenology can or needs to be antinaturalistic (in one or another specific meaning of the concept). At the core, this debate unavoidably is situated within general cultural-scientific debates between the dominant received science and autopoiesis and, specifically within autopoietic theory, among basically naturalizing and nonnaturalizing positions. Autopoiesis itself cannot resolve those contrary issues; indeed it is unfolding within them, especially since it is variously interpreted and used within the context of complex dynamic systems theory, which, though substantially opposed to and attempting to supplant much of received science (in regard to causality, predictability, etc.), is itself subject to the same opposed interpretations. Systems theory, in its multiple varieties, is both the hope of those who would pass beyond traditional and naturalizing science and those who see it as the ultimately subtle elaboration and legitimation of just such an epistemology and ontology.

Thus Maturana and Varela's specific work on autopoiesis and living systems, their influence on a variety of other issues and fields of inquiry, and their and others' continuing development of cognitive science and phenomenology return us to open questions, outstanding issues, and disagreements—a good way to end the chapter.

NOTES

1. Francisco Varela, *Principles of Biological Autonomy* (New York: Elsevier, 1979), 241–43.
2. Varela, *Principles of Biological Autonomy*, 9–11; Francisco Varela, "On Defining Life," in *Self-Production of Supra Molecular Structures*, ed. G. Fleischaker, S. Colonna, and P.L. Luisi (Boston: Kluwer Academic, 1994), 29.
3. Humberto Maturana and Fransico Varela, *The Tree of Knowledge: The Biological Roots of Human Understanding* (Boston: Shambhala, 1987).
4. Varela, *Principles of Biological Autonomy*, 11.
5. Varela, *Principles of Biological Autonomy*, 241–42.
6. Varela, *On Defining Life*, 23.
7. Varela, *On Defining Life*, 28.
8. Varela, *On Defining Life*, 29.
9. Humberto Maturana, *From Being to Doing: The Origins of the Biology of Cognition* (Heidelberg: Carl-Auer Verlag, 2004), 67.
10. Varela, *On Defining Life*, 28; Varela, *Principles of Biological Autonomy*, 13, 50–59.
11. Varela, *Principles of Biological Autonomy*, 10.
12. Varela, *On Defining Life*, 28; Varela, *Principles of Biological Autonomy*, 253.
13. Varela, *Principles of Biological Autonomy*, 33.
14. Varela, *Principles of Biological Autonomy*, 33.
15. Humberto Maturano, "Autopoiesis: Reproduction, Heredity, and Evolution," in *Autopoiesis, Dissipative Structures, and Spontaneous Social Orders*, ed. Milan Zeleny, 45–79 (Boulder: Westview Press, 1980).
16. Varela, *On Defining Life*, 31.
17. Varela, *Principles of Biological Autonomy*, 247.
18. See Maturana, *From Being to Doing*, 106.
19. See Jerome Y. Lettvin et al., "What the Frog's Eye Tells the Frog's Brain." *Proceedings of the Institute of Radio Engineers* 47 (November 1959), 1940–1951. See also Jakob von Uexküll, *A Foray into the Worlds of Animals and Humans with a Theory of Meaning* (Minneapolis: University of Minnesota Press, 2010).
20. Francisco Varela, Evan Thompson, and Eleanor Rosch, *The Embodied Mind* (Cambridge: MIT Press), 1993.
21. Pauline Rosenau, *Post-Modernism and the Social Sciences* (Princeton: Princeton University Press, 1992).
22. Varela, Thompson, and Rosch, *The Embodied Mind*, 8, 99–100.
23. Varela, *Principles of Biological Autonomy*, 247; see also Varela, Thompson, and Rosh, *The Embodied Mind*, 1993.
24. See Terry Winograd and Fernando Flores, *Understanding Computers and Cognition: A New Foundation for Design* (New York: Addison-Wesley, 1987).
25. *Embodied Mind* is from 1993. See Francisco Varela, "Making It Concrete: Before, During, and After Breakdowns," in *Revisioning Philosophy*, ed. James Ogilvy (Albany: SUNY Press, 1992),103–11; see also N. Katherine Hayles, *How We Became Posthuman* (Chicago: University of Chicago Press, 1999), 157–58.
26. Varela, *Principles of Biological Autonomy*, 53.
27. Humberto Maturana and Francisco Varela, "Autopoiesis: The Organization of the Living," in *Autopoiesis and Cognition*, eds. Humberto R. Maturana and Francisco Varela (Dordrecht: Reidel, 1980), 108.
28. Maturna, *From Being to Doing*, 84ff, 105ff.

29. See Francisco Varela, Humberto Maturana, and R. Uribe, "Autopoiesis: The Organization of Living Systems, Its Characterization and a Model," *Biosystems* 5, no. 4 (1974): 187–96.

30. See Francisco Varela, "Structural Coupling and the Origin of Meaning in a Simple Cellular Automaton," in *The Semiotics of Cellular Communications in the Immune System*, ed. Eli E. Secarz et al. (Berlin: Springer, 1988). Hayles, *How We Became Posthuman*, 146–47.

31. John Mingers, *Self-Producing Systems: Implications and Applications of Autopoiesis* (New York: Plenum Press, 1995), 63.

32. Francisco Varela, "Describing the Logic of the Living: The Adequacy and Limitations of the Idea of Autopoiesis," in *Autopoiesis: A Theory of Organization*, ed. Milan Zeleny, 36–48 (New York: North Holland, 1981), 22–23.

33. Huberto Maturana, "Response to Jim Birch," *Journal of Family Therapy* 13, no. 4 (1991): 376.

34. Varela, "Describing the Logic of the Living," 38.

35. Varela, "Describing the Logic of the Living," 37–38; cf. Hayles, *How We Became Posthuman*, 154.

36. Varela, "Describing the Logic of the Living," 39–44; see also Hayles, *How We Became Posthuman*, 155.

37. Varela, "Describing the Logic of the Living," 39.

38. Varela, "Making It Concrete," xi.

39. Niklas Luhmann, "The Autopoiesis of Social Systems," in *Sociocybernetic Paradoxes*, eds. Felix Geyer and J. van der Zouwen (London: Sage, 1986), 174.

40. Maturana, *From Being to Doing*, 84ff, 105ff.

41. Hayles, *How We Became Posthuman*, 142–43.

42. Maturana, *From Being to Doing*, 205.

43. Maturana, *From Being to Doing*, 42–48.

44. Francisco Varela, *Ethical Know-How: Action, Wisdom, and Cognition* (Stanford: Stanford University Press, 1999).

45. Varela, Thompson, and Rosch, *The Embodied Mind*.

46. Varela, *Principles of Biological Autonomy*, 30.

47. For DST see Susan Oyama, *The Ontogeny of Information: Developmental Systems and Evolution* (Durham, NC: Duke University Press, 2000); for work on dialectical biology, see Richard C. Lewontin and Richard Levins, *Biology under the Influence* (New York: Monthly Review Press, 2007).

48. Richard C. Lewontin, *Biology as Ideology: The Doctrine of DNA* (New York: Harper Perennial, 1991); Evelyn Fox Keller, *The Century of the Gene* (Cambridge: Harvard University Press, 2000).

49. Varela, *Principles of Biological Autonomy*; Humberto R. Maturana, "Biology of Cognition," in *Autopoiesis and Cognition*, eds. Humberto R. Maturana and Francisco Varela (Dordrecht: Reidel, 1980).

50. Varela, Thompson, and Rosch, *The Embodied Mind*, 189–90.

51. Oyama, *The Ontogeny of Information*, 122; and cited in Varela, Thompson, and Rosch, *The Embodied Mind*, 200.

52. Varela, *Principles of Biological Autonomy*, p. 67.

53. Susan Oyama, Paul E. Griffiths, and Russell D. Gray, eds., *Cycles of Contingency: Developmental Systems and Evolution* (Cambridge: MIT Press, 2001), 4.

54. Robert Mugerauer, "The City: A Legacy of Organism-Environment Interactions at Every Scale," in *The Natural City*, eds. Ingrid Leman Stefanovic and Stephen Bede Scharper (Toronto: University of Toronto Press, 2010).

55. Levins and Lewontin, *Biology under the Influence*, 90–93, 91; Mugerauer, "The City," 262.

56. Kevin N. Laland, F. John Odling-Smee, and Marcus W. Feldman, "Niche Construction, Ecological Inheritance, and Cycles of Contingency in Evolution," in *Cycles of Contingency,* eds. Susan Oyama, Paul E. Griffiths, and Russell D. Gray. (Cambridge: MIT Press, 2001), 118–20; Kim Sterelny, "Niche Construction, Developmental Systems, and the Extended Replicator," in *Cycles of Contingency,* 336.

57. Varela, Thompson, and Rosch, *The Embodied Mind,* 190–191, 200.

58. Maturana and Varela, *The Tree of Knowledge,* 103.

59. Maturana and Varela, *The Tree of Knowledge,* 100.

60. Maturana and Varela, *The Tree of Knowledge,* 107–17.

61. Varela, *Principles of Biological Autonomy,* 218.

62. Alfred I. Tauber, *The Immune Self: Theory or Metaphor?* (New York: Cambridge University Press, 1994), 172; cf. Francisco Varela and Antonio Coutinho, "Second Generation Immune Networks," *Immunology Today* 12 (1991): 159–66.

63. Varela, *Principles of Biological Autonomy.*

64. Varela, *Principles of Biological Autonomy,* 218.

65. See Varela, *Principles of Biological Autonomy*; Varela and Coutinho, "Second Generation Immune Networks"; Tauber, *The Immune Self.*

66. Francisco Varela and Jonathan Shear, eds. *The View From Within: First-Person Approaches to the Study of Consciousness* (Bowling Green, Ohio: Imprint Academic, 1999).

67. Francisco Varela, "On Defining Life," in *Self-Production of Supramolecular Structures,* eds. Gail R. Fleischaker, Stefano Colonna, and Pier Luigi Luisi (Boston: Kluwer Academic, 1994), 10–11.

68. See Varela, "On Defining Life."

69. Maturana, *From Being to Doing,* 109.

70. Robert Mugerauer, "Anatomy of Life and Well-Being: A Framework for the Contributions of Phenomenology and Complexity Theory," *International Journal of Qualitative Studies of Health & Well-Being* 5, no. 2 (2010), doi: 10.3402/qhw.v512.v512.5097.

71. Varela, "On Defining Life," 9–11.

72. Maturana, *From Being to Doing,* 109.

73. Varela, *Principles of Biological Autonomy,* 6.

74. Varela, *Principles of Biological Autonomy,* 271.

75. Petitot et al., *Naturalizing Phenomenology: Issues in Contemporary Phenomenology and Cognitive Science* (New York: Cambridge University Press, 1999).

76. Jean Petitot et al., *Naturalizing Phenomenology,* 42–43, 83–110, 226–44, 317–29, 440–63.

77. Francisco Varela, "The Naturalization of Phenomenology as the Transcendence of Nature: Searching for Generative Mutual Constraints," *Alter: Revue de Phenomenlogie* 5 (1997): 355–81.

78. Evan Thompson, *Mind in Life: Biology, Phenomenology, and the Sciences of the Mind* (Cambridge, MA: Harvard University Press, 2007), 355–81.

79. Thompson, *Mind in Life,* 81–87, 237–42, 356–59.

80. Shaun Gallagher and Dan Zahavi, *The Phenomenological Mind* (New York: Routledge, 2008), 28–40.

REFERENCES

Gallagher, Shaun, and Dan Zahavi. *The Phenomenological Mind.* New York: Routledge, 2008.

Hayles, N. Katherine. *How We Became Posthuman.* Chicago: University of Chicago Press, 1999.

Keller, Evelyn Fox. *The Century of the Gene.* Cambridge: Harvard University Press, 2000.

Laland, Kevin N., F. John Odling-Smee, and Marcus W. Feldman. "Niche Construction, Ecological Inheritance, and Cycles of Contingency in Evolution." In *Cycles of Contingency,* edited by Susan Oyama, Paul E. Griffiths, and Russell D. Gray, 117–26. Cambridge: MIT Press, 2001.

Lewontin, Richard C. *Biology as Ideology: The Doctrine of DNA.* New York: Harper Perennial, 1991.

———, and Richard Levins. *Biology under the Influence.* New York: Monthly Review Press, 2007.

Lettvin, Jerome Y., Humberto R. Maturana, Warren S. McCulloch, and Walter H. Pitts. "What the Frog's Eye Tells the Frog's Brain." *Proceedings of the Institute of Radio Engineers,* 47 (November 1959), 1940–1951.

Luhmann, Niklas. "The Autopoiesis of Social Systems." In *Sociocybernetic Paradoxes,* edited by F. Geyer and J. van der Zouwen, 172-92. London: Sage, 1986.

Maturana, Humberto R. "Biology of Cognition." In *Autopoiesis and Cognition,* edited by Humberto R. Maturana and Francisco Varela, 2–58. Dordrecht: Reidel, 1980.

———. "Autopoiesis: "Reproduction, Heredity, and Evolution." In *Autopoiesis, Dissipative Structures, and Spontaneous Social Orders,* edited by Milan Zeleny, 45–79. Boulder: Westview Press, 1980. Originally published 1970.

———. "Response to Jim Birch." *Journal of Family Therapy* 13, no. 4 (1991): 375–93.

———. *From Being to Doing: The Origins of the Biology of Cognition.* Heidelberg: Carl-Auer Verlag, 2004.

———, and Francisco Varela. *Autopoiesis and Cognition.* Dordrecht: Reidel, 1980.

———. "Autopoiesis: The Organization of the Living." In *Autopoiesis and Cognition,* edited by Humberto R. Maturana and Francisco Varela, 63–134. Dordrecht: Reidel, 1980. Originally published 1973.

———. *The Tree of Knowledge: The Biological Roots of Human Understanding.* Boston: Shambala, 1987.

Mingers, John. *Self-Producing Systems: Implications and Applications of Autopoiesis.* New York: Plenum Press, 1995.

Mugerauer, Robert. "The City: A Legacy of Organism-Environment Interactions at Every Scale." In *The Natural City,* edited by Ingrid Leman Stefanovic and Stephen Bede Scharper, 147–64. Toronto: University of Toronto Press, 2010.

———. "Anatomy of Life and Well-Being: A Framework for the Contributions of Phenomenology and Complexity Theory." *International Journal of Qualitative Studies of Health & Well-Being* 5, no. 2 (July 2010). doi:10.3402/qhw.v512.5097.

Oyama, Susan. *The Ontogeny of Information: Developmental Systems and Evolution.* Durham, NC: Duke University Press, 2000.

———, Paul E. Griffiths, and Russell D. Gray, eds. *Cycles of Contingency: Developmental Systems and Evolution.* Cambridge: MIT Press, 2001.

Petitot, Jean, Francisco Varela, Bernard Pachoud, and Jean-Michel Roy, eds. *Naturalizing Phenomenology: Issues in Contemporary Phenomenology and Cognitive Science.* New York: Cambridge University Press, 1999.

Rosenau, Pauline. *Post-Modernism and the Social Sciences.* Princeton: Princeton University Press, 1992.

Sterelny, Kim. "Niche Construction, Developmental Systems, and the Extended Replicator." In *Cycles of Contingency,* edited by Susan Oyama, Paul E. Griffiths, and Russell D. Gray, 333–49. Cambridge: MIT Press, 2001.

178   Bob Mugerauer

Tauber, Alfred I. *The Immune Self: Theory or Metaphor?* New York: Cambridge University Press, 1994.
Thompson, Evan. *Mind in Life: Biology, Phenomenology, and the Sciences of the Mind.* Cambridge, MA: Harvard University Press, 2007.
Uexküll, Jakob von. *A Foray into the Worlds of Animals and Humans with a Theory of Meaning.* Minneapolis: University of Minnesota Press, 2010.
Varela, Francisco. *Principles of Biological Autonomy.* New York: Elsevier, 1979.
———. "Describing the Logic of the Living: The Adequacy and Limitations of the Idea of Autopoiesis." In *Autopoiesis: A Theory of Living Organization,* edited by Milan Zeleny, 36–48. New York: North Holland, 1981.
———. "Structural Coupling and the Origin of Meaning in a Simple Cellular Automaton." In *The Semiotics of Cellular Communications in the Immune System,* edited by Eli E. Secarz, Franco Celada, N. Avrion Mitchison, and Tomio Tada, 151–71. Berlin: Springer, 1988.
———. "Making It Concrete: Before, During, and After Breakdowns." In *Revisioning Philosophy,* edited by James Ogilvy, 103–11. Albany: SUNY Press, 1992.
———. "On Defining Life." In *Self-Production of Supra Molecular Structures,* edited by Gail R. Fleischaker, Stefano Colonna, and Pier Luigi Luisi, 23–31. Boston: Kluwer Academic, 1994.
———. "The Naturalization of Phenomenology as the Transcendence of Nature: Searching for Generative Mutual Constraints." *Alter: Revue de Phenomenologie* 5 (1997): 355–81.
———. *Ethical Know-How: Action, Wisdom, and Cognition.* Stanford: Stanford University Press, 1999.
———, and Antonio Coutinho. "Second Generation Immune Networks." *Immunology Today* 12 (1991): 159–66.
———, Humberto Maturana, and R. Uribe. "Autopoiesis: The Organization of Living Systems, Its Characterization and a Model." *Biosystems* 5, no. 4 (1974): 187–96.
———, and Jonathon Shear, eds. *The View From Within: First-Person Approaches to the Study of Consciousness.* Bowling Green, Ohio: Imprint Academic, 1999.
———, Evan Thompson, and Eleanor Rosch. *The Embodied Mind.* Cambridge: MIT Press, 1993.
Winograd, Terry, and Fernando Flores. *Understanding Computers and Cognition: A New Foundation for Design.* New York: Addison-Wesley, 1987.
Zeleny, Milan, ed. *Autopoiesis, Dissipative Structures, and Spontaneous Social Orders.* Boulder: Westview Press, 1980.
———, ed. *Autopoiesis: A Theory of Organization.* New York: North Holland, 1981.

8 Eugene Odum and the Homeostatic Ecosystem
The Resilience of an Idea

Joel B. Hagen

INTRODUCTION

Although the ecosystem is an important ecological concept, it has been highly contested. The idea originated from a dispute over the nature of biological communities.[1] During the early twentieth century, the prominent American ecologist Frederic Clements claimed that plant communities could be thought of as "complex organisms" that underwent a predictable pattern of development (ecological succession) leading to a mature, climax community in harmony with its physical environment. The idea that communities of living organisms are themselves organisms was controversial, and in 1935 the British ecologist Arthur Tansley proposed the ecosystem as a more philosophically acceptable concept.[2] Inspired by developments in the physical sciences, as well as his deep interests in philosophy and Freudian psychology, Tansley claimed that biotic communities and abiotic environments formed interacting systems.[3] Because these systems overlap and are always parts of more encompassing systems, Tansley argued that ecosystems were mental constructs. Nonetheless, in many cases ecosystems corresponded closely to a physical reality. For example, ponds or lakes often have well-defined boundaries that partially separate them from surrounding areas. But even in cases where boundaries are less distinct (e.g. a forest intergrading into grassland) the ecologist could mentally construct a system of interacting physical and biological components, at least some of whose properties could be measured. After World War II, ecosystem ecology flourished as an important area of research. With the rise of environmental movements in the 1960s and '70s, the ecosystem concept also entered popular culture.[4]

Although ecosystem ecologists usually avoided Clements's overt organicism, traces of organismal thinking continued and indeed expanded in novel ways. The idea that ecosystems develop in an orderly way through the process of succession remained important for many ecologists. The flow of energy and cycling of chemicals through the ecosystem was often described as a form of metabolism. Most importantly for the purposes of this essay, ecosystems were conceived as capable of self-regulation through a form of homeostasis.

It is probably no coincidence that the maintenance of stability in an eco-system was often described as homeostatic or cybernetic. During the 1930s when the ecosystem was first proposed, ideas of organic self-regulation were already well established in physiology. The term "homeostasis" was coined by the prominent Harvard medical physiologist Walter Cannon, who popu-larized the idea in his influential book *The Wisdom of the Body.*[5] Cannon's research on nerves and hormones had a profound effect on the develop-ment of cybernetics and systems thinking in general (Hammond 2003). After World War II, biologists in a number of fields, including ecology, genetics, and developmental biology, employed homeostasis and cybernet-ics to explain the self-regulation they found at various levels of biological organization.

EUGENE ODUM AND THE CYBERNETIC ECOSYSTEM

The idea that ecosystems are self-regulating in a homeostatic or cybernetic way was perhaps most thoroughly developed during the post-World War II period by Eugene Odum.

Although not necessarily representative of all ecosystem ecologists, Odum played a pivotal role in the development of the specialty.[6] Together with his brother, Howard Thomas Odum, he pioneered large-scale studies of various ecosystems. He forged a special relationship with the Atomic Energy Commission, which funded much of his early research and provided him the financial resources to build a highly successful institute of ecology at the University of Georgia. He was a leading figure in professional ecol-ogy, serving as president of the Ecological Society of America during the late 1960s when the organization was growing rapidly in size and influence. He effectively used this position as a bully pulpit for promoting ecosystem ecology, particularly in his influential but controversial presidential address "The Strategy of Ecosystem Development."[7] Through his many textbooks and other semipopular writing, Odum presented ecosystem ecology to a very broad audience. His *Fundamentals of Ecology,* first published in 1953, was revised and republished several times and was one of the most influ-ential textbooks of the 1960s and early 1970s.[8] In his textbooks, Odum effectively distilled the highly technical and sometimes arcane ideas of math-ematical systems ecologists in a way that students and nonspecialists could easily grasp. Thus, Odum became the most prominent advocate for ecosys-tem studies but also the most visible target for critics of systems thinking in ecology.

In some respects Odum's use of homeostasis to explain self-regulation, stability, and resilience in ecosystems is unexceptional. Beginning in the 1930s, prominent ecologists had argued that populations and communities are homeostatic,[9] and the idea that ecosystems are self-regulating entities was a commonplace notion that appealed to a broad spectrum of ecologists during the 1960s.[10] During the same period, homeostasis was also highly influential in the social sciences, and Odum's progressive commitment to the social responsibility of scientists as highly trained environmental problem solvers resonated with social thought of the post-World War II era.[11] However, Odum was unusual in the persistence and tenacity with which he argued for ecosystem homeostasis in the face of mounting criticism during the late twentieth century. Thus considering the development of Odum's ideas is important not just because he was an influential ecologist, but also because this episode sheds light on broader changes in ecological thinking during the second half of the twentieth century and the early years of the present century.

Looking back on his career, Odum claimed that the idea of ecosystem homeostasis was a natural extension of a well-documented physiological phenomenon to a higher level of organization.[12] Thus, homeostasis was an exemplar for Odum's holistic commitment to unifying science through the application of fundamental concepts across a "spectrum" of biological disciplines.[13] For example, Odum's doctoral research involved measuring the heart rate of wild birds in their nests using a remote sensing device. He hoped to use heart rate as an indicator of the overall physiological condition of the whole animal, and in his dissertation he attempted to correlate heart rate with metabolism, temperature regulation, and other physiological processes. He saw this as an interdisciplinary bridge between traditional laboratory physiology and ecology:

> In the study as a whole the primary interest has been in the physiology of the intact wild bird rather than in the functioning of the heart as an organ. An attempt has been made to combine the methods and viewpoints of the laboratory physiologist and the field ecologist and thus to bridge the all too wide gap between animal physiology and animal ecology.[14]

Odum also recalled that as a graduate student he read Cannon's *The Wisdom of the Body* and later used it as required reading in physiology courses that he taught as a young faculty member.

Despite his recollections that homeostasis was central to his thinking from the beginning, Odum's use of ecosystem homeostasis actually developed gradually. Although he discussed stability and self-regulation in a general way and even compared population regulation to the governor on a steam engine, Odum did not mention homeostasis in the original edition of his influential textbook, *Fundamentals of Ecology.*[15] In the second edition of the textbook (1958), Odum briefly discussed ecosystem homeostasis in the chapter on biogeochemical cycles. Unlike energy that flowed through the ecosystem in a linear fashion and was constantly lost in the form of heat, chemical substances could, in theory, cycle endlessly between the biotic and abiotic components of the ecosystem. The elaborate food webs were key components of this process, as were the bacteria and fungi that functioned as decomposers to return organic compounds to the abiotic environment in inorganic form. The important carbon and nitrogen cycles had numerous "compensating mechanisms" that ensured a constant exchange of elements between the abiotic and biotic components of the ecosystem. This idea of compensating mechanisms that maintained ecosystem homeostasis was much more thoroughly developed in the third edition of *Fundamentals of Ecology* (1971), where Odum explicitly linked the physiological concept of self-regulation to cybernetics and systems theory.

The gradual development of Odum's ideas about homeostasis closely tracks important external influences on his thinking but also reflects some inherent intellectual conservatism on his part. The second edition of Odum's textbook was significantly shaped by his brother, Howard Thomas, who contributed most of an entirely new chapter on energy flow. This chapter was based heavily on Howard Odum's groundbreaking study of ecosystem energetics in Silver Springs in Florida, but it more broadly reflected approaches to studying energy flow and biochemical cycling pioneered by Howard's dissertation advisor G. Evelyn Hutchinson and his students at Yale University.[16] Hutchinson had been active in the Macy Conferences, and although Howard Odum was unimpressed by his experience at one of the meetings that he attended, the general idea of circular causal mechanisms became a central part of the way both Odums thought about ecosystems. This broader intellectual context undoubtedly encouraged Eugene Odum to more explicitly articulate his ideas on self-regulation and homeostasis, but it is noteworthy that in the second edition of *Fundamentals of Ecology* there is no mention of cybernetics or other forms of systems thinking associated with the Macy conferences. This linkage occurred gradually during the 1960s as Odum became more familiar with the formal systems ecology that was being developed by theoretical ecosystem ecologists, most notably his brother Howard and Bernard C. Patten, who was a colleague at the University of Georgia. The third edition of *Fundamentals of Ecology* was written at the same time that H. T. Odum was completing his highly innovative *Environment, Power, and Society* (1971) and Patten was finishing *Systems Analysis and Simulation in Ecology* (1971). The formal systems ecologies developed by Patten and H. T. Odum, strongly shaped Eugene Odum's use of cybernetic descriptions of homeostasis in his later writings.[17]

In his mature writings, Odum used homeostasis in three broadly overlapping ways: as a universal characteristic of living systems, as a metaphor for self-regulation and stability, and as a philosophical perspective or general way of thinking about ecosystems. As part of his holistic approach to science, Odum's strongest claim about homeostasis was that it was a principle that operated at all levels of biological organization, from cells to ecosystems. Although the exact mechanisms of negative feedback differed from system to system, the general principle applied broadly. For example, Odum described experiments on laboratory populations of house flies and parasitic wasps demonstrating that the amplitude of population fluctuations decreased over many generations.[18] Odum used this example frequently to illustrate self-regulation and to argue that parasitism and other "negative" interactions between species tended to stabilize over time. He also suggested that species produced ectocrine substances that influenced the behavior of other species in a way analogous to hormonal control within an organism. At the level of the ecosystem, Odum claimed, energy flow and nutrient cycling generated self-correcting homeostatic controls that both maintained stability and produced resilience in the face of perturbations.[19]

Homeostasis also served as a metaphor for stability and harmony that had broader implications for human behavior. Odum believed that the before-mentioned experiments with flies and parasitic wasps illustrated a general tendency for parasitism and other "negative" relationships to evolve toward more harmonious interactions. Thus extensive mutualism and cooperation were characteristics of mature ecosystems. An example of this progressive evolution that Odum discussed in all of the editions of his textbook involved lichens. Lichens are a symbiotic association of a fungus and either photosynthetic green algae or cyanobacteria. Odum claimed that in primitive lichens the fungi were parasitic on their photosynthetic hosts. In these associations, the fungal filaments or hyphae penetrated the cells walls of the algae and extracted the products of photosynthesis. However, Odum believed that in more advanced lichens, a true mutualistic partnership evolved with the fungus providing inorganic nutrients and protection from desiccation and the algae providing energy-rich sugars and other organic compounds. This "lichen model" provided an important symbolic lesson for human impacts on the environment: "If man does not learn to live mutualistically with nature, then, like the 'unwise' or 'unadapted' parasite, he may exploit his host to the point of destroying himself."[20]

An unfortunate development of Odum's metaphorical use of homeostasis in this context was the implication that it was contrary to Darwinian evolution. Odum complained that the emphasis on "survival of the fittest" had led ecologists to put too much emphasis on competition and predation while minimizing the importance of mutualism and cooperation.[21] Thus, homeostasis (particularly in its cybernetic formulations) also provided a broad perspective on ecosystem studies that Odum increasingly couched in non-Darwinian evolutionary terms.[22] Instead of the "chaotic" results of natural selection, Odum argued, evolution was both predictable and progressive. This perspective was explicitly articulated in Odum's presidential address to the Ecological Society of America.[23] Here Odum drew strong parallels between ecological succession as an orderly, directional, and highly predictable developmental process and longer-term progressive trends in evolution. Odum claimed that both processes led to increased homeostasis in ecosystems and the biosphere as a whole. He presented a "tabular model" that outlined twenty-four successional changes that one could expect as ecosystems developed toward maturity. These were highly controversial claims, particularly at a time when evolutionary ecologists were arguing for the importance of natural selection. Not surprisingly, this high-profile professional address highlighted a rift between ecosystem ecologists and evolutionary ecologists that developed during the final three decades of the twentieth century.[24] It also encouraged a view on both sides that ideas of ecosystem homeostasis were antithetical to Darwinian evolutionary theory.[25]

CONTROVERSY: ARE ECOSYSTEMS CYBERNETIC?

Odum's ideas about the homeostatic ecosystem were part of the broad mainstream of biological thought during the late 1950s and early 1960s; however, by the time he was expressing his mature views on the subject, a backlash had set in.[26] A mostly younger group of evolutionary biologists argued against the pervasive cooperation and stability that Odum believed were characteristic of nature. For these evolutionary ecologists, individuals and populations rather were of greater interest than ecosystems.

Ironically, given this rift in ecology, the most incisive criticism of the cybernetic ecosystem came not from evolutionary ecologists but from two medical researchers. In a short article published in the *American Naturalist,* the biophysicist Joseph Engelberg and physiologist Louis Boyarsky presented a detailed critique of Odum's claims about homeostasis. According to the two medical researchers, cybernetic systems had three characteristics that were absent in ecosystems.[27] First, cybernetic systems such as organisms, computers, automated machines, and societies were characterized by "global information networks" that integrated the parts of the system. Second, this integration took the form of feedback loops that could be described as goal seeking. Third, this feedback always involved low-energy signals that controlled high-energy processes. Hormones and nerves controlling physiological processes in an organism was the paradigmatic example of this type of cybernetic or homeostatic regulation, but automated machines and human societies also met these criteria. Both Engelberg and Boyarsky denied that a feedback loop between predator and prey populations was cybernetic, because it involved "brute force" energy transfers rather than low-energy signals controlling high-energy processes. For the same reason, they denied that the carbon or nitrogen cycles acted to integrate ecosystems in the same way that hormones regulated the body of an organism or that automatic control systems regulated a complex machine. In short, Engelberg and Boyarsky argued that organisms were a bad analogy for ecosystems. An ecosystem might be a collection of cybernetic systems, but was not, itself, cybernetic.

Engelberg and Boyarsky's critique elicited heated responses from several ecologists that were duly published in later editions of the *American Naturalist.*[28] The reactions demonstrated how deeply invested many ecosystem ecologists were in the concept of homeostasis but also that the concept was often accepted rather uncritically. There was considerable grousing about laboratory scientists addressing ecological issues on which they had no expertise. Most of the articles repeated examples of mutualism, food chains, and nutrient cycling as evidence for ecosystem homeostasis without specifically addressing the criticisms of Engelberg and Boyarsky in detail. More telling, some of the articles made the unwarranted claim that accepting the views of Engelberg and Boyarsky was tantamount to denying the very existence of ecosystems: if ecosystems weren't truly cybernetic, then they couldn't exist. Patten and Odum couched this view in a way that placed their cybernetic viewpoint in opposition to a Darwinian worldview:

> Either the ecosystem is orderly in the way we have described, or its lack of chaos just happened to develop from unregulated Darwinian struggles between competing populations, all alone and uninfluenced except by each other, on a neutral stage of life. The latter seems implausible to us.[29]

This comment is telling for two reasons. First, Patten and Odum dichotomized order and chaos in a way that seemed to deny the possibility that ecosystems might be organized systems, but not in quite the same way as organisms, computers, or automated machines. Second, by claiming that natural selection (i.e. Darwinian evolution) could not account for order in nature, Patten and Odum reinforced the division that was occurring between ecosystem ecology and a population-based evolutionary ecology.[30]

This exchange in the pages of the *American Naturalist* might be viewed as a rhetorical impasse with the two sides largely talking past one another, except that one article specifically targeted the key criticisms of Engelberg and Boyarsky by raising what appeared to be a testable cybernetic hypothesis. Like the other respondents, Samuel McNaughton and Michael Coughenour (1981) claimed that ecosystems were truly cybernetic, but they also provided a fairly detailed example of negative feedback systems of sufficient complexity to be considered information networks in the sense used by Engelberg and Boyarsky. Specifically, the ecosystem-level feedback that they described involved low-energy signals regulating high-energy processes.

McNaughton and Coughenour described the interaction between the western pine beetle (*Dendroctonus brevicomis*) and the ponderosa pine (*Pinus ponderosa*), one of the dominant tree species in western forest ecosystems. Although the pine beetles caused high mortality in pines, there was some evidence that much of this death occurred in older, less productive trees. Thus the feedback loop between parasite and host might regulate the productivity and flows of energy and materials through the entire ecosystem. More importantly, McNaughton and Coughenour argued that this self-regulation was at least partly controlled by chemical signals involving volatile compounds produced both by the trees and by pine beetles. These substances acted as highly specific population regulators. For example, at low population densities female pine beetles secreted pheromones that attracted other pine beetles, but when population densities within a tree reached higher levels, females produced repellants. In some cases, these pheromones were metabolites of terpenes produced by the tree and there was also evidence that substances released directly by infected trees also influenced beetle behavior. These information-carrying molecules were all examples of the phenomenon of low-energy signals regulating high-energy ecosystem-wide effects that Engelberg and Boyarsky claimed was characteristic of cybernetic systems, but insisted was missing in ecosystems. Furthermore, the complex interplay among various chemical signals also exemplified other cybernetic characteristics that Engelberg and Boyarsky had ignored, such as amplification and signal specificity. McNaughton and Coughenour argued that this cybernetic regulation was not unique to ponderosa pine forests but was typical of ecosystems in general. They concluded: "This has nothing to do with ecosystems as superorganisms; they are, rather, truly cybernetic. It is impossible, in the context of this comment, to map the global nature of this single system. But note that it includes not just beetle and tree but also atmosphere, soil, beetle predators, tree competitors, and many other elements contributing to flows of information, energy, and matter. The beetles, chemicals, and trees are not cybernetic in and of themselves. Only the ecosystem of which they are a part is."[31]

The cybernetic hypothesis that McNaughton and Coughenour put forward predicted that pine beetles used information about current forest conditions to regulate their reproductive behavior and that this regulation led to greater constancy or stability of photosynthetic productivity in the ecosystem as a whole. Could this be documented? In a study of beetle infestations in various stands of pine forests in Yellowstone and Grand Teton National Parks, three forest ecologists explicitly set out to test this prediction by comparing tree growth rates in forests following a beetle infestation with control forests that were uninfected.[32] They found that even though beetles sometimes destroyed more than 40% of the canopy of the pines, productivity of the forest quickly recovered. This was because the beetles killed primarily older, less productive trees that overshadowed younger pines. Once the old trees were removed, the younger trees grew rapidly. However, in contrast to the prediction that beetles regulated productivity in a way that maintained stability, the productivity of infested stands was actually more variable than that of control stands. Thus, although one might characterize the relationship between beetles and pines as a feedback loop, Romme, Knight, and Yavitt denied that it was cybernetic in a rigorous sense.

McNaughton and Coughenour admitted that the signaling system was complex and that all of the details were not understood. But it was not just the complex effects of the pheromone-induced behavior among pine beetles that was open to question; it was also the interpretation of this behavior. Following earlier studies by forest ecologists, McNaughton and Coughenour suggested that the functions of pheromones and other ectocrine substances were population regulation and, by extension, regulation of forest productivity. This general way of thinking about "function" was increasingly challenged by a group of evolutionary biologists who wanted to restrict this term to goals or adaptations produced by natural selection.[33] Equally importantly, these evolutionary biologists argued that in almost all cases such adaptations or functions evolved to promote survival and reproductive success of individuals only, not groups. Any benefits to the population (much less the ecosystem) should be thought of as fortuitous side effects. This perspective did not necessarily deny the idea of cybernetic regulation of ecosystems, but if such regulation existed it had not evolved for the purpose of stabilizing ecosystems. Such regulation was merely a side effect of competing individuals acting to maximize their own reproductive success. In a popular and more reductive version, it was not so much selfish individuals as it was selfish genes that were the primary target of natural selection.[34]

The behavioral biologist John Alcock (1982) used this line of reasoning to argue against the view that pine beetles were cooperative or that their behavior had evolved for the common good of the population (much less the ecosystem). Instead, Alcock envisioned a situation where secreting or detecting pheromones was part of an individual's strategy to manipulate the behavior of other pine beetles in order to maximize individual reproductive success. Although sometimes pheromones acted as a means of communication, they could also be used for deception. For example, the pheromones that repelled other pine beetles when populations increased had evolved not as population regulators but rather as a mechanism of "deceitful exploitation" used by females to prevent overcrowding of their own developing offspring by competing females who might try to lay eggs in the same gallery. And it wasn't just competing pine beetles that used pheromones to manipulate one another for individual advantage. Beetle predators used a form of "eavesdropping exploitation" to locate their pine beetle prey by the pheromones that were intended to attract mates. Arguing strenuously against the "good of the group" hypothesis, Alcock relied on a thoroughgoing individual selection to explain the function of pheromones. Any group benefits from the beetle pheromones were "purely incidental" to reproductive success of individual pine beetles.

Of course, one might argue that the cybernetic mechanisms that resulted in the stability and resilience of ecosystems were due to the "invisible hand" of natural selection acting on selfish individuals or genes. However, during the late twentieth century there was little enthusiasm for this explanatory approach. Most evolutionary ecologists had relatively little interest in ecosystems, much less cybernetic ecosystems.[35] For those who were interested in ecosystem integration, there appeared to be a stark choice between the type of cybernetic regulation envisioned by Odum and the Darwinian struggle for existence—with the latter being the clear explanatory choice.[36] In the face of this widespread acceptance of individual selection, Odum continued to view evolution as a progressive process and to use the "lichen model" as the paradigm case of evolution leading to greater cooperation and mutualism. But like the pine beetles and ponderosa pines, lichens turned out to be more ambiguous than Odum thought. Mounting evidence supported the multiple origins of mutualism in distantly related groups of lichens rather than a progressive evolutionary trend toward cooperation. From the Darwinian perspective taken by most evolutionary ecologists, mutualism and parasitism were simply alternative strategies that evolved in different contexts to maximize individual fitness. Where Odum saw increasing harmony and cooperation, evolutionary biologists tended to see a "war in the world of lichens."[37]

CONCLUSION: THE RESILIENCE OF HOMEOSTASIS AS AN ECOLOGICAL CONCEPT

An important theme running through Eugene Odum's major writings was a holistic belief in the unity of science. The idea that general principles, including homeostasis, could be applied at all levels of biological organization both motivated Odum's approach to ecology and unified his thinking about science and society. Homeostasis was not just a physiological and ecological principle; it also encapsulated Odum's deep commitment to the responsibility of scientists, including ecologists, to solve pressing social problems—particularly environmental problems.[38] Critics have sometimes linked Odum's thinking with a discredited belief in the "balance of nature."[39] However, his idea of ecosystem homeostasis implied a dynamic rather than static balance. The self-regulation found in ecosystems was delicately maintained and could be easily disrupted by human activities. Thus, homeostasis was part of an argument for wise stewardship of the environment.

Unfortunately, Odum was often caught up in polemics that sometimes obscured rather than clarified issues. When the idea of a cybernetic ecosystem was challenged, Odum restated his position without seriously reconsidering the analogies and disanalogies among organisms, ecosystems, automated machines, and societies. Similarly, his commitment to cooperation, both in nature and in society, led Odum to reject Darwinian evolutionary theory in favor of a progressive evolution that most other evolutionary biologists increasingly rejected. These controversies led to a fragmenting of ecology during the late twentieth century rather than to the unified science that Odum had hoped for.[40] It also led to the questioning or outright rejection of ecosystem homeostasis by many ecologists.[41]

Still, one might ask whether slightly retooled ideas of homeostasis can serve as fruitful interdisciplinary concepts to link field ecology and laboratory physiology in the way that Odum proposed in his graduate studies on heart rates in birds. Some recent evidence would suggest that this is possible. Feedback has always been an important way of discussing ecological interactions,[42] and although ecosystem homeostasis is not widely discussed, it is still sometimes used in the ecological literature. In contrast to the conclusion of both Odum and his critics, ecosystem homeostasis also appears capable of embodying self-regulatory feedback in a Darwinian manner. For example, some ecologists have described the complex multispecies complex in the nests of leaf cutter ants as a "homeostatic fortress."[43] Although this metaphor probably would not have appealed to Odum, it captures the idea that self-regulation can be the outcome of a continuously shifting evolutionary balance of symbiotic interactions including parasitism, competition, predation, and mutualism. Aside from such metaphorical use, there have also been some attempts to theorize ecosystem homeostasis in ways that are consistent with Darwinian ideas based on population genetics. From one perspective, "information" that has been so central to cybernetic discussions of homeostasis should be reconceptualized in terms of evolutionary information embodied both in genes and in extended phenotypes rather than the energy flow emphasized by Odum and earlier systems ecologists.[44] What is particularly attractive about this approach is the deep interactivity of organisms and their environments. Viewing organisms as "ecological engineers" capable of constructing niches is a perspective not all that different from Odum's views. What is different is the innovative idea that constructed niches have important feedback effects on fitness and thus transmit evolutionary information from one generation to the next, just as genes do. These ecologists view their efforts as, among other theoretical goals, an attempt to restore the idea of ecosystem homeostasis in a thoroughly evolutionarily context.

When Engelberg and Boyarsky criticized Odum and his claim that ecosystems are cybernetic, they drew a sharp dichotomy between homeostasis as it occurs in organisms and the interactions between populations that occur within an ecosystem. Engelberg and Boyarsky denied that the intricate homeostatic signaling by hormones and nerves had any analogy in ecosystems, concluding: "Those analyses of ecosystems which include informational pathways, or which imply the existence of informational networks within ecosystems, do so by analogizing the ecosystem to an organism. This is a bad analogy, for organisms are not good analogs of ecosystems."[45] Most ecologists would emphatically agree that ecosystems are not organisms (or superorganisms), but ironically many microbiologists and molecular biologists have come to consider organisms as ecosystems. It is now commonplace knowledge that the body contains approximately ten times more microbial cells than human cells.[46] Microbial cells within this "microbiome" interact with one another and with human cells in a wide range of symbiotic relationships, including competition, parasitism, and mutualism. Furthermore, the multicellular host provides an environmental matrix within which microbial interactions can occur. Understanding the microbiome as an ecosystem has led some microbiologists to turn explicitly to ecological theory to explain such phenomena as the colonization of the gut by various microorganisms and the ways that the distribution and abundance of these microbes are maintained.[47] More strikingly, homeostasis, not only in mammals but also in simpler organisms such as fruit flies, appears to be maintained to a significant degree by molecular signaling between microbes and host cells. This self-regulation involving molecular feedback or "crosstalk" among multiple species within the gut controls the development of both host and microbiome.[48] The recognition of these ecophysiological mechanisms of self-regulation have led some microbiologists to call for a completely new approach to medicine, turning away from the idea of warfare against bacteria and embracing the idea of medicine as a form of wildlife management or applied ecology.[49] This perspective, which fuses ecological and physiological thinking, is certainly in the spirit of Odum's appeal for the unity of science and the social responsibility of ecologists. It also demonstrates the resilience of homeostasis as an ecological concept.

NOTES

1. Joel B. Hagen, *An Entangled Bank: The Origins of Ecosystem Ecology* (New Brunswick: Rutgers University Press, 1992).
2. A. G. Tansley, "The Use and Abuse of Vegetational Concepts and Terms," *Ecology* 16 (1935): 284–307.
3. Hagen, *An Entangled Bank*; Peder Anker, "The Context of Ecosystem Theory," *Ecosystems* 5 (2002): 611–13; Peter Ayres, *Shaping Ecology: The Life of Arthur Tansley* (Chichester, UK: Wiley-Blackwell, 2012).
4. Joel B. Hagen, "Teaching Ecology during the Environmental Age, 1965–1980," *Environmental History* 13 (2008): 704–23.
5. Walter B. Cannon, *The Wisdom of the Body* (New York: Norton, 1932); Stephen J. Cross and William R. Albury, "Walter B. Cannon, L. J. Henderson, and the Organic Analogy," *Osiris* 3 (1987): 165–92.
6. Hagen, *An Entangled Bank*; Frank Benjamin Golley, *A History of the Ecosystem Concept in Ecology: More than the Sum of the Parts* (New Haven: Yale University Press, 1993); Betty J. Craige, *Eugene Odum: Ecosystem Ecologist and Environmentalist* (Athens, GA: University of Georgia Press, 2001).
7. Eugene P. Odum, "The Strategy of Ecosystem Development," *Science* 164 (1969): 262–70; Gary W. Barrett and Karen E. Mabry, "Twentieth-Century Classic Books and Benchmark Publications in Biology," *Bioscience* 52 (2002): 282–86.
8. Hagen, "Teaching Ecology."
9. Gregg Mitman, *The State of Nature: Ecology, Community, and American Social Thought, 1900–1950* (Chicago: University of Chicago Press, 1992).
10. Donald L. DeAngelis, "The Nature and Significance of Feedback," in *Complex Ecology: The Part-Whole Relationship in Ecosystems,* eds. Bernard C. Patten and Sven E. Jørgensen (Englewood Cliffs, NJ: Prentice Hall, 1995), 450–67.
11. Debora Hammond, *The Science of Synthesis: Exploring the Social Implications of General Systems Theory* (Boulder: University of Colorado Press, 2003); Hagan, "Teaching Ecology."
12. Hagen, *An Entangled Bank.*
13. Howard T. Odum, *Environment, Power, and Society* (New York: John Wiley, 1971), 4–5.

14. Eugene P. Odum, "Variation in the Heart Rate of Birds: A Study in Physiological Ecology," *Ecological Monographs* 11 (1941): 299–326; here 301.
15. Eugene P. Odum, *Fundamentals of Ecology* (Philadelphia: Saunders, 1953).
16. Hagen, *An Entangled Bank*; Peter J. Taylor, "Technocratic Optimism, H. T. Odum, and the Partial Transformation of Ecological Metaphor after World War II," *Journal of the History of Biology* 21(1988): 213–44, here 205.
17. Bernard C. Patten and Eugene P. Odum, "The Cybernetic Nature of Ecosystems," *American Naturalist* 118 (1981): 886–95.
18. Eugene Odum, *Fundamentals of Ecology*, 3rd ed. (Philadelphia: Saunders, 1971), 220–21.
19. Eugene Odum, *Fundamentals*, 3rd ed., 34–35.
20. Eugene Odum, *Fundamentals*, 3rd ed., 233.
21. Eugene Odum, *Fundamentals*, 3rd ed., 1971), 228; Jan Sapp, *Evolution by Association: A History of Symbiosis* (New York: Oxford University Press, 1994), 141
22. Patten and Odum, "The Cybernetic Nature of Ecosystems."
23. Eugene Odum, "The Strategy."
24. Hagen, *An Entangled Bank*; Hagen, "Teaching Ecology."
25. Lauri Oksanen, "Ecosystem Organization: Mutualism and Cybernetics or Plain Darwinian Struggle for Existence?" *American Naturalist* 131 (1988): 424–44; Hagen, *An Entangled Bank*; DeAngelis, "The Nature and Significance of Feedback."
26. Hagen, *An Entangled Bank*; Hagen, "Teaching Ecology."
27. J. Engelberg and L. L. Boyarsky, "The Noncybernetic Nature of Ecosystems," *American Naturalist* 114 (1981): 317–24.
28. Carl P. Jordan, "Do Ecosystems Exist?" *American Naturalist* 118 (1981): 284–87; Robert L. Knight and Dennis P. Swaney, "In Defense of Ecosystems," *American Naturalist* 117 (1981): 991–92; S. J. McNaughton and Michael Coughenour, "The Cybernetic Nature of Ecosystems," *American Naturalist* 117 (1981): 985–90; Patten and Odum, "The Cybernetic Nature of Ecosystems."
29. Patten and Odum, "The Cybernetic Nature of Ecosystems," 891.
30. Hagen, *An Entangled Bank*; Hagen, "Teaching Ecology."
31. McNaughton and Coughenour, "The Cybernetic Nature," 986.
32. William H. Romme, Dennis H. Knight, and Joseph B. Yavitt, "Mountain Pine Beetle Outbreaks in the Rocky Mountains: Regulators of Primary Productivity?" *American Naturalist* 127 (1986): 484–94.
33. George C. Williams, *Adaptation and Natural Selection: A Critique of Some Current Evolutionary Thought* (Princeton: Princeton University Press, 1966).
34. Richard Dawkins, *The Selfish Gene* (Oxford: Oxford University Press, 1976).
35. Hagen, "Teaching Ecology."
36. Oksanen, "Ecosystem Organization."
37. Richardson, "War in the World of Lichens," *Mycological Research* 103 (1999) 641–650.
38. Hagen, "Teaching Ecology."
39. John C. Kricher, *The Balance of Nature: Ecology's Enduring Myth* (Princeton: Princeton University Press, 2009).
40. Hagen, *An Entangled Bank*; Hagen, "Teaching Ecology."
41. DeAngelis, "The Nature and Significance of Feedback."
42. DeAngelis, "The Nature and Significance of Feedback."
43. David P. Hughes, Naomi E. Pierce, and Jacobus J. Boomsma, "Social Insect Symbionts: Evolution in Homeostatic Fortresses," *Trends in Ecology and Evolution* 23 (2008): 672–77.

44. F. John Odling-Smee, Kevin N. Laland, and Marcus W. Feldman, *Niche Construction: The Neglected Process in Evolution* (Princeton: Princeton University Press, 2003).
45. J. Engelberg and L. L. Boyarsky, "The Noncybernetic Nature of Ecosystems," *American Naturalist* 114 (1981): 317–24.
46. Ann M. O'Hara and Fergus Shanahan, "The Gut Flora as a Forgotten Organ," *EMBO Reports* 7 (2006): 688–93.
47. Elizabeth K. Costello, Keaton Stagaman, Les Dethlefsen, Brendan J. M. Bohannan, and David L. Relman, "The Application of Ecological Theory Toward an Understanding of the Human Microbiome," *Science* 336 (2012): 1255–62.
48. Seung Chul Shin, Sung-Hee Kim, Hyejin You, Boram Kim, Aeri C. Kim, Kyung-Ah Lee, Joo-Heon Yoon, et al., "Drosophila Microbiome Modulates Host Developmental and Metabolic Homeostasis via Insulin Signaling," *Science* 334 (2011): 670–74.
49. Costello, "The Application of Ecological Theory"; Carl Zimmer, "Tending the Body's Microbial Garden," *New York Times*, June 18, 2012, D1, http://www.nytimes.com/2012/06/19/science/studies-of-human-microbiome-yield-new-insights.html?pagewanted=all.

REFERENCES

Alcock, John. "Natural Selection and Communication among Bark Beetles." *Florida Entomologist* 65 (1982): 17–32.

Barrett, Gary W., and Karen E. Mabry. "Twentieth-Century Classic Books and Benchmark Publications in Biology." *Bioscience* 52 (2002): 282–86.

Cannon, Walter B. *The Wisdom of the Body.* New York: Norton, 1932.

Costello, Elizabeth K., Keaton Stagaman, Les Dethlefsen, Brendan J. M. Bohannan, and David L. Relman. "The Application of Ecological Theory toward an Understanding of the Human Microbiome." *Science* 336 (2012): 1255–62.

Craige, Betty J. *Eugene Odum: Ecosystem Ecologist and Environmentalist.* Athens, GA: University of Georgia Press, 2001.

Cross, Stephen J., and William R. Albury. "Walter B. Cannon, L. J. Henderson, and the Organic Analogy." *Osiris* 3 (1987): 165–92.

Dawkins, Richard. *The Selfish Gene.* Oxford: Oxford University Press, 1976.

DeAngelis, Donald L. "The Nature and Significance of Feedback." In *Complex Ecology: The Part-Whole Relationship in Ecosystems,* edited by Bernard C. Patten and Sven E. Jørgensen, 450–67. Englewood Cliffs, NJ: Prentice Hall, 1995.

Engelberg, J., and L. L. Boyarsky. "The Noncybernetic Nature of Ecosystems." *American Naturalist* 114 (1981): 317–24.

Golley, Frank Benjamin. *A History of the Ecosystem Concept in Ecology: More than the Sum of the Parts.* New Haven: Yale University Press, 1993.

Hagen, Joel B. *An Entangled Bank: The Origins of Ecosystem Ecology.* New Brunswick: Rutgers University Press, 1992.

———. "Teaching Ecology during the Environmental Age, 1965–1980." *Environmental History* 13 (2008): 704–23.

Hammond, Debora. *The Science of Synthesis: Exploring the Social Implications of General Systems Theory.* Boulder: University of Colorado Press, 2003.

Hughes, David P., Naomi E. Pierce, and Jacobus J. Boomsma. "Social Insect Symbionts: Evolution in Homeostatic Fortresses." *Trends in Ecology and Evolution* 23 (2008): 672–77.

Jordan, Carl P. "Do Ecosystems Exist?" *American Naturalist* 118 (1981): 284–87.

Knight, Robert L., and Dennis P. Swaney. "In Defense of Ecosystems." *American Naturalist* 117 (1981): 991–92.

McNaughton, S. J., and Michael Coughenour. "The Cybernetic Nature of Ecosystems." *American Naturalist* 117 (1981): 985–990.

Mitman, Gregg. *The State of Nature: Ecology, Community, and American Social Thought, 1900–1950*. Chicago: University of Chicago Press, 1992.

Odling-Smee, F. John, Kevin N. Laland, and Marcus W. Feldman. *Niche Construction: The Neglected Process in Evolution*. Princeton: Princeton University Press, 2003.

Odum, Eugene P. "Variation in the Heart Rate of Birds: A Study in Physiological Ecology." *Ecological Monographs* 11 (1941): 299–326.

———. *Fundamentals of Ecology*. Philadelphia: Saunders, 1953.

———. *Fundamentals of Ecology*. 2nd ed. Philadelphia: Saunders, 1958.

———. *Fundamentals of Ecology*. 3rd ed. Philadelphia: Saunders, 1971.

———. "The Strategy of Ecosystem Development." *Science* 164 (1969): 262–70.

Odum, Howard T. *Environment, Power, and Society*. New York: John Wiley, 1971.

O'Hara, Ann M., and Fergus Shanahan. "The Gut Flora as a Forgotten Organ." *EMBO Reports* 7 (2006): 688–93.

Oksanen, Lauri. "Ecosystem Organization: Mutualism and Cybernetics or Plain Darwinian Struggle for Existence?" *American Naturalist* 131 (1988): 424–44.

Patten, Bernard C. *Systems Analysis and Simulation in Ecology*. New York: Academic Press, 1971.

Patten, Bernard C., and Eugene P. Odum. "The Cybernetic Nature of Ecosystems." *American Naturalist* 118 (1981): 886–95.

Richardson, David H. S. "War in the World of Lichens: Parasitism and Symbiosis as Exemplified by Lichens and Lichenicolous Fungi." *Mycological Research* 103 (1999): 641–50.

Romme, William H., Dennis H. Knight, and Joseph B. Yavitt. "Mountain Pine Beetle Outbreaks in the Rocky Mountains: Regulators of Primary Productivity?" *American Naturalist* 127 (1986): 484–94.

Sapp, Jan. *Evolution by Association: A History of Symbiosis*. New York: Oxford University Press. 1994.

Shin, Seung Chul, Sung-Hee Kim, Hyejin You, Boram Kim, Aeri C. Kim, Kyung-Ah Lee, Joo-Heon Yoon, et al. "Drosophila Microbiome Modulates Host Developmental and Metabolic Homeostasis via Insulin Signaling." *Science* 334 (2011): 670–74.

Tansley, A. G. "The Use and Abuse of Vegetational Concepts and Terms." *Ecology* 16 (1935): 284–307.

Taylor, Peter J. "Technocratic Optimism, H. T. Odum, and the Partial Transformation of Ecological Metaphor after World War II." *Journal of the History of Biology* 21 (1988): 213–44.

Williams, George C. *Adaptation and Natural Selection: A Critique of Some Current Evolutionary Thought*. Princeton: Princeton University Press, 1966.

Zimmer, Carl. "Tending the Body's Microbial Garden." *New York Times,* June 18, 2012, D1. http://www.nytimes.com/2012/06/19/science/studies-of-human-microbiome-yield-new-insights.html?pagewanted=all.

Part II
Systems Thinking in Sociology

Introduction to Part II
Systems Thinking in Sociology

Darrell P. Arnold

Part two of the book examines systems thinking in sociology. It begins with a depiction of the development of Talcott Parsons's systems views from his incipient early period, where he had some interaction with systems theoreticians and cyberneticists at the Macy Conferences, to his full-blown sociological systems perspective. Following that is a chapter on Niklas Luhmann, who has developed the most influential form of systems theory in the field of sociology today, though its influence has remained largely confined to Europe. This part concludes with a chapter on Immanuel Wallerstein and world systems analysis. World systems analysis is influenced not so much by early cybernetics and general systems as by an alternative set of ideas on systems traceable in lineage to Marxist and Hegelian thought. A chapter focusing on Wallerstein is included here because it is an influential form of systems thinking in sociology today and because the Hegelian, Marxist trajectory of systems thought with which it aligns needs to be acknowledged in any comprehensive treatment of the field of systems literature. If general systems theory and cybernetics represents a secret history of the twentieth century, then world systems analysis represents a renewed version of the Marxist, Hegelian tradition that is less secret, but vitally important to a contemporary understanding of systems interactions in the area of politics and economics.

In Chapter 9, "Talcott Parsons: A Sociological Theory of Action Systems," Betinna Mahlert provides a historical introduction to Parsons's thought. After examining some of his earliest views, for example as developed in *The Structure of Social Action* (1937), she looks at advancements toward a structural functionalism and the development of Parsons's AGIL system. Parsons draws attention to the social, cultural, behavior, and personality systems. Ends and norms constitute the two fundamental poles of Parsons's systems approach in his earliest work.[1] The further development of his theory occurs, as Mahlert notes, as he refashions key ideas of his early view as "analytic systems." Norms, she notes, then constitute "the structural elements of a social system," while values become "building blocks of a cultural system"; meanwhile the "actor" of the early system becomes "a human personality-system" and later "the behavioral organism."[2] She shows how action is treated as "an emergent property of the contributions of these four subsystems."[3] In his famous systems formulation, Parsons develops the famous fourfold scheme, "AGIL"—including adaptation, goal attainment, integration, and latent pattern maintenance. Every system is to fulfill these functions. After laying out such basic ideas of Parsons's systems theory, in her final section Mahlert compares and contrasts Parsons's systems view with the views of both Niklas Luhmann and Immanuel Wallerstein. She admits that Parsons is susceptible to the criticism of world systems analysis, that he overlooked imperialism and colonialism, but does point to recent work that accepts his views emphasizing a cultural component to modernization efforts, some that might be of value in the ecological crisis. Her final assessment of Luhmann's social theory is that while the focus on systems autonomy is fruitful, the theory would benefit from renewed attention to Parsons's original focus on "the interdependencies of social systems and personalities." Among other things, this might allow renewed interdisciplinary work, which ongoing Luhmann-based systems theory eschews.

While Niklas Luhmann's work has been required reading for German social theorists for over three decades, he still remains little known in the United States. Chapter 10, "Luhmann: Three Key Concepts, System, Meaning, Autopoiesis," by Walter Reese-Schäfer, provides one more opportunity to bridge that intellectual lacuna. Reese-Schäfer introduces Luhmann's thought by describing it in reference to three key concepts: system, meaning, and autopoiesis. His reference point is not Luhmann's 1997 *Die Gesellschaft der Gesellschaft* (the second volume of which is only now being translated into English as *Theory of Society II*). It is instead *Social Systems*, which was published in German a decade previous to *Die Gesellschaft der Gesellschaft*.[4] The German version of *Social Systems* was subtitled "Groundwork of a General Theory" and the work is generally still thought to serve as a fundament for Luhmann's work despite Luhmann's later developments.[5]

Reese-Schäfer begins his discussion of systems by highlighting the role of a particular paradox in Luhmann's work that is related to systems—namely, that while Luhmann is a constructivist, he also thinks "systems are real." Luhmann does not think his constructivism contradicts that statement. Rather, he views the two observations as paradoxical. The paradox results because it is precisely the real systems (with their inevitable blind spots) that allow the constructs in the first place.

Fundamental to Luhmann's view of social systems is that they consist of communications;[6] and while there are clear and direct influences of Claude Shannon and Warren Weaver on Luhmann's view of communication,[7] Reese-Schäfer draws attention to how Luhmann takes Talcott Parsons's views on communication and expands them "to a theory of symbolically generalized communication media, which steer the contexts of social communication."[8] In Luhmann, this presupposes the system-environment differentiation, wherein the system reduces the complexity of the environment, always in a particular system-specific way, filtering and ordering information from a complex world, using the codes of the particular system.

In developing his systems views along these lines, Luhmann applies the idea of autopoiesis from Maturana and Varela to social systems. Like biological systems, which simplify the information from the environment in a way that contributes to their self-maintenance, varying social systems also follow system-internal codes that allow them to simplify the complex information of their environments in a manner that facilitates their self-maintenance.

"Meaning" is another vital idea in Luhmann's theory. He understands it as a functional concept, applicable to humans and social systems, making observations within a system possible. However, the primacy of the human vantage point is denied in Luhmann's systems view, since the human access to the environment is merely one among many, and Luhmann sees no reason to privilege it. Nevertheless, Reese-Schäfer drives home the importance of psychic systems, which Luhmann is so often criticized for ignoring, quoting Luhmann himself: "Meaning enables psychic and social system formations to interpenetrate, while protecting their autopoiesis; meaning simultaneously enables consciousness to understand itself and continue to affect itself in communication, and it enables communication to be referred back to the consciousnesses of the participants."[9]

One of the most controversial ideas in Luhmann's thought is his very foundational one of applying autopoiesis to social systems. Humberto Maturana and Francisco Varela view it as illegitimate. Jürgen Habermas views it as a mere unproven presupposition. Despite its controversial character, numerous sociologists familiar with Luhmann have regretted the meager reception of his work in Anglo-American sociology. Zygmunt Bauman, one of those sociologists, has indicated that he thinks Luhmann's sociology might well be—and certainly deserves to be—discovered in the Anglo-Saxon world posthumously.[10] For now, his thought is primarily being assimilated into the United States through the channels that opened the Anglo-American world to French philosophy of the 1960s—literature departments. This is taken up by Andrew McMurry here in Chapter 14, and discussed by Philipp Schweighauser in Chapter 2.

In Chapter 11, "Systems Historicized: Wallerstein's World-Systems Analysis," W. L. Goldfrank offers a succinct analysis of global systems analysis, a variety of systems thought lying to a great extent outside the reach of the mid-twentieth-century developments of general systems theory and cybernetics and influenced instead by Marxism, German/Austrian institutional economics, French "Annales" historiography, and Latin American dependency theory. The focus of world systems analysis is on "socio-economic totalities," of which Goldfrank notes there have been three kinds: minisystems, world empires, and world economies. Goldfrank describes these, understanding them as "systemic, contradictory, and conflict-ridden totalities historically understood as the fundamental units within which social change occurs."[11] He particularly lays out how the core countries of Europe have dominated peripheral ones since the emergence of the modern world system in around 1600, highlighting tensions that this causes and ways that crises are dealt with *in* systems. After taking up criticisms of world systems analysis, he raises what he believes are the two most likely scenarios should the crisis *of* the current world system become full-blown: (1) an authoritarian global order, dominated by corporate elites, and (2) a future "democratic, socialist world polity."

This influential form of neo-Marxist thought makes a vital contribution to understanding contemporary systems, in part by virtue of its early shift in emphasis away from the analysis of the nation states and their respective social systems toward an analysis of global phenomena. Here, world systems analysis pays due and sustained attention to the role of coercion in creating and maintaining political and economic unities, where some forms of systems thought might be wont to see emergence or some less pernicious structural couplings.[12]

While world systems analysis certainly has lessons for other forms of systems thinking, it might, for its part, also benefit from further integration of elements of other systems thought—such as Prigogine's ideas might spur. Indeed, exchanges integrating Prigogine's views have occurred. Wallerstein has indicated the importance of Prigogine's concepts of the arrow of time and the end of certainty for social science.[13] For his part, Prigogine has asked what similarities there might be between a network society and the complex physical systems that emerge far from equilibrium.[14] Besides this, world systems analysis is also fruitfully applied to domains beyond sociology and history, such as literature. In Chapter 12 Andrew McMurry offers a glimpse of this, although his focus is also generally on other systems views.

NOTES

1. See pp. 205–6 in this volume.
2. See p. 207.
3. See p. 207.
4. Cf. Niklas Luhmann, *Die Gesellschaft der Gesellschaft,* 2 vols. (Frankfurt: Suhrkamp, 1997). Volume 1 has been translated into English as *Theory of Society*, vol. 1, trans. Rhodes Barrett (Stanford: Stanford University Press, 2012).
5. Cf. Helmut Willke's succinct treatment of this work, "Flexibilitaet als Formprizip," in *Schlüsselwerke der Systemtheorie,* ed. Dirk Baecker (Wiesbaden: VS Verlag, 2005), 291–303.
6. Cf. p. 233.
7. Cf. p. 29 in this volume.
8. See Niklas Luhmann, *Social Systems,* trans. John Bednarz, Jr. with Dirk Baecker (Stanford: Stanford University Press, 1995: 171). See also p. 233 in this volume.
9. See Luhmann, *Social Systems,* 219.
10. See Zymunt Bauman, "Review of *Observations on Modernity,*" Journal of the Royal Anthropological Institute 6, no. 3 (September 2000), 554.

11. See p. 243 in this volume.
12. Cf. Jürgen Osterhammel and Niels P. Peterson, *Globalization: A Short History*, trans. Dona Geyer (Princeton: Princeton University Press, 2005), 20f.
13. These remarks were made in Wallerstein's "The Heritage of Sociology, The Promise of Social Science," Presidential Address, XIVth World Congress of Sociology, Montreal, July 26, 1998, accessed March 7, 2013, http://www2. binghamton.edu/fbc/archive/iwprad2.htm.
14. See Ilya Prigogine's article in honor of Wallerstein's work, "The Networked Society," *Journal of World Systems Research* 6, no. 3 (2000), accessed March 7, 2013, http://www.jwsr.org/wp-content/uploads/2013/05/jwsr-v6n3-prigogine.pdf.

REFERENCES

Bauman, Zymunt. "Review of *Observations on Modernity*." *Journal of the Royal Anthropological Institute* 6, no. 3 (September 2000), 554.
Luhmann, Niklas. *Social Systems*. Translated by John Bednarz, Jr., with Dirk Baecker. Stanford: Stanford University Press, 1995.
——. *Die Gesellschaft der Gesellschaft*. 2 vols. Frankfurt: Suhrkamp, 1997.
——. *Theory of Society*. Vol. 1. Translated by Rhodes Barrett. Stanford: Stanford University Press, 2012.
Osterhammel, Jürgen, and Niels P. Peterson. *Globalization: A Short History*. Translated by Dona Geyer. Princeton: Princeton University Press, 2005.
Prigogine, Ilya. "The Networked Society." *Journal of World Systems Research* 6, no. 3 (2000). Accessed March 7, 2013. http://www.jwsr.org/wp-content/uploads/2013/05/jwsr-v6n3-prigogine.pdf.
Wallerstein, Immanuel. "The Heritage of Sociology, the Promise of Social Science." Presidential Address, XIVth World Congress of Sociology, Montreal, July 26, 1998. Accessed March 7, 2013. http://www2.binghamton.edu/fbc/archive/iwprad2.htm..
Willke, Helmut. "Flexibilitaet als Formprizip." In *Schlüsselwerke der Systemtheorie*, edited by Dirk Baecker, 291–303. Wiesbaden: VS Verlag, 2005.

9 Talcott Parsons

A Sociological Theory of Action Systems

Bettina Mahlert

1 INTRODUCTION

Systems theory was first introduced into sociology by the US-American sociologist Talcott Parsons (1902–1979). He laid the foundation for what was to become known as structural functionalism and developed a general theory of action. Parsons was probably the most influential sociologist during the 1940s–1960s, maybe even of the twentieth century. Perhaps as is to be expected, he was and is one of the most criticized sociological writers as well. Parsons was said to ignore the conflicts of social life and to miss the dynamic aspect of social change.[1] To many colleagues, Parsons seemed to present an "oversocialized conception of man"[2] that underrated the creativity and autonomy of human actors.[3]

Both Parsons's enormous influence and the heavy criticism of his work are closely linked to the breadth of his work, this breadth itself being intimately connected to his systems thinking. Parsons's work is broad in at least two respects. First, as a sociologist, Parsons dealt with an immense diversity of sociological themes—to name just a few: democracy; evolution; fascism; family and socialization; youth culture; the United States civil rights movement; modernity; the school class; the professions; and social stratification. Second, Parsons, who called himself an incurable theorist, developed not only a *sociological* theory but also a theoretical framework that was intended to integrate all disciplinary efforts concerned with human action in the cultural sciences, anthropology, psychology, and biology.

This breadth of Parsons's work is intimately linked to his commitment to a systems theoretical approach. For Parsons, to understand social phenomena requires seeing them within the broader context they are embedded in. Thus, he already very early in his academic career criticized economics for misunderstanding the profit-orientation of economic actors for an anthropological universal ("self-interest"). This mistake obviously resulted from isolating the modern economy from the larger social and cultural context it was embedded in. It thus resulted from an atomistic approach to the subject matter. But Parsons felt a need not only to regard the embeddedness of social phenomena but also to attend to a corresponding need for conceptual "context-sensitivity": when developing or using a theoretical concept, one is constantly to take into account the precise logical relationship of this to other concepts belonging to the same frame of reference. From both requirements, for Parsons, a systems theoretical approach logically followed.

The core concept of this approach, to Parsons, clearly had to be "action." Right from the beginning of his scientific career, social life for Parsons was to be understood in terms of human action. At the same time, he was convinced that the concept of action could integrate the disciplinary efforts of the social and cultural sciences (including psychology) into one general frame of reference. From this intuition Parsons developed an action theory that is informed by two basic ideas.

First, action is to be understood as a dynamic relationship between two poles or between two categories of elements, "conditions" and "ideas." Here, Parsons refers to the Kantian distinction between the two realms of the "physical" and of the "ideal." Kant's dichotomous use of this distinction had, according to Parsons, informed social thought throughout the eighteenth and nineteenth centuries—with positivism and idealism as the two great antagonists. Moreover, he discovered a corresponding distinction in biology: the distinction between heredity and environment. The overall aim of Parsons's theoretical efforts was to couch social scientific explanation in terms of the interdependence between these two poles rather than to perceive them in either-or terms.[4]

The second core idea of Parsons's work also takes hold of a distinction that polarized academic debates, at least within sociology. This idea is summed up by a formula that Parsons himself has created: "Action is system."[5] While many scholars claim that action theory and systems theory define two alternative and even hostile sociological approaches, Parsons was convinced that action could be conceived only as a system.

In what follows, it will be shown how Parsons translated these two basic ideas into a theoretical framework and how this framework developed in the course of Parsons's academic life (sections 2 and 3). Parsons's idea of modernity will then be briefly discussed (section 4). The final section relates Parsons's work to that of two other systems theorists (Wallerstein, Luhmann) (section 5). Before the details of Parsons's systems thinking are explored, a short biographical note is added.

Parsons grew up in a protestant home, the son of a protestant priest and headmaster. His mother was a member of the early feminist movement. Parsons studied biology, sociology, and philosophy at Amherst College and at the London School of Economics; he later earned his PhD in economics and sociology from the University of Heidelberg in Germany. From 1927 to 1973 he taught at Harvard, where he cofounded the Department of Sociology and, later, the Department of Social Relations. Through his life, Parsons combined his scientific engagement with an interest in political issues. Thus, for example, as a fierce enemy of Nazism, he joined the Harvard

Defense Group in the 1940s. He later opposed McCarthyism, and he also commented on the Cold War.

2   THE EARLY WORK: A VOLUNTARISTIC ACCOUNT OF SOCIAL ACTION

Parsons called his first theoretical account the voluntaristic theory of action. He presented this theory in his first monograph, *The Structure of Social Action*, where he developed it from a close examination of important lines of social theory.[6] A special feature of *The Structure of Social Action* is that Parsons does not distinguish his own theory by contrasting it with those other theoretical approaches he examines. Rather, he rather wants to make sure that he integrates the fruits of their intellectual work into his own theoretical perspective. Thus, he tries to show that he, Parsons, just picked up his theory in the books of the other writers he is discussing. In particular, he argues that the contributions of Emile Durkheim and Max Weber converged into one single theoretical framework—the voluntaristic theory of action. In this way, Parsons presents his own systems approach as a product of the evolution of social scientific thinking.

But which idea of a system underlies this synthesis? At this early phase of his theoretical work, Parsons compares his analytical frame of reference with that of classical mechanics.[7] He conceives of systems as *relations between analytical elements* that are nonrandom. Underlying this systems concept is an epistemological approach that Parsons calls analytical realism. Analytical realism basically means that the concept of action can logically be broken down into analytical elements. These elements do not themselves constitute unit acts, but they are necessary preconditions for those acts to come about. Action is thus understood as an emergent property of analytical elements and their interrelations. The sociologist can gain an understanding of social phenomena by asking: Which are the logically necessary elements of the concept of action, without which action cannot be conceived of? Which elements have to be present for action to take place? While asking these questions, he or she not only has to look at a single unit act but must also consider the relations between multiple actions. Empirically, these relations show a certain regularity. Individuals do not choose their actions randomly, and social interaction between two or more individuals normally is not chaotic. When breaking down the unit act into its analytical elements, the social theorist has to look for those elements that allow for this regularity and order.

The *Structure of Social Action* is like a journey through the intellectual universe of a couple of writers, undertaken in search of these analytical elements of social action. The starting point of this journey is an illuminating critique of some utilitarian writers, including Thomas Hobbes and Karl Marx. The last and major part of the journey discusses the work of

Durkheim and Weber. Both of them were, according to Parsons, at the beginning of their intellectual life committed to an influential intellectual tradition—Durkheim to individualistic positivism, Weber to idealism; both of them fell upon logical impasses within their respective conceptual paradigms; and both of them then transcended the immanent limitations of the conceptual paradigm they initially were bound to. Finally, both *converged* in the voluntaristic theory of action that fuses the true insights of positivism and idealism.

What then, according to the voluntaristic theory, are the analytical elements of action? Parsons gives the following answer:[8] For action to take place there must be an *actor*. His action takes places in a *situation,* and by acting the actor tries to realize an *end.* In order to complement this, he finds in his situation some factors that he cannot manipulate—these are the *conditions* of action; and he finds some aspects that he can manipulate and thus use as a *means* to realize his end. Last, "there is inherent in the conception of this unit (the unit act, BM) a certain mode of relationship between these elements"[9]: In choosing between possible means to his end, the actor applies a *selective standard,* a norm. Thus, for an actor, a situation consisting of means and conditions, an end and a norm, are necessary elements of action.

Of particular importance here are two of these elements—the end and the norm—for these elements establish the two above-mentioned core ideas of Parsons's systems approach. *Ends* are defined by Parsons in the following way: "An end [. . .] is a future state of affairs to which action is oriented by virtue of the fact that it is deemed desirable by the actor(s) but which differs in important respects from the state which they would expect to supervene by merely allowing the predictable trends of the situation to take their course without active intervention."[10] With this definition, Parsons establishes the idea that action is a dynamic relationship between conditions and ideas. For action is thought to be motivated by a difference between the *situation* as it is experienced by the actor and his *idea* of a desirable future state of affairs. Action is the process that dissolves this difference by modifying the situation in accordance with the idea, the actor's end. The effective relationship between ideas and conditions thus is constituted by a human will that mobilizes energy. The term "voluntarism" refers to this basic understanding of action. It refers both to the autonomy of the actor in choosing the end and to his commitment to realizing this end. In contradistinction to the voluntaristic theory of action, idealism and positivism each analytically reduces social action to one of the two poles. Positivism tries to explain action by deducing it from its "objective" conditions, thereby undermining the autonomy of action that lies in the imagination of an end. Idealism holds that action is fully determined by the actor's ideas, thus overlooking that action is possible only under concrete circumstances that enable and at the same time constrain it.

Now let's turn to norms, i.e. to the selective standards that establish meaningful relations between the different elements of action. This "systemic" function of norms becomes very clear in Parsons's discussion of what he calls "utilitarianism." Parsons's understanding of utilitarianism largely corresponds to what has now been developed as "rational choice" theory. In terms of a history of ideas, this is rather problematic, as Parsons ignores such writers as Bentham and includes, for example, Thomas Hobbes as a prominent utilitarian writer. But as a contribution to the problem of social order, Parsons's discussion of "utilitarianism" is highly illuminating. Utilitarianism is conceived by Parsons as a line of positivism—a line that has already transcended the inherent limits of positivism in one important respect: it defines the end of action as an independent analytical element. Utilitarianism conceives of actors as purposively striving to realize their own subjective and free ends. With this, it shares the basic intuition of voluntarism. But utilitarianism is under-complex when it comes to translating this intuition into a theory that comprises not only a single unit act but also action systems. For this to be completed, an adequate understanding of selective standards—of norms—is necessary. By enabling the actor to choose between different possible means and between different possible ends, norms interrelate the diverse ends and means that are part of an action system in meaningful ways. "Thou shalt not kill," for example, is a norm that prohibits killing as a means to realize a given end and in this way prevents social interaction from falling into a Hobbesian "war of all against all."

The crucial mistake of utilitarianism obviously is not that it denies this function of norms as a prerequisite of social order. For example, the Hobbesian contract—which, again, Parsons views as "utilitarian" in the broad sense—is nothing but a corpus of norms especially designed to stabilize social relations. The mistake of utilitarianism, in Parsons's reading, lies in the analytical place that it gives to norms within the action frame of reference: it locates norms on the condition-pole of action while they correctly must be located at its ideas-pole. Hobbes's contract theory reduces norms to conditions by assuming that actors have a purely instrumental relationship to those norms. Actors are thought to refrain from killing only because they fear negative sanctions, not because they themselves assign a value to the life of their fellowmen. They therefore conceive of the norm not to kill as a pure condition of their action whose implications for the actor have "rationally" to be taken into consideration. In a complex argument, Parsons shows that under these premises social order cannot be explained. If all members of society had a purely instrumental relationship to the prohibition of killing and to other central norms, social life would resemble a Hobbesian state of nature. Social order can be explained only by assuming that the members of society (or a crucial part of them) themselves *want* those norms. They must have the same *motivational attachment* to core social norms as to their "private" ends. Therefore, norms have to be placed on the ideas-pole of action.

Parsons accounts for this insight by subsuming norms and ends under the same general category of analytical elements: Norms and ends are normative elements, "normative" being defined as an "aspect, part or element of a system of action if, and only in so far as, it may be held to manifest or otherwise involve a sentiment attributable to one or more actors that something is an end in itself, regardless of its status as a means to any other end (1) for the member of a collectivity, (2) for some portion of the members of a collectivity, or (3) for the collectivity as a unit. . . . A norm is a verbal description of the concrete course of action thus regarded as desirable."[11]

Parsons's distinctive contribution to the sociological critique of utilitarianism lies in the proposition that ends or "interests" and norms or values are not to be set in a dichotomic relation. There is in social scientific debates an often stereotyped juxtaposition of "moral norms" against "material interests." This juxtaposition is dissolved in *The Structure of Social Action*, and so is the idea that conformity to norms necessarily implies a constraint on the "egoistic" pursuit of "individual" ends. Against this view Parsons holds: The ultimate basis of social order is not that actors feel "constrained" by norms. It is that the members of a given social system themselves have a normative commitment to the system's norms and "want" these norms to be realized.

3 FURTHER ADVANCEMENTS IN THE THEORY OF ACTION: STRUCTURAL-FUNCTIONALISM AND THE AGIL SCHEME

How did Parsons advance his theory after *The Structure of Social Action*? How did he elaborate the formula "action is system," and what did happen to the basic distinction between conditions and ideas? The focus of Parsons's theoretical efforts from the 1940s on was on the elaboration of the systems component of action. At that time, Parsons introduced a new systems concept into his theory. This concept is partly a personal creation of Parsons himself. He developed it by interlinking the two dimensions of "action" and "system" through a procedure of cross tabulation. Through this procedure, Parsons generated a fourfold scheme into which he integrated concepts from nonsociological systems thinking. Thus, during the 1940s, he was influenced by the physiologist Cannon and his book *The Wisdom of the Body*.[12] Parsons also participated in the Macy conferences and adopted several concepts from cybernetics and information theory.[13]

Roughly speaking, Parsons implemented his new idea of an action system by reframing central concepts of his early theory as analytical systems. Norms, for example, now constituted the structural elements of a social system; values or "ultimate ends" were understood as building blocks of a cultural system; and the "actor"-element of the early theory was transformed into a human personality-system plus, later on, the behavioral organism. These four systems were understood by Parsons as subsystems of the general action system. Action was now thought to be an emergent property of the contributions of these four subsystems.

In an intermediary period with *The Social System* as its main publication, Parsons identified three different subsystems of action.[14] But later on, he became increasingly convinced that there should be exactly four such subsystems—and neither three nor five nor six. This conviction was a result of his specific technique of cross tabulation.[15] Parsons developed his final systems theory by cross tabulating two pairs of variables. One of these pairs represents the action aspect of the formula "action is system"; the other one represents the system aspect. The pair that is located on the horizontal axis of the scheme identifies two different aspects of action: the "instrumental" and the "consummatory." The "instrumental" refers to the means that are to be mobilized to realize a given end. The "consummatory," in contrast, refers to the satisfying condition that results when the end of action has already been achieved. The vertical axis distinguishes between the "internal" and the "external." It denotes the external relations of the system, on the one hand, and the internal structures of the system, on the other hand. By cross tabulating these variables, Parsons arrives at four boxes. Each subsystem of the action subsystem fills one of these boxes.

To each of these boxes, Parsons assigns a specific function that results from combining the respective two variables. The combination of external and instrumental orientations for Parsons means adaptation: the system "instrumentalizes" its external relations as a means to produce satisfying relationships between itself and environment. In the social system, this function is performed by the economy. A second type of external relationship is realized by the combination consummatory/external. Here, Parsons speaks of "goal attainment," and he refers to the function of realizing a satisfying state of affairs in the present. In the social system, this is the function of the political system: while the economy provides resources for later use, politics has "to get things done" here and now. The third box combines "internal" and consummatory." Here, satisfying internal conditions are at stake, and these are thought to be realized by "integration." A system can realize satisfying internal conditions by integrating the actions of its multiple members. Finally, to the combination of "internal" and "instrumental" Parsons assigned the function of "latent pattern maintenance." This term reflects the necessity of stabilizing the internal structures of the system during periods of nonrelevance, that is, of latency. Nobody is acting in all his roles all the time; but the roles somehow have to be stabilized in the meantime. Thus, Parsons gets a fourfold scheme called "AGIL"—adaptation, goal attainment, integration, latent pattern maintenance.

Parsons is convinced that all of these and only these four functions have to be fulfilled by every system. AGIL is thus to be applied to the action system as well as to all of its subsystems. Thus, for example, the personality system provides motivation to act "here and now" to the action system. But to fulfill this function it must itself be stabilized as a system—it must fulfill the four functions for itself. It must somehow, for example, integrate different action motives, and it has to establish structures that remain intact

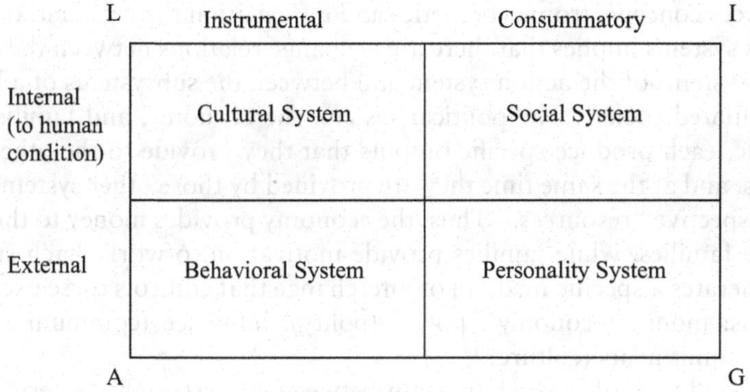

	Instrumental	Consummatory	
L			I
Internal (to human condition)	Cultural System	Social System	
External	Behavioral System	Personality System	
	A		G

Figure 9.1 The action system. A = Adaptation, G = Goal Attainment, I =Integration, L = Latent pattern maintenance.
Source: Parsons, Human Condition, 361

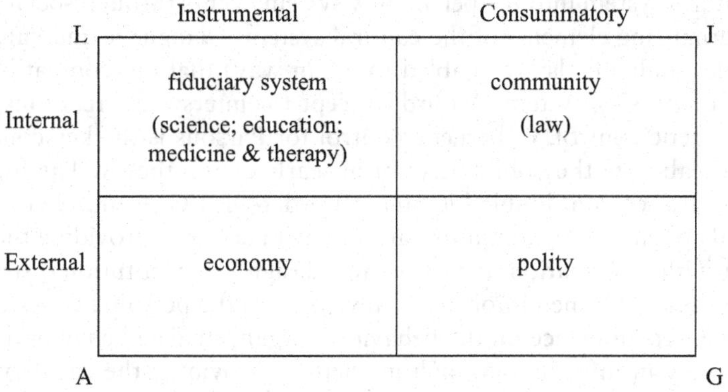

	Instrumental	Consummatory	
L			I
Internal	fiduciary system (science; education; medicine & therapy)	community (law)	
External	economy	polity	
	A		G

Figure 9.2 The social system.
Cf. Parsons, University, 37.

during times of latency. As a result, to each box of the action system the same cross tabulation can be applied, the same procedure being repeated at the level of sub-subsystems, and so on. The degree to which this procedure is to be applied is an empirical question. AGIL delineates a combinatory space of *necessary* functions and at the same time a route of *possible* differentiation. That is, in a given social system—ancient Greece, modern China, etc.—there can be more or less specialized structures (norms, roles) to fulfill the respective functions. Thus, it is an empirical variable in how far systems differentiate.

The more a system is differentiated, the more this differentiation is to be balanced and controlled by intersystem relationships. At this point, Parsons introduces concepts from cybernetics and information theory. First, the idea of open systems implies that there are exchange relations between the different subsystems of the action system and between the subsystems of a highly differentiated society. The political system, the economy, and families, for example, each produce specific outputs that they provide to the other subsystems, and at the same time they are provided by those other systems with their respective "resources." Thus, the economy provides money to the state and the families, while families provide motivation to work. Each subsystem generates a specific medium of interchange that controls these exchange relations: money (economy), power (polity), influence (community), and value commitments (culture).[16]

A second type of interrelationship between subsystems is "interpenetration."[17] Interpenetration occurs when two systems somewhat overlap, and it, too, makes available the "achievements" of one system to another system. Interpenetration of the cultural system into the social system means institutionalization: cultural ideas are specified in terms of social norms that make these ideas available for social interaction. Interpenetration of the cultural system into the personality system occurs through socialization. By internalizing elements of the cultural systems—language and values, for example—individuals are enabled to act in ways that are compatible with the encompassing system. A third concept for intersystem relations is that of cybernetic control. Cybernetic control for Parsons is the key concept to further elaborate the voluntarism of his early action theory. The four subsystems are set in a double hierarchical order—L I G A and A G I L. The cultural system is "high in information, low in energy," providing the social system with information as to how to "design" its institutional structure. The social system then informationally controls the personality system that in turn exerts influence on the behavioral organism. The behavioral organism is "low in information, high in energy," providing the capacity to act and thus to realize the cultural ideas. It is important to note that it is not only culture that is controlling but that culture is conversely controlled by the other subsystems. Thus, not all "good ideas" are compatible with the need-dispositions of human beings. In this way, cybernetic control realizes the dynamic interrelationship between ideas and conditions that already was present in the early action theory. We will now look at how Parsons specified institutionalization and cybernetic control for modern society.

4 THEORY OF MODERN SOCIETY

Parsons's understanding of modern society is heavily influenced by Max Weber's work. Of special importance here are Weber's contributions on capitalism and rationalization as distinguishing features of Western modernity. In contradistinction to the "materialist" interpretation of Marx, Weber traced back the emergence of modern capitalism to the ideas of ascetic Protestantism. Parsons similarly puts a premium on Christianity when it comes to gaining an understanding of modernity.[18] He assumes that the cultural system of modern society is ultimately informed by Christian ideas. This culture then controls the structure and dynamic of modern society. Closely linked to this is the high degree of differentiation (and thus rationalization) of modern society.[19]

But what does this Christian "imprint" mean in terms of the theory of the action system? And what does it concretely imply for the institutional design of modern society? As regards the first question, Parsons tentatively developed a scheme for the classification of cultural systems.[20] His idea is that cultural systems vary according to which variables of the AGIL-scheme they mark as primary normative orientations for action. In this way, it is "possible not only to assert that such and such value-commitments exist in the society but that these are, in determinate ways, selections as between a set of meaningful alternatives."[21] Thus, the cultural system had to determine if the social system primarily realizes an internal or an external orientation, and if primacy is given to the consummatory or to the instrumental variable.[22] Additionally, cultural systems vary according to where they locate the primary source of "moral sanction," i.e. regarding whether "it is conceived to reside within the world of empirical experience . . . or in cognate terms to lie in a transcendental reality or entity of some sort."[23]

The religious ideas of Christendom and thus of modern culture are reconstructed by Parsons as a combination of the instrumental, external, and transcendent variables. Parsons summarized this combination in the formula of "instrumental activism." "Instrumental activism" is the ultimately Christian cultural value pattern of modern society. Its implications for social structure can easily be illustrated by the Calvinistic idea of a future Kingdom of God on Earth. Instrumental activism can be read as a mission to mobilize all available resources in order to get prepared for this future Kingdom. But the concrete outlook of this future Kingdom is unknown to God's "children." Against this background, *activism* means an active engagement in manipulating this world in its natural and social aspects. That this activism is *instrumental* means that there is no vision of the concrete shape of the final result of this engagement. Modern culture could thus be understood as a vision of a society that is at any time able to realize any action, project, or any larger intervention in its environment—a society with a maximum capacity of action that is to a historically singular degree able to mobilize commitments to concrete goals in case there should be some demand. Instrumental activism fosters the "development of normative institutional frameworks for the higher-order organization of secular society."[24]

Among these institutional frameworks are, for example, formal organizations such as business firms, bureaucracies, schools, hospitals, and armies. They are more "modern" than other types of collective actors because they can coordinate and thus effectively increase the capacities of many individual actors. The action capacity of the nation is formally organized by the state bureaucracy and government. Another and very obvious correlate of instrumental activism is modern society's high normative emphasis on economic productivity and efficiency. Like profit-seeking economic actors, though less obviously, the professions are related to the modern effort to maximize action-capacity. Teachers, doctors, and psychotherapists are concerned with developing, "upgrading," and stabilizing the human potential to act.[25] In this way, the members of modern society are being enabled to participate in the preparation for the future Kingdom of God on Earth. In this context, Parsons's understanding of individualism becomes clear. A demand is made on everyone to participate actively in the building of God's Kingdom on Earth. That the concrete shape of this Kingdom is unknown means that there are no specifications for the individual regarding how to realize this engagement in detail. Thus, the individual has a broad range of "freedoms." But at the same time this individualism is restrictive in one sense, namely that fatalistic retreat from an active engagement in social affairs is not tolerated. The demand for individual achievement thus becomes the most important demand made on members of modern society. Of course, then, individual achievement—primarily in occupational roles—is the most important criterion for social status in modern societies.

5 SYSTEMS THINKING IN SOCIOLOGY: THE INFLUENCE OF PARSONS AND HIS RELEVANCE TODAY

Though Parsons's theory today is rarely used as an analytical instrument for research, his influence within sociology is considerable. Parsons's theory has been adopted and integrated into new theoretical frameworks by such different scholars as Jürgen Habermas,[26] Jeffrey C. Alexander, and Niklas Luhmann. Furthermore, many writers show in some aspects a Parsonian understanding of their subject matter without explicitly referring to Parsons. The world-polity-school around John W. Meyer is a case in point here. Finally, the critique of Parsons played a role in stimulating new sociological approaches, among them the interpretative paradigm.

But what is the more specific heritage of Parsons's *systems* theory, and how does Parsons relate to other sociological systems theorists? The most important writer here certainly is Niklas Luhmann. He adopted systems theoretical concepts from Parsons and from more recent lines of general systems thinking (i.e. autopoiesis) and created a new sociological systems theory out of them. Before discussing some continuities and discontinuities between his work and that of Parsons, we do well to take a short look at a quite different line of sociological systems thinking, namely the systems theory of Immanuel Wallerstein.

SOCIOLOGICAL PERSPECTIVES ON THE GLOBAL SYSTEM: IMMANUEL WALLERSTEIN VERSUS TALCOTT PARSONS?

Since the late 1960s, Immanuel Wallerstein has elaborated an account of a global social order, the world system. As this account is inspired by Marx, it is not surprising that it in important points differs from a Parsonian perspective. According to Wallerstein, the world system is neither culturally nor politically integrated. It is an economic entity that comprises plural polities (nation states) and plural cultures.[27] Therefore, today's world is dominated by an economic logic. The systemic character of the world system is incorporated in this economic logic. Thus, the capitalist world system *systematically* (re)produces a threefold economic stratification; it runs through Kondratieff cycles and so forth. For Parsons, in contrast, a systems perspective is tantamount to negating the primary economic character of the global social system: a systems perspective means to situate the global economy within a broader social and cultural context. Without such a broader context, for Parsons a global social *order*—unlike global chaos, conflict, anomie—would be unthinkable. Thus, if he had to identify a global social system, he first had to ask if there were some elements of global normative integration. He should ask if a global or world culture existed. The world economy would then be conceived as a structural manifestation of this global culture.

Parsons indeed embarked on this path in a few short texts, among them being some comments on the Cold War.[28] Here, he argued in a rather unconventional manner that the parties of the Cold War were tied together by shared normative commitments. The evidence for this was to be found in the fact that there was a worldwide commitment to modernization—that is: to institutionalize the social correlates of the cultural pattern named instrumental activism. Thus, did not the parties of the Cold War converge in their strong interest in industrialization and in economic productivity more generally? "From the communist point of view, the essential immorality of capitalism does not consist in its having abandoned the virtues of preindustrial economic systems; nor, from the other side is it the 'crime' of Soviet Russia to have promoted industrialization. Quite the contrary on both sides, as is evidenced by the continuing stress in Soviet pronouncements on their imminent 'catching up' with the United States and a less obvious, sometimes indeed grudging, Western admiration for Soviet achievements."[29] Another piece of evidence of the trend toward the worldwide institutionalization of modern values was to be seen in the growth of organizations in every societal sector. Thus, hospitals, schools, parties, business organizations were to be found in ever growing numbers in ever more countries. This clearly was an expression of the high degree of legitimation of effective collective action in modern world culture. Also, "a demand for equal status as societies, with its bearing on political independence"[30] and "a drive [. . .] toward the development of a 'modern state' "[31] were to be understood as expressions of a shared commitment to modernity.

The modernization view of the 1940s–1950s was criticized for ignoring imperialism, colonialism, and the inequalities between global North and global South more generally. Wallerstein's account of the world system was, alongside *Dependencia,* one of the answers to this problem. This critique also applies to Parsons's contribution.[32] At the same time, more recent lines of globalization research have turned exactly to the cultural aspects that Parsons and other modernization theorists pointed to long ago.[33] They have affirmed Parsons's view that the worldwide concern for modernization and economic productivity are not an expression of a "natural" interest in profit or a natural concern to enhance the quality of life. There is in the meantime a vast corpus of empirical research that powerfully reveals the cultural foundations of the modernization efforts. To Parsons, the worldwide commitment to modernity was a reason to celebrate. Today, it seems at least a dubious blessing, as we are now faced with the ecological limits of the worldwide realization of "instrumental activism." A potentially fruitful line for bringing Parsons back into contemporary research would be to relate "instrumental activism" to the ecological crisis.

AUTONOMY AND DIFFERENTIATION: TALCOTT PARSONS AND NIKLAS LUHMANN

While there are few points of contact between the systems theories of Immanuel Wallerstein and that of Parsons, Niklas Luhmann's work can be understood as the follow-up to Parsons's systems theory. In the second half of the twentieth century, Niklas Luhmann built up a sociological systems theory that is similarly comprehensive to that of Parsons, and while doing so he integrated several Parsonian ideas and concepts. Like Parsons, Luhmann put a premium on functional differentiation when it came to characterizing modern society. He adopted—and modified—Parsons's concept of symbolic media of interchange, and he integrated Parsons's theorem of double contingency. At the same time, Luhmann at different points diverged considerably from Parsons. In order to remove some restrictions he found in Parsons's analytical framework, he drew on more recent concepts from general systems theory, among them autopoiesis and second-order cybernetics.[34]

A very central point of departure from Parsons is Luhmann's abandonment of analytical realism. Luhmann conceives of systems not as analytical but as concrete systems. The economy, the political system, a school class, a social interaction—they all are thought to be empirical entities existing "out there" and reproducing themselves by maintaining a concrete boundary between themselves and their environment. This has important consequences for how Luhmann conceives of differentiation. Refusing analytical realism to him meant abandoning the AGIL scheme. Thus, Luhmann conceives of functional differentiation as a contingent process that starts at some point in history and then enables and constrains possibilities of further differentiation. The specific functions that are differentiated in a given society and the specializations that are structurally implemented are not predetermined. The number of functional subsystems thus is historically variable. Another important consequence of the concrete systems concept concerns the autonomy of social systems. For Parsons, a necessary prerequisite for social order was normative integration by common values or norms. In this way, Parsons constructed a close connection between the motivational orientations of human actors and the structures of social systems. Due to his concrete systems concepts, Luhmann abandons the prerequisite of normative integration. As a result, he gains a much more sophisticated understanding of the autonomy and of the independent logic of social systems. But at the same time, an important theme disappeared from view. The more Luhmann became interested in the autonomy of social systems, the less he was interested in the interrelationship between these systems and their human environment. Themes such as socialization and the motivational foundations of social processes that were central to Parsons are not prominent in Luhmann's work. Accordingly, the interest in the relevant neighboring disciplines, such as psychology, was reduced. This is not to say that Luhmann's systems theory offers no possibilities to reflect on these issues. Quite the contrary: Luhmann's insights into the autonomy of social systems could be combined with Parsons's original interest in the interdependencies of social systems and personalities. This would possibly advance the understanding of these interdependencies and reopen prospects for interdisciplinarity that for many years have been left unexploited.

NOTES

1. John W. Meyer et al., "World Society and the Nation-State," *American Journal of Sociology* 103 (1997): 144–81.
2. Dennis Wrong, "The Oversocialized Conception of Man in Modern Society," *American Sociological Review* 26 (1961): 183–96.
3. Cf. Alan Sica and Stephen Turner, eds., *The Disobedient Generation: Social Theorists in the Sixties* (Chicago, IL: University of Chicago Press, 2005).
4. Cf. Talcott Parsons, "Unity and Diversity in the Intellectual Disciplines: The Role of the Social Sciences," in *Sociological Theory and Modern Society*, ed. Talcott Parsons (New York: Free Press, 1967), 180.
5. Cf. Talcott Parsons, "The Position of Identity in the General Theory of Action," in *The Self in Social Interaction*, vol.1, eds. Chad Gordon and Kenneth J. Gergen (New York: Wiley, 1968), 14.
6. Talcott Parsons, *The Structure of Social Action: A Study in Social Theory with Special Reference to a Group of Recent European Writers* (New York: Free Press, 1937; reprint 1968).
7. Parsons, *Structure of Social Action*, 27ff.
8. Parsons, *Structure of Social Action*, 43ff.
9. Parsons, *Structure of Social Action*, 44.
10. Parsons, *Structure of Social Action*, 75.
11. Parsons, *Structure of Social Action*, 75.

12. Walter B. Cannon, *The Wisdom of the Body* (New York: Norton, 1963). Originally published 1933.
13. Important publications are: Talcott Parsons, *The Social System* (New York: Free Press, 1951); Talcott Parsons and Edward Shils, eds., *Toward a General Theory of Action* (Cambridge, MA: Harvard University Press, 1951); Talcott Parsons and Gerald M. Platt, *The American University* (Cambridge, MA: Harvard University Press, 1973); Talcott Parsons, *Social Systems and the Evolution of Action Theory* (New York: Free Press, 1977); Talcott Parsons, *A Paradigm of the Human Condition* (New York: Free Press, 1978).
14. Cf. Parsons, *The Social System*; Parsons and Shils, *Toward a General Theory.*
15. Cf. the following summary: Niklas Luhmann, *Einführung in die Systemtheorie* (Heidelberg: Carl Auer. 2002), 26ff.
16. Cf. Parsons, *Evolution of Action Theory,* 362ff., 374ff.
17. Cf. Parsons, *Evolution of Action Theory,* 177–203.
18. Parsons and Talcott, "Christianity and Modern Society," *in The Talcott Parsons Reader,* ed. Bryan S. Turner (Malden, MA: Blackwell, 1999).
19. Among Parsons's contributions on modern society are: Talcott Parsons, *Structure and Process in Modern Society* (New York: Free Press, 1960); Talcott Parsons, *Societies: Evolutionary and Comparative Perspectives* (New York: Englewood Cliffs, 1966); Talcott Parsons, *The System of Modern Societies* (Englewood Cliffs, NJ: Prentice-Hall, 1971).
20. Talcott Parsons, "A Tentative Outline of American Values," in *Talcott Parsons: Theorist of Modernity,* eds. Roland Robertson and Bryan S. Turner (London: Sage, 1991), 37–65.
21. Parsons, "American Values," 41.
22. Parsons, "American Values," 43.
23. Parsons, "American Values," 42.
24. Talcott Parsons, "Order and Community in the International Social System," in *The Talcott Parsons Reader,* ed. Bryan S. Turner (Malden, MA: Blackwell. 1999), 248.
25. Cf. Talcott Parsons and Winston White, "The Link between Character and Society," in *Culture and Social Character,* eds. Seymour M. Lipset and Leo Loewenthal (New York: Free Press, 1957), 89–135.
26. Habermas adopts Parsonian concepts for his account of the "system" in contradistinction to the "lifeworld." The starting point for this adoption is his impression that Parsons adheres to the core of utilitarian thinking: he interprets the actor's freedom of decision as a freedom of choice between different alternatives, while ends are conceived as given. Cf. Jürgen Habermas, *Zur Kritik der funktinalistischen Vernunft,* vol. 2 of *Theorie des kommunikativen Handelns* (Suhrkamp: Frankfurt am Main, 1999), 320f.
27. Cf. Immanuel Wallerstein, "The Rise and Future Demise of the World Capitalist System: Concepts for Comparative Analysis," in *The Capitalist World Economy: Essays* (Cambridge: Cambridge University Press, 1980), 1–36.
28. Parsons, "Order and Community"; Talcott Parsons, "Communism and the West: The Sociology of Conflict," in *Social Change: Sources, Patterns, and Consequences,* eds. Amitai Etzioni and Eva Etzioni (New York: Basic Books. 1964), 390–99; Talcott Parsons, "Polarization of the World and International Order," in *The Talcott Parsons Reader,* ed. Bryan S. Turner (Oxford: Blackwell, 1999), 237–53.
29. Parsons, "Communism," 391.
30. Parsons, "Polarization," 254.
31. Parsons, "Order and Community," 248.
32. Even if Parsons makes one fruitful point on global inequality, he points out that "development differences" were not only economic. They also

functioned as status differences, with the developing countries being the "have-nots" and the industrialized being the "haves" of the international stratification system. Cf. Parsons, "Communism."

33. Cf. Meyer et al., *Nation State*; Frederick Cooper and Randall Packard, *International Development and the Social Sciences: Essays in the History and Politics of Knowledge* (Berkeley: University of California Press, 1997).
34. Cf. Niklas Luhmann, *Social Systems* (Stanford: Stanford University Press, 1995).

REFERENCES

Cannon, Walter B. *The Wisdom of the Body.* New York: Norton, 1963. Originally published 1933.

Cooper, Frederick, and Randall Packard. *International Development and the Social Sciences: Essays in the History and Politics of Knowledge.* Berkeley: University of California Press, 1997.

Habermas, Jürgen. *Zur Kritik der funktinalistischen Vernunft.* Vol. 2 of *Theorie des kommunikativen Handelns.* Suhrkamp: Frankfurt am Main, 1999.

Luhmann, Niklas. *Social Systems.* Stanford: Stanford University Press, 1995.

———. *Einführung in die Systemtheorie.* Heidelberg: Carl Auer, 2002.

Meyer, John W., John Boli, George M. Thomas, and Francisco O. Ramirez. "World Society and the Nation-State." *American Journal of Sociology* 103 (1997): 144–81.

Parsons, Talcott. *The Structure of Social Action: A Study in Social Theory with Special Reference to a Group of Recent European Writers.* New York: Free Press, 1937; reprint 1968.

———. *The Social System.* New York: Free Press, 1951.

———. *Structure and Process in Modern Society.* New York: Free Press, 1960.

———. "Communism and the West: The Sociology of Conflict." In *Social Change: Sources, Patterns, and Consequences,* edited by Amitai Etzioni and Eva Etzioni, 390–99. New York: Basic Books, 1964.

———. *Societies: Evolutionary and Comparative Perspectives.* New York: Englewood Cliffs, 1966.

———. "Unity and Diversity in the Intellectual Disciplines: The Role of the Social Sciences." In *Sociological Theory and Modern Society,* edited by Talcott Parsons, 166–91. New York: Free Press, 1967.

———. "The Position of Identity in the General Theory of Action." In *The Self in Social Interaction,* vol.1, edited by Chad Gordon and Kenneth J. Gergen, 11–23. New York: Wiley, 1968.

———. *The System of Modern Societies.* Englewood Cliffs, NJ: Prentice-Hall, 1971.

———. *Social Systems and the Evolution of Action Theory.* New York: Free Press, 1977.

———. *A Paradigm of the Human Condition.* New York: Free Press, 1978.

———. "A Tentative Outline of American Values." In *Talcott Parsons: Theorist of Modernity,* edited by Roland Robertson and Bryan S. Turner, 37–65. London: Sage, 1991.

———. "Christianity and Modern Society." In *The Talcott Parsons Reader,* edited by Bryan S. Turner, 23–50. Malden, MA: Blackwell, 1999.

———. "Order and Community in the International Social System." In *The Talcott Parsons Reader,* edited by Bryan S. Turner, 237–52. Oxford: Blackwell, 1999.

———. "Polarization of the World and International Order." In *The Talcott Parsons Reader,* edited by Bryan S. Turner, 253–70. Oxford: Blackwell, 1999.

————, and Gerald M. Platt. *The American University.* Cambridge, MA: Harvard University Press, 1973.

————, and Edward Shils, eds. *Toward A General Theory of Action.* Cambridge, MA: Harvard University Press, 1951.

Wallerstein, Immanuel. "The Rise and Future Demise of the World Capitalist System: Concepts for Comparative Analysis." In *The Capitalist World-Economy: Essays by Immanuel Wallerstein,* 1–36. Cambridge: Cambridge University Press, 1980.

Wrong, Dennis. "The Oversocialized Conception of Man in Modern Society." *American Sociological Review* 26 (1961): 183–96.

10 Luhmann
Three Key Concepts, System, Meaning, Autopoiesis

Walter Reese-Schäfer

"All knowing systems operate as real systems in the real world."[1]

"There are systems." This is one of Luhmann's basic theses, expressed in this and other forms. Many readers of Luhmann have been taken aback by this: hadn't they, with much effort and against their common sense understanding, gotten used to one of the basic dogmas of system theory—that systems are supposed to be nothing other than constructions of our understanding. Precisely this is what Luhmann doubts. "The concept of the system (as we use the term in our investigations) always stands for a real state of affairs. Thus by 'system' we never mean a purely analytical system, a mere conceptual construction, a bare model."[2] Added to this is that the process of observation is also a real process, which for its part can be taken for, and described as, a fact. Luhmann thus no longer accepts the traditional dualism of the observer and the object, because he also always integrates the observation of the observer itself, that is, second-order observation, into his theory.

The benefit of this turned-around definition consists in the fact that it can solve or at least avert the continuing and, in his view, unproductive controversy between realism and constructivism. Realists believe in the reality of the external world; constructivists take it to be a product of our perceptive capability. Luhmann accepts a view differing from both of these positions and also explains the operation of relating to something—that is, of referring, whether that be to the external world or to the elements of our perceptive ability—as a real operation. Then what is real is no longer only the object to which one refers, but also the process of referring. "However, it is not enough merely to change to the opposing view and to adhere to the reality of the operation referred to. For this is inaccessible to itself, and for an observer it would only be something that can be referred to, which he characterizes. So one arrives at the already existing controversy between realism and constructivism—as if this were a matter of incompatible positions."[3]

Here, we are dealing with the famous "blind spot" of the observer. This means that a differentiation that is made for the purpose of the observer cannot itself be observed. "The true/untrue differentiation cannot itself only be true or untrue; it cannot observe itself; it is own blind spot."[4] Or in other words: the differentiation uses the observing as a blind spot. This is also true if the level is changed and one now observes the observing. The differentiation used in this is not brought into view either. On the operative level this second-order observing must also proceed naively because it cannot simultaneously critically observe its own reference. In Luhmann's thought there are "no hierarchies of reflexivity."[5] Blind spots and operative naivety are the two characteristic attributes of that ever so simple "starting operation" known as observation.

In order to properly assess Luhmann's thought it is important to understand its simplicity. Luhmann was very offended precisely by the reproach for epistemological naivety.[6] Thus he attempted to counter this reproach, employing a basic motif of nonnaïve thought, namely paradox. If one does not speak of knowledge [Erkenntnis], but of the environment, then the following ensues: "likewise, if one prescinds from knowledge, there are not systems. (For this reason, we said above, there are systems.)"[7] The result is the same: through paradox, the question fizzles out, and one reaches the conclusion that it is sensible to observe knowledge processes with an empirical mindset. By the way, here, as in Richard Rorty, it can be seen that where an epistemological theory is employed that is in principle simple, considerable work is required of irony and paradox. Because Luhmann characterizes the observer's self-observation as reflection and because he occasionally is happy to cite Hegel, the decisive difference from this approach should at least be mentioned here: Luhmann thinks that a basic error of the subject-theoretic approach to thinking (and thus also of Hegel) consists in conferring a hierarchically higher position to second-order observation. "From the view of system theory the question can only be whether the observer in direct reference to reality has a thing (a concept, symbol, etc.) in mind or an observer, who, for his part, observes beyond a boundary, what is for him an environment."[8] A hierarchy of levels of reflection cannot come into existence in this way. There is always the possibility of observing an observer: however, one must differentiate him from something, and thus use a different differentiation than this. Thus everyone participates in the observation game, at least if and for as long as anyone observes. There is no outside position. This consideration is connected with the view of the Chilean neurobiologist, Humberto Maturana, "that it is not possible in the act of perception to differentiate between reference to reality and illusion."[9]

If there is no outside and no higher standpoint, where then is the starting point for knowledge? Luhmann here proposes beginning with a *differentiation*, namely with the difference between the de facto existing and the possible. Through this basic difference, all experience gains an informational value. It makes it possible to correlate sense and the otherwise unstructured manifoldness of appearances. "Thus one begins not with identity but with difference. Only thus can one give accidents informational value and thereby construct order, because information is nothing more than an event that brings about a connection between difference—a difference that makes a difference."[10]

For Luhmann, *meaning* is a basic concept of sociology. Already in his debate with Habermas at the beginning of the 1970s he devoted an important article to this topic.[11] From the point of view of theory construction, the idea of meaning is considered extremely important. "Not the property of a specific kind of living being, but the referential wealth of meaning enables the formation of social systems through which human beings can have consciousness and life."[12]

The concept of meaning applies to both psychic and social systems. It is especially powerful because it can conceptually present its reciprocal permeation, and it thus enables both "communication to be referred back to the consciousness of the participants"[13] and the observation of communication processes in their independent development. "Meaning" is not an idea used to characterize a certain existing state of affairs; rather, it characterizes the form employed in organizing human experience.[14] So, it is understood functionally. Our experience is characterized by a certain "surplus of possibility." It must be structured by a program to steer choice. What we have grown accustomed to calling "meaning" serves this end. Experience and action are selections that occur though ascribing sense criteria. Here, that which is not chosen is not wasted but, as an undetermined manifold, preserved as a *world*—possibly for future selection according to somewhat changed sense criteria. The choice according to meaning points of view is an important evolutionary development. "Not all systems process complexity and self-reference in the form of meaning; but for those that do, it is the *only* possibility."[15] These are personal and social systems.

As Luhmann understands it, the concept of meaning is "an unnegatable category, a category devoid of difference."[16] The typical talk of meaninglessness is thus, however, difficult to accommodate within this model: "Meaninglessness is a special phenomenon, which is, after all, possible only in the domain of signs and resides in a confusion of signs. A muddle of objects is never meaningless. A pile of rubble, for example, is immediately recognizable as such and one can immediately tell whether it is attributable to time, to an earthquake, or to 'enemy action.'"[17] In everyday language one likes to speak of "meaningless destruction." However, the concept of a "heap of ruins" is an ascription of sense to which further ones can be added arbitrarily, up to and including the most disgusting ascription of guilt to the enemy, to oneself, or to war as such.

It is necessary to warn against confusing these two uses of the concept. Luhmann uses *meaning* to refer to the sense that something has for an observer. By contrast, the concept of meaning that is intended when one speaks of meaninglessness is the sense or purpose of life. The intended loss is a loss in value.[18] In accord with Luhmann's categories, a loss in value can surely have a meaning. There are two different concepts that unfortunately are characterized by the same word. It is an error in reasoning, a classical logical equivocation, to conclude from the impossibility of the loss of one type of meaning to the impossibility of the other. Unfortunately, Luhmann is not entirely immune to this mistake. Using his special concept of meaning, he in fact argues against talk of "a loss of meaning" in modern society generally: "In particular, today the formula 'loss of meaning' incorporates what can be experienced into the self-description of society. But meaning is still an unavoidable form of experience and action. Without meaning, society and every social system would simply cease to exist. This formula does not adequately indicate what it means, but exaggerates in order to pronounce society guilty."[19] Now and then in Luhmann one comes across such a case, where "the clarity of the conceptual determinations . . . leaves something to be desired."[20] That is due to his tendency to formulate quick, merely stimulating but often not worked out, definitions.

Besides system and meaning, *autopoiesis* is the third key concept of Luhmann, which I would like to explain at the outset, because of its cross-sectional character. The concept is an artificial word, influenced by the circle of the cognitive biologist, Humberto Maturana, from the Greek *autos* (self) and *poiesis* (creation, poetics), which can be translated as self-creation or self-generation. The reason that one is better off leaving it untranslated will become clear momentarily.

Living systems, as, for example, bodily cells, are among the autopoietic systems. A cell:

> produces, as a network with a division of labor, the specific components (complex, organic molecules) of which it consists. Simultaneously the cellular components make possible the existence of the production network in the first place that emerges through the 'border' (the cell membrane) and the environment. All internal cellular processes are directed to the self-generation and self-maintenance of the cell, that is, to continuation of autopoiese. The cell has a strong internal dynamic, for inner-cellular processes are conditioned by the interactions between the elements (that is, recursivity). Environmental effects merely interrupt ('perturb') the cells and lead to balancing reactions. Organisms require the milieu (environment) in order to absorb nutrition, etc., or in order to emit waste into the environment, but they do not adapt to it.[21]

In contrast to living systems, for example, machines are not autopoietic systems, because they are not oriented toward generating and maintaining their own structure but toward producing a product, that is, thus, to something else. Both machines and cells have *input* from the environment and *output*. Autopoiesis thus does not mean, as one might easily be led to believe with the translation "self-creating," that there is self-generation out of nothing. The concept rather is meant to describe a system that is oriented to its own continuance, on the basis of its own dynamic.

Luhmann's *Social Systems* is an attempt to transfer this concept to sociology. One can even speak of an "autopoietic turn" in his theory, which was initiated at the end of the 1970s and became increasingly clear from about

1980.[22] Luhmann himself spoke of a paradigm shift in system theory.[23] Originally, system theories proceeded from a differentiation between the part and the whole. The second major paradigm of system theoretic thinking was the differentiation between system and environment. Luhmann, from the late 1970s, attempts to give foundation to a third, auotpoietic one.

LUHMANN'S OPERATIVE LOGIC AND RADICAL CONSTRUCTIVISM

In all of his more recent publications Luhmann set out from the operative logic of George Spencer Brown, which begins with the directive: "Draw a distinction!"[24] We cannot identify something without demarcating a difference. In order to observe anything at all, a system requires a border over which it can look. It is thus necessary to draw a boundary. It is an issue of boundaries of meaning or sense. Every self-observation "presumes the arrangement of the appropriate internal differences."[25] A differentiation requires that one cannot be on both sides at the same time. One can certainly change perspectives and also observe something from the other side; but only afterwards. One must cross the boundaries (to use the term of Spencer Brown), and that takes time, at least the renowned logical second. This time difference serves to dislodge paradoxes, to obviate the paradox that the observer is simultaneously external and internal. Fully implemented, the observing can observe differently, but its differentiation cannot. That is his blind spot. Luhmann pounds this thought into his readers with the help of an (of course, ironically intended) tautology: "It can only see what it can see with this difference. It cannot see what it cannot see."[26]

Nevertheless it is possible to observe this difference itself again. "That can (but need not) occur in one and the same system. In this way what we will call self-observation is possible in one system."[27] Thus within the same system a change in perspective occurs, a crossing, that is oriented to the operation of the system itself. The original differentiation then appears again in the differentiated.[28] Spencer Brown calls this re-entry. Relativizing Spencer Brown's logical correctness a bit, Luhmann perceives it as "a kind of veiled paradox,"[29] which he gladly adopts. In terms of system theory, in the system there is a re-entry of the differentiation between system and environment. "A differentiation marks off an area and is then re-introduced to it through this. It thus occurs twice: as an originating differentiation and as a differentiation in that which is differentiated by it. It is the same and not the same. It is the same because what is funny about *re-entry* is evident precisely when applying the differentiation recursively to itself; it is not the same because it is introduced in something else, in an already differing sphere."[30] For Luhmann, it is important to present the treatment of the paradox so that the relationship to the paradox is still able to be recognized.[31]

Readers schooled in philosophy certainly recognize here a simple form of the thought process known as reflection.

If the system is now viewed as a whole (in contrast to the environment), as unified, but in-itself differentiated, thus as a unity of unity and difference, then the problems begin; for then one is smack in the middle of a classical paradox. How can one begin with a differentiation if to do so one already has to have chosen a difference? George Spencer Brown's happy solution is: just start, and then later, upon re-entry, see whether it has been useful. It is basically a question of an operation employing a typical technique for solving the paradox, namely the sequence of temporalization. (The paradoxical character of a considerable number of the paradoxes that are well known in the history of ideas can be traced back to the fact that one attempts to think certain thing simultaneously.)

The reflection or observation of the observer is not hierarchically of a higher order—this basic theorem of system thinking (compare the section "There Are Systems") should be called to mind again. In the one case, things (or concepts or symbols) are observed; in the other case, observers, who for their part observe what is for them an environment, beyond their boundary and with a blind spot. Even second-order observation, second-order cybernetics or second semiotics (Luhmann has in particular von Foerster in mind and Maturana) has a blind spot, but another one, and it can, through this, see the blind spot of first-order observation.[32] By the way, it is also only an *operation that de facto occurs* that for its part can be observed. In the view of this epistemology, operations are not artificial forms, created by reflection; rather, they are factual occurrences. To observe is to describe occurrences—thus Luhmann's use of the term "operative," a word whose use in this function he appropriates from Heinz von Foerster's *Sicht und Einsicht: Versuche zu einer operativen Erkenntnistheorie.*

It is a testament to Luhmann's metaphysical *esprit* that he does not just retain these appeasing formulations, even though they are very useful for understanding the matter that is supposed to be at hand. Readers who are afraid of getting confused might rather skip the next section. However, then they will only be able to claim to understand the objects of Luhmann's thought, not the spirit of it. After all, it is a question of the recursiveness of the observer and the observed, thus of the problem of self-reference. If the same operation of the "differentiated-characterized observation" can again be applied to each differentiation, some surplus always remains. "It must be assumed that the world (whatever that is) tolerates differentiations and that, depending on the differentiation that violates it, it confuses in various ways the observations and descriptions that emerge from it. . . . The world thus appears a bit like an intricate invisible object or like a hint of a conclusion that is only recursively possible."[33] Every differentiation is able to be deconstructed—in this view Luhmann is in full agreement with Jacques Derrida. However, he is not prepared to follow him in his *worlds of style* on the "expressive possibilities of writing errors" in order to share these paradoxes.[34] Another way to self-reflexively deal with the paradoxes would be to attempt to construct a many-valued logic that works like Gotthard Günther's but with binary schematized operations. Luhmann, who very much liked and had great respect for Gotthard Günther, nonetheless in the last analysis does not follow him, for if a rejection value is introduced in every differentiation—that is, a metadifferentiation that poses the question of the acceptance or the rejection of this differentiation—then one is faced with a paradox if one applies this thought to itself.[35]

The world, as something imperceptible that gives itself up through observation, is a temporalizable paradox and "thus can only be grasped with a non-stationary logic, not fixed on 'objects.' "[36] Luhmann finds the simplest and most elegant attempt of this type in Spencer Brown's logic, which "positions its paradox until the calculation is complex enough that it can assume the form of a re-entry of the difference in that which through it differing (or a form in the form)."[37] "Form" is the term used by Spencer Brown for the differentiation that separates two sides and thereby requires time to cross the lines of separation.[38]

The English logician, philosopher, and computer specialist, George Spencer Brown, was hardly read by anyone in Germany other than Luhmann. In 1967 he presented Bertrand Russell with a logical calculation showing the lack of need for the principle of Russell's and Whitehead's logical type theory from the *Principia Mathematica* of 1910, which showed that the reflexive proposition was not allowed, that the self-maintenance of a set is thus impermissible. Russell was impressed and congratulated him.[39] His calculation, however, did not become common knowledge, and Luhmann found it important that in his reliance on ideas of Spencer Brown's, this calculation need not be presumed to be correct; only its epistemological context did.[40] Heinz von Foerster had seen the importance of Spencer Brown's conception of knowledge, which was developed in the work of the Biological Computer Laboratory of the University of Illinois in Urbana. More precisely, it is not Spencer Brown's logic that Luhmann uses but the conception of knowledge that is connected to it.[41]

Luhmann's theory understands itself as a program that precisely spurs on paradoxes, contradiction, and tautologies, that is, all of what logic finds objectionable.[42] All three can become extremely interesting elements from a functional point of view. In order to quickly elucidate this I will single out contradictions, because they are most meaningful for social theory.

In dealing with the explosive "self-reference," he is served by two concepts that I concisely introduced at the beginning of this article: the sentence "there are systems" and his concept of sense. There are contradictions; they occur—and it is possible to inquire into their function. For theories that are "addicted to unity," they are of course a horror.[43] A theory that views contradictions only as logical mistakes runs the danger that it, or even its objects of knowledge, will be excluded from the range of possible knowledge (SY 489). "The law of non-contradiction (the contradiction to be avoided) corresponds to this thesis of a contraction-free world."[44] At best, an exclusively logically oriented theory allows so-called "fuzzy sets" for indeterminates and poorly defined problems. Luhmann wants to go further and is prepared to accept tutelage from Hegel, for "[i]f social life does not work in a purely logical way, then a theory of it cannot be formulated as free of logical contradictions."[45] This statement must not be read as a statement of fact, but as a typical opening provocation. Luhmann by no means makes things as simple as it appears at first sight. He rejects the traditional Marxist talk of "social contradictions," for the "contradiction of labor and capital" is merely concerned with antagonistic interests. Competition is not a contradiction either. Two persons can certainly strive for the same good. Contradictions, as Luhmann wants to see them, arise in another way, namely as moments of the self-reference of sense. That requires an explanation. "Communication brings about unity (and with it possible contradiction) by integrating a threefold selection. Information, utterance, and understanding (with or without acceptance) are practiced as a unity. . . . Only communication's expectation of unity constitutes a contradiction, by choosing what.[46]

A series of contradictions arise through this so that one might nearly think of developing a special social therapy program, analogous to psychological assistance for paradoxical malformation of the psychic system. But the instability that such contradictions create is not necessarily functionally harmful. Contradictions can be forms of processing "by which one can induce a situation that would end of itself when one wants to enable connections nonetheless"[47] Or expressed with recourse to the concept of autopoiesis: In order to reproduce itself, the system needs unstable elements, and self-reproduction is a precondition of evolution. Contradictions have a "function of warning and alarming": "*For an instant they destroy the system's total pretension to being ordered, reduced complexity. For an instant, then, indeterminate complexity is restored, and everything is possible. But at the same time contradictions possess enough form to guarantee the connectivity of communicative processing via meaning.*"[48] Autopoiesis can then continue. That contradictions are a moment of the development and not simply something to be excluded is a central thought of Hegel to which Luhmann continually alludes in such contexts. However, that is once again to be emphasized with two important differences: First, he speaks of autopoiesis, not of a subject, be that spirit or the Left-Hegelian collective subject, society. Second, in a form that can be missed, but that stands in complete opposition: Luhmann speaks—here consistently aligned with the difference principle of Spencer Brown—of the difference between identity and difference, Hegel's dialectic and its unity.[49] Contradictions, as alarm signals, build in a sort of immune system, which Luhmann understands to be by no means metaphorical, but rather functional.[50] "The system does not immunize itself against the no but with the help of the no; it does not protect itself against changes but with the help of changes against rigidifying. . . . The immune system protects not structure but autopoiesis, the system's closed self-reproduction."[51] The concept of the immune system can nearly be taken literally, for the example for society is the legal system, which does not serve to prevent conflicts but to regulate them. Contradictions are thus "syntheses constituted within the system, combining semantic features under the perspective of incompatibility."[52]

The excursus over operative logic and Luhmann's conception of contradiction should close with the presentation of a side view of an application of this concept, namely the epistemology of *radical constructivism*. Today knowledge can no longer be understood as a reduction to subjective certainty, but neither can it be understood as a kind of scientifically practical everyday pragmatism, as the result of applying mere methodological rules. "It is the construction of a difference whereby that which makes the difference has no counterpart in reality. Reality as such (that means without a relation to knowledge) is unknowable."[53] The radicality of the constructivism consists in an inversion of perspective. If one earlier asked: "How is knowledge possible, although it has no access to reality external to itself?," radical constructivism begins with an empirical statement: "Knowledge is only possible because it has no access to reality outside of itself." (EK 8f) "The brain is not a reflex system open to the environment, but a functional, closed system that only understands its own 'language' and deals with its own conditions. . . . Because the brain has no direct access to the world, it is a part of the nervous system, cognitively and semantically closed. It is . . . self-referential and self-explicative."[54] For epistemology, that means that every apperception is already an interpretation. That is not particularly new, especially in philosophy, where, since Kant, one of the basic insights has been that we do not know the thing-in-itself, but only appearances. Many constructivists are even quite proud to be able to refer to their agreement with Kant. However, Luhmann very rightly objects that the thesis that all knowledge is a construction naturally applies to that sentence as well.[55] A plausible argument for constructivism can thus only be gained elsewhere. What was new and striking was then also the fact that this thought is to be presented as a result of cognitive science research, that is, with the dignity of empirical natural science.

However, the view that there is an empirical proof that empirical knowledge is a construction so obviously pulls the ground from under its own feet that there was little chance of its making a big impression. Luhmann firmly maintains: "knowing systems are real (empirical and that means observable) systems in the real world. Without the world, they could not even exist or know anything. The world is thus only cognitively accessible to them."[56] The point of constructivism is completely different: namely, that that it describes knowledge as an operation of a system (of the brain) that "maintains no qualitative and only a little quantitative contact with the external world."[57]

Luhmann thus suggests obtaining an argument for constructivism "from an explication of the self-observation and self-description of observing systems."[58] To do this, the differences must first of all be changed. Classical ontology differentiated thinking from being, Kant, the transcendental from the empirical. Both should now be replaced with the difference between *observation*, which is an action of the system, and *operation*, which is concerned with an empirical event in the environment. This can be pictured as follows:

Table 10.1

Old Europe	Ontology	Thinking	Being
Modern	Kant (Epistemology)	Transcendental	Empirical
Postmodern	Luhmann (Cognition)	Observation	Operation

He thus wants to expand radical constructivism to include an element of the laws of form (difference theory), because this "has not yet sufficiently finished its homework"[59] and because certain dramatizations have been worked out in this area that are merely replicates of age-old doubts about a proof for the existence of the external world that have been cast as subjectivist or idealist. For an empiricist, however, this problem is already solved. The difference between system and environment thus replaces both the traditional subjectivist and objectivist epistemologies.[60] The differentiation between an operation and an observation takes the place that "the unity-dependent reflective logic has hitherto had."[61] Precisely this differentiation is the particular contribution of systems, which nothing corresponds to in the environment. The old differentiation between knowledge and objects is only a construction, that is, itself a differentiation that is to be observed from the side "from which the world is damaged, fragmented, and observed."[62] This is all a real process in a real environment and it avoids being arbitrary only because a selectivity that is controlled by evolution underlies it. It is not arbitrary, but like every evolution, it is contingent, in a philosophical sense, coincidental, because nothing is to be found in its essence that would necessitate or preclude its development.[63] Observing is no longer attributed to "humans"—and that is what is new about radical constructivism. "Although constructivism has thus far tended to benefit from researchers of biology, neurology, and psychology (Maturana, Varela, Piaget, von Glasersfeld) it in effect benefits a sociological epistemology. The Quinean program of a "naturalized epistemology" must be expanded to include sociology; yes, it can only then do what it promises. What we call knowledge is a product of the communication system, society, on which consciousness indeed actively participates as appropriate, but only in a minimal piecemeal way."[64] However, herewith, epistemology must give up some of its traditional demands. It can no longer serve as the basis for the sciences or provide foundations or certainties. "It reflects the uncertainty of knowledge and thus provides reasons. And then it need not cause us to wonder that no epistemology today can reach the degree of certainty that quantum mechanics or biochemistry has achieved."[65]

SOCIAL SYSTEMS: AN OUTLINE AND MAP OF
LUHMANN'S THEORY

Until the appearance of the *Theory of Society, Social Systems* long was considered Luhmann's main work. In any case, it was in his view the first book that elevated itself above the "null series in theory generation."[66] It fulfilled the subtitle of the German edition—Outline of a General Theory (*Grundriß einer allgemeinen Theorie*)—although strictly taken it does not contain a theory of anything, but serves rather as a systematically reflecting compendium of the basic conceptual determinations and definitions of Luhmann's teaching. Its goal is to erect a universal theory for sociology that unifies the discipline. That it is universal does not mean that it disqualifies truth claims of other theories, but that it is concerned with a universal apprehension of objects, a theory of everything social and not merely of extracts. If such a theory truly strives to be universal, it must take itself as its own object, that is, it must be self-referential.

Because sociology reads only its classic authors and otherwise has little in the way of theory to offer, Luhmann takes up a discipline-external, interdisciplinary theoretical development that has been successful, namely, the theory of autopoietic, self-referential systems.[67] It is the model of a *super theory*.[68] It carries out two important paradigm shifts: In the first step (around 1960) the traditional view that a system consists of a whole and its parts was replaced with a demarcation between the system and the environment. The second step (since the 1970s) moves toward self-referential, autopoietic closedness. Initial impulses came from thermodynamics, later from the biological theory of organisms, and then neurophysiology, cell theory, and computer theory, as well as from the interdisciplinary constructs such as information theory and cybernetics. "Not only was sociology excluded from cooperative research, it proved incapable of learning within this interdisciplinary context."[69] Luhmann aimed to help out by importing the theory of autopoietic systems into sociology and simultaneously testing its robustness on sociological material. In Luhmann's view, "the explosive of self-reference" is not something to avoid;[70] it is rather a matter of solving the paradoxes that arise or assuaging them in some other way.

Luhmann's method is that of a consistent functional analysis. He is always concerned with the functions, not the structures. By thinking through the function, what is well known and trusted is shifted into a different context. Because of the many possibilities for linkages, an object of functional analysis may appear to be more complex than it is for itself.[71] This functionalism has three sources from which one can see that Luhmann is indeed an opponent of sterile classical interpretation but is not against using it as a productive source of inspiration: The first source is the ethnological sociology of Alfred R. Radcliffe-Brown and Bronislaw Malinowski, whose work he had already read in the 1950s.[72] This is the origin of the emphasis on the improbability of the probable, which I will come back to shortly. Second is the issue of the deep effect of philosophy. Based on his work in mathematics and the foundations of exact science, in 1910 Ernst Cassirer was prompted to dissolve substance concepts into functional ones.[73] Above all, however, functionalism is a main tendency of sociology, from Emile Durkheim to Talcott Parsons to today, which Luhmann admittedly altered in one essential way.[74] In traditional functionalism, the function serves to secure the continued existence of concrete social systems. Luhmann, by contrast, elevates the concept of function above that of structure and can thereby free himself from the exasperating assumption that the functions exist in order to secure the continued existence of the structure, facts of the case or the system.[75] Herewith, however, quasi substances were presumed to which happenings were related. In such structural functionalism, it was always difficult to explain social transformation.[76] Luhmann's shift to autopoietic self-movement has likely overcome this problem.

The methodological formula emerges from the functional analysis "to search for theories that can succeed in explaining the normal as improbable."[77] This "inversion of the natural attitude about the world (*Weltein-stellung*)"[78] with its "disregard [for] experience and habit" and its breaking through "the illusions of noramality"[79] is in a certain sense connected with Edmund Husserl's phenomenological reduction, that method of bracketing the entire world and observing it with an internal distance.[80] Luhmann continually explicitly draws attention, from this range, even if he sharply criticizes Husserl's thesis as "transcendental positivism," to the notion that one can reach ultimate certain insights in this way.[81] This type of reflection leads rather to the opposite of ultimately certain evidence, for it transforms all certainties into problems.

The question is thus: How is social order possible at all?[82] Here a problem must be solved that has been known since Talcott Parsons as "double contingency":[83] No action can occur "if alter makes his action dependent on how ego acts, and ego wants to connect his action to alter's."[84] This problem concerns the conditions for the possibility of action. With reference to a value consensus and to long-term structures, Parsons relegated it to socialization and tradition. Luhmann attempts a completely different solution, which we are already familiar with from his treatment of logical paradoxes: "Nothing forces one to seek the solution for the problem of double contingency exclusively in an already-existing consensus, thus in the social dimension. There are functional equivalents—for example, those in the temporal dimension. At first alter tentatively determines his behavior in a situation that is still unclear. He begins with a friendly glance, a gesture, a gift—and waits to see whether and how ego receives the proposed definition of the situation."[85] Parsons starts with tradition, Luhmann with experimental action. An already accepted value consensus is not necessary; the theory is open to chance, in alignment with the "order from noise principle" of general systems theory.[86] In Parsons we find theory conservatism. In Luhmann, by contrast, conservatism is not required of the theory, and where it does come through, in his political side comments (often these are anticonservative), this is rather due to his personal temperament.

The concept of contingency "results from excluding necessity and impossibility. Something is contingent insofar as it is neither necessary nor impossible; it is just what it is (or was or will be), though it could also be otherwise."[87] The basic situation is simple: two black boxes end up having something to do with one another. In their complexity, they remain opaque to one another. For the emergence of a social system, however, it is completely irrelevant. There must be only so much "wisdom" that an interaction is possible.[88] The decisive question is how the system can start up in the first place. Since Thomas Hobbes, one has thought of the individual interest of the actors. Luhmann inverts this perspective: "The pursuit of one's own advantage is much too demanding an attitude to be a general presupposition. . . . ." The initial question is whether one's partner in conversations "react[s] positively or negatively to his communication"[89] and the position of one's self-interest is secondary, dependent on the partner's reaction to a suggestion. The problem of double contingency is self-solving because the emergence of it initiates a problem-solving process and thereby can even incorporate coincidences and mistakes. The thesis is "that double contingency necessarily leads to the formation of social systems and in this sense operates autocatalytically as an enduring problem (and not just as an impulse)."[90] It reacts sensitively to coincidence and thereby sets evolution in motion. "Without it there would be no sociocultural evolution."[91] The system generator in this approach to thought is thus a functionally introduced paradox, continually emerging and resultant everywhere, with a built-in tendency, once it emerges, to initiate processes of resolution. This makes it possible to eliminate a venerable traditional concept, namely that of the subject. "The rejection of the subject by system theory is closely linked to the idea that the world is not something that can be described from one point. The last attempt to do this was the theory of the subject."[92] After having served as the basis for knowledge and action, the concept of the subject from the philosophical tradition is hereby given up. In contrast, Luhmann preserves concepts such as the human, the individual and the person.[93] However, these three concepts loose some of their humanistic emphasis. The person becomes "collages of expectation."[94] The "I" then becomes something like what Claude Lévi-Strauss had described for many in the twentieth century: "I never had, and still do not have, the perception of feeling my personal identity. I appear to myself as the place where something is going on, but there is no 'I', no 'me', Each of us is a kind of crossroads where things happen. The crossroads is purely passive; something happens there."[95] This is the thought when Luhmann, at the beginning of *Social Systems*, explains that it is as if the book "wrote itself."[96] The issue here is a methodological antihumanism, not a normative one.[97] Unlike Arnold Gehlen, Luhmann does not demand that individuals subordinate themselves to institutions and he rejects such a demand just as much as a comparable moralization from the Left. "When there is a highly developed but poorly defined conscious-ness of problems, the result is a hasty array of embarrassing claims about theses of post-history, the end of the individual, one-dimensionality, tech-nocracy, the crisis of the capitalist state, etc., which do more to cloud things than to clarify them."[98]

His methodological antihumanism consists in carrying out the system theoretic differentiations and viewing people not as a part of society itself but as a part of their environment.[99] A posthumanist conception results from this—that the subject, that is, the singular human being, cedes its posi-tion as the guarantor of the unity of knowledge and entitlement to society and that he is also no longer needed in order to understand society.[100] More abstract identification standpoints will be needed than "that special thing, the human being."[101]

In Luhmann's theory, the social system thus does not consist of human beings, nor, as is the dominant view today, of actions, but of communication, which then only in a second step is broken down, and actions are ascribed. "The elementary process constituting the social domain as a special reality is a process of communication."[102] Actions are not to be separated from this, but they are indeed to be differentiated from it. This is the reason that Luhmann resists the suggestive temptation to treat them both, in parallel, as communicative action, as Jürgen Habermas does.

Then, specifically in the form of intersubjectivity, a residual of the old subject is retained. That comes down to a decision about the type of theory. What is more important, however, is that both Habermas and Luhmann attempt to move beyond the version of action theory that is dominant in academic sociology and that tends toward dogmatism, which is built upon a "very vague concept of the individual (to some extent only able to be explicated by pointing to people)."[103] Action theories of this sort teach that in fact only individuals—that is, subjects—can act, not systems (Luhmann 1984, 595).[104] In this "mere linguistic customs are repeatedly presented as factual knowledge"[105]—for language requires that we insert subjects. The common understanding that is generated by this—that it must be someone who acts, someone who observes, etc.—"has no theoretical grounding."[106]

Language does indeed provide this specification, but it by no means requires it because it is through and through possible to transform such verbs into nouns (action, observation, expectation, explanation) to establish a self-referential system as a medium that need not work with a subjective consciousness. The boundaries between language and the expressive pos-sibilities are greater than everyday understanding suggests, and concluding that a linguistic subject implies an acting subject is a typical fallacy. This is once again a place in which the theoretical sense behind Luhmann's linguis-tic mannerisms (and those of his model, Talcott Parsons) is recognizable. Wittgenstein's utterance "The limits of my language are the limits of my world" does not prohibit the use of a theoretical language to reach beyond the everyday world.[107] It must be admitted that this point makes it difficult for himself and his readers because it is typical in philosophical and social scientific theory to differentiate action from ("mere") behavior on the bases of an orientation toward a goal or purpose, the pursuit of an intention, or the possession of meaning, the goals, intentions, and meanings normally being sought in the acting subject. However, because Luhmann conceives of the concept of sense (or meaning) without a subject, he can also consistently conceive of actions without a subject, thus without already having to employ the contrasting concept, behavior. The meaning of the concept is transformed independently of a transformation in the theory that Luhmann carries out; however, the relation to the opposing concept, behavior, remains. The short circuit in the conceptual system that is always possible in this sort of reconstruction is avoided here. Because no action can be constituted without a system and no system without an action, it is advisable to dispense with the contrast between action theory and systems theory.[108] "So action theoretically, by all means the warning can be lifted."[109]

"Once embroiled in communication, one can never return to the paradise of innocent souls."[110] It is much more than language and it is also possible without language (e.g. also through looks, smiles, clothing, absence, etc.). Language, however, makes possible a stronger differentiation and thus participates in the differentiation of social systems. Communication is a highly improbable affair. It is improbable that one person even understands another. "It is improbable for a communication to reach more persons than are present in a concrete situation,"[111] and even if someone is reached and understood, it by no means need be accepted. Luhmann quotes Goethe's *Ottilie's Journal,* from *Elective Affinities:* "Every assertion provokes its contrary."[112] In any case, it is not completely imaginable that at the end of the communication everyone would sit there in understanding if there were not external problems. In Luhmann's view it is rather a continually arising double contingency that generates and regenerates the problem situations from inside communication itself.

Leaning on Talcott Parsons, the concept of communication is here expanded to a theory of symbolically generalized communication media, which steer the contexts of social communication. It is, for example, truth, love, power, and above all money, in part also art, and religious belief or its secularized form of "basic values." Communication is thus something like the continual "self-excitation that inundates the system with meaning."[113] To reduce the complexity that arises from this it is sensible to differentiate between the system and the environment. Society consists solely of communications. It should be clear "that the highly complex arrangement of individual macromolecules, individual cells, individual nervous systems, and individual psychic systems belongs to its environment."[114] Society can shift its complexity to the outside, so to say, and lavishly treat it in order to obtain capacity to develop a high degree of complexity of its own.

Humans, after all, about seven billion psychic and organic systems, are apportioned to the environment.[115] They are thereby not less important, even if the idea of classical humanism, that "man" is the measure of society, is abandoned. "But the distinction between system and environment offers the possibility of conceiving human beings as parts of the societal environment in a way that is both more complex and less restricting than if they had to be interpreted as parts of society, because in comparison with the system, the environment is the domain of distinction that shows greater complexity and less existing order. The human being is thus conceded greater freedom in relation to his environment, especially freedom for irrational and immoral behavior."[116]

In order to be able to more precisely determine the relationship between humans and social systems, Luhmann uses the concept of interpenetration, a term originating with Talcott Parsons. Interpenetration exists if two "systems enable each other by introducing their own already-constituted complexity into each other."[117] Both systems remain environments for one another. "Thus one could say that psychic systems supply social systems with adequate disorder and vice versa."[118] The relationship of the interpreting system is determined by double contingency; consequently one is to answer the question of how social systems can develop at all. One mustn't proceed from the consciousness of humans, nor from intersubjectivity, but from a reciprocal configuration context configuration for autopoietic systems. "The social system, based on life and consciousness, makes the autopoiesis of these conditions possible in that it enables them to renew themselves constantly in a closed nexus of reproduction."[119] Different kinds of autopoiesis, such as organic life, consciousness, and communication are thus able to connect with one another. This can best be conceived with reference to the concept of sense, and retrospectively the key position of this concept for the theory construction should be clear: "Meaning enables psychic and social system formations to interpenetrate, while protecting their autopoiesis; meaning simultaneously enables consciousness to understand itself and continue to affect itself in communication, and it enables communication to be referred back to the consciousnesses of the participants."[120] By reintroducing the concept of meaning here, we arrive at a point where the patience for conceptualization ends. Because there is only one short introductory article, rather than 128, I have laid out only a few, albeit decisive, cards; but the system should have become clear, and also that it all not only "somehow" fits together.

The complex and thick work, *Social Systems,* is much better suited to provide an authentic understanding of Luhmann than the multiple individual studies that Luhmann has provided since then, because in it an integrated level of abstraction is consistently maintained, and digressions and excurses are avoided. Every single chapter is thus worthy of a thorough and intensive discussion, and the work makes it possible for the reader finally to do his or her own theoretical work on the basis of these concepts. Luhmann is an author whose work has now been productively received beyond the discipline of sociology, in art, literature, religious studies, and political theory, and even in areas such as ecology and education.

NOTES

1. Niklas Luhmann, *Erkenntnis als Konstruktion* (Bern: Benteili, 1988), 294.
2. Niklas Luhmann, *Social Systems*, trans. John Bednarz Jr. with Dirk Baecker (Stanford, CA: Stanford University Press, 1995), 442.
3. Niklas Luhmann, *Die Wissenschaft der Gesellschaft* (Frankfurt: Suhrkamp, 1990), 706.
4. Luhmann, *Die Wissenschaft der Gesellschaft*, 520.
5. Luhmann, *Die Wissenschaft der Gesellschaft*, 85.
6. Luhmann, *Erkenntnis als Konstruktion*, 13.
7. Luhmann, *Erkenntnis als Konstruktion*, 16.
8. Luhmann, *Die Wissenschaft der Gesellschaft*, 86.
9. Luhmann, *Die Wissenschaft der Gesellschaft*, 87; Humberto Maturana, "Autopoietische Systeme: eine Bestimmung der Lebendigen Orgranisation," in *Erkennen: die Organisation und Verkörperung von Wirklichkeit: ausgewählte Arbeiten zur biologischen Epistemologie*, ed. Humberto Maturana (Braunschweig: Vierweg, 1985), 225.
10. Luhmann, *Social Systems*, 75. Luhmann here refers to Gregory Bateson, *Steps to an Ecology of Mind* (Chicago: University of Chicago Press, 2000), 459: "In fact, what we mean by information—the elementary unit of information—is a *difference which makes a difference.*"
11. Niklas Luhmann, "Sinn als Grundbegriff der Soziologie," in *Theorie der Gesellschaft oder Sozialtechnologie: Was leistet die Systemforschung?*, eds. Jürgen Habermas and Niklas Luhmann, 25–101 (Frankfurt: Suhrkamp, 1971).
12. Luhmann, *Social Systems*, 219.
13. Luhmann, *Social Systems*, 219.
14. Luhmann, "Sinn als Grundbegriff der Soziologie," 32.
15. Luhmann, *Social Systems*, 61.
16. Luhmann, *Social Systems*, 62.
17. Luhmann, *Social Systems*, 62.
18. Cf. Georg Lohmann, "Autopoiesis und die Unmöglichkeit von Sinnverlust," in *Sinn, Kommunikation und soziale Differenzierung*, ed. Hans Haferkamp and Michael Schmid (Frankfurt: Suhrkamp, 1987), 166f.
19. Luhmann, *Social Systems*, 432.
20. Jürgen Gerhards, *Wahrheit und Ideologie: eine kritische Einführung in die Systemtheorie von Niklas Luhmann* (Cologne: Janus, 1984), 23.
21. Volker Riegas, "Glossar," in *Zur Biologie der Kognition, Ein Gespräch mit Humberto R. Maturana und Beiträge zur Diskussion seines Werkes*, eds. Volker Riegas and Christian Vetter (Frankfurt: Surhkamp, 1990), 327. Cf. for a foundation, especially the article from Humberto Maturana and Francisco J. Varela, "Autopoietische Systeme: eine Bestimmung der lebendigen Organisation," in *Erkennen: die Organisation und Verkörperung von Wirklichkeit: ausgewählte Arbeiten zur biologischen Epistemologie*, ed. Humberto Maturana (Braunschweig: Vierweg, 1985), 170ff.; see also Francisco J. Varela, "Autonomie und Autopoiese," in *Der Diskurs des Radikalen Konstruktivismus*, ed. Sigfried Schmidt (Suhrkamp, 1987), 119ff.

236 Walter Reese-Schäfer

22. Gábor Kiss, *Grundzüge und Entwicklung der Luhmannschen Systemtheorie* (Stuttgart: Enke, 1990), 1, 17.
23. Luhmann, *Social Systems*, 1f.
24. George Spencer Brown, *Laws of Form* (New York: Crown Publishers, 1972), 1f.; cf. Niklas Luhmann, *Soziologie des Risikos* (Berlin: Walter de Gruyter, 1992), 23ff.
25. Luhmann, *Die Wissenschaft der Gesellschaft*, 79.
26. Luhmann, *Die Wissenschaft der Gesellschaft*, 85.
27. Luhmann, *Die Wissenschaft der Gesellschaft*, 83.
28. Luhmann, *Die Wissenschaft der Gesellschaft*, 190.
29. Luhmann, *Die Wissenschaft der Gesellschaft*, 189f.
30. Luhmann, *Die Wissenschaft der Gesellschaft*, 379f.
31. Luhmann, *Die Wissenschaft der Gesellschaft*, 190.
32. Heinz von Foerster, *Observing Systems* (Seaside, CA: Intersystems, 1981); cf. Luhmann, *Soziologie des Risikos*, 238.
33. Luhmann, *Die Wissenschaft der Gesellschaft*, 94.
34. Luhmann, *Die Wissenschaft der Gesellschaft*, 94.
35. Luhmann, *Die Wissenschaft der Gesellschaft*, 94, cf. Gotthard Günther, *Beiträge zur Grundlegung einer operationsfähigen Dialektik*, vol. 1 (Hamburg: Meiner, 1976), 228ff, 350f.
36. Luhmann, *Die Wissenschaft der Gesellschaft*, 93.
37. Luhmann, *Die Wissenschaft der Gesellschaft*, 94.
38. Luhmann, *Soziologie des Risikos*, 23. Luhmann's ability to apprehend these problems as pointed paradoxes is of course indebted to work he had done with the theology of Nicholas of Cusa, who is referenced already in his first publication, as well as to his work on Hegel's Logic, which opens precisely with the question: With what shall science begin? There temporalization is already anticipated as a possible resolution.
39. Paul Watzlawick reports this in his edited volume, *Die erfundene Wirklichkeit: Wie wissen wir, was wir zu wissen glauben; Beiträge zum Konstruktivismus*, 6th ed. (Munich: Piper, 1990), 230ff.
40. Luhmann, *Die Wissenschaft der Gesellschaft*, 84.
41. Ralph Schumacher pointed out this important difference.
42. Niklas Luhmann, "Tautologie und Paradoxie in den Selbstbeschreibungen der modernen Gesellschaft," *Zeitschrift für Soziologie* 16 no. 3 (1987): 161ff.
43. Niklas Luhmann, "Autopoiesis als soziologischer Begriff," in *Sinn, Kommunikation und soziale Differenzierung*, eds. Hans Haferkamp and Michael Schmid (Frankfurt: Suhrkamp, 1987), 320.
44. Niklas Luhmann and Stefan H. Pfürtner, *Theorietechnik und Moral* (Frankfurt: Suhrkamp, 1978), 22.
45. Luhmann, *Social Systems*, 359.
46. Luhmann, *Social Systems*, 364f.
47. Luhmann, *Social Systems*, 368.
48. Luhmann, *Social Systems*, 373, emphasis in the original.
49. Luhmann, *Social Systems*, 9.
50. Luhmann, *Social Systems*, 371.
51. Luhmann, *Social Systems*, 371f.
52. Luhmann, *Social Systems*, 385.
53. Luhmann, *Die Wissenschaft der Gesellschaft*, 698.
54. Siegfried J. Schmidt, "Der Radikale Konstruktivismus: Ein neues Paradigma im interdisziplinären Diskurs," in *Der Diskurs des Radikalen Konstruktivismus*, ed. Sigfried J. Schmidt (Frankfurt: Suhrkamp, 1987), 14f.
55. Luhmann, *Die Wissenschaft der Gesellschaft*, 512.

56. Niklas Luhmann, *Soziologische Aufklärung*, vol. 5, *Konstruktivistische Perspektiven* (Opladen: Westdeutscher, 1990), 41.
57. Luhmann, *Soziologische Aufklärung*, vol. 5, 40.
58. Luhmann, *Die Wissenschaft der Gesellschaft*, 512.
59. Luhmann, *Die Wissenschaft der Gesellschaft*, 521.
60. Luhmann, *Soziologische Aufklärung*, vol. 5, 35.
61. Luhymann, *Soziologische Aufklärung*, vol. 5, 39.
62. Luhmann, *Soziologische Aufklärung*, vol. 5, 51.
63. One can compare Spinoza's definition of the contingency of individual objects, presented in the *Ethics* according to the geometric method. See *The Ethics and Selected Letters*, trans. Samuel Shirley (Indianapolis: Hackett, 1982), Part IV, Definition 3, 155; see also Immanuel Kant, *Critique of Pure Reason*, trans. and ed. Paul Guyer and Allen W. Wood (Cambridge: Cambridge University Press, 1998), B 142.
64. Luhmann, *Soziologische Aufklärung*, vol. 5, 54. Willard Van Orman Quine's article "Epistemology Naturalized," which Luhmann often cited as confirming his theses, can be found in *Ontological Relativity and Other Essays* (New York: Columbia University Press, 1969).
65. Luhmann, *Soziologische Aufklärung*, vol. 5, 59.
66. Dirk Baecker and Georg Stanitzek, eds., *Archimedes und wir* (Berlin: Merve, 1987), 142.
67. Luhmann, *Social Systems*, xlix.
68. Luhmann and Pfürtner, *Theorietechnik und Moral*, 9.
69. Luhmann, *Social Systems*, 11.
70. Luhmann, *Social Systems*, 485.
71. Luhmann, *Social Systems*, 56.
72. Cf. Baecker and Stanitzek, *Archimedes und wir*, 131. First of all, Bronislaw von Malinowski (1884–1942) is to be mentioned. See his *Eine wissenschaftliche Theorie der Kultur* (Zürich: Pan Verlag, 1949) and *Sex and Repression in Savage Society*, 2nd rev. ed. (New York: Routledge, 2003); from Alfred R. Radcliffe-Brown (1881–1955), see *Structure and Function in Primitive Society* (New York: The Free Press, 1965).
73. Cf. Niklas Luhmann, *Soziologische Aufklärung*, vol. 1 in *Aufsätze zur Theorie sozialer Systeme* (Opladen: Westdeutscher, 1970), 72; see also Ernst Cassirer, *Substanzbegriff und Funktionsbegriff: Untersuchung über die Grundfragen der Erkenntniskritik*, 6th ed. (Darmstadt: Meiner, 1990).
74. See Durkheim, *Die Regeln der soziologischen Methode* (Frankfurt: Suhrkamp, 1984). Originally published 1895.
75. Cf. Kiss, *Grundzüge*, 1, 75ff.
76. This is the standard objection to Parsons, formulated most precisely by Ralf Dahrendorf in "Struktur und Funktion: Talcott Parsons und die Entwicklung der soziologischen Theorie," in Dahrendorf, *Pfade aus Utopia*, 4th ed., 213–41 (Munich: Piper, 1986).
77. Luhmann, *Social Systems*, 114.
78. That is Jürgen Habermas's fitting description of this technique. Cf. Habermas's description of this technique in *Der philosophische Diskurs der Moderne* (Frankfurt: Suhrkamp, 1985), 443.
79. Luhmann, *Social Systems*, 114.
80. Cf. Luhmann, *Social Systems*, 114. For a comparison, see especially §§ 27–51 in Husserl's *Ideen zu einer reinen Phänomenologie und phänomenologischen Philosophie* (Tübingen: Niemeyer, 1913/1980) 48–96; for more, see Peter Prechtl, *Husserl zur Einführung* (Hamburg: Junius, 1991). The difference consists in Luhmann's rejection of the claim to a transcendental theory.
81. Luhmann, *Soziologische Aufklärung*, vol. 1, 78.

82. Niklas Luhmann, *Gesellschaftsstruktur und Semantik,* vol. 4 in *Studien zur Wissenssoziologie der modernen Gesellschaft* (Frankfurt: Suhrkamp, 1993), 195ff.

83. Talcott Parsons and Edward A. Shils, eds., *Toward a General Theory of Action: Theoretical Foundations for the Social Sciences* (Cambridge, MA: Harvard University Press, 1951), 3ff.

84. Luhmann, *Social Systems,* 103.

85. Luhmann, *Social Systems,* 104.

86. Cf. Luhmann, *Social Systems,* 104f.; Heinz von Foerster, "On Self-Organizing Systems and their Environments," in *Self-Organizing Systems,* eds. Marshall C. Yovits and Scott Cameron (Oxford: Pergamon, 1960), 31–48.

87. Luhmann, *Social Systems,* 106.

88. Cf. Luhmann, *Social Systems,* 109f. Cf. Ranulph Glanville, "The Form of Cybernetics: Whitening the Black Box," in *General Systems Research: A Science, a Methodology, a Technology,* 35–42 (Louisville, KY: Society for General Systems Research, 1979).

89. Luhmann, *Social Systems,* 112.

90. Luhmann, *Social Systems,* 126.

91. Luhmann, *Social Systems,* 133.

92. Dirk Baecker and Georg Stanitzek, eds., *Archimedes und wir* (Berlin: Merve, 1987), 120.

93. Since Foucault spoke of the "death of man," there has been much confusion in this discussion. Manfred Frank clarifies some of it. See his "Subjekt, Person, Individuum," in *Tod des Subjekts?,* eds. Herta Nagl-Docekal and Helmuth Vetter, 54–77 (Munich: Oldenbourg R. Verlag, 1987).

94. Cf. Luhmann, *Social Systems,* 127. Hans Grünberger, "Dehumanisierung der Gesellschaft und Verabschiedung staatlicher Souveränität: das Politische System in der Gesellschaftstheorie Niklas Luhmanns," in *Pipers Handbuch der politischen Ideen,* vol. 5, Iring Fetscher and Herfried Münkler (Munich: Piper, 1987), 624.

95. Claude Lévi-Strauss, *Myth and Meaning* (New York: Schocken Books, 1979), 3–4.

96. Luhmann, *Social Systems,* lii.

97. Jürgen Habermas very clearly differentiated this, such that many objections of Luhmann critics adjusted and above all clarified that Luhmann is not to be equated with Arnold Gehlen. Cf. Habermas's *Der philosophische Diskurs der Moderne* (Frankfurt: Surhkamp, 1985), 436.

98. Niklas Luhmann, *Soziologische Aufklärung,* vol. 2 in *Aufsätze zur Theorie sozialer Systeme* (Opladen: Westdeutscher, 1975), 186.

99. Luhmann, *Social Systems,* 212.

100. Cf. Luhmann, *Soziologische Aufklärung,* vol. 5, 53.

101. Luhmann, *Social Systems,* 314.

102. Luhmann, *Social Systems,* 138f.

103. Niklas Luhmann, "Neuere Entwicklungen in der Systemtheorie," *Merkur* 42 (1988): 298.

104. Cf. Stefan Jensen, *Systemtheorie* (Stuttgart: Kohlhammer, 1983), 91. Luhmann turned against Wolfgang Schluchter. See "Gesellschaft und Kultur: Überlegungen zu einer Theorie institutioneller Differenzierung," in *Verhalten, Handeln und System: Talcott Parsons' Beitrag zur Entwicklung der Sozialwissenschaften,* ed. Wolfgang Schluchter (Frankfurt: Suhrkamp, 1980), 119f.

105. Luhmann, *Social Systems,* 607, fn. 7.

106. Luhmann, *Social Systems,* 439.

107. Luhmann, *Social Systems*, 439f. Luhmann thus reacts gruffly to linguists and the literati, who complain about terminology, the use of foreign words, and the incomprehensibility of scientific prose, but should rather concern themselves with making a plural possible for a concept like "differing" *(das Unterscheiden)* so that the norminalization sounding "differings" *(Unterscheidungen)* can be avoided. [Translators' note: "Differing" has been chosen for "das Unterscheiden" since it displays the problem of the German better than the more typical translation for such a context, "differentiation."]
108. Niklas Luhmann, *Gesellschaftsstruktur und Semantik*, vol. 1. *Studien zur Wissenssoziologie der modernen Gesellschaft* (Frankfurt: Suhrkamp, 1980), 246.
109. Johannes Berger, "Wie 'systemisch' ist die Theorie sozialer Systeme?," in *Sinn, Kommunikation und soziale Differenzierung*, eds. Hans Haferkamp and Michael Schmid, 129–54 (Frankfurt: Suhrkamp, 1987), 132.
110. Luhmann, *Social Systems*, 150.
111. Luhmann, *Social Systems*, 158.
112. Luhmann, *Social Systems*, 148.
113. Luhmann, *Social Systems*, 171.
114. Luhmann, *Social Systems*, 182.
115. Translator's note. The number here has been changed to reflect shifts in demographics since Luhmann's text was written.
116. Luhmann, *Social Systems*, 212f.
117. Luhmann, *Social Systems*, 213.
118. Luhmann, *Social Systems*, 214.
119. Luhmann, *Social Systems*, 219.
120. Luhmann, *Social Systems*, 219.

REFERENCES

Baecker, Dirk, and Georg Stanitzek, eds. *Archimedes und wir*. Berlin: Merve, 1987.
Berger, Johannes. "Wie 'systemisch' ist die Theorie sozialer Systeme?" In *Sinn, Kommunikation und soziale Differenzierung*, edited by Hans Haferkamp and Michael Schmid, 129–54. Frankfurt: Suhrkamp, 1987.
Cassirer, Ernst. *Substanzbegriff und Funktionsbegriff: Untersuchung über die Grundfragen der Erkenntniskritik*. 6th ed. Darmstadt: Meiner, 1990. Originally published 1910.
Dahrendorf, Ralf. "Struktur und Funktion: Talcott Parsons und die Entwicklung der soziologischen Theorie." In *Pfade aus Utopia*, 4th ed., edited by Ralf Dahrendorf, 213–41. Munich: Piper, 1986.
Durkheim, Émile. *Die Regeln der soziologischen Methode*. Frankfurt: Suhrkamp, 1984. Originally published 1895.
Foerster, Heinz von. *Sicht und Einsicht: Versuche zu einer operativen Erkenntnistheorie*. Braunschweig: Vieweg, 1985.
———. *Observing Systems*. Seaside, CA: Intersystems, 1981.
———. "On Self-Organizing Systems and their Environments." In *Self-Organizing Systems*. Edited by Marshall C. Yovits and Scott Cameron. Oxford: Pergamon, 1960.
Frank, Manfried. "Subjekt, Person, Individuum." In *Tod des Subjekts?*, edited by Herta Nagl-Docekal and Helmuth Vetter, 54–77. Munich: Oldenbourg: R. Verlag, 1987.

Gerhards, Jürgen. *Wahrheit und Ideologie: eine kritische Einführung in die System-theorie von Niklas Luhmann*. Cologne: Janus, 1984.

Glanville, Ranulph. "The Form of Cybernetics: Whitening the Black Box." In *General Systems Research: A Science, a Methodology, a Technology*, 35–42. Louisville, KY: Society for General Systems Research, 1979.

Günther, Gotthard. *Beiträge zur Grundlegung einer operationsfähigen Dialektik*. 3 vols. Hamburg: Meiner, 1976–1980.

Grünberger, Hans. "Dehumanisierung der Gesellschaft und Verabschiedung staatlicher Souveränität: das Politische System in der Gesellschaftstheorie Niklas Luhmanns." In *Pipers Handbuch der politischen Ideen*, vol. 5, edited by Iring Fetscher and Herfried Münkler. Munich: Piper, 1987.

Habermas, Jürgen. *Der philosophische Diskurs der Moderne*. Frankfurt: Surhkamp, 1985.

———, and Niklas Luhmann. *Theorie der Gesellschaft oder Sozialtechnologie: Was leistet die Systemforschung?* Frankfurt: Suhrkamp, 1971.

Husserl, Edmund. *Ideen zu einer reinen Phänomenologie und phänomenologischen Philosophie*. Tübingen: Niemeyer, 1980. Originally published 1913.

Jensen, Stefan. *Systemtheorie*. Stuttgart: Kohlhammer, 1983.

Kant, Immanuel. *Critique of Pure Reason*. Translated and edited by Paul Guyer and Allen W. Wood. Cambridge: Cambridge University Press, 1998.

Kiss, Gábor. *Grundzüge und Entwicklung der Luhmannschen Systemtheorie*. Stuttgart: Enke, 1990.

Lévi-Strauss, Claude. *Myth and Meaning*. New York: Schocken Books, 1979.

Lohmann, Georg. "Autopoiesis und die Unmöglichkeit von Sinnverlust." In *Sinn, Kommunikation und soziale Differenzierung*, edited by Hans Haferkamp and Michael Schmid, 165–86. Frankfurt: Suhrkamp, 1987.

Luhmann, Niklas. *Social Systems*. Translated by John Bednarz Jr., with Dirk Baecker. Stanford, CA: Stanford University Press, 1995.

———. *Gesellschaftsstruktur und Semantik: Studien zur Wissenssoziologie der modernen Gesellschaft*. Vol. 4. Frankfurt: Suhrkamp, 1993.

———. *Soziologie des Risikos*. Berlin: Walter de Gruyter, 1992.

———. *Die Wissenschaft der Gesellschaft*. Frankfurt: Suhrkamp, 1990.

———. *Soziologische Aufklärung*. Vol. 5. *Konstruktivistische Perspektiven*. Opladen: Westdeutscher, 1990.

———. "Neuere Entwicklungen in der Systemtheorie." *Merkur* 42 (1988): 292–300.

———. *Erkenntnis als Konstruktion*. Bern: Benteili, 1988.

———. "Tautologie und Paradoxie in den Selbstbeschreibungen der modernen Gesellschaft." *Zeitschrift für Soziologie* 16 no. 3 (1987): 161–74.

———. "Autopoiesis als soziologischer Begriff." In *Sinn, Kommunikation und soziale Differenzierung*, edited by Hnas Haferkamp and Michael Schmid. Frankfurt: Suhrkamp, 1987.

———. *Gesellschaftsstruktur und Semantik*. Vol. 1. *Studien zur Wissenssoziologie der modernen Gesellschaft*. Frankfurt: Suhrkamp, 1980.

———. *Soziologische Aufklärung*. Vol. 2. *Aufsätze zur Theorie sozialer Systeme*. Opladen: Westdeutscher, 1975.

———. *Soziologische Aufklärung*. Vol. 1. *Aufsätze zur Theorie sozialer Systeme*. Opladen: Westdeutscher, 1970.

———, and Stefan H. Pfürtner. *Theorietechnik und Moral*. Frankfurt: Suhrkamp, 1978.

Malinowski, Bronislaw von. *Eine wissenschaftliche Theorie der Kultur*. Zürich: Pan Verlag, 1949.

———. *Sex and Repression in Savage Society*. 2nd rev. ed. New York: Routledge, 2003. Originally published 1927.

Maturana, Humberto R. *Erkennen: Die Organisation und Verkörperung von Wirklichkeit, Ausgewählte Arbeiten zur biologischen Epistemologie.* 2nd ed. Braunschweig: Vieweg, 1984.

Maturana, Humberto R., and Francisco J. Varela. "Autopoietische Systeme: eine Bestimmung der lebendigen Organisation." In *Erkennen: die Organisation und Verkörperung von Wirklichkeit: ausgewählte Arbeiten zur biologischen Epistemologie,* edited by Humberto Maturana. Braunschweig: Vierweg, 1985.

Parsons, Talcott, and Edward A. Shils, eds. *Toward a General Theory of Action: Theoretical Foundations for the Social Sciences.* Cambridge, MA: Harvard University Press, 1951.

Prechtl, Peter. *Husserl zur Einführung.* Hamburg: Junius, 1991.

Quine, Willard Van Orman. "Epistemology Naturalized." In *Ontological Relativity and Other Essays* (New York: Columbia University Press, 1969).

Radcliffe-Brown, Alfred R. *Structure and Function in Primitive Society.* New York: The Free Press, 1965. Originally published 1952.

Riegas, Volker. "Glossar." In *Zur Biologie der Kognition, Ein Gespräch mit Humberto R. Maturana und Beiträge zur Diskussion seines Werkes,* edited by Volker Riegas and Christian Vetter. Frankfurt: Surhkamp, 1990.

Schluchter, Wolfgang, ed. *Verhalten, Handeln und System: Talcott Parsons' Beitrag zur Entwicklung der Sozialwissenschaften.* Frankfurt: Suhrkamp, 1980.

Schmidt, Siegfried J. "Der Radikale Konstruktivismus: Ein neues Paradigma im interdisziplinären Diskurs." In *Der Diskurs des Radikalen Konstruktivismus,* edited by Sigfried J. Schmidt, 11–88. Frankfurt: Suhrkamp, 1987.

Spencer Brown, George. *Laws of Form.* New York: Crown, 1972.

———. "Autonomie und Autopoiese." In *Der Diskurs des Radikalen Konstruktivismus,* edited by Sigfried Schmidt. Frankfurt: Suhrkamp, 1987.

Watzlawick, Paul, ed. *Die erfundene Wirklichkeit: Wie wissen wir, was wir zu wissen glauben; Beiträge zum Konstruktivismus.* 6th ed. Munich: Piper, 1990.

11 Systems Historicized
Wallerstein's World-Systems Analysis
W. L. Goldfrank

INTRODUCTION

One of the more unusual recent appropriations of "systems" as an organizing concept has been the development of world-systems analysis, associated above all with the prodigious scholarship and voluminous writings of Immanuel Wallerstein (b. 1930).[1] Many of the basic ideas of the world-systems approach had been articulated in the 1960s and prefigured in the era around World War I. But it was not until the early 1970s that Wallerstein synthesized, codified, and promulgated world-systems analysis. It was to become a formidable alternative to the three prevailing "modernizationist" schools of thought in the macrohistorical social sciences: Parsonian functionalism, neo-Weberian state-centrism, and traditional Marxism. In addition, it both drew upon and superseded the antimodernizationist "dependency" school that had arisen primarily in Latin America.

Into the present century, with its radical de-centering of the national society as the typical unit of analysis in the study of social dynamics, the world-systems approach had not only critically anticipated the blather about globalization ("modernization" revisited?) but had become an influential tendency in many social science disciplines and in the humanities as well. This spreading influence was in large part due to Wallerstein's intellectual innovations, to his collaborations with such contemporaries as Terence Hopkins (1928–1997), Giovanni Arrighi (1937–2009), Andre Gunder Frank (1929–2005), and Samir Amin (b. 1931), and to his formidable institution-building: a PhD program and research center at the University of Binghamton; a new section (PEWS) of the American Sociological Association, which since 1977 has held annual conferences and published a volume of conference papers; and an interdisciplinary journal (REVIEW). This chapter sketches the genealogy of world-systems analysis, adumbrates its major tenets, and notes some of its significant contributions, including an assessment of its hypotheses about possible future world-systems.[2]

GENEALOGY

In constructing and reworking the basic ideas of world-systems analysis, Wallerstein drew upon four important intellectual traditions, all of which run counter to the predominant Anglo-American social science emphases on universalist liberalism, scientistic positivism, and unidirectional modernizationism.

The older pair of these traditions is Marxism and German/Austrian institutional economics, the more recent pair "Annales" historiography from France and dependency theory from Latin America.

From Marxism comes the basic underlying conception of systemic, contradictory, and conflict-ridden totalities historically understood as the fundamental units within which social change occurs. Modern capitalism is one such totality, with its emergence, consolidation, reconfigurations, and eventual demise as primary objects of study. Capital accumulation, competition, and class struggle are at its heart, and in analyzing it, so too are the impulses both to identify and to help along the collectivities capitalism creates that may prove to usher in its supersession by world socialism. Other strains in Marxist thought fed into Wallerstein's synthesis as well: Rosa Luxemburg's emphasis on the persistence of "primary" (or "primitive") accumulation long after the initial transition to capitalism, Lenin's understandings of labor aristocracies and interimperialist rivalry, and Mao Ze-Dong's insistence that class struggle continues after self-styled "socialist" revolutions. And in his empirical work, Wallerstein often draws on the writings of European Marxist historians. But he also broke from conventional Marxism in one absolutely essential respect by rejecting the view that each national society goes through the evolutionary stages (slavery, feudalism, capitalism, etc.) commonly associated with the Marxist paradigm. It goes without saying that he had no use whatever for the Soviet Union's boast that it had created a separate "socialist world-system."

World-systems analysis draws importantly on the Germanic tradition as well, with echoes as far back as Friedrich List. Among the most significant ideas from this rich vein are Max Weber's insistence on interstate conflicts—above all the competition for mobile capital—as the political framework of capitalism and his emphasis on ethnonational status-group struggles as central to politics. Another three main ideas are Joseph Schumpeter's interpretation of economic cycles, his enduring metaphor of "creative destruction," and his forecast that capitalism will eventually undermine itself. From Karl Polanyi came the model of three fundamental types of socioeconomic totality in world history, the reciprocal, the redistributive, and the market-based. Wallerstein would rechristen them as mini-systems, world-empires, and world-economies, the latter two being variants of world-systems.

Another crucial strand derives from the *Annales* school of historiography, most importantly from its second-generation leader, Fernand Braudel, for whom Wallerstein named the research center he and Hopkins established at Binghamton University in 1976. Braudel focused historical study on the *longue durée,* i.e., enduring and deep historical structures, rather than on transitory events or instances of alleged universals such as "economic man." He also invented the use of the term "world" in the technical sense of a socioeconomic space with multiple polities and cultures, as in his book on the "Mediterranean world" in the long sixteenth century. The Annalistes revived the study of rural history and of peasantries (note the contrast with Marxism's focus on urban industry) as the underpinning of modern economies. And their empirical histories provided considerable grist for the mill of volume one of Wallerstein's *The Modern World-System* (1974, reissued 2011).

What came to be called "dependency theory" in the 1960s provided the final ingredient in the world-systems stew. This approach critically confronted both liberal (modernizationist) and Marxist development studies by arguing that divergent and highly unequal trajectories of change characterize countries in the imperialist center compared with those in the dominated, often colonized peripheries. At that time liberals called for foreign aid (technology and capital) to jumpstart Third World development, and Marxists called for bourgeois revolutions to do the same. But the dependentistas rather advocated for "de-linking" from exploitative center-periphery relationships and for "self-centering" economic growth. Wallerstein agreed with the diagnosis but found the cure unlikely at best and disastrous in practice, as the two most serious attempts at de-linking were to prove, the Burmese military from the right and the Cambodian Khmer Rouge from the left. Theoretically, the dependentista position took three steps forward by positing dominated countries as integral parts of a single systemic whole, but then took two steps backward, both by imagining that (some) parts could detach themselves from that whole to embark on their own self-generated paths and by implicitly treating the wealthy countries as having "developed" without the spoils of colonialism. Here was an instance where Wallerstein's insistence on the "system-ness" of the capitalist world-economy broke decisively with all of the various country-by-country methodological approaches that have long predominated in macro social science and that still refuse to die.

STRUCTURED TOTALITIES

According to the world-systems approach, over the entire course of human history three types of socioeconomic totality have existed: mini-systems and two kinds of world-systems, world-empires and world-economies. (A fourth potential type is envisioned as one possible twenty-first- or twenty-second-century future, a democratic socialist world polity.) Mini-systems are—or rather primarily if not entirely *were*—tribal groupings able to provision themselves with basic material necessities and to survive without protection from or taxation by a more powerful political entity. Over long historical time, fewer and fewer such systems have escaped either (1) domination and thus incorporation into some kind of world-system, or (2) extinction. It is doubtful that any mini-systems remain in today's world, except perhaps in the anthropological imaginary.

World-systems entail two or more—often many, many more—cultures with regionally distinct economic activities. The world-empire type ranges from simple kingdoms ruling over two or three tribal communities to the great civilizations of the premodern epochs with their multiple far-flung domains of differing economic strength and their complex administrative and religious hierarchies. Most important, world-empires are governed from a single political center that exacts taxes or tribute from the outer realms. Typically they experience cycles of expansion and contraction, and they often interact with other totalities via luxury trade, cultural borrowing, and military encounters on their frontiers. It is crucial that world-empires in this usage not be confused with the modern-era empires governed by individual dynasties or nation-states, such as the Hapsburg Empire or the British Empire: such empires are political units within the larger totality variously known as the modern world-system or the capitalist world-economy.

Like world-empires, world-economies entail multiple cultures and regionally distinctive economic activities. But unlike world-empires, world-economies feature multiple polities, unequal in power to be sure, but not so unequal that a single state can govern the whole. While for considerable periods in the past world-economies existed in several parts of the world (e.g., the Mediterranean, Southeast Asia), their typical fate was to become absorbed into world-empires (e.g., Rome in the Mediterranean). The uniqueness of the modern world-system, according to Wallerstein, is that the emergent capitalist world-economy of the long sixteenth century survived the seventeenth-century Hapsburg attempt to convert it into an updated version of the Holy Roman Empire. Instead it developed multiple centers of national power (the Dutch Republic, the United Kingdom, and France initially the strongest of them) that would contest for supremacy via war and diplomacy but would respect, if sometimes grudgingly, the Westphalian system of independent states, each with its sovereign ruler. Having survived the Hapsburg threat, the core countries of the capitalist world-economy expanded the system's reach in spurts over the ensuing three centuries, eventually incorporating all the remaining territories of the globe, whether mini-systems or world-empires, via trade, diplomatic invitation, war, or colonial rule. Most of these territories were incorporated as peripheral zones, a few as semiperipheral; we now turn to defining these structural parts of the world-system.

All systems are structured into parts with distinctive functions, and world-systems are no different in this regard. Wallerstein designated the parts as core, semiperiphery, and periphery. In contrast to the aforementioned replicationist views of modern world history in which each national state is portrayed as destined to undergo roughly the same stages of development, the zones of the capitalist world-economy have a strong tendency to reproduce their specialized roles, albeit with one crucial exception: as the modern world-system as a whole expanded geographically and economically between the seventeenth and twentieth centuries, opportunity space opened up for some peripheral zones to become semiperipheral (e.g. Brazil), and for some semiperipheral zones to become part of the core (e.g. Japan).

At any given time, core zones feature the most technologically advanced productive activities (e.g. textiles and shipbuilding in the seventeenth century, steel and railroads in the mid-nineteenth, computers and biotechnology in the early twenty-first); the most educated, skilled, and free labor forces including a sizable middle class; the militarily and administratively strongest states; the lion's share of world finance; and perhaps an even larger share of scientific research. Peripheral zones are the opposite in all respects, with low levels of productivity, coerced or semicoerced labor, weak states (or none at all, if formally colonized), and neither financial clout nor scientific prowess. The periphery functions to supply low-cost labor and low-cost raw materials to the wealthier zones, and its elites are typically allied with core zone capitalists or their commercial representatives. Semiperipheral zones are intermediate on most of these dimensions, sometimes literally so, sometimes as a result of combining within national borders both core-like and peripheral economic activities, as for example in nineteenth-century Spain with industrial Bilbao and Barcelona and agricultural Galicia and Andalucia. Among the mechanisms that historically reproduce and even widen the core/periphery divide are military domination, plunder, unequal trade, labor migration (when the laborers are sufficiently skilled, this is called "brain drain"), and the virtual monopolization of scientific and engineering innovations, including the armaments that facilitate continued domination of the world-system.

The discovery of the semiperiphery and the insistence on its importance are among the most significant advances of world-systems analysis. All prior macrohistorical conceptualizations were basically dichotomous: traditional/modern, feudal/capitalist, dominant/dependent. Semiperipheral zones have existed since the sixteenth-century inception of the capitalist world-economy and continue into the present, as sources both of stabilization (e.g., the subimperial role) and of radical challenge (e.g., the Russian Revolution). The most careful quantitative study of the semiperiphery in the twentieth century found remarkable stability in its membership between 1938 and 1983,[3] suggesting that this intermediate structural part is not only durably persistent, but that once it is ensconced in a particular world-system position, it is extremely difficult for a country to move into another one. Economically, the semiperiphery supplies relatively low-wage products to the core and intermediate-level products to the periphery. In times of profit squeeze in the richer countries, it serves as a site of industrial relocation, especially for industries that are no longer cutting-edge monopolies. In times of boom, it is a major source of skilled labor migration. Because of their importance to both system maintenance and system change, and because their politics are often the most dramatic and conflict ridden, semiperipheral countries have been a major locus of research for world-systems scholars.

Another major research topic has been exploration of the commodity chains of the world-economy. The idea was first proposed by Wallerstein and Hopkins in the 1970s to describe the way in which the production and commercialization of many major goods satisfying daily needs routinely cross national borders and have done so since the sixteenth century, when American treasure facilitated European commercial and financial growth, serf-produced Baltic grain and slave-produced Caribbean sugar fed parts of northwest Europe, and Scandinavian timber and pitch enabled Dutch ship-building. Commodity-chain analysis, including that of illegal goods such as cocaine, has itself become a growth industry over the last twenty-five years.

Differentiated geographic zones and the commodity chains that unite them are the material bases of the capitalist world-economy. To understand its political side, Wallerstein started from Weber's crucial interpretation of interstate competition as a necessary foundation for capitalism. From there he elaborated two ideas, state strength as a variable, and hegemony as a transitory phenomenon. State strength has internal and external dimensions. Internally, it is less a question of bureaucratic mass than of class compromises that facilitate efficient administration by lessening the need for a cumbersome apparatus of surveillance and repression. Externally, it derives from economic advantage, class alliances, and geopolitical position. Core states are typically efficient internally and powerful externally, peripheral ones inefficient and weak, and semiperipheral ones in between. Core states compete with one another for predominance in the interstate system, and on three occasions one such state has become hegemonic for a delimited period of time. This is a situation of dominating leadership, and it is achieved by simultaneous superiority in production, commerce, and finance, along with military prowess.[4] Hegemony has occurred thrice in the modern world-system's history: under the Dutch Republic in the mid-seventeenth century, the United Kingdom in the mid-nineteenth, and the United States in the mid-twentieth. But given the competitive structure of the capitalist world-economy, hegemony is necessarily transitory, as rival centers of capital accumulation emerge while the costs to the hegemon of policing and stabilizing the world grow ever less affordable.

PROCESSUAL DYNAMICS: CYCLES AND TRENDS

Some critics have faulted the world-systems perspective for overemphasizing system-maintenance, the reproduction of the tripartite structure, the observation (distressing to some) that anticapitalist rebellions have thus far been recuperated and redirected into new instances of competitive accumulation, typically state-led when claiming to be "socialist." But Wallerstein's vision includes dynamic processes as well, cycles intersecting with trends that presage the eventual demise of the capitalist world-economy and its transformation into a new kind of totality or perhaps its reversion to a (global) world-empire. To speak of "historical systems" is to posit dynamics that ultimately result—much as Ilya Prigogine models—in fluctuations that the usual equilibrating processes can no longer manage. Periodic crises *in* the system can be overcome; a terminal crisis *of* the system cannot. How close we are today to a terminal crisis is a matter of great controversy.

Drawing on the Russian Nikolai Kondratieff as well as on Joseph Schumpeter, Wallerstein argues that from its sixteenth-century origins, the capitalist world-economy has experienced 50–60-year economic cycles. The A-phase, or first half of a long cycle, features expansive growth, while the B-phase is marked by stagnation. Typically, the two phases differentially affect the three world-system zones. During A-phases, most areas in each zone show increased prosperity. But during B-phases, the core zones merely undergo slower growth, while much of the periphery and semiperiphery experience regression (e.g., Latin America's "lost decade" of the 1980s) and greater misery. At the same time, a very few exceptional cases of dramatic ascent are also occurring and being extolled as "miracles" and "models" of development (e.g., Taiwan, South Korea in those same 1980s). Over long historical time, this repeated pattern exacerbates core/periphery inequality. As in the perspectives of Marx and Schumpeter, recurrent crises are understood as necessary parts of the capitalist process rather than as failures of monetary or fiscal policy. They are caused by overproduction given the scale of the market, and they usually entail a shift by leading capitalist entities from productive to financial investments. Historically, they have been overcome when a combination of geographic expansion, technological innovation, and income redistribution downward recreates the conditions for newly profitable investment in production by lowering costs and expanding markets.

While consideration of economic cycles draws on a long if controversial legacy of social science research, the world-systems view of political cycles—the rise and decline of hegemony—is highly original and antedates the heated recent debates about the existence, the nature, and the extent of the United States's decline from its post-World War II position of dominance. We referred earlier to the three Wallersteinian instances of hegemony (Dutch, British, American) and should add that Arrighi posits two prior ones at the dawn of capitalism, Venice in the fourteenth century and the Hapsburg monarchy (buoyed by Genoese finance) around the turn of the sixteenth. As the capitalist world-economy came into robust and long-term existence with the defeat of the Hapsburg project, a pattern of hegemonic cycles emerged. First, great power rivalry and "world" war: the Thirty Years' War (1618–1648); the Napoleonic Wars (1793–1815); World Wars I and II (1914–1945).

Next comes a mostly peaceful period of hegemony proper. Then follows a period of hegemonic decline as competitors begin to match the hegemon's economic prowess and begin to challenge its leadership of the world-economy. Finally, this competition evolves into serious rivalry and, historically, breakdown of the international order and a new world war. Were this cyclical pattern to continue in an era of nuclear armaments, human life on the planet might well cease. Can a hegemonic transition occur without war? Is it likely that a new hegemon (say, China) will assume global leadership in the next fifty years? Such questions about potential changes *in* the system are inextricably linked to questions about changes *of* the system.

If "historical system" is indeed the most fruitful model for thinking about socioeconomic totalities, then there must be dynamic change processes beyond cycles, processes that eventually will cause a system's demise. Some historical world-empires eventually expanded beyond their capacity to exercise control while others destroyed their ecological material bases. In Marx's model of capitalist self-immolation, a majoritarian social class is first created and aggregated in factories and cities, and then educated through repeated crises to see the necessity of organizing politically to overthrow its exploiters and usher in a new system. In Thorstein Veblen's model, it is the engineers who see the irrationality of capitalism and take the lead in replacing it. In Schumpeter's view, capitalism's gravediggers will be hostile intellectuals and social-democratic majorities pursuing welfare-state guarantees who together will squelch the entrepreneurial spirit. So the idea that capitalism as a system will undermine itself is hardly a new one. In the world-systems view, however, it will take more than urban workers (as revolutionaries or as voters) and more than "rational" intellectuals faced with the irrationalities of the market to cause a terminal crisis *of* capitalism, although both these groups will doubtless play a part. Rather, a number of trends that in the past have enabled capitalism to overcome its cyclical crises and to renew the accumulation process seem to be approaching limits. These trends are understood as essential dynamic processes of the capitalist world-economy as a historical system.

The first dynamic trend is geographic expansion. The capitalist world-economy came into being in the long sixteenth century with Iberian conquest and plunder in the Western hemisphere, the onset of the Atlantic slave trade, and the regular provisioning of parts of northwest Europe with Baltic grain. Roughly speaking, then, the tripartite structure of the nascent world-economy came to involve a northwest European core, a southern European semiperiphery, and a periphery including parts of eastern Europe, Scandinavia, and Iberomerica. This system had consequential interactions with other systems, such as Imperial Russia, the Ottoman Empire, Mughal India, and Ming China. (Some world-system scholars, following the later works of Frank, downplay the rise of a European-centered system, arguing instead for a five-thousand-year Asia-centric world system— no hyphen—with the modern European irruption a relatively minor blip.)

After the institutionalization of this young world-economy by the Treaty of Westphalia in 1648, uneven waves of trade-based and colonial incorporations expanded its reach over the next centuries to encompass the entire globe. The analysis of incorporation followed by peripheralization is probably one of the most impressive accomplishments of world-systems analysis. Nowhere is it more strikingly available than in Wallerstein's account of essential similarities among the post-1750 absorption of four very different cultural areas into the system: Russia, India, West Africa, and the Ottoman Empire.[5] In each case, new export production and new imported products were introduced, local manufactures declined, and enterprise size increased along with additional coercion of the labor force. With variations due to greatly different initial conditions, in each case the state was strengthened internally and weakened externally.

As a potentially crisis-superseding trend, geographic expansion has obvious limits. The entire globe has been incorporated, with the possible exception of the seabed and a few extremely remote areas—hence the talk of mining or colonizing in outer space. In fact geography could now be said to be fighting back, in three forms: resource depletion, costly pollution, and, most ominously, climate change. Capitalists have heretofore been able to externalize most of their environmental costs, but that is becoming less and less possible. And while "green" technology may become a new source of profitable investment, the threat to capital from environmental damage seems at least as great as—if not considerably greater than—the potential profits from "greening."

A second major historical trend is commodification. If capitalism is at its heart a system of production of goods and services for sale in a market, then it follows that capitalists will seek to turn whatever they can into commodities. Once upon a time it was the basic material products of daily life plus luxuries for the rich. Now it is clean air and pure water, food preparation and child care, medicine and entertainment, with a push to privatize many public services formerly believed to be the province of governments, such as administering prisons or educating a citizenry. It is difficult to estimate how much further the commodification trend could run, since new "needs" are being created all the time along with new products to fill them. But there is considerable popular resistance to many of the latest efforts to turn public services into commodities, as in the South American struggles over water privatization and the widespread distrust of voucher systems for US K-12 education. Biotechnology firms are meeting strong opposition to their efforts to patent human genes. Commodification probably has more current possibilities than geographic expansion, but those possibilities may well be shrinking.

A third trend that has historically helped the world-economy recover its buoyancy is proletarianization, the conversion of peasants into low-wage workers, the commodification, as it were, of labor-power. This trend cheapens the costs of production and hence renews profitability. During the relatively stagnant B-phase of the last thirty-odd years, much of the Asian region has been the exceptional site of dynamic economic growth, due in no small part to its huge reserves of peasants in the process of becoming wage-workers. Likewise, many core zones have benefited from peasant labor migration, both legal and undocumented, cushioning them somewhat from the effects of recession. Roughly one-third of the world population, some 2.5 billion peasants remain in the countryside. Thus of the system-rescuing trends, proletarianization would appear to have the most robust future in the short to medium term. On the other hand, proletarianization typically brings with it labor unrest, and the urban growth it entails creates further potential for disruptive protest and increasingly radical political challenges to world order. Irregularly employed young adults, many of them with secondary and even university education, have recently proved to be potent antisystematic activists in parts of the world, most notably the Middle East.

CRISES AND TRANSFORMATION

Over its five-hundred-year history to date, the capitalist world-economy has experienced economic crises of stagnating profitability and political crises of hegemonic transition. Geographic expansion, new commodification via technological innovation, and increased proletarianization served to overcome the economic crises; war among core states has given rise to new periods of hegemonic stability. Past crises *in* the system have thus been resolved. In the present moment, the world-system is once again in crisis, economically stagnant and with US hegemony in clear decline. The economic crisis may be overcome by a combination of innovation (e.g., biotechnology, software, robots, clean[er] energy) and proletarianization in Asia and Africa. The political crisis may also be overcome, certainly not by war, but by diplomatic realignments leading to a temporarily stable trilateral condominium of core powers in North America, east Asia, and western Europe. "May" is the operative word here: if the world-economy manages a new A-phase and a workable international order, the system could well be sustained for much of the twenty-first century.

According to Wallerstein, however, beyond this current crisis *in* the system, the capitalist world-economy has already begun its demise via a crisis *of* the system. Following Prigogine's model of increasingly wild fluctuations and chaotic turbulence, his futuristics resemble those of current climate scientists though he articulated them before such science became well known. The underlying image of capitalism as a historical system is that it has expanded and hence overcome recurrent crises occasioned by relentless ingestion, converting all the earth's people and resources into commodities. Such a historical process cannot go on forever, because on the one hand population and resources are finite, and on the other hand it engenders resistance and revolt from its victims and their ideological champions.[6] As with climate science, too many variables are interacting to predict with any certainty how soon the fluctuations will become unmanageably chaotic and with what consequences for the otherwise possible systemic recuperation and ongoing reproduction. If Wallerstein's hypothesis is correct, decoding the present era becomes especially difficult, because one must try to disentangle the predominantly cyclical crisis manifestations from the symptoms of a terminal crisis *of* the system.

Barring nuclear catastrophe or a climatic crash, we can ask, finally, what might be the long-term outcome after the modern world-system has met its demise. In Wallerstein's view, there are two possibilities. One is an authoritarian global order dominated by future generations of transnational corporate managers and core-country government officials, a reversion to world-empire on a global scale. The other is an egalitarian and democratic socialist world commonwealth. He sees the germ of the former in annual gatherings of the World Economic Forum at Davos and the germ of the latter in the meetings of the World Social Forum, with its slogan "Another World is Possible." We are left to wonder whether either of these possible future world-systems would someday succumb to historical forces we cannot now envision.

NOTES

1. For a complete bibliography, see http://www.iwallerstein.com.
2. For a recent compendium of ongoing theorizing and research among world-system scholars, see *Routledge Handbook of World-Systems Analysis,* eds. Salvatore Babones and Christopher Chase-Dunn (London: Routledge, 2012).
3. Giovanni Arrighi and Jessica Drangel, "The Stratification of the World-Economy: An Exploration of the Semiperipheral Zone," *Review* 10, no. 1 (1986): 9–74.
4. For Arrighi's slightly different version of world-systemic hegemony, see Giovanni Arrighi, *The Long Twentieth Century* (New York: Verso, 1994).
5. Immanuel Wallerstein, *The Second Era of Great Expansion of the Capitalist World-Economy, 1730–1840s,* vol. III in The *Modern World-System* (New York: Academic Press, 1998), ch. 3.
6. This formulation restates both Polanyi's "double movement" and Marx's model of capitalist self-destruction.

REFERENCES

Babones, Salvatore, and Christopher Chase-Dunn, eds. *Routledge Handbook of World-Systems Analysis.* London: Routledge, 2012.
Arrighi, Giovanni, and Jessica Drangel. "The Stratification of the World-Economy: An Exploration of the Semiperipheral Zone." *Review* 10, no. 1 (1986): 9–74.
Arrighi, Giovanni. *The Long Twentieth Century.* New York: Verso, 1994.
Wallerstein, Immanuel. *The Second Era of Great Expansion of the Capitalist World-Economy, 1730–1840s.* Vol. III in *The Modern World-System.* New York: Academic Press, 1998.

Part III

Further Contemporary Developments

Introduction to Part III
Further Contemporary Developments
Darrell P. Arnold

The final part of the book examines further contemporary developments in systems thinking, largely beyond sociology. It includes an examination of the relationship between systems theory and literature, a discussion of the systems thought as relative to digital culture, a short introduction to one form of ecosystems thought with some salience (under the name of evolutionary cultural ecology) in Germany, but that has similarities to views of Fritjof Capra, and resonates with ideas of Donella Meadows, along with some thought in deep ecology, and ecological economics, as well as other general environmental thought focused on sustainability. It includes an examination of Prigogine's influential view and an expansive overview of the development of systems theory as related to organizational and management theory that briefly introduces a few of the main present trends in these areas. The concluding excursus is a metalogue on Gregory Bateson and a call in the end to integrate the ideas of systems theory and cybernetics into one's intellectual toolbox in such a manner that they fundamentally affect how we live our lives.

In Chapter 12, "Systems Theories and Literary Studies," after exploring why systems theories have traditionally had so little impact on literature, Andrew McMurry introduces some of the main applications of systems theories in literature today. He highlights work of N. Katherine Hayles, Cary Wolfe, and Bruce Clark, but also notes the use of ecosystems views and world systems analysis. McMurry's view is that systems theory has traditionally had so little impact on literature, in part, because neither the command and control character of much of early cybernetics nor Parsonian functionalism was attractive to literary theorists. And even now, in McMurry's witty albeit apt formulation: "[D]espite its modern mission to decenter texts, authors, and readers while exploring the posthuman possibilities offered up by the open text, literary studies remains disdainful of concepts drawn from fields that a) use mathematics or b) build robots or c) theorize business management."[1] He explores other reasons, arguing that the most important of them is that until Luhmann's work was available, there was simply no theorist whose work was quite so appropriate for the job. McMurry's view is that systems theories will have greatest influence on "those critics who consider how literary works condition or are conditioned by events, trends, conditions, and so forth in the social world."[2] He concludes that "[i]t is perhaps at this confluence of posthumanism, media, and mass culture that much of the most exciting work in literary studies is now focused, and there, too, that systems approaches may find the most fertile ground."[3]

In Chapter 13, "Systems Heuristics and Digital Culture," Raphael Sassower and Nimrod Bar-Am show how systems theory can serve a useful heuristic function for the study of digital culture and for other fields. They argue that since there is no one systems theory, and no neat way that all systems fit together as parts of ever increasing wholes, we are best served using systems theories as heuristics, which serve to counter simple reductionist accounts of reality. That is the approach they accept as they explore in which ways systems theories illuminate the digital age and the concomitant ways the digital age might illuminate our understanding of systems. Their account of modern systems is of broader historical scope than most articles in the volume. Beginning with an analysis of eighteenth-century economics, they note a modern trend toward explaining wholes as comprised by interactions that are greater than the sum of their parts and that lead to outcomes different than those of the intentional actors who make up the systems. Systems theories, on this broad account, are found then throughout the eighteenth and nineteenth centuries, not only in the work of Adam Smith, but also in the theories of Thomas Malthus, Charles Darwin, and Karl Marx, as well as Claude Bernard, Walter Bradford Cannon, and James J. Gibson. However, Sassower and Bar-Am do note that with Norbert Wiener and cybernetics, there is a full-fledged attempt to apply such thinking to virtually all mechanisms. What they particularly admire in Wiener's thought is its open-endedness. Since he does not characterize machines "as such," he needn't decide about what type of functions machines in the future might have. After looking at some of the historical developments of thought on systems, the chapter takes up questions of whether the conditions for system functioning are strictly system-internal or whether they require system coupling. Does the economic system or do technical systems function one way per se? Are they not rather dependent on coupling with other systems external to themselves? In their view, such coupling is important for understanding all kinds of systems. For capitalism itself only functions under certain conditions; and similarly, digital culture will have preconditions of its own—some certain forms of economic order, for example. In this sense—i.e., that they examine these varying systems as parts of larger environments that function only with certain conditions of those environments—their framework is ecological in a very broad sense. And it is then within this type of "ecological systems view" that the article continues to examine the preconditions for digital culture and how the digital world, for its part, affects various systems and our understanding of systems. What they provide is thus an analysis of the digital world, not as a mere development of some system or another, but as a world that for its part then enters into a complex relationship with the other systems, together with which it shifts and changes. The last section of their chapter drives home the view that systems theory constitutes not a full-blown research program but a perspectival approach. Especially for the digital age, they emphasize that attempts to understand systems need to be open-minded, critical, testable, and carried out with a view toward sustainability. In short, they encourage the employment of a constructivist and fallabilist spirit, open to shifts, changes, and surprises.[4]

In Chapter 14, "A Brief Outline of Evolutionary Cultural Ecology," Peter Finke presents an introduction to one of the other main strands of systems thinking that is widespread today—systems thinking as applied to the environmental problematic. Finke in various work acknowledges his own indebtedness to Gregory Bateson, thinkers like Jakob von Uexküll, Eugene Odum, and Ludwig von Bertalanffy.[5] Yet his thought also has uncanny similarities to that of Kenneth Boulding.[6] Like Boulding, he views cultural systems as emergent from and influential upon natural ones. Like Boulding, he thinks that the social systems need to aim at sustainability. Various developments in present environmental philosophy (or ecological philosophy) run parallel to the ideas Finke presents here. Indeed, the spirit of this is evident in developments of ecological economics, which both Boulding and Donella Meadows strongly influenced. Finke's view, like the views of the mentioned theorists, highlights the importance of recognizing the basis of all social systems in the basic earth system and the need for the varying social systems—or what Bateson characterized as the "ecosystems of ideas"—to be sustainable.

Chapter 15, "Prigogine: The Interplay of Cosmos, Complexity, and Culture," by Dorothea Olkowski, is important for outlining some of the basic ideas of chaos and complexity theory, which in many areas has eclipsed original systems theoretic positions. Indeed the development of views in the form of the dynamic system model that she outlines is certainly one of the areas in which systems theory is alive, but the earlier developments are somewhat secret. This chapter is predictably heavy on ontology: Are order and simplicity rather an exception in the universe than chaos? Is there a singular universe, or does the introduction of the observer into physics mean that, as Bergson intuited, there are "multiple lived times"? These and many similar questions are pursued here as Olkowski characterizes the shift from classical Newtonian mechanics to Prigogine's dynamic systems view. Olkowski quickly introduces key elements of the deterministic Newtonian worldview before contrasting this with the new world that Ilya Prigogine and Isabelle Stengers argue we now inhabit—one characterized by pluralism, deterministic and stochastic processes, reversible and irreversible ones.[7] Her initial focus is on the nuts and bolts of Prigogine and Stengers's account of the physical world—including descriptions of the butterfly effect, order emerging far from equilibrium, dissipative systems. While pursuing the above-noted ontological issues and describing Prigogine and Stengers's views, she contrasts their position with Einstein's, noting that what they take from Einstein is not so much his view that there is a timeless singular universe (which they view as a relic of the alleged observer-independent Newtonian worldview), but rather that the universe is an evolving process. Her focus here is on the processes involved in this evolution.

In her short conclusion, she links the study of nature with culture, offering some cultural factors that may have hindered research on the type of theories discussed here. In particular, she suggests that it is related, among other things, to gender issues, and that, along with demographic changes, the interest in the type of scientific questions studied may itself shift. In a culturally changed future, we may expect more emphasis on process and relational theories like the one she describes. Olkowski's remarks on the effect that cultural shifts have on our views of nature do align in an uncanny way with observations, familiar not only from feminist philosophy of science and phenomenology, but also from Gregory Bateson, who is quoted in the final chapter of this book as making the following comment about the role of the observer in the observation: "The social scientist is not only in the sort of position that Ashby has suggested for his observer but, worse, he is investigating a dynamic system more or less in the dark with a flexible stick, his own personality, the characteristics of whose flexibility he does not fully know. There is, therefore, a set of unknowns in the observer, which are also subject to investigation." In a somewhat different but not irrelevant context, he continues, "the premise about myself is built into my conclusion. The whole gamut of projection phenomena follows. 'There are premises about one's self, in terms of which one understands something else.' "[8]

In Chapter 16, "Systems Theory and Practice in Organizational Change and Development," Debora Hammond offers a general overview of systems developments, especially in the area of management and organizational theory, up to the present. While starting with a general introduction to some basic ideas of Ludwig von Bertalanffy, the piece has the merit of focusing on a variety of early developments that are often overlooked in accounts of general systems theory. Hammond discusses a very wide range of work, from the views of Russell Ackoff and Peter Senge to the systems dynamics approach taken up by the Club of Rome. Fundamental to her analysis of recent developments is the distinction between hard and soft systems approaches. Recent proponents of "hard" systems approaches have tended to emphasize the importance of top-down decision-making—incidentally, much as one tendentially finds among proponents of Niklas Luhmann's sociological systems theory—where proponents of "soft" approaches have often built on West Churchman's view that there are no experts on systems and emphasized the need for participatory, democratic approaches to decision making.[9] Hammond traces applied systems theory in part back to the work of Kenneth Boulding, one of the founders of the Society for General

Systems Research, who set it on a trajectory emphasizing the need for participatory decision making and who influenced critical systems approaches. The work of Ackoff at the Wharton School of Management is also aligned with this tradition and is critical of the technically dominated approaches to management, whether in alternative "hard" forms of systems theory or in other management theories.

Hammond's own sympathies lie with the sociotechnical systems approach developed by Fred Emery, which emphasizes the necessity of designing systems for humans. Proponents of this position underline the importance of workplace democracy and participatory forms of organization more generally. Such approaches align to a certain extent with "critical systems approaches" developed in recent work by Robert Flood and Michael C. Jackson as well as Gerald Midgley. These latter thinkers, while clearly in some sense aligning more with soft than hard systems approaches, view the "soft" systems approaches as limited by a failure to reflect on the role of power in influencing the basic assumptions of systems thinking. Such critical systems approaches, as Hammond puts it, are characterized by "three basic commitments: critical awareness, methodological pluralism and, perhaps most importantly, a commitment to emancipation."[10] The sociotechnical systems view that Hammond favors balances the need for knowledge of the technological infrastructure in modern society with a need for knowledge of social organization.[11] It emphasizes that in the last analysis, systems are to serve human ends.

The systems views Hammond outlines here thus move along quite different paths from those of Talcott Parsons and Niklas Luhmann, the preeminent figures of systems theory in sociology. Yet in very general terms, the views tend to maintain an action-theoretic framework akin to Parson's sociological systems view rather than eclipsing the individual so fully in the manner typical of Luhmann's systems perspective.

The book concludes with "Systems, Tools, and Bateson's Cybernetics: A Joint Metalogue." This transcript of a Skype conversation between Nora Bateson, a documentary filmmaker and the daughter of Gregory Bateson, and Phillip Guddemi, a former student of Gregory Bateson, highlights main points of Bateson's cybernetics. It discusses some of the historical roots of Bateson's thought in his broader family background and in his anthropological work with Margaret Mead. It also emphasizes Bateson's special interest in cultivating an understanding of the relational character of reality and of the role of the observer in the observed. Both Nora Bateson and Phillip Guddemi further emphasize his view that cybernetics and systems thinking are tools, and that while these and other tools allow us to change the world, they also allow us to change ourselves. The conversation ends with something of a plea to cultivate a cybernetic understanding and, as Ranulph Glanville also emphasizes in this volume, ultimately to live cybernetics.

CONCLUSION

Though this book does offer about as broad a theoretical account of systems theories as is available, given the truly breathtaking number of alternative theories, this book too is only partial. The contributions here, however, do go a long way toward filling in the gaps in knowledge about the varying systems views, making interconnections between them, and elucidating their allure. They show hidden influences that general systems theory and cybernetics have exuded and ways that more explicit forms of systems thinking continue to wield influence. Given that the ways in which parts and wholes fit together and mutually influence each other and influence other wholes and parts still, one can expect systems thinking, in its complex and myriad forms, to enjoy a long life span. The hope is that this volume facilitates reflection not only about its recent history but also about systems and the way we conceptualize them. Maintaining some of the pragmatic spirit of early cybernetics and systems theory, we can hope that this makes a significant difference in how we live and shape our lives.

NOTES

1. See p. 264 in this volume.
2. See p. 269.
3. See p. 272.
4. See pp. 289–90.
5. See, for example, Finke, *Die Ökologie des Wissens: Exkursionen in eine gefährdete Landschaft.* Freiburg: Karl Alber, 2005.
6. For an introduction to Boulding's thought, see Debora Hammond, *The Science of Synthesis: Exploring the Social Implications of General Systems Theory.* Boulder: University Press of Colorado, 2003.
7. See pp. 310–11.
8. See p. 361
9. See p. 331.
10. See p. 331.
11. See pp. 332–35.

REFERENCES

Finke, Peter. *Die Ökologie des Wissens: Exkursionen in eine gefährdete Landschaft.* Freiburg: Karl Alber, 2005.
Hammond, Debora. *The Science of Synthesis: Exploring the Social Implications of General Systems Theory.* Boulder: University Press of Colorado, 2003.

12 Systems Theories and Literary Studies

Andrew McMurry

If there is a literary system its existence has likely gone unnoticed by writers, the very people whose work supplies its elements. They are concerned with generating texts. For any first-order observer, a system of which she is a part is of no account. Only second-order observers find value in system descriptions. The circulatory system proceeds, and blood cells could not care less. A cardiologist cares. A writer writes; she is in the writing. A literary critic observes the writing from outside the writing. It is from that displaced position I make the observations that follow.

More precisely, my focus in this chapter is on the slight but growing influence of systems theory in Anglo-American literary studies, particularly in the United States, where systems approaches to literature are less common than in Europe, notably Germany. It's worth pondering that dichotomy: Is there something Germans know that Americans don't about systems theory? Or do Americans know something that Germans don't? Systems theory's failure to capture the imagination of American literary studies is due to a number of factors, which I'll discuss in some detail below, but the short version is that the dramatic shifts in scale and focus that systems thinking requires, the reductionism and scientism that systems theory seems to imply, and the incomprehension that systems concepts are met with by literary scholars are all factors contributing to the neglect of systems theory in American literary critical circles. Systems theories (of almost any stripe) appear so removed from the traditional methods and materials of American literary criticism that the latter would seem to require an extraordinary "reboot" of its fundamental precepts (author, meaning, narrative, and so on) in order to benefit from systems insights—insights that, frankly, often look to be inimical to what is still an essentially humanist discipline.

One might argue, as some have, that there is indeed value in such a reboot, not only because standard literary critical methods are suffering from a certain exhaustion, in dire need of posthumanist perspectives, but also because systems approaches promise to connect literary studies to other allied disciplines—and beyond, to the sciences and social sciences. Yet systems approaches demand of the critic enormous commitment to recondite concepts and models whose interpretive benefits have yet to be demonstrated powerfully over a sustained period by a leading figure (in the manner in which, say, Marxism, has been unpacked in the literary scholarship of Fredric Jameson). The basic stance of most critics continues to be that literary texts are intelligible to close reading; that these texts are constructed from, are constrained by, and comment upon some version of our world and the subjects within it; and that such texts constitute palpable ideological stakes as we read, interpret, and contest their meanings. Systems theories seem not to supply ready tools for the work associated with this stance. To paraphrase Niklas Luhmann, whom I will discuss later in this essay, systems theory is not easy, and one could die quite happily without having had a taste of it.[1] So the question for literary critics and theorists, who can take any number of easier, more comfortable paths into the heart of literature: of what value is the systems approach?

If one sets the bar for the deployment of systems theory this high, one must expect that systems theory will continue to have only a minor impact on literary studies. But one can also argue that, if we peel back the onion, systems theories actually offer a relatively straightforward framework and a useful toolkit of concepts that can produce new and important insights about the nature and role of literature in a world-historical context. For example, Luhmann's basic diagnosis of modernity can be immediately helpful to working literary critics, who are not chiefly theorists but bricoleurs and magpies. The question, then, to which systems theory can be usefully directed in this case is simple: of what sort of modernity is literature a part? A satisfying answer to that question opens up a space for many further and related insights into the operations and functions of modern literature, at both the level of genre and the level of specific authors and texts. Systems theory provides a compelling new language to frame as-yet unasked questions about modern literature.

In this chapter, I will (1) discuss the obstacles to systems thinking stemming from the entrenched humanism and historicism of American literary criticism; (2) review some of the key insights of systems theories as they relate to literature; and (3) speculate as to the future of systems theory in America.

OBSTACLES TO SYSTEMS APPROACHES

Before I discuss the intransigence of literary studies to systems approaches, I need to acknowledge that "literature" is itself a problematic term, at least for literary critics and theorists, whose work thrives on dialogue not only about the meaning of literary texts but also about what constitutes them in the first place. The limited appeal of systems theories, at least in North America, has to be understood alongside the implosion of the "high literature" conceit and a concomitant explosion of literary critical approaches.

At one time, literature essentially referred to well-regarded written works, primarily fictional and poetic ones, along with drama, certain genres of non-fiction (such as the personal essay), and those texts of sufficient age and stylistic brio that they had passed from immediate scientific or historical relevance yet continued to excite the imagination (e.g., classical Greek and Roman histories, biographies, and so on). But literature today is a term *sous rature,* in the sense that a central development in contemporary literary studies is the opening of the field to all manner of what had hitherto been agreed were nonliterary, subliterary, and extraliterary forms. Marginalized genres—popular novels, comics, pulp fiction—are now fair game, as are many forms of media—film, television, online texts such as blogs, and video games. These come up for scrutiny as literary studies transforms itself into a more capacious cultural studies discipline. As the only defining criteria for literary studies becomes language—in particular, language that has been troped and schemed away from conventionality—any kind of text, regardless of its explicit origins, can be fodder for literary studies. Even the principle works of other disciplines—philosophy and psychology are good examples—are now reread as if they were novels, whose characters are concepts like Subject and Object or Ego and Id. Methodologically, literary studies is incapable of excluding any materials not only for analysis but also as contextual items that bear on more classically understood literary objects. It's fair to say that to literary studies, nothing is alien.

If literary studies has become omnivorous in its hunt for primary materials, it has also become hungry for concepts and theories from outside its field proper. By the 1970s literary studies had moved on from considerations of taste, archetype, myth, symbol, biography, and aesthetic integrity, toward a variety of approaches (structural anthropology, phenomenology, Marxism, philosophy of language, to name but a few) that vitiated the conception of literary texts as discrete objects possessing exclusive and extraordinary merit. Instead texts became nodes in vaster constellations of meaning where questions of literary merit were less pressing than questions of location, construction, function, ideology, and reception. At times the literary text seemed lost under a cloud of extraliterary concerns, but the great benefit was that the closed authorities of author or text were at last rejected and their situatedness in the welter of worldly fact and experience was revealed.

Pieces of literature thus came to be understood as open texts (cf. Barthes' *SZ, Eco's The Open Work*), fully enmeshed in the semiotic web. This view, unrelinquished to the present day, would eventually lead literary studies to consider its relationship to a number of analogous holisms, including ecology,[2] physics,[3] neurobiology,[4] and chaos and complexity theory.[5] Concepts salutary to the open text (particularly contingency, perspectivism, recursivity) made these scientific fields attractive sources of ideas and models. A whole subfield of literary studies grew up around the interconnections between these scientific perspectives and literary criticism, going under the name of Literature and Science studies. By rights, systems theories should have been among the first of these holisms to be ransacked by literary theory for congenial concepts. But systems theories, which since Bertalanffy had sought a system of systems that could close the loop on the scattered isomorphisms of a variety of fields of knowledge, did not make a discernible impression on literary thought until well after these above-named approaches had already been unpacked in the context of literary studies. If systems theory was the answer, evidently it was to a question very few were asking.

There is no definitive history of the idea of system in literary studies, although the sustained attention of Katherine Hayles on cybernetics and systems across a number of books provides some of that history (see especially *Chaos Bound* and *How We Became Posthuman*). But there appear to be at least four reasons why systems theories made little impression:

First, in their earliest manifestations systems theories were linked to command and control regimes on the one hand and Parsonian theoretical sociology on the other. Neither of these held great appeal to literary critical culture in the 1950s and 1960s, which was neck-deep in the New Criticism, an approach to textual elucidation that had no want or need for systemic viewpoints that would undermine the integrity of literature's "well wrought urns," to borrow Cleanth Brooks's memorable repurposing of Keats' "Ode on a Grecian Urn." In essence, Parsons's action theory and the first-order systems approaches of this period could not find fertile ground in a discipline that prided itself on adducing, through close reading, fundamentally poetic truths about texts, truths that were important precisely because they were unchanging in the face of external stimuli and could not be reverse engineered as if they were symbolic productions of the cultural action system. Poetic truth did not want to be functionalized; it was an interior state of unity-in-tension that hinged on concrete formal elements and spoke only to the poet's mastery of the form/content dialectic and the audience's capacity to perceive it. Despite enormous changes in the literary landscape since the age of Brooks et al., the baseline defensive humanism of literary studies remains, as does the abiding sense that systems theory is for engineers, not artists (although in a bit of irony the autotelism of the poem under New Criticism seems to have a filial connection to second-order systems theory, particularly the concept of autopoiesis). This protectiveness should not be read as parochialism or insularity on the part of literary studies: literary critics and theorists are quite eager to borrow from anywhere. But they want to do so on their own terms, and for many literary scholars systems theories, rightly or wrongly, still smack of goal attainment, normativity, scientism, and, yes, even militarism. To put it even more baldly, despite its modern mission to decenter texts, authors, and readers while exploring the posthuman possibilities offered up by the open text, literary studies remains disdainful of concepts drawn from fields that a) use mathematics or b) build robots or c) theorize business management.

The second obstacle to systems theory was the allure of French semiotics and structuralism, which probably sucked all the air from the room when it came to looking for linkages between literary forms and other sociocultural patterns. It's obvious why the Saussurean tradition would have a more organic connection to literary studies than, say, what emerged from the Bell Labs or the Macy Conferences: there is a common intellectual heritage (e.g., philology, linguistics, rhetoric) between the two domains. Yet one wonders if in the right hands the emerging insights about information and meaning from the first wave of systems theory could not have similarly been made to jibe with the then-ambitions of literary studies. Structuralism occupied the metarole that, in an alternate dimension, systems theory might have filled. In point of fact, there is yet to be a good account of the fuzzy relationship between structuralism and systems theory. But we do know that literary criticism had a short affair with structuralism before abandoning it (for a lengthy marriage with post-structuralism, some might say) on charges of ahistoricism and mechanical inflexibility. Vaguely congenerous with "structure," perhaps "system" was tarred with that same brush.

The third obstacle appears only in the rearview mirror: the embrace of systems theoretical concepts by the counterculture discourse of 1960s with the resultant taint of "flakiness." The "hippie era of wholeness," as Bruce Clarke calls it, was marked by the counterculture's keen interest in systems thinking, particularly ecosystemic approaches that could model and support sociopolitical goals of interconnection, global consciousness, environmentalism, and egalitarianism.[6] Literary critical culture being what it was—still a highbrow sport—it took up these themes only spottily. In retrospect, it is perhaps easier to understand why extraordinary systems thinkers like Gregory Bateson and Anthony Wilden did not gain wide readership in English departments. They modeled exciting, generative systems approaches to language, narrative, and symbolic exchange that on first blush should have appealed to literary scholars. But the intrinsic conservatism of the discipline held sway. As with McLuhan, the potency of their work seemed mostly lost on the literature and communication specialists who were meant to be the primary audiences. The case of Wilden is particularly revealing: *System and Structure* was a heady brew of Lacan, Bertalanffy, Saussure, Spencer Brown, Parsons, and Sebeok, to mention only a few of his influences, and the book engaged directly with many of the political/ideological issues that would occupy literary studies for the next several decades: sexism, racism, power, subjectivity, and academic politics.[7] Language was at the center of it all. Yet the work had no appreciable impact on literary studies. Aligning himself against mainstream science and the commodification of knowledge, Wilden critiques the institutionalized violence perpetrated by the university, identifying himself as a "negative academic."[8] Very much an anti-"The System" system approach, Wilden's work, like Bateson's, crossed disciplinary boundaries and inserted itself into the social issues with a vigorousness that many literary scholars of the day simply could not stomach or did not want to understand.

The final and likely most powerful reason for the slowness of systems theory to enter into the literary critical discussion was that until Luhmann was introduced to the English-speaking world, there was no systems theorist whose work contained a sufficient amount of clear discursive/conceptual overlaps to catch the eye of literary scholars. (And this is not to say that Luhmann was by any means the ideal vessel.) As I've noted, literary scholars have absolutely no compunction about helping themselves to concepts produced in other disciplines; much literary theoretical innovation depends on the jerry-rigging of theories drawn from elsewhere. But when it comes to the integration of systems theory and literary theory, the attachment has had to be forced, for even with Luhmann (with his for-literary theorists-attractive emphasis on meaning and symbolically generalized communication media) there is a noticeable distancing effect in play, which is due not entirely to his theory's notable difficulty but rather to his enervating writing style and the devitalized worldview that this style seems to exude. Moeller suggests that Luhmann's off-putting idiom was actually quite acceptable at home in Germany, where his " 'soporific' style"⁹ helped soften the radical substance of his writings and "made him appear unsuspicious to his peers," who were for the most part mainstream humanists. But the bar was set higher for North America, where the discourse—political, academic, popular—still "relies heavily on the semantics of the 'old-European' Enlightenment tradition of the eighteenth century."¹⁰ Jokisch extends this view, arguing that the stylistic obstacles only mask a deeper cultural disconnect, "one that is based on the attitude that the individual has to his state."¹¹ In essence, American culture is not disposed favorably to theories that sideline the agency of the individual subject/creator. And this is not to say that American literary critics are uncomfortable thinking about the decentered, postmodern subject; they can, and do, in spades. But always with a view to the way forward for this problematic creature, not with a view to leaving it behind, so to speak, for the system to mop up. Whatever the case, to the uninitiated, systems theory often reads as if its job were to suck the lifeblood from the world and replace it with embalming fluid. Worse, systems theorists seem to have no interest in parts, only wholes, as if they are librarians who never deign to read a book. Configuring systems theory for application to literary or cultural texts is not easy. Just reading it is hard. Moeller admits, "The material sometimes makes me fall asleep."¹²

SYSTEMS INSIGHTS

If there have been four main stumbling blocks to the adoption of systems approaches in the United States, there are at least three areas of humanistic inquiry where systems theory has begun to bear some fruit. Of course, these areas are not mutually exclusive; there is much overlap. But they do broadly express the aims of those working with systems theoretical concepts.

INTEGRATIVE APPROACHES

This trajectory finds theorists positing that literary or cultural objects and processes are analogous, homologous, or isomorphic to other entities in the universe and that there may be common principles or laws underpinning or directing these organized complexities. The strong version says that novels or poems create effects, or are themselves effects, consonant with forces in play elsewhere and at profounder levels of existence. In the strong version, literary systems are not simply "like" other systems in nature (analogous) but, in an evolutionary sense, share a common, underlying origin or propensity (homologous) that may be explicable with reference to biology, ecology, nonlinear dynamics, self-organization, or neurophysiology. In *The Noise of Culture,* for example, William Paulson notes that "the question of how there can be complex cultural meaning in spite of textual dissemination . . . appears homologous to the question of how there can be complex natural structures in spite of the physical law of increasing entropy in a closed system."[13] Joseph Meeker suggests, "Literary forms must be reconciled if possible with the forms and structures of nature as they are defined by ecological scientists. Characters in literature may also be analyzed as typical or atypical representatives of the human species, and their behavior compared to patterns of behavior among other animals as described by contemporary ethology."[14] Meeker asserts a tight kinship between the methods of ecologists and literary comparatists: both are "students of process," and "if the world were schematically represented as an organization chart, ecologists and comparatists would study the various lines which connect the little boxes, while disciplinarians would scrupulously examine the contents of each box."[15] The thorny issue for theorists advocating the strong program is obvious: how tight are the couplings between the literary and biophysical systems? In other words, isn't the strong thesis more or less the standard reductionism, with a unity of knowledge established by a downward absorption of messy human sciences into the physical sciences, so that the foundations of even poetic activity lie in genetic or other biophysical predispositions? When interdisciplinarity starts to look like reductionism, those whose methods and materials are being reduced typically react with great indignation, for the upshot of the strong version appears to them tantamount to, as Tzevtan Todorovputs it, "ceding to the biological glutton the meaning of the creative arts and the direction of our moral and political actions."[16]

The more palatable, weaker version is that there are sets of ideas—artistic, scientific, and technological in particular—circulating in the wider culture that come to the attention of workers in specific domains and prompt them to think and create along parallel lines. Katherine Hayles uses the term "cultural field" to signal the resonance effect of broad cultural themes on the nascent paradigms and problematics of specific disciplines. These fields create "feedback loops among theory, technology and culture [that] develop and expand into complex connections between literature and science which are mediated through the cultural matrix."[17] This "interzone" between the self-organizing systems studied by the sciences and the self-referential works studied by literary and cultural theory is the focus of what Ira Livingston dubs "autopoetics."[18] Both Hayles and Livingston are less interested in discovering and defining systems or unifying the agendas of the various disciplines than in showing how systems thinking allows us to perceive and create cultural connectivity between the "hard" and "soft" disciplines—in a certain way, systems approaches help us overcome the "Two Cultures" problem identified by C. P. Snow. If there are epigenetic rules or systems homologies that apply equally to poems and slime molds, they are only distantly apposite to questions of literary meaning, whose high-level semantics are for most intents and purposes fully detachable from the substratum of gene determination or ecosystemic conditioning. To put it bluntly, even were we biologically predisposed to fear the snake underfoot, there is very little that datum can tell us about the exultant figurations of the serpent in the first eight stanzas of Stevens's "Auroras of Autumn," which include the following: "This is form gulping after formlessness, / Skin flashing to wished-for disappearances / And the serpent body flashing without the skin."[19] Paulson puts it this way:

> [I]f I practice interdisciplinarity by importing terms and concepts such as those of information theory and self-organization, violating conventional boundaries by identifying textual ambiguity and rhetoricity with noise, I do not do so to produce a Grand Synthesis but to disturb, enrich, and perhaps displace the study of literature by injecting into it some information sufficiently foreign as to function initially as "noise," the only possible source of new patterns. From the interference between disciplines can arise new forms of explanation, new articulations between levels of phenomena in a world of emergent complexity.[20]

SOCIOHISTORICAL APPROACHES

Some scholars are interested in identifying and exploring the workings of putative literary and cultural systems as they have unfolded over time.[21] Luhmann's systems version of modernity has been the most influential to date. But the work of Siegfried Schmidt deserves more attention because it provides much common ground with traditional literary historical methods and approaches. Schmidt's oeuvre, little known in America, has begun to filter in with the publication of a collection of his essays in English under the title *Worlds of Communication*. Over several decades Schmidt developed an empirical study of literature—which incorporated the apparatuses of text and discourse analysis and, eventually, the systems approach of Luhmann. Schmidt wanted to leave behind questions of hermeneutics and deal more directly with the operations of literary production, distribution, reception, education, etc.; in short, to "concentrate on social processes which resulted in literary phenomena."[22] "Interpretation" in this view is just one aspect of literary understanding, something Schmidt includes in the category of "post-processing."[23] The advantage of systems theory to an empirical approach is that while it provides a radical constructivist framework (like, say, deconstruction), it does not fail (again, like deconstruction) to deliver on more than simply a terminological shift (and one can point to the conclusion of many literary scholars that deconstruction is only New Criticism turned on its head, "disunity" and "fragmentation" replacing "unity" and "coherence" as the prized literary traits). Schmidt argues that literature and culture under systems theory are now amenable to a rational, scientific method, whereby clear questions can be posed and determined. One salient departure from Luhmann is Schmidt's inclusion of human actors in his empirical method, so that literary systems must be modeled as admixtures of symbolic communications media, programs, and institutions along with symbol emitters and their unique cognitive domains. Luhmann, by contrast, echoes Foucault at the end of *The Order of Things,* claiming that "I reject any invitation to speak about man as such—human images, how dreadful. Man as such does not interest me, if I may put it so harshly."[24]

The power and scope of Schmidt's systems approach notwithstanding, as I've already argued, systems approaches that cannot contribute to the main currents of literary and literary historical thought will likely have only modest appeal within the discipline. Where systems theory may generate greater interest is among those critics who consider how literary works condition or are conditioned by events, trends, conditions, and so forth in the social world. Here systems theories can inform critics' engagement with the form and content of specific texts. Tom LeClair's *In the Loop,* for example, investigates the thematization of systems by several contemporary writers: Gaddis, Pynchon, Barth, and, preeminently, DeLillo. LeClair's choice of title signals the embedded recursivity of the "systems novel," which is a kind of feed-forward/feed-backward device for exploring the constantly moving target that is networked, globalized, mediatized postindustrial America.[25] The processes and products of this culture cycle back into that culture, regenerating its organization from moment to moment—but also, as a result of noise, perturbations, and "copy errors," transforming its structure. Tracking and embodying this dynamic, the systems novel must approach its mercurial subject less with the aim of representing it than with that of capturing, in terms, style, and mood, its unceasing communicational flow. LeClair argues that these novelists "pursue innovative and often demanding stylistic strategies in order to imitate living systems, to be both spatial paradigm and temporal process, to give the medium of the text the illusion of reciprocal simultaneity, growth to complexity, and ecosystemic plenitude."[26] LeClair's project involves, then, both close readings of systems-influenced postmodern novels and a consideration of that genre's significance within a longer historical trajectory of systems growth and differentiation.

Another literary historical approach, orthogonal to those adumbrated above but also keenly aware of the centrality of genre, has been developed by Franco Moretti via Immanuel Wallerstein's world-system theory. In *Modern Epic: The World System from Goethe to Garcia Márquez*, Moretti was focused on the disconcerting evolution and diffusion of the modern epic since the Early Modern period away from the traditional centers of England and France.[27] "Disconcerting," as he explains in a later essay, "because between 1650 and 1950 these two literatures are unquestionably the core of the world literary system—and yet, in the most ambitious genre of all, they are replaced by German, American, Irish, Latin American writers . . . Why?"[28] The modern epic, the novel of all things, which hearkens back to the great classical poems of Homer and Virgil, seems to have emerged at the same time as the great capitalist expansion of the eighteenth century. Works by Goethe, Wagner, Melville, Joyce, Pound, and Eliot, among others, present a remarkable opportunity to understand cultural production within the context of world-systems analysis. In Moretti's application of Wallerstein, "a common ground emerges: they are all writers from the semiperiphery, who were probably encouraged by their intermediate and dynamic position to grapple with the world as a whole." The value of world-systems theory, then, is in moving us away from studying a thematics of "globalization" or "the world-system" as expressed overtly in literary works to a view of such works as actual embodiments of those very forces of world-system formation and expansion. Epics are not simply texts about the whole but texts that "mix a plot from the core, and a style from the periphery."[29]

EPISTEMOLOGICAL APPROACHES

One of the preoccupations of Modernist writers was the relationship of the (allegedly) knowing self to world. In American prose writing, as early as the American Romantic period questions were being raised as to our capacities to calibrate knower and known. For Emerson, who began as a by-the-numbers Idealist, the reliability of "seeing" (read, first-order observation) came up for scrutiny: "Where do we find ourselves? In a series of which we do not know the extremes, and believe that it has none."[30] By the mid-twentieth century, the full-blown epistemological crisis that marked High Modernism had emerged with the likes of Wallace Stevens, whose work was characterized by a poetic grappling with the infelicity of subject to object and word to world. Cary Wolfe's systems approach to literary figures like Emerson and Stevens has mapped precisely this evolution of second-order perspective onto the thematics of their most self-reflexive prose and poetry. In both cases, Wolfe draws on Luhmann's point that observation is blind to its own distinction, that only second-order observation can "deparadoxize" first-order observation. When the "imperial self" (to borrow Quentin Anderson's term for the traditional liberal, humanist subject) is shaken by events or realizations that call into question its stability and durability, well, if that shaken subject is a certain kind of poet or thinker, the results can be quite interesting. Emerson reveals his felt awareness of this "unhandsome condition" in key essays such as "Experience" and, particularly, "Circles," about which Wolfe claims "the only way for the Emersonian self to 'stand' is to not stand, to not stand still, but to move in 'abandonment' beyond the self of 'apprehension' that one was only a second ago."[31] With Stevens, the epistemological doubt that accompanies second-order observation is taken even further when it is placed within the context of the poetico-philosophic probing of external reality that is central to his aesthetic. Wolfe writes that "in Luhmann's terms . . . observation is multiple, contingent, and paradoxical in its self-reference [and] cannot be overcome, and it's a good thing, too. It both creates and partakes of a world that is 'imperfect,' that 'lies in flawed words and stubborn sounds.' "[32] Wolfe's point is that for Stevens— and many other Modernist poets, doubtlessly—poetry hinges precisely on the issue of how to figure the lamentable contingency of reality that so often forms the thematics of the poetic project. This unhandsome condition of contingency is exactly one of the features of systems that Luhmann's work, in particular, has opened up for us with great precision and power.

The problematics of first-, second-, and even third-order observation as they relate to literary understanding have also been explored by Joseph Tabbi and, to an unparalleled degree, by Bruce Clarke.[33] In *Posthuman Metamorphosis: Narrative and Systems*, Clarke locates in Varela's and Maturana's concept of autopioesis and Luhmann's elaboration of the concept in social systems an extraordinarily rich set of tools for considering the evolution (and transgression) of the idea of the "human" in a variety of target texts, from Shakespeare's *A Midsummer Night's Dream* to David Cronenberg's *The Fly*. What Clarke shows, with an expansiveness that to date no one else has managed, is that systems concepts not only are amenable to a variety of well-known narrative schemes (e.g., those developed by Mieke Bal and Gerard Genette) but that they also can be deployed in a manner complementary to the preoccupations of our own environmentally-precarious, media-saturated, transdisciplinary, poststructural, posthumanist moment.

SYSTEMS THEORIES AND LITERATURE: PROSPECTS

It is perhaps at this confluence of posthumanism, media, and mass culture that much of the most exciting work in literary studies is now focused, and there, too, that systems approaches may find the most fertile ground. But let us back up for a moment to reflect on the basic terrain that systems theories occupy, and why their extension into the cognitive ecologies of contemporary mediatized culture might prove attractive, if not altogether painless.

One of the challenges of thinking across academic disciplines (or, for that matter, many divisions of knowledge and techné) is that eventually we find ourselves coming up against what appear to be incommensurable views of what constitutes the objects and ambits of knowledge: the venerable Two Cultures debate, by any other name. Systems, as we have noted above, are meant to overcome this dualism by foregrounding relations rather than things, connections rather than compartments. This much is well known. But we could also say that within systems thinking itself there is another somewhat challenging dichotomy, that between mechanical and natural systems, and those that are made of lighter stuff, like information or consciousness. Apropos this dichotomy, a once-useful distinction was made by Checkland between hard and soft systems. Hard systems are those that for all intents and purposes appear to exist objectively in the world: well-defined systems like amoebas, radiators, and economies, in which the elements, boundaries, inputs, outputs, and feedbacks can be specified and measured concretely. Soft systems are those that, to use Ion Georgiou's apt phrase, are only "answerable to consciousness."[34] Soft systems rise and fall on the motivated perspective of an observer; their components are shifty and evanescent, and they don't stick around. To give but one example: every time we engage in conversation with another we are creating a soft system (what Luhmann calls an interaction system). The elements here are symbols, put into a systemic relationship via the thoughts and actions of the speakers, who draw on the resources of a cultural semantics and an expectation regime to establish a meaningful exchange. Soft systems emerge in the process of drawing distinctions, and such distinctions depend on the variable and multifarious activity of human agents, who observe, define, and participate in systems constantly, whether they know it or not—or, perhaps more importantly, whether they choose to identify their activity as system-generative or, more likely, as something else (e.g., shooting the breeze, having a chat). While hard systems are empirically verifiable, soft systems are in the eye of the beholder, so to speak.

Thus this division illustrates some of the difficulty of conceiving as systems—or even as entities subject to systems constraints—literary artifacts and processes, which as a result of their "softness" are labile or dissipate very quickly, perhaps as quickly as they are distinguished by an observer. Luhmann, for the purposes of his grand sociological project, took a great conceptual leap in extending the work on autopoietic living systems to social systems, despite the misgivings of Maturana, who had less tolerance for the soft systems approach. Luhmann came up with ways to ensure the longevity and robustness of social systems, including temporal binding and structure. But the basic challenge for literary scholars wishing to outline a soft system of literature is that the old literary critical lexicon proves hard to give up. As we work to understand and make use of systems theory, we find ourselves translating its audacious conceptual vocabularies into more familiar equivalents. Basically, we task systems theory with confirming what we already know, albeit in a new and startling language. But in this translation, unfortunately, we reassert the concepts and values we are trying to move beyond (author, intention, context, influence, and so forth). To the extent that systems theory is deployed only to give a systems patina to prior understandings of, say, modernity, globalization, and subjectivity, to the same extent has systems theory failed to live up to its potential.

Instead, where systems theory could make a difference (that makes a difference) is precisely in the undoing of what is also holding it back: the abiding humanism of literary studies and cultural in general. We do not yet know all that systems approaches to literature can do—though we have hints from the likes of Wolfe, Hayles, Clark, et al. We are still beholden to the precepts and vocabulary of traditional literary studies, with its deep roots in Enlightenment subjectivity, progressive rationality, and anthropocentrism. So it is at this very point of entrenched strength that systems theorists and their literary critical fellow travelers must aim their blows. They must assume the burden of risk that Luhmann outlines at the outset of his monumental *Social Systems:* "the concept of system refers to something that is in reality a system and thereby incurs the responsibility of testing statements against reality."[35] What this means for literary scholars is quite demanding and deeply provocative. It means that no longer can they adhere unselfconsciously to the old divisions of literary knowledge and the long lading lists of inherited pieties, values, and oppositions—the literary and the nonliterary, to name one obvious example, and the human and the nonhuman, to name a less obvious but more searching one. It means replacing such oppositions with the distinction between systems and environments. It means understanding "meaning" not as what a text is "about" but as the milieu in which literature handles internal and external complexity. It means, above all, jettisoning interpretation for the observation of observations.

NOTES

1. Niklas Luhmann, *Social Systems,* trans. John Bednarz Jr., with Dirk Baecker (Stanford: Stanford University Press, 1984/1995), 1.
2. Joseph Meeker, *The Comedy of Survival* (New York: Charles Scribner's Sons, 1972).
3. Robert Nadeau, *Readings from the New Book on Nature: Physics and Metaphysics in the Modern Novel* (Amherst: University of Massachusetts Press, 1981).
4. Frederick Turner, *Natural Classicism* (Charlottesville: University of Virginia Press, 1992).
5. N. Katherine Hayles, *Chaos Bound* (Ithaca: Cornell University Press, 1990).
6. Bruce Clarke, "Steps to an Ecology of Systems: Whole Earth and Systemic Holism," in *Addressing Modernity: Social Systems Theory and U.S. Cultures,* eds. Hannes Bergthaller and Carsten Schinko (Amsterdam: Rodopi, 2011), 261.

7. Anthony Wilden, *System and Structure* (London: Tavistock, 1972).
8. Wilden, *System and Structure*, xxv.
9. Hans-Georg Moeller, *The Radical Luhmann* (New York: Columbia University Press, 2012), 3.
10. Moeller, *The Radical Luhmann*, 20.
11. Rodrigo Jokisch, "Why Did Luhmann's Social Systems Theory Find So Little Resonance in the United States?," in *Addressing Modernity: Social Systems Theory and U.S. Cultures*, eds. Hannes Bergthaller and Carsten Schinko (Amsterdam: Rodopi, 2011), 203.
12. Jokisch, "Why?," 10.
13. William Paulson, *The Noise of Culture* (Ithaca: Cornell University Press, 1988).
14. Meeker, *The Comedy of Survival*, 9–10.
15. Meeker, *The Comedy of Survival*, 13.
16. Tzvetan Todorov, "'The Surrender to Nature,' Review of E.O. Wilson's *Consilience: The Unity of Knowledge*," *The New Republic* (April 1998): 29–33.
17. Hayles, *Chaos Bound*, 3–4.
18. Ira Livingston, *Between Science and Literature: An Introduction to Autopoetics* (Urbana: University of Illinois Press, 2006), 1–2.
19. See Wallace Stevens, *The Collected Poems* (New York: Vintage, 1982), 411.
20. William Paulson, "Literature, Complexity, Interdisciplinarity," in *Chaos and Order: Complex Dynamics in Literature and Science,* ed. N. Katherine Hayles (Chicago: University of Chicago Press, 1991), 49.
21. See Cary Wolfe, *Critical Environments* (Minneapolis: University of Minnesota Press, 1998); William Rasch, *Niklas Luhmann's Modernity* (Stanford: Stanford University Press, 2000); Andrew McMurry, *Environmental Renaissance* (Athens: University of Georgia Press, 2003).
22. Siegfried Schmidt, "Literary Studies from Hermeneutics to Media Culture Studies," *Comparative Literature and Culture* 12 no. 1 (2010): 5, doi:10.7771/1481-4374.1569.
23. Seigfried Schmidt, *Worlds of Communication* (Oxford: Peter Lang, 2011), xxi.
24. Niklas Luhmann, "A Conversation with Niklas Luhmann on Art and Society," *Logos: A Journal of Modern Society and Culture* 1, no. 3 (2002): 117, http://www.logosjournal.com/issue_1.3.pdf.
25. Tom LeClair, *In the Loop: Don DeLillo and the Systems Novel* (Urbana: University of Illinois Press, 1987).
26. Luhmann, "A Conversation with Niklas Luhmann," 18.
27. Franco Moretti, *Modern Epic*, trans. Quintin Hoare (London: Verso, 1996).
28. Moretti, "World-Systems Analysis, Evolutionary Theory, Weltliteratur," in *Immanuel Wallerstein and the Problem of the World: System, Scale, Culture,* eds. David Palumbo-Liu, Bruce Robbins, and Nirvana Tanoukhi (Durham: Duke University Press, 2011), 68.
29. Moretti, *World-Systems Analysis,* 74.
30. Emerson, Ralph Waldo, "Experience" (1844), in *Essays: First and Second Series* (New York: Vintage, 1990), 241.
31. Cary Wolfe, "'The Eye Is the First Circle': Emerson's 'Romanticism,' Cavell's Skepticism, Luhmann's Modernity," in *The Other Emerson*, eds. Branka Arsic' and Cary Wolfe (Minneapolis: University of Minnesota Press, 2010), 194.
32. Carly Wolfe, *What Is Posthumanism?* (Minneapolis: University of Minnesota Press, 2010), 281.

33. See Joseph Tabbi, *Cognitive Fictions* (Minneapolis: University of Minnesota Press, 2002). See Bruce Clark, *Posthuman Metamorphosis: Narrative and Systems* (New York: Fordham University Press, 2009).
34. Ion Georgiou, *Thinking Through Systems Thinking* (New York: Routledge, 2007), 29. For Peter Checkland's work on this see, *Systems Thinking, Systems Practice* (Chichester: Wiley, 1981).
35. Luhmann, *Social Systems*, 12.

REFERENCES

Barthes, Roland S/Z: *An Essay*. Translated by Richard Miller. New York: Hill and Wang, 1970/1975.

Checkland, Peter. *Systems Thinking, Systems Practice*. Chichester: Wiley, 1981.

Clark, Bruce. *Posthuman Metamorphosis: Narrative and Systems*. New York: Fordham University Press, 2009.

———. "Steps to an Ecology of Systems: Whole Earth and Systemic Holism." In *Addressing Modernity: Social Systems Theory and U.S. Cultures*, edited by Hannes Bergthaller and Carsten Schinko. Amsterdam: Rodopi, 2011.

Eco, Umberto. *The Open Work*. Translated by Anna Cancogni. Cambridge, MA: Harvard University Press, 1962/1989.

Emerson, Ralph Waldo. "Experience." In *Essays: First and Second Series*. New York: Vintage, 1844/1990.

Georgiou, Ion. *Thinking Through Systems Thinking*. New York: Routledge, 2007.

Hayles, N. Katherine. *Chaos Bound*. Ithaca: Cornell University Press, 1990.

———. *How We Became Posthuman*. Chicago: University of Chicago Press, 1999.

Jokisch, Rodrigo. "Why Did Luhmann's Social Systems Theory Find So Little Resonance in the United States?" In *Addressing Modernity: Social Systems Theory and U.S. Cultures*, edited by Hannes Bergthaller and Carsten Schinko. Amsterdam: Rodopi, 2011.

LeClair, Tom. *In the Loop: Don DeLillo and the Systems Novel*. Urbana: University of Illinois Press, 1987.

Livingston, Ira. *Between Science and Literature: An Introduction to Autopoetics*. Urbana: University of Illinois Press, 2006.

Luhmann, Niklas. *Social Systems*. Translated by John Bednarz Jr., with Dirk Baecker. Stanford: Stanford University Press, 1984/1995.

———. "A Conversation with Niklas Luhmann on Art and Society." *Logos: A Journal of Modern Society and Culture* 1, no. 3 (2002): 106–18. http://www.logosjournal.com/issue_1.3.pdf.

McMurry, Andrew. *Environmental Renaissance*. Athens: University of Georgia Press, 2003.

Meeker, Joseph. *The Comedy of Survival*. New York: Charles Scribner's Sons, 1972.

Moeller, Hans-Georg. *The Radical Luhmann*. New York: Columbia University Press, 2012.

Moretti, Franco. *Modern Epic*. Translated by Quintin Hoare. London: Verso, 1996.

———. "World-Systems Analysis, Evolutionary Theory, Weltliteratur." In *Immanuel Wallerstein and the Problem of the World: System, Scale, Culture*—edited by David Palumbo-Liu, Bruce Robbins, and Nirvana Tanoukhi. Durham: Duke University Press, 2011.

Nadeau, Robert. *Readings from the New Book on Nature: Physics and Metaphysics in the Modern Novel*. Amherst: University of Massachusetts Press, 1981.

Paulson, William. *The Noise of Culture*. Ithaca: Cornell University Press, 1988.

————. "Literature, Complexity, Interdisciplinarity." In *Chaos and Order: Complex Dynamics in Literature and Science,* edited by N. Katherine Hayles. Chicago: University of Chicago Press, 1991.

Rasch, William. *Niklas Luhmann's Modernity.* Stanford: Stanford University Press, 2000.

Schmidt, Siegfried. "Literary Studies from Hermeneutics to Media Culture Studies." *Comparative Literature and Culture* 12, no. 1 (2010). doi:10.7771/1481-4374.1569.

————. *Worlds of Communication.* Bern: Peter Lang, 2011.

Stevens, Wallace. *The Collected Poems.* New York: Vintage, 1982.

Tabbi, Joseph. *Cognitive Fictions.* Minneapolis: University of Minnesota Press, 2002.

Todorov, Tzvetan. "The Surrender to Nature." Review of E. O. Wilson's *Consilience: The Unity of Knowledge. The New Republic* (April 1998): 29–33.

Turner, Frederick. *Natural Classicism.* Charlottesville: University of Virginia Press, 1992.

Wilden, Anthony. *System and Structure.* London: Tavistock, 1972.

Wolfe, Cary. *Critical Environments.* Minneapolis: University of Minnesota Press, 1998.

————. " 'The Eye Is the First Circle': Emerson's 'Romanticism,' Cavell's Skepticism, Luhmann's Modernity." In *The Other Emerson,* edited by Branka Arsić and Cary Wolfe. Minneapolis: University of Minnesota Press, 2010.

————. *What Is Posthumanism?* Minneapolis: University of Minnesota Press, 2010.

13 Systems Heuristics and Digital Culture

Raphael Sassower and Nimrod Bar-Am

As digital culture permeates every facet of our life, it deserves to be studied not merely as a large set of new forms of communication, but because every novel form of interaction redefines those who make use of it. In order to appreciate this new identity in a critical manner, systems heuristics may be usefully applied. Systems heuristics in their various incarnations remain steadfastly antireductionist: they depict various limitations to approaches to complex problems that (merely) break them into their elementary components. Applying them to the investigation of digital culture will enrich both our knowledge of systems and attempts to appraise the impact of digital culture on our economic life and political future.

I

There are two claims that we wish to make here: First, systems theory is not and can never be a full-fledged theory, because there is no "one size fits all" mechanism according to which systems merge into larger systems, and so no single mechanism by which systems emerge into our world.[1] Since this is so, systems theory should be considered a heuristics, rather than a theory proper. Its main feature serves to guide us in searching for and identifying valid criticism of reductionist models of a given field. Second, since the study of systems is heuristic rather than algorithmic, with each new system that we stipulate or intend to inspect, we should inquire into the manner in which the new system expands our understanding of systems as such, if it does this at all. The aim of this chapter, then, is to raise this question with respect to some of the defining interaction-systems of the Digital Age. In other words, we wish to ask, first, in what manner does systems heuristics help us understand the digital age? And second, in what manner does the digital age expand our understanding of systems?

In order to answer both questions, we intend to first provide a brief historical account of the gradual wearing down of reductionism as the reigning heuristic principle for Western science. To be sure, reductionism still enjoys immense success because of its simplicity and clarity, and because it is the only heuristic principle that seems to mesh perfectly with our reigning explanatory model, with its focus on the deductive inference from natural laws; indeed, it stems from it. However limited and unsatisfying these principles and this model may be, their success is undeniable: all of us dissect as a step toward comprehension, and all of us strive to formalize our theories as a means of making their deductive structure as apparent as possible. Reductionism, then, allows scientists both to replace nebulous problem-settings with clearer ones and to simplify various complex questions into simpler ones. Our account is not intended as a detailed or comprehensive history of the interesting process of discovering reductionism's limits and improving upon them, which is still in its early stages, but rather as a series of personal signposts that may help us formulate our observations regarding digital age systems and their impact upon society.

As a preliminary, it is perhaps helpful to remind the reader that classic Aristotelian science was neither reductionist nor mechanistic. (Mechanism is the metaphysical framework with which most reductionists have worked since Galilei.) Final causes and essences do not fit well into the clockwork cosmos of Galilei and Newton. Essences presuppose the existence of substances, entities that cannot be broken up into elements that can explain their conduct; and final causes invite teleological explanations, which are irreducible to purely formal deductive ones. Science turned mechanistic and reductionist as it became modern, that is, by the sixteenth and seventeenth centuries. The Age of Modernity was extremely successful not only in its theoretical framing of natural laws and the predictive powers of its models, but also in the lasting effects of its methods on contemporary thinking, on our very standards for successful explanation as such.[2] The idea, to repeat, was that any explanation of a fact or an event is to be given solely by means of an accurate description of an initial setting of elements plus the recursive general laws that govern their conduct.

Today, we are becoming more and more aware of the limits of such explanations. One clear sign of such awareness is that the standard paradigm for scientific research is no longer physics but biology, no longer mechanics but evolution by natural selection. Too many biological facts, it seems, cannot be reduced to mechanical descriptions without losing their gist. Biology, therefore, invites, as Robert Rosen (1991) insisted, a paradigm shift in Thomas Kuhn's (1962/2012) sense. Can the modern worldview, from thermodynamics to sociology and economics, be unified by means of reduction to elementary physics? Can physics, psychology, and sociology presuppose the exact same explanatory apparatus? We do not offer answers to these questions here, though it seems to us that the answer to them is in the negative. Our aim here is merely to point out that in an important sense the pendulum now swings back from reductionism to attenuated reductionism, or systemism. This does not mean that we shall find ourselves in the near future, or ever again, resorting to essences and teleological principles (Aristotelian or others). But it does mean, as Richard Lewontin (1993) convincingly argued, that more and more of us nowadays recognize the limits of reductionism and therefore the indispensability of some nonreductionist notions while explaining complex phenomena. Chief among these notions is that of the emerging functions of a system, an unexpected (and thus inherently unpredictable) property of a whole that could not have been realized by a thorough investigation of the laws governing the operation of its parts. The point was highlighted, for example, by Ernst Mayr (1989) when explaining why in some cases genetic information is relevant and sometimes not when analyzing diseases. Environmental factors may overwhelm or suppress certain genetic tendencies or propensities in unexpected ways, thus eschewing standard models of predictability.

It seems to us that economists were among the first to have taken note of the interesting fact that a set of conditions within a supersystem (or environment) may have overwhelming impact upon the conduct of the systems that it comprises. Thus, they seem to have been the first to have resorted to what would later be called an *ecological* or *systemic* explanation. A systemic explanation is any explanation of the conduct of some subject matter that takes into account the fact that it is not merely a sum of elements but rather a meaningful part of a larger whole. This whole, the system, has its own dynamics and function: it, thus, imposes limiting or boundary conditions upon the conduct of the internal parts of the system under study. Understanding systems dynamics is crucial for explaining the conduct of their parts and the outcome of their internal interactions. And, since the dynamic is emergent and often cannot be stipulated by merely observing the isolated elements, it can be attributed to such elements, with exact certainty, only in hindsight. Some have called these *exogenous* (outside) conditions, factors, or variables to distinguish them from *endogenous* (inside) ones. It is fascinating to observe that at times exogenous factors that were considered negligible in the old classical economic sense of *ceterus paribus*—all things being equal (or remaining as they were)—have become so powerful that they dwarf in their impact whatever internal conditions hold (for example, drought conditions in an agriculture society, or devaluation of foreign currency in the global financial markets).

And so, when Adam Smith (1776/1937) argued that the happy free market is an inevitable result of the sum of rational choices made by its members as rational beings (*homo economicus*), he was in fact still presenting a mechanistic worldview, still implying that the environment is not an important variable for determining whether or not a marketplace can function efficiently and thereby contribute to the growth of society's wealth.[3] However, Thomas Malthus (1798/1970), whom we regard as the father of ecological explanations, had argued that this would only be true if the environment was unlimited in its resources. Malthus's environment, then, imposes limiting conditions (how much food can be produced) upon the set of possible actions to be taken by the individuals who live in it (he took birthrate as more or less given, and so wars and famine as inevitable). The ecological setting, then, becomes a crucial variable in the economic explanation so that without it, the explanation remains incomplete, and therefore, strictly speaking, false. Observing the individual rational human as a means of explaining his social dynamics, then, is often misleading. However, the addition of exogenous factors into one's equations (if quantitative-mathematical solutions are provided) is not simply an addition of more variables, since they do not operate as independent variables but rather impact other endogenous variables. As such, they transform other variables (that are dependent on them) and contribute a new level of complexity.

The ecological explanation became the cornerstone of all major theories of the nineteenth century: Karl Marx, Charles Darwin, Claude Bernard, have all used it in various ways. One crucial aspect of that new form of explanatory framework is that it accents two complementary forces. The first is the inherently blind and often unpredictable force of chance. The second is the tendency of all systems for balance and self-preservation (known today as "robustness"). This self-regulating balance can be the interdependence between predators and their prey in a given eco niche (Darwin) or the body's tendency to maintain a fixed temperature (Bernard, and later Cannon), or it can be an eye's tendency for preserving certain features of the environment regardless of variations in ambient light (Gibson). The integration of these complementary forces into physics by means of statistical thermodynamics was achieved by Ludwig Boltzmann: we thus received entropy, on the one hand, and order or various types of orders, on the other hand; entropy, on the one hand, and system or various types of systems, on the other.[4] But it was only around the middle of the twentieth century that attempts were made to incorporate some of the aspects of this new paradigm into a new and expanded theory of mechanisms. This was the leap undertaken by Norbert Wiener (1948/1961) and his many collaborators. Wiener noticed that the seventeenth–eighteenth-century model for a machine (Rene Descartes, Gottfried Wilhelm Leibniz, and Isaac Newton), and consequently of a mechanistic explanation, was that of the clock. And, he added, it cannot explain even the most basic of interactions, such as self-regulation to an environment through feedback. Not having a more elaborated model for a machine, observed Wiener, forced Leibniz to explain away all interactions, all communication, as unreal: he reduced it to a preestablished harmony between his monads. Interestingly, Wiener neither abandoned nor pledged allegiance to the mechanistic model. He merely expressed his conviction that it is much more open-ended than Descartes and Newton had ever imagined, and possibly open-ended in principle. He stressed that we have no idea what machines will be able to simulate and explain in the future, because there may be no final and closed theory of machines-as-such. This open-endedness was an invitation for system theory to step in. (It is also why we regard system theory as heuristics rather than a full-fledged theory.) The difference between holding onto reductionist heuristics and allowing new explanatory principles to step in becomes merely semantic when we admit that the set of reduction mechanisms that we aim to study is open-ended in principle and knowable only in hindsight.[5]

II

One way to approach the uniqueness of Digital Age systems is to inquire about the economic conditions within which they have flourished. These economic conditions are both endogenous and exogenous insofar as they have not merely provided the conditions under which digital technologies could proliferate (as has been argued about capitalism as a necessary, though not sufficient, condition for the development of the Industrial Revolution) but have become constitutive. One of the fascinating features of these economic conditions is that they are the product of two incompatible theoretical systems, capitalism and socialism.

The set of principles and conditions under which capitalism functions, including institutionalized individualism, personal freedom of choice, and equal opportunities to participate in an open marketplace, operate, according to Adam Smith, with an Invisible Hand. For him, this mode of operation is accompanied by a division of labor and market efficiencies that produce wealth through market growth. The laws of supply and demand for commodities and labor, for example, determine prices without regulatory intervention and thus exemplify the notion of the Invisible Hand. The ideal of *laissez-faire* (leave everyone alone) remains the cornerstone for competition among individuals with the provision that it should cause no harm to others (just as liberty is constrained by protecting the liberty of others). But can this idealized system operate according to its own internal laws? Are there environmental conditions necessary to guarantee its functionality? In contemporary literature we appreciate a legal system wherein property rights, for example, are preserved, and where contractual relations among individuals are enforced. For Smith, though, what became known as the classical model of capitalism was dependent on the conditions of a small village where moral sentiments were fostered (1976/1759). Within small communities, he suggested, mutual trust can be built, and one's moral sentiment can be repeatedly tested (with positive results). Social networks are bound to flourish because all the individuals within the community appreciate the fundamental principle of voluntary interdependence, anchored in tradition and reinforced through customs and habits (to use David Hume's notion) by what Smith termed the Impartial Spectator. Though seemingly exogenous, these social and moral conditions are crucial for a *laissez-faire* marketplace. Once one system is juxtaposed with another, it's clear how it will function. But what happens when the conditions are radically transformed? What happens when the British village of the eighteenth century is replaced by a global village that is digitally interconnected? Under contemporary conditions, it stands to reason that repeated encounters of the same people may not take place, as marketing tools reach millions with a few keystrokes. Likewise, personal encounters are less likely when communicating across oceans via the Internet.[6] What kind of community can one count on when commercial transactions are underway? How likely is it that one's moral sentiment will remain a positive factor in decision making? Though it's obvious that Smith's village has been superseded and that therefore some of the salient features of his marketplace have been compromised (and that therefore outcomes cannot be easily predicted), there are other, even opposite, transformations that are detected as well. And here the Marxian or socialist economic model comes into play.

The economic functioning of socialism depends on markets as well, but now they are centrally coordinated with long-term planning in mind. Because private property rights have been subsumed under communal property rights, competition for capital accumulation is no longer necessary or even feasible. Moreover, since the socialist model assumes a classless society, class struggle that is fermented because of alienation and exploitation disappears, allowing for greater collaboration among individuals for the good of the whole. The Marxian ideal that historically transforms feudal (barter) society into a capitalist and eventually into a socialist (communist) one depends on the accumulation of national wealth so that in fact everyone can contribute according to ability and receive according to needs. Communal success overshadows the individual, and its measure isn't in terms of personal wealth anymore.[7] However alien this way of thinking may be in a hypercapitalist system, we can see its practical manifestation in the digital age more clearly than in any period of the recent past.

Digital culture fosters what Lawrence Lessig (2008) has called a "sharing" economy in addition to the "commercial" economy. He recounts all kinds of examples of the "software sharing economy": Project Gutenberg, Distributed Proofreaders, Distributed-Computing projects, The Internet Archive, The Mars Mapping Project, The Open Directory Project, Open Source Food.[8] For him, the hybrid economy combines the commercial economy with the sharing economy, using free software as the paradigm. Perhaps this isn't exactly a merger between capitalist and socialist economic systems in their theoretical purity—often enough it seems like two systems battling for domination—but it's a hybrid economy nonetheless, because some of their distinguishing features (competition and collaboration, respectively) find common ground for the proliferation of digital technologies. Lessig distinguishes between "community spaces" that are virtual spaces for sharing information, "collaboration spaces" where a specific task, goal, or work is undertaken by many people, and the third type of "communities," such as Second Life, where one chooses how and where to "live" among others.[9] Because the values are different between a sharing and commercial economies, it's important to keep them apart; otherwise what seems like a "gift economy"—where one willingly gives away a technoscientific secret or tool without recognition or financial reward—will turn into or fall back into a profit one, thus undermining the "culture of generosity" and turning it into the ethic of profit.[10] But can they be kept apart?

Our focus on digital culture, then, forces us to rethink the neatness of relations between a system and its environment as well as among competing or complementary systems. Indeed, it seems to us that one of the striking features of the Digital Age is that its systems are now cradled by hybrid environments. Consider contemporary hybrid economy, called "postcapitalism" by some.[11] Is it the environment within which digital-age systems operate, or is it the case that such digital systems constitute the economy's environment? According to William Davidow, there are several levels of connectivity that are historically dictated. But can history help us untangle this new and considerably more complex Gordian knot? His concern is to examine how "overconnected environments perform, how they feed upon themselves and become unpredictable, accident-prone, and subject to contagions."[12] In what he terms "primitive cultures" one can find the state of being "underconnected." In an "interconnected state" the environment changes gradually, and all systems have enough time to adjust and keep pace with the changing environmental conditions. In a "highly connected state . . . businesses, economic systems, and government institutions are driving change . . . society can still cope and prosper." The prime example of this stage has been Silicon Valley in California. Finally, in an "overconnected state . . . institutions change so quickly that the environment in which they are embedded is unable to cope." This, he argues, is what happened to Iceland in the last economic crisis of 2008–2010.[13] As we can see from this classification, there are points at which multiple systems can adjust to each other's transformations and growth, while there are other points at which adjustments fail because of the pace at which they are expected.

To put it in our own terms, complexity is a relational term: it depicts a certain distance between the questions that we pose and the apparatuses that we use in order to answer them. In this sense, complexity is an aspect of digital technologies. The Digital Age, then, has presented us with a reality so complex that it is at times no longer clear how to approach some of the traditional economical questions within it. This is fascinating since traditionally economic systems are considered the most complex of systems, and so the hardest to predict, whereas individual decisions are considered more or less obvious and rational (or at least irrational and yet predictable as some economical psychologist would have it, as argued by Ariely in 2008). But the Digital Age has brought upon us hybrid-reality that is considerably more complex than the traditional market, and in order to understand it we desperately need new tools.

Recalling classical economics of the eighteenth century, Davidow admits that "[a]s interconnection technologies have extended the reach of business and helped it migrate from physical to virtual space, the bonds between the pursuit of self-interest and the social control Smith envisioned have been further weakened. To see how this is happening, we need merely compare

Smith's time to our own."[14] The environment in which economic systems operate provide for the proliferation of digital technologies that have to "match" or feed each other without undermining or overheating each other's progress or the environment as a whole. For Davidow, then, there is an optimal approach: "instead of an overconnected world we return to a highly connected one . . . [we] need to focus more attention on prevention . . . introduce controls. . . . Regulation is one important way to reduce risk to depositors . . . to the economy as a whole."[15] We should note that this is a very traditional reaction to an old problem in a highly new setting: exerting an external force to control the internal workings of a system. It may or may not work well within the digital hybrid environment and its intricate multifaceted context. Regulations in the Digital Age very often fail because of the diffuse environment in which they attempt to exert power or authority. Even if they somewhat succeed here and there, they may in the long run be as ineffective as the breaking of looms by the Luddites. Also, if they do succeed, because they occur in an arena where it is too easy to violate privacy, for example, results may be downright dangerous insofar as they may impose surveillance strategies that are overly oppressive.

The call for prevention and regulation from one traditional system—political and legal authorities—so that another system—hybrid-digital-businesses and hybrid-digital marketplaces—will not implode when overheating is only one solution. Can system heuristics offer alternatives, or at least some complementary aids? We do not know. But it is clear that if they can, the first step would be to analyze the novelty of our situation by means of such novel heuristic frameworks so as to try to figure out in what manner alternative solutions can become testable. For example, questions about boundary conditions can be posed so that clearer delineation between systems can be ascertained, as well as questions about the multiple roles participants play in multiple systems and the distinguishing characteristics they display in each one of them (consumers, producers, distributers, and the like). Is one system used exclusively for entertainment? Does it have a commercial application?

Concluding this section, I would like to give one concrete example of the manner by which novel system concepts have enriched our understanding of digital-age systems, and were in turn expanded by them. My example is by now a classic of systems heuristics, but its many implications for digital-age systems are still under lively debate. It goes back to Pierre-Paul Grassé, the famous zoologist who studied the formation dynamics of termite mounds and tagged the special form of communication that enables them "stigmergy." Stigmergy, for him, was a form of intention-less communication that allows very simple agents to bond as if to create a superintelligent that is capable of completing incredibly complex tasks, tasks that transcend the abilities of any single agent. Instead of the familiar back-and-forth message transmission between individual agents, in stigmergic communication we find the agents changing the features of their immediate environment in a manner that determines future behavior and decisions of other agents who may follow it.[16]

Here is one classic example. Given two or more alternative routes to a food source, an ant colony will almost always find the shortest one, and follow it until that food source is exhausted. This fact is puzzling, since clearly no ant is capable of conceiving the dilemma that it helps, at some level, to solve. It doesn't have the "hardware" for it: ants cannot count steps, they certainly cannot do sums, and they definitely do not analyze an optimal solution to a problem. Since the ant colony seems to act intelligently (from an external perspective), and in a seemingly coordinated manner that is hard to explain when observing the single ant, sociobiologists sometimes call ant colonies superorganisms. Debates about what a superorganism is, debates that sometimes border on the fanciful science-fictional, are widespread since they excite our imagination. Let us skip them here. It hardly needs stressing that a conscious, problem-solving entity does not emerge from the fascinating cooperation among ants. But it is worth mentioning that in many senses the single ant does not qualify as an individual organism: except for the queen ant, ants are sterile, and so cannot possibly transmit their genes, and without perpetual contact with their colony they do not even seem to subsist.

The solution to our problem, then, is found in the special manner by which ants communicate. Foraging ants go about looking for food more or less randomly (not entirely, but for the sake of simplification let us assume that they do). When they find food, they use carefully laid pheromones to mark their way back to their colony. These pheromones induce other ants to follow the same trail. Thus, pheromones are their means of communication. The reaction pattern of ants to pheromones is fixed within their organic structure, so it is not, for them, a matter of choice whether to follow a marked trail or not; and they would always follow the trail with the strongest scent. Finally, since pheromones evaporate quickly, every ant that reaches the food source will continue to re-mark the trail on its way back, else the way to the food source will be lost. And so, the shorter trail quickly acquires the stronger scent, as it allows for more ants to tread it back and forth to the food source. Thus, in a remarkably short time the shortest trail is chosen and maintained. As such, the ant colony forms a system with marked internal dynamics and a unique environment, but without conscious intentional life; the purpose of this dynamic is externally explicable, then, only by presupposing a communal goal, a quasi intention, if you like. Perhaps this is what systems theory has always urged us to appreciate: that without presupposing some such quasi intentions, certain facts about our environment will remain inexplicable. The fact that some such quasi intentions (say survival or transmission of genes) are presupposed by all biological explanations is the crucial distinction between system heuristics and reductionism. For clearly intentions and even quasi intentions are the reductionist's worst nightmares. What is even more interesting, though, is the repeated observation of all students of complexity at all levels that new and surprising such quasi intentions emerge naturally in our universe, and that they comprise new agendas for the systems with which they emerge. In so doing, they habitually set novel and unexpected agendas for their parts.

Stigmergy occurs frequently between humans, too. A very simple and old example is the dynamics of path formations. When crossing a dense and high cornfield, for example, we partially and unintentionally clear a path for anyone who may wish to cross that field in the near future. The path that we have cleared is considerably easier to follow, as clearing an alternative path is often a tedious task. It may also be unsuccessful when the field is very large or if the stalks are too high for us to see the field's end. A cleared path, then, even a partially cleared path, invites treading, as it seems to signal to anyone that it has been tested, that it leads somewhere rather than nowhere. By crossing the field, we modify its features in a manner that influences future decisions by those who may find themselves facing it, too. A completely cleared path, a leveled one, is thus a signal of joint efforts, a mini-tradition, and most likely a relatively successful one, or else a new and more successful path would have wiped out the old one, and new stalks would have covered it. The cleared path, then, is a mark of joint stigmergic intelligence.

It is no wonder that nowadays stigmergic systems are studied by everyone from city planners to computer engineers, and from bookies to marketers. Nowhere, it seems, do such systems become as effective as when they meet the digital space, which combines unprecedented overconnectedness with incredibly low costs of networking. From Facebook to Wikipedia, it is all stigmergic interfaces shaping and reshaping their own makeup and our own. Search engines utilize stigmergic principles to determine the relative importance or ranking of sites so as to perform the incredible task of sifting through an astonishing amount of data to find exactly what we were looking for; marketing programs utilize them to offer us purchases that fit the profiles of people who made choices similar to ours; viral marketers attempt to find the secret of redirecting the human ant colony to their products (food source); and political activists utilize them, often with unprecedented success, to achieve political unity and impact, and so on.

The most interesting general question that can be asked about such cases, then, is how stigmergic dynamics change when connectedness meets overconnectedness and when the ant is replaced by a human, that is to say, when the mindless heteronomous agent is replaced by a conscious, relatively autonomous, sometimes highly intelligent, at times free-minded, often humorous and artistic, and certainly political one. Let us stress that this is a novel question, one that we owe entirely to digital technologies. One important difference seems to be that the human-based stigmergic system is in principle considerably less predictable. Attempts to prevent this unpredictability are often built into our interfaces, especially those that define for us sets of prefixed alternatives to choose from. Is this desirable? In which contexts is it so, and why? Another important and closely related difference seems to be that human agents are often very much aware of the dynamics that they help to create, or in which they are expected to operate. And despite the fact that individual choices rarely influence the overall dynamics, often enough they do, and significantly so. (Even whimsical diverting of search results is not uncommon nowadays.) When and how does such awareness influence stigmergic dynamics? Finally, and most importantly, many digital age stigmergic interfaces were designed by individuals, or by small groups of individuals, with very traditional agendas. Facebook, for example, as Barabási (2002) has stressed, charmed people into giving up (for free!) some of their most valuable innermost secrets, mapping out their entire social relationships, their hobbies, their "likes" and "dislikes" on almost every imaginable subject. These data are a fortune to advertisers but not only for them. Facebook owners, then, can now use this unprecedented knowledge for their own, rather mundane, personal agendas. They thus created a hybrid stigmergic system, one that potentially does exactly the opposite of what the original stigmergic system was designed to do: it grants certain individuals (about whom we know very little) the ability to exercise unprecedented control over the workings of an entire community. This is why we regard as crucial the study of possible conflicts between such personal agendas and the emergent dynamics of the digital-stigmergic-human system. It may become one of the most important questions of our age.

And consider this: a very simple digital stigmergic infrastructure can be designed so as to allow unprecedented levels of democratic participation by its users: every policy issue could be brought for public discussion, and town-hall-like meetings could ensure public debate and an actual vote by all participants. What would such a system do to standard politics and standard political roles? Would such increased participation change the nature of political discourse? Would it optimize the ideal of "crowd intelligence" that James Surowiecki (2004) has portrayed so eloquently? Would this hold for political debates? Or would large and semi-interested crowds prefer short-term solutions to long-term ones, and simple to complex ones, as behavioral economists remind us is the case? On the other spectrum of political results associated with stigmergic overconnectedness is the fact that regimes find it harder and harder to perform harsh acts of oppression secretly, which is, of course, a benefit of the Digital Age. The rising costs of such cover-ups become crucial factors in the stability prospects of those regimes, especially when the outcomes of failed cover-ups and of inaction are so hard to predict. Though one kind of oppression is extremely effective given a set of social and technological conditions, it becomes counterproductive or even disastrous for the oppressor. When one system—the oppressing regime—tries to ignore or suppress the dynamics of another system—the stigmergic network of its populace—which has become a dominant factor in its environment (and even a metasystem, rapidly shaping and reshaping that regime's environment), the result is often self-mutilation. System heuristics, then, can outline at least some of the parameters and matrices according to which such new dynamics can be recognized and their effectiveness measured. For example, it can offer tools for estimating, if only roughly, the overall scope and impact of some stigmergic dynamics, and even help monitor to some extent their "direction," or quasi intentions. It foretells explicitly that accounting for the dynamics of any new environment, a new metasystem, is essential in order to appreciate the future workings of any system that functions in its midst. This, by the way, is not holism, as some have mistakenly argued.[17] For systems heuristics dismisses the idea that there exists an uppermost supersystem, the whole, emanating goals to its parts. Rather, the very configuration of "wholes" and their "parts" is context dependent. At times this discussion is undertaken by postmodernists when they insist on contextualization so as to frame the system they wish to examine and explain. But this point follows just as easily the critical rationalist tradition of "the logic of research" as a set of tentative understandings regarding the proper manner for seeking truth,[18] guided by tentative metaphysical frameworks.[19] Indeed, this perspectival approach has its origins in diverse traditions ranging from Friedrich Nietzsche all the way to modern communication theory.[20]

III

Systems heuristics, then, is a metaphysical framework, a still budding set of guidelines for research, not a full-fledged theory that enables unequivocal predictions. Unequivocal predictions, it teaches us, are results of ideal apparatuses, of mechanical models that we can approach only by artificially reducing the complexity level of that which we try to explain. By doing so, we gain clarity at the price of exactness. This may seem like a paradox, since analytic philosophy has taught us that exactness and clarity are one and the same thing. But digital technologies, and the new culture that they have ushered in, made us realize better than ever that this is simply not so. They allowed us to construct institutions that are unprecedented in their complexity and provided us with partial tools to appreciate the breathtaking scale of that complexity. In doing so, they have directed our attention to the fact that reductions (our best known means of simplification) almost always come at a price that is often too high: they cut off some of the desiderata that they come to explain. They do so in principle, for in order to have a full-fledged reductionist explanation of our universe, one would need to have the full list of possible systems that can emerge within it, and that list, it argues, is open-ended in principle. Thus, by reducing the mind to a machine we lose its vital consciousness, its subjective experience of its environment; by reducing digital culture to its members we lose the uniqueness of the network that unites them and its emerging, often surprising dynamics; by reducing the cosmos to a machine we lose freedom and beauty and morality.

Systems heuristics offers us a new model of knowledge. It challenges the feasibility of the project of unification of science by reduction to a single explanatory layer and forces us to reconsider the criteria according to which complexity can be understood, even when its results cannot be predicted. Since we have mentioned the biological model as a more sophisticated and in some ways more accurate model for systems analysis because of its internal variations and therefore its emergent qualities (that are unpredictable by comparison to a mechanical model whose components have functional limits), we should also mention the recent work of Edward O. Wilson (2012) in regard to human evolution. As mentioned above, the unit of selection always bothered evolutionary scientists and was distorted by social Darwinists, for example, who justified capitalist competition under the rubric of the "survival of the fittest" individuals in the marketplace.[21] Wilson's latest salvo in the ongoing debate over the units to be examined within an evolutionary system (for Richard Dawkins [2006/1976], for example, it's the selfish gene) includes a multilevel selection process of individuals on one level—with competitive tendencies to ensure survival—and groups on another level—with cooperative and even altruistic tendencies of self-sacrifice for the sake of group survival.

Notions of *system* and *environment* according to this schema are rearranged so that a *purpose* can be established (e.g. survival). But the system at times includes individuals and at times groups, and the environment includes other individuals at some level and other groups at another, not to mention the surrounding jungle or city. This multilevel systems approach exemplifies the kind of conceptual difficulties we have outlined, and the need to come up with some operational criteria as heuristics in a digital culture that mimics in some strange ways biological processes and systems. Though diametrically opposed on one methodological and conceptual level—individual ants or humans seem to behave independently from each other even when observed in large groups while coordinated behavior is observed at other levels—there is some conjunction of purposes that emerge as if on their own. It is exactly this phenomenon of interconnected and self-organizing systems that baffles reductionists.

Perhaps what can be said in the Digital Age about understanding (as opposed to controlling) any system or set of interlocked systems is that we ought to fulfill some operational and conceptual criteria. These include in broad terms (a) *open-mindedness* that reflects a deep appreciation of the open-endedness of systems and their mutual influence; (b) *criticism* insofar as some of the goals ascribed to systems undergo self-adjustment and therefore are unpredictable; (c) *sustainability* in terms of the incremental changes and transformations perceived within and among systems so that whatever has been learned from one moment can be partially used in future analyses (or what Popper calls "piecemeal engineering");[22] and (d) *testability* so that some kernel of rationality is maintained even when feedback loops seem random, at times, but in fact allow for the detection of patterns or (external) tendencies, and what some would suggest are also (internal) propensities.[23] All of these criteria would enhance current tendencies to attenuate reductionism and facilitate our view that even when human intelligence cannot fully comprehend its surroundings (as interconnected systems), it can at the very least approach them intelligently.

If we add our criteria to the four values mentioned by Robert Merton (1942) of communism (common ownership of scientific discoveries), universalism (impartiality to personal differences), disinterestedness, and organized skepticism, there would be a reasonable way to navigate the Digital Age, a way to recognize the limits of human knowledge and the boundary conditions under which they might expand over time. To expect at this juncture the kind of perspective recorded by the giants of the scientific revolutions is a mistake we are dearly paying for, since we make outlandish general claims in the name of scientific knowledge when at best we can offer informed guesses. This doesn't mean we are relieved from responsibilities, but rather that we should more carefully express our opinions with a great deal of humility and anticipation, inviting criticism from any source.

NOTES

1. Mario Bunge, *Emergence and Convergence: Qualitative Novelty and the Unity of Knowledge* (Toronto: University of Toronto Press, 2003), 22.
2. Robert Rosen, *Life Itself* (New York: Columbia University Press, 1991), ch. 3.
3. See critical neoclassical treatment by Martin Hollis and Edward Nell, *Rational Economic Man: A Philosophical Critique of Neo-Classical Economics* (Cambridge: Cambridge University Press, 1975).
4. See the critical survey of Ilya Prigogine and Isabelle Stengers, *Order Out of Chaos: Man's Dialogue with Nature* (Toronto: Bantam Books, 1984).
5. Nathaniel Laor and Joseph Agassi, *Diagnosis: Philosophical and Medical Perspectives* (Dordrecht: Kluwer Academic, 1990), 92.
6. A contemporary response to some of these questions can be seen in Yochai Benkler, *The Wealth of Networks: How Social Production Transforms Markets and Freedom* (New Haven: Yale University Press, 2006).
7. Karl Marx, *The Communist Manifesto,* ed. Fred Bender (New York: W. W. Norton, 1988).
8. Marx, *The Communist Manifesto,* ch. 6.
9. Marx, *The Communist Manifesto,* ch. 7.
10. Marx, *The Communist Manifesto,* 232–33.
11. Raphael Sassower, *Postcapitalism: Moving beyond Ideology in America's Economic Crises* (Boulder: Paradigm, 2009).
12. William H. Davidow, *Overconnected: The Promise and Threat of the Internet* (Harrison, NY: Delphinium Books, 2011), 6.
13. Davidow, *Overconnected,* 22–22.
14. Davidow, *Overconnected,* 185–86.
15. Davidow, *Overconnected,* 189–92.
16. See Pierre-Paul Grassé, *Termitologia,* 3 vols. (Paris: Masson, 1982–86).
17. Fritjof Capra, *The Web of Life* (New York: Anchor Books, 1996).
18. Karl R. Popper, *The Logic of Scientific Discovery* (London: Routledge, 1992).

19. Joseph Agassi, *Science in Flux* (Dordrecht: Reidel, 1975).
20. Marshall McLuhan, *Understanding Media: The Extensions of Man* (London: Routledge, 1964).
21. Richard Hofstadter, *Social Darwinism in American Thought* (Boston: Beacon Press, 1992).
22. Karl R. Popper, *The Poverty of Historicism* (London: Routledge, 1997).
23. James Gleick, *Chaos: Making a New Science* (New York: Penguin, 1987).

REFERENCES

Agassi, Joseph. *Science in Flux*. Dordrecht: Reidel, 1975.
Ariely, Dan. *Predictably Irrational: The Hidden Forces That Shape Our Decisions*. New York: Harper Collins, 2008.
Barabási, Albert-László. *Linked*. New York: Perseus Books Group, 2002.
Benkler, Yochai. *The Wealth of Networks: How Social Production Transforms Markets and Freedom*. New Haven and London: Yale University Press, 2006.
Bunge, Mario. *Emergence and Convergence: Qualitative Novelty and the Unity of Knowledge*. Toronto: University of Toronto Press, 2003.
Capra, Fritjof. *The Web of Life*. New York: Anchor Books, 1996.
Davidow, William H. *Overconnected: The Promise and Threat of the Internet*. Harrison, NY: Delphinium Books, 2011.
Gleick, James. *Chaos: Making a New Science*. New York: Penguin, 1987.
Grassé, Pierre-Paul. *Termitologia*. 3 vols. Paris: Masson, 1982–86.
Hofstadter, Richard. *Social Darwinism in American Thought*. Boston: Beacon Press, 1992. Originally published 1944.
Hollis, Martin, and Edward Nell. *Rational Economic Man: A Philosophical Critique of Neo-Classical Economics*. Cambridge: Cambridge University Press, 1975.
Kuhn, Thomas S. *The Structure of Scientific Revolutions*. Chicago: University of Chicago press, 2012. Originally published 1962.
Laor, Nathaniel, and Agassi, Joseph. *Diagnosis: Philosophical and Medical Perspectives*. Dordrecht: Kluwer Academic, 1990.
Lessig, Lawrence. *Remix: Making Art and Commerce Thrive in the Hybrid Economy*. New York: The Penguin Press, 2008.
Lewontin, Richard C. *Biology as Ideology: The Doctrine of DNA*. New York: Harper Perennial, 1993.
Mayr, Ernst. *Towards a New Philosophy of Biology: Observations of an Evolutionist*. Cambridge: Harvard University Press, 1989.
McLuhan, Marshall. *Understanding Media: The Extensions of Man*. London: Routledge, 1964.
Malthus, Thomas Robert. *An Essay on the Principle of Population and A Summary View of the Principle of Population*. Edited by Anthony Flew. New York: Penguin Books, 1970. Originally published 1798 and 1830.
Marx, Karl. *The Communist Manifesto*. Edited by Fred Bender. New York: W. W. Norton, 1988. Originally published 1872.
Popper, Karl R. *The Poverty of Historicism*. London: Routledge, 1997. Originally published 1957.
———. *The Logic of Scientific Discovery*. London: Routledge, 1992. Originally published 1959.
Prigogine, Ilya, and Stengers, Isabelle. *Order Out of Chaos: Man's Dialogue with Nature*. New York: Bantam Books, 1984.
Rosen, Robert. *Life Itself*. New York: Columbia University Press, 1991.
Sassower, Raphael. *Postcapitalism: Moving beyond Ideology in America's Economic Crises*. Boulder: Paradigm, 2009.

Smith, Adam. *The Theory of Moral Sentiments*. Indianapolis: Liberty Classics, 1976. Originally published 1759.

Smith, Adam. *An Inquiry into the Nature and Causes of the Wealth of Nations*. Edited by E. Cannan. New York: The Modern Library, 1937. Originally published 1776.

Surowiecki, James. *The Wisdom of Crowds: Why the Many Are Smarter than the Few and How Collective Wisdom Shapes Business, Economies, Societies, and Nations*. Garden City: Doubleday, 2004.

Wiener, Norbert. *Cybernetics*. Cambridge, MA: MIT Press, 1961.

Wilson, Edward O. *The Social Conquest of Earth*. New York: Liveright, 2012.

14 A Brief Outline of Evolutionary Cultural Ecology

Peter Finke

1 BACKGROUND OF EVOLUTIONARY CULTURAL ECOLOGY (ECE)

Evolutionary Cultural Ecology (ECE) is a new cultural theory based largely on recent transdisciplinary studies in evolutionary theory and in the structure and function of ecosystems.[1] Therefore it is partially rooted in natural science, where it is related, for example, to the powerful and nonconformist thinking of the biologist Jakob von Uexküll (1864–1944). But there are important roots in the humanities, too. For instance, new research allowing a fuller understanding of the mind, anthropological theory, and the ecological philosophy of Arne Naess (*1912) have had a strong influence on ECE;[2] but the most important source for its ideas is the creative work of Gregory Bateson (1904–1980), especially his groundbreaking research on an "ecology of mind." Therefore, although actually developed in Europe, ECE bears heavily on European and American transdisciplinary research.[3] It is no simple refinement, however, of other conceptions calling themselves "Cultural Ecology" or similar developments such as Julian H. Steward's influential theory of cultural adaptation.[4]

Whereas most other theories of culture—the classical as well as more recent ones developed by Steward, Geertz, Rappaport, Luhmann, Assmann, or Bhaba—have largely been based on ethnological, sociological, anthropological, or other human-related fundaments, ECE takes a broader view of the problem. It includes a thorough study of some results of modern biological research that have not been sufficiently appreciated by those working with other theories. Yet one should not be mistaken: ECE is not natural scientific approach in general or a sociobiological one in particular; but these do place knowledge at our disposal that can no (longer) be neglected by any academically rigorous explanation of cultural phenomena. One weakness in conventional cultural theory has long been its insufficient assimilation of important results from the natural sciences, despite that it is surely of major importance for a better understanding of man and human culture. While ECE integrates such research, at least two facts show that ECE does not favor biologisms: (1) although it is indebted to modern biological insights, it fundamentally assumes a critical stance toward the current physicalist foundation of biological thinking (e.g. the "normal" conception of an eco-system); and (2) it explains culture as a system of conventional rules rather than of natural laws. (Both points will be taken up below.)[5]

2   THREE FUNDAMENTALS OF ECE

ECE can be characterized by three fundamental convictions:

(I)   *The world consists of two realms, the realm of nature and the realm of culture. There is not a third.* Nature is older, culture younger. Culture has developed out of nature by evolutionary processes; and since this development has begun, culture has accompanied and influenced nature, but it does not replace it. Therefore, the two realms are not entirely distinct. Culture in particular still shows traces of its evolutionary mother nature. Besides, the two are not strictly separated but are rather linked by a transitional zone that has to be carefully studied if culture is to be adequately explained.

(II) *The evolution of culture has produced a second level of manifold varieties, mirroring the natural diversity that was produced by the earlier evolution of nature.* Nevertheless, there are universal features of culture as well as particular ones. Generally, cultures resemble ecosystems functionally and structurally for evolutionary reasons; this is the central hypothesis. However, they also exhibit character-istic differences from them. Nevertheless, they can be understood as representing an evolutionarily new type of ecosystem.

(III) *Culture is neither fully restricted to the human sphere, nor is it iden-tical with the good, the true, and the beautiful.* The latter is only a small part of culture; and our actions fail to live up to these ideals. Like their positive counterparts, these failings also become a part of culture. Our cultural behavior is ambivalent. There is a striking gap between our cultural aims or ideals, on the one hand, and our cultural everyday performance, on the other. As a consequence, we have to extend our cultural theorizing to include normative argu-ments, too, and to include the negative as well as the positive in the study of culture.

The following paragraphs will explain these features in more detail.[6]

3   METHODICAL PRINCIPLES OF ECE

There are some rather general principles ECE takes as a guideline for its new approach to culture: it places culture within an evolutionary context; it uses a broad conception of culture; and it fosters a consciousness of the remarkable complexity of culture.

3.1 The Evolutionary Context

Cultural scholars coming from a traditional perspective may be astonished by the weight ECE places on the earliest facts of culture, when normally such facts are of only marginal interest or are even neglected altogether. From the point of view of ECE, there is no reasonable alternative to an evolutionary explanation of our world. And we have to thoroughly study the beginning of the evolutionary process because that beginning is likely to have left lasting traces in the systems generated in the course of that development.

Long before culture came into existence, the evolution of nature began. It is not the task of cultural theory to explain natural evolution, but it is of major importance that a sufficiently developed nature preexists culture and is a precondition for any cultural process. It is important because an awareness of the structural relics of nature that are present in culture is required for an adequate understanding of culture. In ECE, nature is defined as the realm of relations governed by natural laws. This is equivalent to speaking of a realm not constructed by human action or capable of being fundamentally changed by human action. We can change the rules of the culture we are living with, but we are not able to change the natural laws. All we can do is unveil and obey them. This does not mean natural laws are invariable constants. Although this is the widely believed conservative position, there are some serious arguments that natural laws change.[7] But such change is not instigated and controlled by man; we have no influence over it. In the cultural sphere, however, we construct and influence our cultural rules—and we do so every day. We tend not to be fully aware of this constant change in culture; but even without being conscious of it, we engage in changing culture.

In the strict sense the term "cultural evolution" refers to the processes that took place during the evolution of life, which eventually led to the addition of the new dimension of psychic life to the older, physical life. It entails the emergence of new species, the systemic tools that are able to influence behavior (e.g. semiotic systems),[8] and the emergence of humans and their language and culture. Cultural evolution refers to the processes that bring about this somewhat different "daughter evolution" by means of mechanisms of the natural "mother evolution." However, "cultural evolution" is often used in a second sense, too, referring to later developments of the different cultural systems (e.g. "technical evolution," "the evolution of the computer," etc.). This usage is problematic because it commingles evolution in its strict sense with the history of human activities. Evolution is a process of self-organizing systems, whereas human history is full of personal or institutional organizers. Nevertheless, evolution is an ongoing process in human history, too, and it entails cultural evolution; but one has to bear that conceptual problem in mind.

3.2 A Broad Conception of Culture

The evolutionary context of the problem leads to the broadest conception of culture possible: nature is a predecessor to culture; and culture is its evolutionary offspring. This results in a concept of culture that is not identical with the human sphere. If the origins of culture occur well before man appeared in the world, then we have to consider the living world around us in order to fully understand culture. There is no need to describe the extrahuman cultural world in the same detail as the human world, or even to concentrate on it; but to neglect it as a vital source for information about culture is a fatal mistake of conventional cultural theories. This mistake is mirrored in the obscurity and vagueness of the common definitions of culture, and it is missing in some clear definitions like that provided by Princeton biologist J. T. Bonner, which emphasizes that "[c]ulture is the transmission of information by behavior and communication,"[9] rather than the transmission of information by genetic means, as is found in nature.

The fact that nature is seen to be a predecessor to culture does not mean that culture is viewed generally as succeeding nature. This too is a common mistaken view. Culture did not replace nature when it emerged; but since that emergence, it has accompanied its evolutionary mother and—certainly—has affected her in many respects. But nature is obviously still existent today, and it influences culture in many respects. Indeed, it remains fundamental for all culture. Because nature is the energized and carrying basis system, the disappearance or death of nature, or merely severe damage to it, would undoubtedly result in the disappearance of culture or in considerable damage to it. If we destroy the vital functions of nature, there will no longer be any culture.[10]

Everything that is not natural belongs to the cultural sphere, and vice versa. This does not imply a strict borderline between the two spheres. On the contrary: there is an important (and growing) intermediate zone between them that has played a vital role in the past evolutionary process and that continues to play a vital role today.[11]

3.3 Cultural Complexity

Culture is an extremely complex phenomenon that, again, is paralleled by the complexity of nature. There are at least four dimensions of cultural relations: (1) the relations between nature and culture; (2) the relations between the different levels of culture; (3) the relations between cultures of the same level; and (4) the relations between parts of the same culture.

There are three different levels of culture: the psychic, the social, and the ethnic levels. Cultures on the psychic level are innate or acquired systems of personality; these are characterized by the beliefs, knowledge, and ways of life of individuals. They entail considerable cultural diversity. The social cultures distinguish between groups and subcommunities within a given society. They are more or less related to institutions that have been built on that sociocultural basis. The cultural diversity on the ethnic level ("the cultures of the world") represents a cultural manifoldness that is mainly based on the linguistic and religious systems used in apprehending the world. Today ethnic cultures are strongly affected and modified by forceful social cultures, especially science, politics, and economics.

This indicates that the intermediate level of social cultures is of special importance.[12] It has been developed into institutional forms, producing the most influential and well-defined institutions and institutes. Religion and churches, science and schools, and the economy and money are examples. On this level, we can best study the various changing strategies of intercultural immissions and emissions, influence and divergence. The narrow conceptions of culture ("music, museums, literature," etc.) that have traditionally been popular refer to this level as well.

The whole realm of culture therefore forms a complex net of relations on different levels; and the elements are parts of the whole. One of the reasons for the hitherto unsatisfactory state of cultural theory is that the complexity of the cultural net is usually only partially perceived.

4 THEORETICAL PRINCIPLES OF ECE

Following these general lines, there are three theoretical principles that distinguish ECE from other cultural theories: (1) on the basis of a functional view it understands culture as an ecological means by which it becomes possible for living beings with a psychic dimension of life to handle the new problems of that dimension; (2) it has a central structural view of culture, showing it to be a new type of ecosystem; and (3) it highlights the characteristic series of interconnected new developmental stages of natural evolution called "cultural evolution" (in the strict sense of the word), most prominently bound to the origin and further development of humankind and its language.

4.1 The Function of Culture

An explanation of the function of culture inevitably relies on the concepts of life and the living. Although important parts of culture, as it is conventionally understood, are related to nonliving objects or institutions, it is the life of the living beings that needs, makes use of, and shapes culture, cultural objects, and institutions.

Culture provides these living beings with a suitable psychic environment. It places psychic structures at their disposal that they need similarly to the way they need a suitable physical habitat in order to meet their continuing natural needs. Long before man entered the stage, many animals appeared that were endowed with certain different but well-defined cognitive abilities.

Therefore, they already needed the substantially adequate psychic extensions of their physical environment that had developed with them in the process of coevolution. In ECE these are called "proto-cultures," the systems of animal behavior. J. v. Uexküll, one of the great independent thinkers in the field of biology, already engaged in deep investigations of these "inner worlds" that codetermine the ecology of animals.[13] Such protocultures are the first evolutionary experiments dealing with the construction of useful psychic habitats, many of which have proved to be very successful and can be observed up to the present. One of their most important and conspicuous features is their use of rather species-specific interactive means for communication, which establish the species-specific webs of communicative relations. Humans still use many nonverbal skills to structure their cultures that are akin to those prehuman achievements, but the emergence of language has provided us with an important new means for cultural advancement.

The cultural environment is essential to us in a similar way to the physical environment. Human life requires the fulfillment of specific cultural needs as much as many forms of animal life require the fulfillment of protocultural needs. Therefore, any description of human life limited solely to physical life and omitting the psychic level is insufficient. The usual biological definition of an ecosystem, which makes reference only to physical parameters ("biomass," "material energy flow," and "trophic circularity"), is insufficient as a characterization of an ecosystem, even when only the nonhuman world is concerned. The web of cognitive and communicative relations that is spread out in all of those systems by the populations living with them contributes to their unity and consistency, not only externally and superficially, but even centrally and vitally. They prove the natural ecosystems to be the birthplaces of culture.

Whereas its function already clearly indicates the ecosystemic role of culture, it is especially its structural aspects that lead ECE to the conclusion that by developing culture, evolution created a new type of ecosystem.

4.2 The Structure of Culture

Culture is a systemic phenomenon. This is not a new insight, but in ECE new consequences are drawn from it. However, they will not become apparent if the systemic quality of culture is not substantially stated much more precisely than in conventional cultural theorizing, which has overlooked the key role of nature for the explanation of culture. Since everything can be described as a system, we have to characterize the special features of the cultural systems in a rather detailed way in order to cull substantial lessons from the insight that nature plays a key role in explaining culture. Bateson's ability to do this is the most innovative aspect of his thinking. To a certain extent, it could be called the kernel of the theory.[14]

If we describe culture structurally, we are often struck by the extreme differences between such structures and the structures we know from nature and by the novelties of such structures in comparison with natural structures. But the view that such differences are deep-seated only indicates the superficiality of conventional cultural analyses. In fact, a culture does resemble a woodland or a lake not only in a functional sense—since they both benefit the creatures living in them—but also in some decisive structural sense, which in present culture is largely masked by other superficial structures of later origin. What is the system-specific structure of an ecosystem? It is not only the openness to an environment or the creativity of such systems, which we can find in some nonecological systems too. The structural specificity of an ecosystem lies in its dependence on an ongoing stream of energy from outside of the system that makes possible the assembly and maintenance of the very typical and characteristic nonlinear dynamics of its internal systems organization: a circularly organized interconnection of productive, consumptive, and reductive processes. Only a system that exhibits such a structure is rightly to be called an ecosystem.

This type of circular organization, well known from natural ecosystems, can be found in cultures, too, although they are neither found there to be governed by natural laws nor directed toward a material product (biomass). Instead, they exist there as rule-governed processes that deal with the circulation of nonmaterial information. Obviously, evolution has made a second use of the structural form of the ecosystem, which initially proved very successful within the material world and has now been redesigned to organize the immaterial world of information. Basically, Bateson already had that insight,[15] and he consequently spoke of an "ecology of mind" as an extension of the well-known ecology of matter into the psychic world of mental processes. Although this is still not very widely known or held in great esteem, this was one of the great scientific discoveries of the twentieth century, along with Watson's discovery of the genetic double helix and Chomsky's discovery of the syntactical creativity of language. In ECE, we consequently call cultures "cultural ecosystems" and relate them to their ancestors, the natural ecosystems. We thus call the new theory "evolutionary cultural ecology."

Therefore, the cultural theory that constitutes the core part of ECE is a theory of new ecosystems that have developed from their natural ancestors and have become more and more (although not fully) autonomous. In this process of the growth of culture, semiotic evolution and especially the development of a language faculty play important roles.

4.3 The Innovations of Culture

Like every evolutionary process, the emergence of culture from nature involved conservative and nonconservative processes. The fundamental conservativeness of evolution is explained by the fact that the capacity for copying a given object is its basic type of process; we call it "replication" and an object with the ability to do the copying a "replicator." The non-conservativeness of evolution is mainly based on "mistakes" happening spontaneously during these copying processes ("mutations"). As pointed out, structurally the conservative aspects seem to dominate. But there are quite a few innovations accumulating through mutations. During the whole process that eventually led to the emergence of *Homo sapiens,* a typical bundle of joint developments took place. Probably, none of these clearly preceded the other; they are typical examples of coevolutionary processes. All of them are the results of evolutionary experiments, loosening the bounds of natural determination and extending the scope for free behavior and interaction. Analyzing that coevolution, there are at least six developments of major importance to be singled out:

(1) The cognitive faculties allow more and more abstract thinking, which replaces the concrete objects observed by the senses with signs handled by thought. This involves a sort of disembodiment or abstraction from spatio-temporal bindings that is quite typical for the whole of cultural evolution.

(2) Whereas the natural evolution of living beings is based on a single type of replicator, the material gene, its cultural offspring begins with the emergence of a new type of replicator, the meme, and uses the new substitutional objects as carriers of information. By this, it starts and accelerates what has been called the semiotic evolution: the evolution of signs.[16]

(3) The continued semiotic evolution subsequently adds new types of signs to the older natural signs: from indexical signs that already play a part in animal communication to icons that already arose in nature, albeit reluctantly and not extensively, and from those icons to symbols quite typical for the human cultural sphere. There are many intermediate stages that could be illustrated by adapted communication systems and early forms for visualizing language (writing).

(4) Action supplements and partly replaces behavior. Whereas behavior is cause driven, governed by natural laws, and lacking the possibility for free will, action allows aim-driven intentional behavior and deviations from behavioral tendencies anchored in the laws of nature.

(5) Rules supplement natural laws. Rules permit the construction of new systems with organizational structures that are not to be taken for granted and that are not to be viewed as unamenable to change, but that should rather be viewed as amenable to modifications through intentional action and the development of new conventions. ECE therefore views rules and conventions as the evolutionary cultural offspring of the laws of nature.

(6) The development of language (see 4.4 below).

The whole process of cultural evolution had two important effects shaping the new ecosystems: Firstly, they no longer needed roles partitioned in reference to special groups of living beings, as is characteristic of the materially based natural ecosystems. With these material systems, the production, consumption, and reduction of biomass are distributed to well-defined types of organisms ("the producers—green plants; the consumers—animals; the reducers—bacteria and fungi"). By contrast, in the circulation of immaterial information, not only is such partitioned role-playing rendered superfluous, but it also benefits new creatures who learn to act on the basis of information in all of these roles, switching easily among them. Producing information (e.g. "speaking"), consuming information (e.g. "understanding"), and reducing information (e.g. "forgetting") are three roles in the information cycle that must be mastered by each partner of an informational process. Secondly, cultural ecosystems further depend on the existence and proper functioning of their natural ancestors, and therefore on the ongoing flow of the energy of the sun. However, because of their own immateriality they do not make use of that physical energy themselves; for their own development and perseverance they need psychical energies. It is a striking fact that modern cultural theorizing (in accordance with most of the conventional humanities) entirely lacks a conception that the cultural processes need a form of energy in order to become possible at all. There is considerable evidence that the cultures themselves, especially the highly original ones, possess faculties that make it possible to perceive that energy. Given our scientific understanding of culture, however, we have to relearn that energy is not only a concept of physics.[17] It is a clear misconception to argue that, within an ever-changing world, the diverse and forceful psychic processes can be carried out with no energy at all. ECE proposes a view different from this, influenced by the thinking of the famous physicochemist Wilhelm Ostwald and other pioneers of the theory of psychic energy.[18]

These innovative views describe culture by comparing it to its mother nature. They clarify the status of the cultural theory of ECE, showing it to integrate learning from the research of natural scientists but not as belonging to natural science itself.

4.4 The Link: Language

Within that innovative framework, new means of communication became possible, language being the most effective since it allows a creative use of abstract symbols. Language certainly is the most important innovation in the process of cultural evolution. Modern linguistics supports the view that it is not only a refinement of some recent system of animal communication but also a newly generated system adapted and restricted to the powers of the human brain. In this respect, language was the first and only developmental tool for the generation and maintenance of culture. Human culture is strictly bound to language. A different language opens a new view of the world; it renders a different culture possible. Each case of language diversity on all possible levels of linguistic diversity indicates a diversity of cultures on all possible levels of cultural diversity.

As with the signs, the rules have developed, preserving all intermediate stages up to today. The preserved, rich rule systems of natural languages might be taken as proof for this hypothesis, indicating the succession of language growth during the process of the evolution of language. In the vast structures of our natural languages they are finely assembled, spread out through the whole range of linguistic regulations. They range from strict natural laws (phonetics, neurology, and physiology of language) to rules that are still very strictly valid but that are no longer natural laws (most rules of pragmatics, parts of syntax) to those of a midrange validity (large parts of syntax, elementary semantics) further on to less strictly valid ones (most parts of semantics) to conventions toward which there is low and very low commitment (stylistics): a series mirroring the different ages of the respective parts of natural language. (The same series is to be found in complex systems of cultural rules of every kind, ranging from strictest law-like ones to various conventions toward which there is an intermediate-level obligation, to rules to which there is very little obligation: beginning with instincts and rituals, progressing through animals and man, to dogmas in the state, society, or the church, to norms like orders or decrees, to laws in the legal order, to traffic rules and rules for many games, to the directions given by composers or novelists, to usages, styles, and fashions, to advice, rules of behavior, and "etiquette," to purposes, loose recommendations, and, finally, inspiration and fancies of the moment.)

Modern linguistics has shown language to exhibit ecosystemic structures; in light of ECE this is not surprising. Language links the natural with the cultural sphere in a chronological development, and its structure mirrors the basic conservative tendency of evolution.[19]

5 PRACTICAL PRINCIPLES OF ECE

There are some properties of a cultural ecosystem that invariably determine its vibrancy. They insure its prospects for survival. Among the most important are diversity, flexibility, transitoriness, creativity, and cooperation. All of these properties have in principle developed on the basis of sustainable conditions in the natural sphere; they are already indispensable for nature.

Cultural diversity, for instance, is an evolutionary clone of biodiversity. Although natural ecosystems exist in many variations, including variations with rich diversity and variations with poorer diversity, less diverse systems, too, are built on a minimally required inner diversity, necessary for their functions. Diversity is as important a means for culture as it is for nature. Not only does the latter result from nature, but it also provides a starting point for later evolutionary processes. Today, the importance of this cultural diversity is widely ignored, as is the importance of natural diversity; and cultural inflexibility is often mistaken for cultural power. A necessary precondition for the needed flexibility is an intelligent regime at the borders of a culture.

No culture could forever rest on its own creative powers; so learning from external cultural sources is necessary in order to augment cultural creativity, too. The cooperative ideas especially have to be developed creatively since we, as inhabitants of the one earth, have no alternative to the development of symbiotic lifestyles. If we want to learn from the long experience of natural evolution, then our attention is not to be directed primarily to the survival of the fittest but to win-win cooperative relationships. Yet, cooperation does not entail that one give up one's cultural identity; rather, it enables us to participate in the cultural net and to learn from alternative forms of cultural life.

Culture consists of matters of fact as well as evaluations. It allows descriptive and normative characterizations. A science of culture without that normative component is blind to differences of major importance. It cannot discriminate between democracy and tyranny, humanity and inhumanity, good and evil. All that belongs to the realm of culture.

The diversity of cultures misleads many to think that there are no universal parameters for cultural evaluation. But this is not the case. In protocultures there is little need for evaluation since the lack of alternative possibilities for behavior means that alternative structures are out of reach. In human cultures things have become much more differentiated. Our freedom to act, and not only to behave, has led to the development of possible alternative actions that enable us to develop our cultures in one or the other direction. There are some important evaluation systems, especially moral, legal, and aesthetic ones. Although the different systems of morals are tightly bound to the different cultures, we nevertheless conceive of a universal set of ethical principles, which form the basic kernel of human rights. Similarly, we conceive of some basic aesthetic features as probably universal, although they are still less well defined than the ethical universals.

Mostly, culture is discussed as either an ethnic or a social phenomenon; but as has been shown, it is false to maintain that we must choose between these two. Culture is intertwined in a complex net of relations between all three of its levels ("the cultural net," cf. 3.3), and every more specified definition of culture fails to include some important features of it. ECE leads us to the conclusion that, within this complex cultural net, the role of individuals is more important than is largely perceived in the "sociological age": it is the persons who have ideas, discover new problems, and invent new ways of solving them. Since we are the agents of creativity, our cultural future is heavily dependent on the cultures of the individuals. The often hailed "wisdom of the crowds" is a biologism that is misleading and dangerous.

There are two types of life conditions: natural ones and the cultural ones. In recent decades, the growing risks to our natural life conditions have been widely discussed; and, consequently, some political steps have been taken to better them. It is a cultural issue of major importance that these steps are to be reenforced, since nature bears all of culture on its shoulders. But many involved in the discussion on this issue also fail to perceive that there are conditions for cultural life, too.

Therefore, ECE states a "principle of the intelligent learning from nature" as one of the leading principles for cultural action related to our cultural future. It does not imply a form of biologizing which would recommend that every solution nature has come up should be strictly copied in the domain of culture; that would be a rather unintelligent strategy. But it means that it is rewarding to consider whether nature has found a solution to a problem that recurs in a modified garment within the new cultural sphere. Sustainable systems are the most striking examples of natural systems that we must try to copy in cultural processes. Sustainable systems are by no means a genuine invention of man; the most perfect examples are to be found as unspoiled and fully intact natural ecosystems. An example of the original form is the sustainability of a natural woodland or river that is capable of maintaining its ecological balances over long periods of time: our practices of sustainable forestry or fishery have only intelligently imitated those. Presently we are trying to learn this for all of our economic activities.

The principle of the intelligent learning from nature makes use of what has been called the rationality of nature. It is a rationality that has long been developed by the trials and errors of natural evolution. Although by no means all cultural problems can be solved by applying that principle, many of the systems in the natural world have faced problems similar to the problems now faced in culture, and we can learn from such natural systems. Yet the learning process at times also requires conscious deviations from the ways of nature. Nature has often preferred solutions that cannot be intelligently used as cultural guides for moral reasons. In contrast to nature, the cultural capacities of mankind allow ethical reasoning; and this certainly excludes some natural solutions from being applied to the human sphere as inadequate or shortsighted. For instance, a social Darwinism, the insipid cultural propagation of the survival of the fittest, is one example of an ethically wrong cultural strategy, a biologism, unacceptable when applied to culture. However, in the attempt to establish a sustainable economy, we find an example of intelligent learning from nature.

6   SHORT REMARK ON "WESTERN CIVILIZATION"

In view of the factual influence of the cultural world powers, it is of vital importance that cultural development continues concomitant with ongoing strivings for cultural change. This needs to be undertaken in all cultures but especially the leading ones. So-called "Western civilization," a complex superculture with its own combination of religious, scientific, and economic features, is surely a leading force in the present global developments; and its de facto course of development is ambivalent and laden with problems. It is an economically, not ecologically, driven culture; sustainability has come to be known as a rational guide, but political actors still do not pay it its deserved attention; our globalization endeavors are carried out in ways more reminiscent of the win-lose scenarios of predators and their prey than of the win-win scenarios of symbiotic systems. Cultural diversity is severely threatened and being thinned out. We still think of borders more typically as lines of exclusion than as transitional zones of learning, and so on. However, the problems of our world are only to be solved culturally; and this requires many modifications, even hard turns, in our leading contemporary cultures.

Undoubtedly, in Western civilization many important cultural achievements are to be saved and defended: the pursuit of a rational view of the world, the models of democracy and freedom of thought, the equality of the sexes, the ideal of fraternity, and several other things besides. But there is a marked gap between those ideals and the reality of our Western culture. This is mainly caused by the ambivalent course of the globally acting cultural powers that—openly or concealed—follow the dubious ideals of egoism, marking the starting point for necessary cultural change. The aggression of the Islamic civilization, for instance, can be understood as a reaction to another more subtle aggression: the dangerous ideals in Western culture accompanying its politics of global economic and ideological dominion and control. Therefore one of the main cultural aims of our age is a substantial reform of Western civilization from the present "Wall-Street culture" to a new liveliness of its real ideals.

7 ANTHROPOLOGICAL ISSUES RELATING TO ECE

It is not difficult to understand that ECE has some major consequences for anthropological theory and for our collective self-understanding at the present time. They are drawn not only from the practical principles we have considered, but also from the more fundamental theoretical and methodological ones. This becomes apparent once we are confronted with some common views that have arisen and become popular during the past century.[20]

The fragmented views of twentieth century scientific specializations have contributed to an image of mankind that in many respects does not align with the views of ECE. We are broadly viewed as refined constructed machines, driven by egoism and barely concealed instincts, hardly capable of real communication and moral advancement, much more endowed with destructive than constructive powers. The yes-no scheme of digitalization, far from resulting merely in a leading technology, has come to characterize our general approaches to and views of the world. Two-valued logic, computer science, the theory of abstract automatons, radical constructivism, psychoanalysis, sociological systems theory, sociobiology, and the study of our aggressions, along with other specified fields of research, have each contributed to that image. Nevertheless, it provides a distorted picture, emerging from the isolated perspectives of separate disciplines, without vision of a coherent culture of knowledge. The age of transdisciplinarity, of which Bateson's ideas and ECE are products, could contribute to some major corrections in that antiquated understanding of knowledge and man. Skeptical of the powers of our ruling paradigms, ECE strengthens the cooperative forces instead of the confrontational ones; it strengthens the consciousness of change and of the ongoing dependency of all culture on the fundamental natural processes. Man may resemble a complex machine if viewed through the superficial lenses of computer scientists, but a deeper analysis shows that it is no longer difficult to perceive the limitations of such a view, which can be seen as reflecting the tunnel vision of specialization. We are increasingly once again learning of our existential, vital rootedness in the nonhuman world; and we increasingly conceive of ourselves as partners in a comprehensive energy-flow and communication system. Led by the insights of transdisciplinary research in such various fields as quantum physics, neurobiology, cognitive linguistics, and ecological economics, we are again learning to relativize materiality and direct attention to the immaterial world. We are learning that creativity—rather than schematic skills and routines—is the most important cultural competence in life, and sustainable lifestyles, the best kind at which to aim.

ECE has not invented that emerging new picture of ourselves, but it shares the basic outlines of that view and adds information to help clarify it.

NOTES

1. For a thorough introduction to this theory, see my recent monograph, *Die Ökologie des Wissens: Exkursionen in eine gefährdete Landschaft* (Freiburg: Karl Alber, 2005.). I have also dealt with this in numerous other works including "Identity and Manifoldness: New Perspectives in Science, Language and Politics," in *The Ecolinguistics Reader: Language, Ecology and Environment*, Alwin Fill and Peter Mühlhäusler, eds, 84–90 (New York: Continuum, 2001).
2. For an introduction to Naess's view, see *Ecology, Community and Lifestyle*, D. Rothenberg, ed. (Cambridge: Cambridge University Press, 1989).
3. Heidegger, Bakhtin, Ricoeur, or Foucault, for example, who influenced the alternative ecological theorizing especially in America, played no prominent role within the development of ECE. Nevertheless, there are parallels to be detected.
4. Some conceptions of "human ecology" or "social ecology" are also sometimes referred to as "cultural ecology." There are many parallels, however, nothing more.
5. Presently ECE is mainly being developed by the "Evolutionary Cultural Ecology Research Group" (E.C.E.), which comprises scholars in Europe, Asia, and America from many different fields of research. The group is based at the University of Bielefeld (Germany).
6. See Yüce and Plöger, *Die Vielfalt der Wechselwirkung: Eine transdisziplinäre Exkursion im Umfeld der Evolutionären Kulturökologie* (Freiburg: Karl Alber, 2003); see also Finke, "Kulturökologie," in *Konzepte der Kulturwissenschaften: Theoretische Grundlagen – Ansätze – Perspektiven*, ed. Ansgar Nünning and Vera Nünning (Stuttgart: Metzler, 2003) and "Die Evolutionäre Kulturökologie: Hintergründe, Prinzipien und Perspektiven einer neuen Theorie der Kultur," *Literature and Ecology* (2006): 175–217.
7. Rupert Sheldrake, *The Presence of the Past: Morphic Resonance and the Habits of Nature* (New York: Times Books, 1988).

8. It is in this respect that J. v. Uexküll has influenced ECE to quite a great extent; cp. Jakob von Uexküll, *Umwelt und Innenwelt der Tiere* (Berlin: Springer, 1909) and *Kompositionslehre der Natur: Ausgewählte Texte*, ed. Thure von Uexküll (Frankfurt: Ullstein, 1980).

9. John Tyler Bonner, *The Evolution of Culture in Animals* (Princeton, NJ: Princeton University Press, 1980), 17.

10. Fortunately, man's capabilities for the destruction of nature are limited. Even destroying himself as a species (not only human populations) or life in general (not only special forms of life) or earth (not only parts of the earth) is not equivalent to destroying nature. The nonliving or the extraterrestrial world may not be affected to a noticeable extent. Culture, however, would certainly have to start anew.

11. This is not equivalent to saying nature is gradually fading away into culture (a slogan of popular philosophy). If nature is defined by the scope of the natural laws, nothing is lost by the progression of culture.

12. Many influential theories of culture therefore entirely restrict themselves to this level, e.g. Luhmann.

13. Uexküll, *Umwelt und Innenwelt der Tiere*. Being one of the founders of modern biology, Uexküll hoped to anchor not only the outer-worlds conception of the environment in biological ecology, but also the dimension of the inner-worlds of cognition and behavior. He was disappointed that most biologists were unwilling to learn that lesson.

14. See Peter Finke, "Kultur als Ökosystem: Eine kurze Beschreibung, Erklärung und Anwendung," *Living* 3 (1993). Among Bateson's significant work on this are his *Mind and Nature: A Necessary Unity* (New York: Hampton Press, 1979) and *Sacred Unity: Further Steps to an Ecology of Mind*, R. Donaldson, ed. (New York: Harper Collins, 1991).

15. As Gregory Bateson notes: "[L]let me say that a redwood forest or a coral reef with its aggregate of organisms interlocking in their relationships has the necessary general structure." *Steps to an Ecology of Mind* (Chicago: University of Chicago Press, 2000), 490. Redwood forests or coral reefs represent what biologists call "ecosystems." Bateson obviously speaks in a more acute way than many of his interpreters, most of whom tell us his insight is merely into the pattern that connects a system. There are many types of systems, however; Bateson clearly thought of a system with a rather special structure and function: an ecosystem. Speaking of an "ecology of mind," he meant that mode of speech literally, not as a metaphorical expression only.

16. The theory of the meme as being an evolutionary new replicator following the physical gene was originally published by Richard Dawkins, *The Selfish Gene* (Oxford: Oxford University Press, 1976), ch. 11, "Memes, the New Replicators"; but, unfortunately, the author neglected the role of signs. For a discussion of the consequences to the understanding of language and culture, see Finke, "The Memory of Language: New Research in Cultural Evolution," in *Language, Signs, Nature: Ecolinguistic Dimensions of Environmental Discourse. Essays in Honour of Alwin Fill* (Tübingen: Stauffenburg, 2008). For another important work on memes, see Susan Blackmore, *The Meme Machine* (Oxford: Oxford University Press, 1999).

17. Cf. most textbooks on the energy problem, e.g. A. L. Lehninger, *Bioenergetics: The Molecular Basis of Biological Energy Transformations*, 2nd ed. (Menlo Park: Addison-Wesley, 1971).

18. Wilhelm Ostwald, *Der energetische Imperativ* (Leipzig: Akademische Verlagsgesellschaft, 1912).

19. Peter Finke, "The Memory of Language."

20. Ervin Laszlo, *The Whispering Pond* (Boston: Element Books, 1999).

REFERENCES

Bateson, Gregory. *Steps to an Ecology of Mind.* New York: Chandler, 1972. Reprinted with a foreword by Mary Catherine Bateson. Chicago: University of Chicago Press, 2000.

———. *Mind and Nature: A Necessary Unity.* New York: Hampton Press, 1979.

———. *Sacred Unity: Further Steps to an Ecology of Mind.* Edited by R. Donaldson. New York: Harper Collins, 1991.

Blackmore, Susan. *The Meme Machine.* Oxford: Oxford University Press, 1999.

Bonner, John Tyler. *The Evolution of Culture in Animals.* Princeton, NJ: Princeton University Press, 1980.

Dawkins, Richard. *The Selfish Gene.* Oxford: Oxford University Press, 1976.

Finke, Peter. "Kultur als Ökosystem: Eine kurze Beschreibung, Erklärung und Anwendung." *Living* 3 (1993): 56–59.

———. "Identity and Manifoldness: New Perspectives in Science, Language and Politics." In *The Ecolinguistics Reader: Language, Ecology and Environment,* edited by Alwin Fill and Peter Mühlhäusler, 84–90 (New York: Continuum, 2001).

———. "Kulturökologie." In *Konzepte der Kulturwissenschaften: Theoretische Grundlagen—Ansätze—Perspektiven,* edited by Ansgar Nünning and Vera Nünning. Stuttgart: Metzler, 2003.

———. *Die Ökologie des Wissens: Exkursionen in eine gefährdete Landschaft.* Freiburg: Karl Alber, 2005.

———. "Die Evolutionäre Kulturökologie: Hintergründe, Prinzipien und Perspektiven einer neuen Theorie der Kultur." Special issue, *Literature and Ecology* (2006): 175–217.

———. "The Memory of Language: New Research in Cultural Evolution." In *Language, Signs, Nature: Ecolinguistic Dimensions of Environmental Discourse. Essays in Honour of Alwin Fill.* Tübingen: Stauffenburg, 2008.

Laszlo, Ervin. *The Whispering Pond.* Boston: Element Books, 1999.

Lehninger, A. L. *Bioenergetics: The Molecular Basis of Biological Energy Transformations.* 2nd ed. Menlo Park: Addison-Wesley, 1971.

Naess, Arne. *Ecology, Community and Lifestyle.* Edited by D. Rothenberg. Cambridge: Cambridge University Press, 1989.

Ostwald, Wilhelm. *Der energetische Imperativ.* Leipzig: Akademische Verlagsgesellschaft, 1912.

Sheldrake, Rupert. *The Presence of the Past: Morphic Resonance and the Habits of Nature.* NewYork: Times Books, 1988.

Uexküll, Jakob von. *Umwelt und Innenwelt der Tiere.* Berlin: Springer, 1909.

———. *Kompositionslehre der Natur: Ausgewählte Texte.* Edited and with a foreword by Thure von Uexküll. Frankfurt: Ullstein, 1980.

Yüce, Nilgün, and Peter Plöger. *Die Vielfalt der Wechselwirkung: Eine transdisziplinäre Exkursion im Umfeld der Evolutionären Kulturökologie (with contributions by Fritjof Capra, Hans-Peter Dürr, Peter Finke, Ervin Laszlo, Adam Makkai and others).* Freiburg: Karl Alber, 2003.

15 Prigogine
The Interplay of Cosmos, Complexity, and Culture

Dorothea Olkowski

A DIFFERENT WORLD

We used to live in a different world but, somehow, the world we lived in has changed. These changes are not historical; they are not political or economic, cultural or intellectual. These changes appear to be actual physical changes. Is this possible? Is it possible that the world, meaning the universe, has physically altered? From the second century AD forward, the discoveries of Ptolemy, Copernicus, Tyco Brahe, Kepler, and Galileo did in fact gradually alter the Ancient worldview of the universe as finite and our solar system as earth centered. These literally world-changing discoveries culminated in the invention of the telescope and, ultimately, in the defeat of the earth-centered view of our solar system and its replacement by the view that the sun is at the center. With this, the stage was ready for the emergence of a new science. This new science no longer relied on the evidence of the senses and geometry but required much a more rigorous mathematical tool, the calculus, to complement the much more accurate technological instrument of perception, the telescope. Isaac Newton's laws of motion plus the universal law of gravitation and the calculus, developed simultaneously by Newton and the philosopher Gottfried Leibniz, created a new universe, a possibly infinite universe, with the sun at the center of our planetary system. It was a machine-like, calculable universe whose planets and stars move as the result of known external forces, without the need for the watchful eye of God.[1]

In *Exploring Complexity: An Introduction,* coauthors Grégoire Nicolis and Ilya Prigogine acknowledge that after Newton, what came to be called "classical science" reached a high point.[2] It was believed that the fundamental laws of the universe had been discovered once and for all, that they are deterministic and reversible laws, and that any process that did not obey this order was considered to be an exception, arising due to ignorance, especially concerning variables. Furthermore, it was indisputable that the scientific investigator stands outside of the system being studied.[3] But since Newton, this view of the world has indeed changed. And, although the Newtonian universe still accounts for many physical phenomenon, a new universe of deterministic but irreversible laws seems to have sprung up to fill numerous gaps in explanation and understanding. Let us begin by clarifying the main features of the old classical deterministic and reversible universe before moving on to the new world.

IRREVERSIBILITY AND DETERMINISM

We will discuss determinism at length below, but an account of irreversibility is necessary and useful, so let us begin with this. Irreversible processes are independent of the direction of time. They become evident in the context of the laws of motion and the use of differential calculus, the tool for describing instantaneous changes in quantities such as position, velocity and acceleration. Since Galileo, a central concern of physics was, for bodies moving uniformly, how can we describe the state of a body at a given instant, and how can we describe the change from rest to motion and motion to rest for a projectile or a falling body?[4] Mathematical dynamics measures quantities so it begins by breaking up the changing motion into an infinite series of infinitely small changes (called infinitesimals), each of which can then be measured.[5] Classical physics focuses on the acceleration at each instant of the points that form a system. "Generally speaking, acceleration itself varies with time, and the physicist's task is to determine precisely the nature of this variation."[6]

However, bodies do not accelerate in a vacuum; forces act on each of these points, and force at any point is proportional to the acceleration the force produces. This is Newton's second law of motion ($F = ma$).[7] Differential equations define each point in the system by means of position, velocity, and acceleration, and this calculation of trajectories provides a complete description of the dynamic system. This takes place in a mathematical conceptual manifold called a *state space*, wherein each dimension corresponds to one variable of the system, and the system traces a path in that space called a trajectory.[8] Force refers to gravity and gravity applies equally to atoms and to large bodies like planets as every body has mass and interacts with other bodies according to its distance and acceleration.[9]

Differential equations allow physicists to calculate trajectories, which are characterized by "*lawfulness, determinism*, and *reversibility*."[10] Starting from an initial position or state, the laws governing motion allow for deduction from the initial state to the entire series of states the system will pass through. It is possible to begin anywhere, with any state and to deduce the entire future and past of the system.[11] This is what makes the system reversible. "If all the points of a system are reversed, the system will . . . retrace all the states it went through during the previous change," exactly restoring the original conditions.[12] Of course reversibility seems to be strongly counterintuitive, but it holds for the idealized world of dynamics.

But do we actually inhabit this ideal world? Nicolis and Prigogine commit themselves to the view that the world has changed, and that we now live in a pluralistic world, which includes both deterministic and stochastic (probable), reversible and irreversible phenomena.[13] What has changed, they argue, is the relative importance of these phenomena. Classical science claimed and in many instances continues to claim that the fundamental laws of the universe are deterministic and reversible. This view of matter, as passive and governed by mechanical forces, of necessity, almost completely excludes the relevance of unexpected events and discoveries.[14] In this sense, classical science could be said to be seeking the ultimate structure governing *all* physical systems. But to understand this, we must clearly define what we mean by "deterministic," a term subject to much confusion, as much among scientists as among philosophers.

The philosopher Karl Popper compares the scientific idea of determinism to a film whose producer is the creator and for whom "those parts of the film which have already been shown constitute the past. And those which have not yet been shown constitute the future."[15] The physicist and philosopher Gaston Bachelard argued that there is a feeling that a fundamental order exists, "a feeling of intellectual repose stemming from the symmetries and certainties inherent in the mathematical analysis."[16] This is because, Bachelard states, the mathematical conception of the world arose from the intuition of simple forms, simple geometries, and determinism followed as a consequence of this in spite of the existence of deformations and perturbations, which were taken to be superficial correctives only.[17]

Perhaps the most succinct explanation of determinism is the idea that if things cannot be otherwise than as they are, the current total state of the universe plus the full set of physical laws governing it should yield an adequate explanation for every event in the universe. Additionally, if prediction is the necessary condition for understanding the universe, then determinism implies that every event can be derived from the initial conditions and the physical laws.[18] At the least, determinism seems to rule out divine intervention (first or final cause) as well as its apparent opposite, mere accident.[19]

Philosopher of science Stephen H. Kellert, citing the common claim that the universe as a whole is a system of some sort, separates out the different senses of determinism into four layers. The first layer is that in a deterministic system, the future depends on the present in a *mathematically specifiable* way, that is, according to a set of differential equations.[20] Differential equations, we saw above, are the rules governing the changing state of a so-called dynamical system where the variables change in a smooth or continuous manner.[21] Furthermore, there will be no probabilities, no stochastic processes, so that any complex behavior comes from the system's internal mathematical structure and the differential equations themselves allow for no branching, choices, or probabilities.[22] The general principle at work here is that the system is able to predict the future by relating it to the past or present with mathematical rules.

An even stronger notion of determinism (sometimes called Laplacian, after mathematician-astronomer Pierre-Simon Laplace), states that a complete and instantaneous description of the system fixes past and future with *no alternatives*; thus the entire universe and not merely a dynamical system is deterministic.[23] A third level requires that physical quantities have exact values. And the fourth level stipulates that the entire universe, not just individual dynamical systems, is predictable. Interestingly, this may occur either through an omnipotent intelligence or an omnipotent computational schema, but in either case it requires a closed physical system. It is this definition of determinism that Prigogine and Isabelle Stengers apparently adhere to, and also question, in their coauthored book *Order out of Chaos: Man's New Dialogue with Nature.*[24] It is a view, they argue, that fails because deterministic trajectories are really "unobservable idealizations for sufficiently unstable systems."[25]

Together they argue that if "in the classical view, the basic processes of nature were considered to be deterministic and reversible. . . . Today we see everywhere, the role of irreversible processes, of fluctuations."[26] Prigogine and Stengers reformulate this world as open, complex, probabalistic, and temporally irreversible. Thus, *Order out of Chaos* is an account of the conceptual transformation of science from classical science to the present, particularly as it applies to the macroscopic scale, the scale of atoms, molecules, and biomolecules, with special attention to the problem of time, a problem that arose out of the realization that new dynamic states of matter may emerge from thermal chaos when a system interacts with its surroundings. These new structures were given the name *dissipative* structures to indicate that dissipation can in fact play a constructive role in the formation of new states.[27]

Prigogine and Stengers thus take us from the static view of classical dynamics to an evolutionary view arising with nonequilibrium thermodynamics, based on time irreversibility. Simultaneously, "one of the main themes of this book is that of a strong interaction of the issues proper to culture as a whole and the internal conceptual problems of science in particular."[28] Thus, the reorientation from the classical to the contemporary view is, for them, equally reflected in the conflict between the natural sciences and the social sciences and humanities. If the development of science has been understood to shift away from concrete experience toward abstraction, this is, the authors believe, a consequence of the limitations of classical science, its inability to give a coherent account of the relationship between humans and nature. Many important results were repressed or set aside insofar as they failed to conform to the classical model. In order to free itself from traditional modes of comprehending nature, science isolated and purified its practices in the effort to achieve greater and greater autonomy, leading it to conceptualize its knowledge as universal and to isolate itself from any social context.[29]

Much of the contention about determinism seems to rest with the distinction between prediction and determinism, a distinction that is often not that clear but should be. Given the determinate state of the universe at any particular moment, it has been argued that all past and future states of the universe must therefore be fixed; whether or not we are able to accurately measure and compute this is another matter. In other words, we can distinguish between the world as it is and the world as we know it; thus, for now at least, there is determinism but also, unpredictability.[30] Against this, Prigogine, with Stengers, argues that determinism fails along with prediction because the universe consists of extremely unstable, intrinsically random systems, and sensitive dependence on initial conditions makes even close approximations ultimately obsolete, illegitimate idealizations.[31] In the end, Prigogine and Stengers appear to retain determinism as a construct while recognizing that it seems to be of limited use in the new science of complexity, the science that interests them the most.[32] An even stronger position would be to claim that "determinism fails because our best theories (as actually used) argue against it," an argument that would eliminate both the notion that past and future are fixed with no alternatives and the idea of total predictability.[33] This solution is one we will return to later, but first let us set out Prigogine's version in more detail.

CHAOS AND COMPLEXITY

We might want to ask why scientists such as Prigogine have come to the conclusion that determinism is limited in scope, and prediction even more so. To a large degree, this is a result of what has come to be called *chaos theory* as well as the accompanying notion of *complexity*. Chaos theory, it has been noted, is not as interesting as it sounds.[34] "Chaos involves a deterministic mechanism that generates the *appearance* of randomness; a genuine randomness has no such deterministic underpinning."[35] But more specifically, what chaos describes is that systems governed by mathematically simple equations can and do result in unpredictable behavior. Nevertheless, the definition of chaos theory as "*the qualitative study of unstable aperiodic behavior in deterministic nonlinear dynamical systems*" calls for greater clarification and explanation.[36] The key terms here are "unstable" and "aperiodic." Instability refers to sensitive dependence on initial conditions of a dynamical system for which, even if two or more initial states differ imperceptibly, they will diverge, evolving into considerably different states.[37]

Aperiodic behavior refers to the state of a system when no variable describing it undergoes a regular repetition of values, thereby producing measurements that appear to be random. Thus, unstable, aperiodic behavior is *complex*. It does not repeat itself and it continues to manifest the effects of its initial condition.[38] Such systems describe colliding humans as much as colliding molecules: a panicked crowd, an auto pileup on the highway, a summer thunderstorm, thermal convection, all qualify. However, unstable and aperiodic behaviors are *not* the same as *molecular chaos*, which refers to the completely disordered, erratic behavior of molecules because they cannot recognize one another over distances greater than a few angstroms (one-hundred-millionth of a centimeter). By contrast, an intricately patterned snowflake, with its "coordinated activity or form or dynamics," the result of the encounter between a cubic centimeter of water and a winter storm, is in fact the result of such an unstable and aperiodic behavior.[39] As every child knows, no two snowflakes are ever alike.

There is one more important concept that must be included in this discussion: the concept of a *strange attractor*. We have already noted the significance of sensitive dependence on initial conditions, the fact that a dynamical system with this characteristic will produce considerably different solutions for two initial states that differ by imperceptible amounts.[40] Importantly, if there is any error at all in observing the initial state, prediction of a future state may be impossible. This is the so-called butterfly effect. Images of this system show two graceful sets of swirling rings positioned more or less like flapping butterfly wings. The term was actually coined by James Gleick in a paper asking if the flapping of butterfly wings in Brazil are the initial sensitive conditions of a trajectory that includes a tornado in Texas, something impossible to predict so also, not the first cause of a causal chain.[41] This last because after a certain *specifiable* amount of time, initial and final states are *causally disconnected,* such that not even an idealization could provide a full causal explanation. Instead, statistical or structural laws, or geometrical mechanisms such as topologies—the mathematical study of the properties that are preserved through deformations, twisting, and stretching objects—are much more relevant for an understanding of the behaviors in question.[42]

Given that extreme sensitivity makes exact prediction of trajectories impossible, other methods were needed. Using a computer to plot the trajectory of a system's unstable, periodic motion produced a picture of a new geometrical object: a strange attractor.[43] Trajectories were known to converge around fixed point attractors (a well-defined end point), limit cycle attractors (a periodic circling orbit), and torus attractors (picture a quasiperiodic line spiraling around a donut without ever precisely circling back on itself). Converging trajectories characterize all attractors, but some trajectories display sensitive dependence on initial conditions. Trajectories that are initially extremely close together rapidly diverge due to stretching and folding behavior, just as a saltwater taffy-pulling machine will rapidly pull apart, stretch, and then fold the taffy so that two pieces of candy placed together at the start will indeed end up far apart.[44] The stretching carries them away, and the folding brings together points that were distant from one another, so they converge.

The two wings of the Lorenz attractor (named for mathematician and meteorologist Edward Lorenz) show how points are stretched and move far apart into opposite wings, but then one trajectory passing through the center gets folded onto the opposite wing so that "nearby points can quickly evolve to opposite sides of the attractor, yet the trajectories are confined to a region of phase space with a particular shape."[45] These shapes are called fractals. Their dimensions are fractal and nonintegral. Integrable systems are representable as sets of independent units, eliminating interactions so that each of them changes in isolation from the others like Aristotle's heavenly bodies or Leibniz's monads.[46] Fractal dimensions quantify complexity as a ratio of change in detail in relation to change in scale.[47]

What characterizes this *order out of chaos* is that even where there is a strange attractor, dynamical chaos remains a deterministic system modeled by differential equations. As such, it is possible to characterize the instability of motion and the randomness of behavior arising with sensitive dependence on initial conditions using methods such as the Lyapunov exponents, which measure initially nearby trajectories that separate exponentially over time.[48] One important and necessary factor operating in deterministic chaos is that the systems we have been discussing are all *dissipative*. Let us now turn to the question of dissipation and what it means.

DISSIPATIVE SYSTEMS

Nicolis and Prigogine begin their discussion of dissipative systems by referring first to conservative systems. Classical mechanics developed and greatly expanded the ancient idea that the universe consists of a primordial element such as water that is untouched by change.[49] The laws of motion established by Isaac Newton along with the calculus developed by both Newton and Gottfried Leibniz became the basis of quantitative calculations to explain the motions of celestial bodies as well as those bodies subject to terrestrial gravity.[50] I noted above that the basic characteristics of trajectories in classical systems are lawfulness, determinism, and reversibility. Lawfulness refers to the laws of motion characterizing inertia, force, and acceleration, action and reaction. Determinism means that "everything is given" because any single state is adequate to define the complete system, past and future.[51] And reversibility refers to the equivalence of cause and effect, insofar as they are simultaneous in an abstract space; thus if the velocities of all points in the system are reversed, the system will retrace all its steps restoring original conditions.[52] The swinging pendulum forming a closed curve along which energy is conserved is a familiar manifestation of these principles.[53]

This system can now be contrasted with a dissipative system that gives rise to irreversible processes. The classical principle of inertia—that a body in motion will stay in motion—neglects the existence of friction by assuming the conservation of energy and the transfer of motion from one body to another.[54] From this point of view, dissipation can mean only the using up and exhaustion of available energy, something that is not supposed to occur.[55] Nicolas Léonard Sadi Carnot uncovered the second law of thermodynamics in 1824 while trying to construct the most efficient steam engine. But it was not until 1840 that Rudolf Clausius realized that in a coal-burning steam engine there must also be a way of heating the engine to compensate for the possible loss of heat in the process of converting heat into work. This brought to light the notion of losses and the formulation by William Thompson of the second law of thermodynamics in 1852, expressing the "universal tendency toward the degradation of mechanical energy."[56] As a universal tendency, this law expresses clearly the principle of irreversibility, the conversion of heat into motion at the price of waste and dissipation tending toward a state of thermal equilibrium called *entropy*, which is dissipated energy that is irreversibly wasted.[57]

In an isolated system, with no exchange with the outside world, entropy either increases or remains steady, an indication of irreversibility, the arrow of time.[58] Irreversible processes exhibit some uncontrolled changes in temperature, volume, and pressure leading to heat loss and friction, and so an increase in entropy.[59] Ideal systems can be reversed and these types of ideal *thermodynamic object*s can be controlled through their boundary conditions. However, thermodynamic objects in nature seem to be isolated since they favor certain states. They are drawn by attractors that the system seems to prefer and the system moves irreversibly toward increasing entropy.[60] Nevertheless, thermodynamic objects modified by exchanges with the outside world do sometimes break from this pattern because, for example, heat and compressibility are independent of the way the system is initially set up. This latter is fundamental to thermodynamic systems, which are complex and on the order of magnitude of 6.10^{23} particles (Avogadro's number, the number of atoms in one gram of hydrogen).[61]

For systems at equilibrium, entropy production, fluctuations and forces affecting the system, are at zero. For close-to-equilibrium systems, thermodynamic forces are not zero but are weak. Both of these systems remain stable and linear, exhibiting spatial and temporal continuity. "A striking difference between linear and nonlinear laws is whether the property of superposition holds or breaks down. In a linear system, the ultimate effect of the combined action of two different causes is merely the superposition of the effects of each cause taken individually."[62] By contrast, "in a nonlinear system adding a small cause to one already present can induce dramatic effects that have no common measure with the amplitude of the cause."[63] When nonlinearity is combined with an appropriate distance from equilibrium, the system gives rise to multiple solutions because some fluctuations may be amplified and compel the entire system to evolve in a qualitatively different manner. These far-from-equilibrium systems are instances of the threshold where fluctuations lead to unstable behavior.[64] In the field of hydrodynamics, for example, once a flow rate threshold is reached, stable flows may become turbulent. Lucretius referred to this as the clinamen, a spontaneous, unpredictable deviation that describes turbulence, irregular on the macroscopic scale but highly organized microscopically.[65] This *transition,* from the macroscopic to the microscopic, from the chaotic to highly organized, coherent behavior, from stable flows to turbulence, is now viewed as *self-organization*.[66]

This behavior returns us to the concept of dissipation and to dissipative structures. Dissipation refers to the close association, in certain structures, between structure and order on one side and dissipation or waste on the other.[67] In classical thermodynamics, in an isolated system, the transfer of heat from a warm to a cool container is a source of energy that is irreversibly wasted. This loss of available energy is an effect of friction so that without an influx of external energy, the system will just wind down to a motionless state.[68] Physicist Ludwig Boltzman recognized that the irreversible entropy growth reflects disorder on the molecular scale, but that it also is a change toward states of *increasing probability* on the microscopic scale, such that the attractor state is one of maximum probability. The explanation in terms of probability was groundbreaking as it makes prediction possible.[69] Whatever the starting point, the system moves toward a macroscopic state of disorder and symmetry that corresponds to maximally probable *microscopic* states where as many particles will be moving in one direction as in the other.[70]

But when a system interacts with the outside world, exchanging energy and matter, these nonequilibrium conditions may be the setting for dissipative structures that do not exhibit the characteristics of energy loss. The heat transfer of an isolated system leads to loss, but in an open exchange system, it becomes a source of order. One model of this type of dissipative system is the Bénard cell for which a layer of fluid lies between two horizontal parallel plates whose dimensions are much greater than the width of the fluid layer. In an equilibrium system, the fluid spreads out homogeneously, as all parts are identical, so any position of an observer in the fluid is indistinguishable from any other position.[71] Because there is no change, there is also no way to measure time, and all instants are identical.[72]

If the fluid is heated from below the bottom plate, something remarkable takes place. The *external* constraint—the application of heat—initially allows the system to remain at equilibrium. However, an increase in temperature or thermal conduction, brought to a critical point, restructures the fluid into a series of small convection cells, the Bénard cells.[73] The cells line up and rotate in the opposite direction of adjacent cells and the fluid itself stratifies into lower density and higher density layers along a heat gradient from low to high, from the bottom to the top, making the system potentially unstable, able to generate ascending and descending currents of the fluid. An observer in this system has a very different experience from the equilibrium system. The differently rotating cells allow the observer to determine position, and the observer can move horizontally from cell to cell, counting to acquire a measure of distance in space.

Such broken symmetry (breaking up of homogeneity) means that the space is defined by what is taking place in the system.[74] "This suggests the existence of *correlations*, that is, statistically reproducible relations between distant parts of the system."[75] These structures are also *supramolecular,* that is, their parameters are macroscopic, not microscopic and so their time scales are seconds, minutes, or hours.[76] This complexity is both coherent and orderly and represents a new type of dissipative system, one that transforms energy from the environment into an ordered system characterized by symmetry breaking, choices, and correlations on the macroscopic scale.[77] Prigogine and Stengers caution that the relation between order and chaos is complex. They ask, "Is a tropical forest an ordered or a chaotic system? . . . [T]he feeling persists that, as such, an overall pattern of a tropical forest, as represented, for instance, by the diversity of species, corresponds to the very archetype of order."[78] Such systems seem to exhibit the interplay between chance and constraint.

Nikolas and Prigogine point out the similarity between fluctuations and biological mutation, stability and biological selection, emphasizing the impact of biological evolution on these ideas.[79] In biology as in physiochemical systems, this complexity producing interplay is characterized by bifurcations of a trajectory, which arise when a critical value is reached and states become unstable so that small external perturbations are not dampened; then the system amplifies them and moves into a new regime that displays broken symmetries.[80] Depending on the number of inputs, bifurcation can produce what mathematicians call *catastrophes.* Catastrophes correspond to parameter values where a fixed point governing the system's behavior becomes unstable and bifurcates. The fold, cusp, swallowtail, and butterfly are three-dimensional figures that correspond to one, two, three, and four inputs respectively. However, the change in stability moves the system to the region of *new stable fixed point,* maintaining the interplay of fluctuations and stability.[81]

CHAOS AND CULTURE

If there is an order in nature or in the universe, it is, for Prigogine and Stengers, grounded in irreversibility, which brings order out of chaos. They point out that, whereas for Albert Einstein, science must be independent of any observer, for them, there can be no measurement or experiments without a relevant theoretical framework: that of the observer.[82] Einstein's single-minded thinking on this led him to dismiss Henri Bergson when Bergson proposed that there are a multiplicity of coexisting lived times, which for Einstein, could be phenomenological but never fundamental since the distinction between past, present, and future stands outside of physics, for which irreversibility is an illusion produced by improbable initial conditions.[83] As Nicolis and Prigogine state, Einstein sought a timeless description of the universe. The model of general relativity proposed that a relation exists between space-time and matter such that space-time became a physical phenomenon, not a temporal one, and following from which, irreversibility had to be an expression of subjectivity; thus it is not scientific.

However, for Prigogine and Stengers, the real lesson to take from Einstein is quite different from what Einstein insisted upon, and that is the concept of an evolving universe. This has much to do with the question of what is fundamental. Classical physics chose to examine macroscopic objects that exhibited simple behavior, objects such as the pendulum and planetary motion.[84] For Newtonian physics, the motions of all bodies in the universe—atoms or planets—were subject to the same law applied universally on every scale. But what if stability and simplicity appear as exceptions rather than as the rule in the universe? Classical homogeneity was shattered by the discovery of "*c*," the constant known as the speed of light, which established a limit beyond which an observer cannot transmit or receive signals. Likewise, "*h*," Plank's constant, establishes a scale based on the mass of an object, and so established that electrons are scaled differently than macroscopic bodies, which are heavy and slow-moving by comparison.[85] Moreover, unlike the Newtonian model, relativity applies only to physically localized observers who are in one place at one time, presupposing an observer situated within the world being observed.[86] Nevertheless, they maintain, it was only the birth of quantum mechanics that allowed physics to depart from the notion of an *immanent* formulation of the universe that would be a complete description of nature, a notion that was merely a reformulation of the classical conception of a transcendent knower observing the entire universe from outside.[87]

We noted above the correlation between nonequilibrium systems and chaos. Their breakthrough in seeking evidence for this seems to arise precisely with the introduction of a concept of time that is internal to what are called *intrinsically random systems*. Internal time is not mechanical; it depends on the global topology of a system, and Prigogine and Stengers associate it with ideas about time in geography; thus they refer to "the timing of space."[88] So, for example, in any geography one finds interacting and coexisting temporal elements that correspond to a well-defined internal age. By analogy, physical systems can be understood to have internal but still objective interacting temporal structures. Utilizing a measure of internal time "*T*" in a specific structure called a *baker transformation,* they note that ink that originally had been set out in horizontal stripes in a square would eventually be distributed uniformly over the entire area, thereby reaching equilibrium. In other words, the distribution goes from being ordered to being disordered. This is a randomization process, and the same occurs when the system is traced in the reverse direction, the so-called past, even though, as we will see, the reverse direction of such systems is dropped. This shows, it is argued, that probability is not merely the result of ignorance; it is not subjective. It is an objective property inside a dynamic system that expresses a basic structure.[89]

The basic structure of the baker transformation is one among many that are time irreversible. The thinking supporting this claim is articulated in a statement by the philosopher Karl Popper. If we were to drop a large stone into a deep and large pool of water and film the resulting circular wave pattern, and then show the film in reverse, something interesting would occur. "The reversed film will show *contracting* circular waves of increasing amplitude," and behind the highest wave crest, in the center, precisely where the stone was dropped, there will be a circular area of *undisturbed* water.[90] The point is that this reverse phenomenon is not a possible classical process. No matter how sophisticated we become technically, there will always be a distance from the center beyond which no contracting wave can be generated by any means. Similarly, if we assume the universe began with the "Big Bang," the implication is that there is a cosmological arrow of time, a cosmological temporal order that is not due merely to ignorance. Of course, reversible as well as irreversible processes are said to coexist inside the expanding universe, but the point of this discussion is that probability presupposes the arrow of time and the increase of entropy (disorder) expresses the increase of probability.[91]

Prigogine and Stenger's evolutionary model includes isolated systems that evolve to disorder following the second law of thermodynamics, but it also takes into account open systems that evolve into higher forms of complexity. This realization alone, they declare, ends the human sense of separation from other processes in the universe, as humans certainly experience the arrow of time.[92] It also reconnects much of philosophy with science. This reconnection has not been without conflicts. Kellert points out that at one time a solution to a problem in physics that contained probabilistic terms was not considered an adequate solution at all. The classical model demanded solutions with relatively simple functional relations whereby prediction and retrodiction (predictions about the past) were a matter of plugging in initial conditions and performing routine mathematical operations. Thus, integrable systems involving two bodies under the influence of a force were the model for dynamic systems.[93] The stable periodic behavior this structure yields has, Kellert argues, produced a world of clockwork hegemony and a fascination with simple and exact solutions. This may have led to a disregard for nonlinear systems, which may still turn out to be simpler than linear systems.[94]

Part of this bias lies with philosophers. The widely accepted model of scientific revolutions put forth by Thomas Kuhn maintains that serious science carried out in universities and research centers emphasizes solutions to paradigmatic problems and leads to specialization and compartmentalization while ignoring general questions. This *normal* science stands in contrast to paradigm shifts, which are moments of crisis in which scientists ask basic questions and compete with one another until a new paradigm emerges and the community returns to the new normal.[95] As Kuhn expresses it, "normal science does not aim at novelties of fact or theory and, when successful, finds none."[96] It is only when nature pushes back and normal methods fail repeatedly to resolve anomalies that crisis looms and scientific activity is forced to change. "The proliferation of competing articulations, the willingness to try anything, the expression of explicit discontent, the recourse to philosophy and to debate over fundamentals, all these are symptoms of a transition from normal to extraordinary research."[97] But for Prigogine and Stengers, this means that innovation in science is driven by the intensely conservative behavior of scientists themselves. Although they recognize that this does occur, they also argue that scientists have asked and continue to ask deliberate and lucid questions in search of new paradigms. This, they conclude, is connected to human history and culture. The rediscovery of time in physics is not and cannot be independent of other aspects of contemporary life.[98]

Kellert adds to this that practical utility as well as social interests delayed research in chaos theory, and he finds that the work of feminist philosophers of science who explore the role of gender ideology in science "amplifie[s] our understanding of the nontreatment of chaos."[99] Evelyn Fox Keller, Sandra Harding, and Helen Longino have all studied how ideology affects science with respect to the choice of what are taken to be important phenomena, which methods are preferred, and judgments about which results are successful.[100] Practical interest in mechanical systems and information transmission technology exhibiting stable periodic behavior tended to steer scientists away from the study of chaotic behaviors. This meant, according to Keller, that certain kinds of mathematics were more tractable than others, and these were favored.[101] Given these interests, a good solution was one that responded to the first two of these concerns.

Insofar as the prediction and control of natural phenomena has been and presumably continues to be a widely held goal of science, Kellert thinks that this lends itself to the manipulation and exploitation of nonhuman nature for human ends. This "cultural and economic interest" calls for "exact closed-form solutions" that favor reducing aspects of the world to objects of human use.[102]

Even if this depiction of normal science is overstated, Kellert still wishes to assert a correlation between the domination of nature and the domination of women. Even in the investigation of nonlinear dynamics, there is a fascination with images of " 'turbulence and chaos,' " which may be identified with the tradition of linking women to "wild, disorderly features of the natural world perceived as needing to be subdued."[103] The mechanistic view of the world, the view of physical matter as inert and dead, the ability to control and manipulate nature, have all contributed to a slowdown in the study of chaotic phenomena as opposed to other contemporary scientific phenomena.[104] It may be, as Prigogine and Stengers attest, that demographic changes in human society are what have led, finally, to a renewed interest in nonlinear dynamics and to new relations between humans and nature and humans and other humans.[105] Instability and fluctuation are notable in human societies; thus it is to be hoped that the increasing concern of science with these realities will make it possible to solve problems of importance for humans and for nature.

NOTES

1. Richard DeWitt, *Worldviews: An Introduction to the History and Philosophy of Science* (London: Blackwell, 2004), 183–84.
2. Grégoire Nicolis and Ilya Prigogine, *Exploring Complexity: An Introduction* (New York: W.H. Freeman, 1989), 2. Nicolis was a professor of theoretical physical chemistry and Prigogine was, of course, a Nobel laureate in chemistry.
3. Nicolis and Prigogine, *Exploring Complexity*, 3.
4. Ilya Prigogine and Isabelle Stengers, *Order out of Chaos: Man's New Dialogue with Nature* (New York: Bantam Books, 1984), 57.
5. Prigogine and Stengers, *Order out of Chaos*, 58.
6. Prigogine and Stengers, *Order out of Chaos*, 58.
7. Prigogine and Stengers, *Order out of Chaos*, 58.
8. Stephen H. Kellert, *In the Wake of Chaos* (Chicago: University of Chicago Press, 1993), 7–8.
9. Prigogine and Stengers, *Order out of Chaos*, 58–59.
10. Prigogine and Stengers, *Order out of Chaos*, 60.
11. Prigogine and Stengers, *Order out of Chaos*, 60.
12. Prigogine and Stengers, *Order out of Chaos*, 61.
13. Nicolis and Prigogine, *Exploring Complexity*, 2.
14. Nicolis and Prigogine, *Exploring Complexity*, 3.
15. Karl Popper, *The Open Universe* (Totowa, New Jersey: Rowman & Littlefield), 5. Cited in Kellert, *In the Wake of Chaos*, 52.
16. Gaston Bachelard, *The New Scientific Spirit*, trans. Arthur Goldhammer (Boston: Beacon Press, 1984), 102; cited in Kellert, *In the Wake of Chaos*, 53.
17. Bachelard, *The New Scientific Spirit*, 102–03.
18. Kellert, *In the Wake of Chaos*, 54–55.
19. J. Earman, *A Primer on Determinism* (Dordrecht: Reidel, 1986), 23; cited in Kellert, *In the Wake of Chaos*, 55.
20. Kellert, *In the Wake of Chaos*, 56; for discrete time units these would be difference equations known as mapping (2).
21. Kellert, *In the Wake of Chaos*, 2.
22. Kellert, *In the Wake of Chaos*, 58.
23. Kellert, *In the Wake of Chaos*, 59.
24. Kellert, *In the Wake of Chaos*, 60–61; Ilya Prigogine and Isabelle Stengers, *Order out of Chaos* (New York: Bantam Books, 1984), 77.
25. Kellert, *In the Wake of Chaos*, 64.
26. Prigogine and Stengers, *Order out of Chaos*, xxvii.
27. Prigogine and Stengers, *Order out of Chaos*, 12. Equilibrium thermodynamics studies the transformation of energy and the laws of thermodynamics recognize that although "energy is conserved," when energy is defined as the capacity to do work," nevertheless, nature is fundamentally asymmetrical; that is, although the total quantity of energy remains the same, its distribution changes in a manner that is irreversible. See P.W. Atkins, *The Second Law* (New York: Scientific American Library, 1984), 8–13.
28. Prigogine and Stengers, *Order out of Chaos*, 19. The French title of this book, an earlier and slightly less developed version, reflects the "new alliance" between science and culture.
29. Prigogine and Stengers, *Order out of Chaos*, 19–22.
30. Kellert, *In the Wake of Chaos*, 63–64.
31. Prigogine and Stengers, *Order out of Chaos*, 177–78; cited in Kellert, *In the Wake of Chaos*, 64.

32. Prigogine and Stengers, *Order out of Chaos,* 272; cited in Kellert, *In the Wake of Chaos,* 66.
33. Kellert, *In the Wake of Chaos,* 67.
34. Kellert, *In the Wake of Chaos,* ix.
35. John L. Casti, *Complexification: Explaining a Complex World through the Science of Surprise* (New York: Harper Collins, 1994), 103. Casti is a mathematician and a fellow at the Santa Fe Institute.
36. Kellert, *In the Wake of Chaos,* ix, 2.
37. Kellert, *In the Wake of Chaos,* 12.
38. Kellert, *In the Wake of Chaos,* 4.
39. Nicolis and Prigogine, *Exploring Complexity,* 6.
40. Kellert, *In the Wake of Chaos,* 12.
41. James Gleick, "Predictability: Does the Flap of a Butterfly's Wing in Brazil Set off a Tornado in Texas?" A paper delivered at the 139th meeting of the American Association for the Advancement of Science, December 29, 1972. Cited in Kellert, *In the Wake of Chaos,* 12 and endnote 9, 13.
42. Kellert, *In the Wake of Chaos,* 105–06. Kellert also cites the brilliant work of Robert Shaw, *The Dripping Faucet as a Model Chaotic System* (Santa Cruz: Ariel Press, 1984), 220.
43. Kellert, *In the Wake of Chaos,* 13. For topologies see: http://mathworld. wolfram.com/Topology.html.
44. Casti, *Complexification,* 91–92. This was the discovery of German theoretical chemist Otto Rössler in the mid-1970s who noticed a taffy-pulling machine in a store window.
45. Kellert, *In the Wake of Chaos,* 14–15.
46. Prigogine and Stengers, *Order out of Chaos,* 71–72, 302.
47. Benoît B. Mandelbrot, *The Fractal Geometry of Nature* (New York: Macmillan, 1983).
48. Kellert, *In the Wake of Chaos,* p. 19. Nicolis and Prigogine, *Exploring Complexity,* 254–55.
49. Nicolis and Prigogine, *Exploring Complexity,* 46.
50. Nicolis and Prigogine, *Exploring Complexity,* 46.
51. Prigogine and Stengers, *Order out of Chaos,* 60.
52. Prigogine and Stengers, *Order out of Chaos,* 60–61.
53. Nicolis and Prigogine, *Exploring Complexity,* 49.
54. Prigogine and Stengers, *Order out of Chaos,* 112.
55. Nicolis and Prigogine, *Exploring Complexity,* 50.
56. Prigogine and Stengers, *Order out of Chaos,* 114–15.
57. Prigogine and Stengers, *Order out of Chaos,* 115–16, 117. Entropy is denoted by "*S.*"
58. Prigogine and Stengers, *Order out of Chaos,* 119.
59. Prigogine and Stengers, *Order out of Chaos,* 120.
60. Prigogine and Stengers, *Order out of Chaos,* 121.
61. Prigogine and Stengers, *Order out of Chaos,* 121.
62. Nicolis and Prigogine, *Exploring Complexity,* 59.
63. Nicolis and Prigogine, *Exploring Complexity,* 59.
64. Prigogine and Stengers, *Order out of Chaos,* 141.
65. Prigogine and Stengers, *Order out of Chaos,* 141. Michel Serres, *The Birth of Physics,* trans. Jack Hawkes (Manchester: Clinamen Press, 2000).
66. Prigogine and Stengers, *Order out of Chaos,* 141.
67. Prigogine and Stengers, *Order out of Chaos,* 143.
68. Kellert, *In the Wake of Chaos,* 13.
69. Prigogine and Stengers, *Order out of Chaos,* 124.

70. Prigogine and Stengers, *Order out of Chaos,* 124–25.
71. Nicolis and Prigogine, *Exploring Complexity,* 9.
72. Nicolis and Prigogine, *Exploring Complexity,* 10.
73. Nicolis and Prigogine, *Exploring Complexity,* 10.
74. Nicolis and Prigogine, *Exploring Complexity,* 11–13.
75. Nicolis and Prigogine, *Exploring Complexity,* 13.
76. Prigogine and Stengers, *Order out of Chaos,* 143–44.
77. Nicolis and Prigogine, *Exploring Complexity,* 15.
78. Prigogine and Stengers, *Order out of Chaos,* 169.
79. Nicolis and Prigogine, *Exploring Complexity,* 73.
80. Nicolis and Prigogine, *Exploring Complexity,* 73–74.
81. Casti, *Complexification,* 53–55, 62.
82. Prigogine and Stengers, *Order out of Chaos,* 292–93.
83. Prigogine and Stengers, *Order out of Chaos,* 214, 294. Einstein and Bergson met at the Société de Philosophie in Paris on April 6, 1922.
84. Prigogine and Stengers, *Order out of Chaos,* 215–16.
85. Prigogine and Stengers, *Order out of Chaos,* 217.
86. Prigogine and Stengers, *Order out of Chaos,* 218.
87. Prigogine and Stengers, *Order out of Chaos,* 218.
88. Prigogine and Stengers, *Order out of Chaos,* 272.
89. Prigogine and Stengers, *Order out of Chaos,* 273–74.
90. Cited in Prigogine and Stengers, *Order out of Chaos,* 258.
91. Prigogine and Stengers, *Order out of Chaos,* 259, 297.
92. Prigogine and Stengers, *Order out of Chaos,* 298.
93. Kellert, *In the Wake of Chaos,* 141–42.
94. Kellert, *In the Wake of Chaos,* 146.
95. Prigogine and Stengers, *Order out of Chaos,* 307–08.
96. Thomas Kuhn, *The Structure of Scientific Revolutions* (Chicago: University of Chicago Press, 1970), 59.
97. Kuhn, *The Structure of Scientific Revolutions,* 91.
98. Prigogine and Stengers, *Order out of Chaos,* 308–09.
99. Kellert, *In the Wake of Chaos,* 148–49.
100. Kellert, *In the Wake of Chaos,* 149.
101. Kellert, *In the Wake of Chaos,* 151. Evelyn Fox Keller, *Reflections on Gender and Science* (New Haven: Yale University Press, 1985), 155.
102. Kellert, *In the Wake of Chaos,* 155.
103. Kellert, *In the Wake of Chaos,* 156. Kellert is citing Carolyn Merchant, *The Death of Nature* (New York: Harper & Row, 1980), 132.
104. Kellert, *In the Wake of Chaos,* 157–58.
105. Prigogine and Stengers, *Order out of Chaos,* 312.

REFERENCES

Bachelard, G. *The New Scientific Spirit.* Translated by Arthur Goldhammer. Boston: Beacon Press, 1984.

Casti, J. L. *Complexification: Explaining a Complex World through the Science of Surprise.* New York: Harper Collins, 1994.

DeWitt, R. *Worldviews: An Introduction to the History and Philosophy of Science.* London: Blackwell, 2004.

Earman, J. *A Primer on Determinism.* Dordrecht: Reidel, 1986.

Gleick, J. "Predictability: Does the Flap of a Butterfly's Wing in Brazil Set off a Tornado in Texas?" A paper delivered at the 139th meeting of the American Association for the Advancement of Science, December 29, 1972.

Keller, E. F. *Reflections on Gender and Science.* New Haven: Yale University Press, 1985.

Kellert, S. H. *In the Wake of Chaos.* Chicago: University of Chicago Press, 1993.

Kuhn, T. *The Structure of Scientific Revolutions.* Chicago: University of Chicago Press, 1970.

Mandelbrot, B. B. *The Fractal Geometry of Nature.* New York: Macmillan, 1983.

Merchant, C. *The Death of Nature.* New York: Harper & Row, 1980.

Nicolis, Gregoire, and Ilya Prigogine. *Exploring Complexity: An Introduction.* New York: W. H. Freeman, 1989.

Popper, K. *The Open Universe.* Totowa, New Jersey: Rowman & Littlefield, 1982.

Prigogine, Ilya, and Isabelle Stengers. *Order out of Chaos: Man's New Dialogue with Nature.* New York: Bantam Books, 1984.

Shaw, R. *The Dripping Faucet as a Model Chaotic System.* Santa Cruz: Ariel Press, 1984.

16 Systems Theory and Practice in Organizational Change and Development

Debora Hammond

INTRODUCTION

Although its roots can be traced back centuries, and even millennia, systems theory—and the corresponding systems approaches to dealing with complex problem situations—emerged as a distinct field of inquiry in the mid-twentieth century through a confluence of developments in science and technology. Revolutionary discoveries in the physical sciences in the early twentieth century—quantum mechanics and the theory of relativity—had already exposed the limitations of the Newtonian framework that had dominated scientific inquiry since the seventeenth century. In the biological sciences, the emerging understanding of feedback processes and the open system nature of living systems pointed to the need for an expanded scientific framework to address the complexity of these systems. Parallel technological developments in the rapidly evolving energy, manufacturing, transportation, and information sectors introduced more complex organizational challenges. The systems movement can thus be seen as an attempt to understand the nature and source of organization in complex systems and to apply that understanding in the design of human systems.

As a result, systems theory has had a significant impact in the applied social and behavioral sciences, particularly in the theory and practice of organizational management. The earliest applications of systems concepts in organizational contexts, in such fields as systems analysis, systems engineering, and operations research, have often been described as "hard" systems approaches. Dominating the organizational landscape during the first half of the twentieth century, these approaches tended to be characterized by top-down decision-making processes and to focus primarily on maximizing productivity, profitability, or other concrete and quantifiable measures of organizational function.

As managers and systems practitioners began to appreciate the limitations of these approaches and of the mechanistic framework in which they were embedded, new orientations emerged, often referred to as "soft" systems approaches. And beyond the hard/soft divide, there was a flowering of the applied systems field beginning in the 1960s, generating an ever-widening

array of approaches to understanding and addressing the increasingly complex, "messy" problems confronting the human community. Growing out
of early theoretical developments in general systems theory, cybernetics and
system dynamics, the field of applied systems thinking grew to encompass
such divergent approaches as organizational cybernetics, systems design,
critical and emancipatory systems theory, sociotechnical systems, organizational learning, and organization development. Although they developed
along relatively separate trajectories, these various schools of theory and
practice embody similar conceptual frameworks and approaches to organizational intervention, including "whole systems" thinking, an appreciation
for the human relational dimension, and, generally, a focus on facilitating
collaborative decision-making processes in organizations.

This chapter will trace the evolution of these communities of practice,
exploring parallels and differences, and evaluating their significance for the
twenty-first century. With rapidly accelerating developments in technology
and the concomitant growth of global institutions, the world is becoming
increasingly complex as human systems become increasingly interdependent. It is critical to the preservation of democratic values, social justice,
and ecological integrity that we learn how to manage the organizations that
structure our lives in ways that honor the needs and purposes of all participants in the system, as well as the larger environment within which that
system functions. The work in this broad array of systems-oriented fields
offers both the theoretical foundation and the practical tools to foster this
objective.

ON ORGANIZATION

Ludwig von Bertalanffy, who has generally been recognized as the "father"
of general system(s) theory, proposed the concept of organismic biology in
the early twentieth century as an alternative to the dominant mechanistic
paradigm in the biological sciences. He argued that the laws of physics and
chemistry were insufficient to explain the complex organization in living systems and their ability to maintain themselves in a far-from-equilibrium steady
state. Unlike the vitalists of that era, Bertalanffy did not appeal to an organizing intelligence, but rather suggested that the laws of organization were emergent properties that could be studied scientifically. Not only did he believe
that the mechanistic worldview was scientifically inadequate, but he also held
it accountable for many of the ills confronting modern civilization, arguing
that "possibly the model of the world as a great organization can help to
reinforce the sense of reverence for the living which we have almost lost."[1]

Probably his most important contribution to the evolution of systems
ideas was the concept of living organisms as open systems, able to import
energy and matter from the environment and export their entropy—or
waste—thus allowing them to maintain their highly organized states in

seeming defiance of the second law of thermodynamics. This insight ultimately led to the concept of self-organization, which allows for creativity
and spontaneity in the behavior and evolution of living systems. Bertalanffy
was profoundly critical of the mechanistic orientation of behaviorist psychology, which he described as the "robot model" of man.[2] Emerging in
parallel with Gestalt psychology, which emphasized the holistic nature of
consciousness, Bertalanffy's insights were significantly influential in the
development of humanistic psychology and, more specifically, in the field of
family systems theory.

In parallel with these theoretical developments, the Industrial Revolution
brought about profound practical changes in the nature of human social
organization and the corresponding challenges in managing and controlling the growing number and size of human systems resulting from the new
technologies. As one of the founders, along with Bertalanffy, of the Society for General Systems Research (SGSR; later renamed the International
Society for the Systems Sciences/ISSS) in 1954, Kenneth Boulding provided
some important perspectives on these changes in *The Organizational Revolution: A Study in the Ethics of Organization*.[3] Building his analysis on
a comparison between organisms and organizations, Boulding described
how lines of communication become limiting factors in the optimum size
of organizations and how emerging information and communication technologies made possible an unprecedented growth in the size and power of
organizations. Anticipating many of the themes that would become central
in the fields of applied systems, he highlighted the importance of considering
the relationships between individuals and organizations, the consequences
of increasingly stratified hierarchical organizational structures, the potential danger of oligarchical concentrations of power, and the psychological
effects resulting from the individual's loss of autonomy.

Gareth Morgan has done a fascinating job of depicting the evolution
of thinking about the nature of human systems in *Images of Organization*, which provides a useful framework for considering the growth of the
applied systems field.[4] Like biological systems in the early twentieth century,
emerging human organizations were initially understood in mechanical
terms, leading to the establishment of bureaucratic systems and "scientific"
approaches to management. With the development of organismic metaphors in the biological sciences, organizations began to be seen as open
systems, necessitating an appreciation for the role of the environment and
the inherent capacity for self-organization. With the growing understanding
of the role of information in complex systems and the emergence of increasingly complex information technology, organizations came to be understood as information-processing systems with the capacity for learning and
innovation. As organizations became larger and more influential, there was
a growing recognition of the cultural and political dimensions of organization, entailing a consideration of values and belief systems, as well as the
role of conflicting interests and power structures. Finally, Morgan concludes

his analysis in exploring the more challenging views of organizations as psychic prisons and instruments of domination.

THE ORIGINS AND EARLY YEARS OF MANAGEMENT SCIENCE

Before the establishment of schools of business administration in the early twentieth century, management was generally understood as a branch of engineering, applying scientific principles in coordinating the myriad processes involved in the unprecedented expansion of large-scale organizations made possible by the Industrial Revolution. The concept of "scientific management" is generally associated with the name of Frederick Taylor, who is most well known for his time and motion studies, through which he sought to maximize the productivity of workers in the growing manufacturing sector. As the first to articulate a scientific approach to management, Taylor is often characterized as an apologist for authoritarian hierarchical structures. Marvin Weisbord offers an alternative perspective, depicting Taylor instead as a social reformer who actually sought to eliminate authoritarian supervision and to cultivate greater cooperation between management and labor, through what he considered a more rational and humane system of management, separating the tasks of planning and implementation, and assigning specialized roles to each employee. In fact, his views were championed by the progressive leaders of that era.[5] Morgan offers a concise summary of the five principles of Taylor's approach:

(1) *Shift all responsibility for the organization of work from the worker to the manager*; managers should do all the thinking relating to the planning and design of work, leaving the workers with the task of implementation.

(2) *Use scientific methods* to determine the most efficient way of doing work; design the worker's task accordingly, specifying the *precise* way in which the work is to be done.

(3) *Select* the best person to perform the job as designed.

(4) *Train* the worker to do the work efficiently.

(5) *Monitor* worker performance to ensure that appropriate work procedures are being followed and that appropriate results are achieved.[6]

Systems concepts entered the management scene through the emergence of three relatively distinct but overlapping fields: systems engineering, systems analysis, and operations research, all of which employed a range of analytical methods based on scientific principles to improve efficiency, increase productivity, and standardize practices through optimization. Systems engineering is generally concerned with the logistics of large-scale technological processes, including the allocation of resources and the coordination of inputs and outputs; the concept was first introduced in the 1940s at Bell Telephone Laboratories. Systems analysis, often described as decision analysis, can be seen as an approach to determining the best course of action within given constraints through sophisticated cost-benefit analyses. Developed in connection with the RAND Corporation, it was applied in the public sector under the leadership of Robert McNamara and contributed to a growing distrust of systems approaches. Operations research, which is most closely related to management science, emerged in the context of World War II as a way of coordinating the complex problems of logistics and resource management in warfare. Although all three fields involve interactions between humans and technology, it is in the related fields of operations research and management science that these concerns become a primary focus.

THE GENERAL SYSTEMS LINEAGE

Two of the most prominent spokesmen for this emerging field, and coauthors (with Leonard Arnoff) of the comprehensive *Introduction to Operations Research,* West Churchman and Russell Ackoff had a significant impact on the evolution of the field beyond purely instrumental concerns to integrate a more human-centered focus.[7] Both became active members of the "general systems" community, embodied in the SGSR/ISSS. Another member of that community, Stafford Beer was also instrumental in the evolution of the field of cybernetics, drawing on the foundations of management science and operations research to develop the field of organizational cybernetics. Although the SGSR was initially founded in 1954 to foster interdisciplinary research into the nature of complex systems, it became increasingly concerned with the practical implications of the emerging field in the 1960s and '70s.

Of the original founders of the SGSR, Kenneth Boulding was perhaps the most influential in this evolution, in his concern with the ethical implications of large-scale organization and his emphasis on the importance of dialogue in decision-making processes in organizations, inspiring the development of methodologies to facilitate more participatory and inclusive approaches. Reflecting similar concerns, West Churchman provided further impetus for work in that field. As a student of E. A. Singer Jr., who was himself a student of William James, Churchman was solidly grounded in the tradition of philosophical pragmatism. Ackoff, in turn, was Churchman's first doctoral student. Together they published an early text on what would become a key concept in applied systems, entitled *Methods of Inquiry.*[8] Systems inquiry highlights the primacy of organizing relationships, drawing on the philosophical and ethical implications of a systemic orientation in developing methodologies to facilitate problem solving in complex systems.

Beginning with basic systems theoretical emphases on the holistic nature of reality and the importance of considering relationships, both among the components of a system and with the larger environment, a systems-oriented ontology highlights organization, interaction, and interdependence, shifting from the atomistic orientation of the mechanistic worldview to an appreciation of networks and the patterns and processes of relationship. In the context of human systems, a systems-oriented epistemology underscores the dynamic and dialectical nature of knowledge; the importance of perception, interpretation, and the creation of meaning; the involvement of the observer in the process of observation; and the importance of considering multiple perspectives. Challenging earlier approaches to management science, Churchman argues that there are no experts in the systems approach.[9] Knowledge thus becomes an active process, dialectical, pluralistic, and participatory, and the ethics of systemic practice reflect a shift from control to collaboration, from competition to interdependence, from hierarchical to participatory decision-making processes, and from objectivity to subjectivity and reflective self-awareness.[10]

Robert Flood describes Churchman as the moral conscience of the operations research/management science field. He believed that scientists were responsible for the social consequences of their discoveries and suggested that science should be devoted to the study and amelioration of serious dilemmas, such as hunger, poverty, and war.[11] His orientation, particularly as elaborated in *The Design of Inquiring Systems,* provided the foundation for Werner Ullrich's work on critical heuristics in the 1980s, which further inspired the development of the critical systems approach, most notably in the work of Flood and Michael C. Jackson.[12] Gerald Midgley describes critical systems thinking as a "research perspective" that encompasses three basic commitments: critical awareness, methodological pluralism, and, perhaps most importantly, a commitment to emancipation. The latter implies a focus on improvement, taking issues of power into account.[13]

Drawing on his work with Churchman, in 1980 Ackoff established the Social Systems Sciences Program at the Wharton School of Business at the University of Pennsylvania, which became one of the first major schools in the United States to foster systems approaches in management. Beginning in the 1970s, he became increasingly critical of "technique-dominated" approaches to operations research, suggesting that although humanity had entered the Systems Age in the 1940s, it was still attempting to solve problems with Machine Age thinking.[14] Based on his understanding of human systems as purposeful systems, composed of purposeful parts and also part of larger purposeful systems, he described the challenge of management as designing human systems in ways that can "serve their own purposes, the purposes of the purposeful parts, and the purposes of the larger systems of which they are a part."[15] Building on this insight, he developed a method for addressing what he called "messes," given the complex nature of the systems involved, based on interactive planning and idealized design:

> Interactivists are not willing to settle for the current state of their affairs or the way they are going, and they are not willing to return to the past.

They want to design a desirable future and invent ways of bringing it about. They believe we are capable of controlling a significant part of the future as well as its effects on us. They try to *prevent,* not merely prepare for, threats and to *create,* not merely exploit, opportunities.[16]

Another approach to idealized systems design was developed by Bela H. Banathy, who was also an active member of the general systems community. Building on the earlier work of Singer, Churchman, Ackoff and Emery, Banathy notes that "idealized design facilitates participation in the design inquiry. It provides opportunity to the designing community to work with others, to think and learn about their system, to contribute their ideas to the design, and thus, to affect the future of the system."[17] Further, such a process enhances the commitment of participants to the implementation of the resulting design. One of the ways in which he sought to foster this approach was through the establishment in 1981 of the International Systems Institute, which hosted annual "conversations" as an alternative to the traditional conference structure. In parallel with his commitment to participatory design, he sought to create an environment that would engage all participants in an interactive learning process. This conversational approach was carried forward in the work of Aleco Christakis and Ken Bausch (also influenced by the work of John Warfield),[[Ed: the preceding parenthetical statement is in 11 pt. font]] through the establishment of the Institute for 21st Century Agoras, a nonprofit organization "dedicated to the vision of democratic transformation of society and culture."[18]

THE BRITISH CONNECTION: SOFT SYSTEMS METHODOLOGY AND SOCIOTECHNICAL SYSTEMS

While most of the early work in systems was based in the United States, there were a number of parallel and interconnected developments in other parts of the world, most notably in the United Kingdom. In 1969, Peter Checkland joined a team of researchers in the department of Systems Engineering at the University of Lancaster who developed Soft Systems Methodology in response to the limitations of then-current systems engineering approaches in dealing with real-world management problems, where there are often very divergent views of what constitutes the problem. Checkland was largely responsible for articulating and popularizing the soft systems approach and was closely affiliated with those members of the general systems community previously mentioned, as reflected in the list of Past Presidents of the SGSR/ISSS: Warfield was president in 1982, Banathy was president in 1984, Checkland in 1986, Ackoff in 1987, and Churchman in 1989.[19] Inspired by Churchman's earlier work, Checkland emphasized what he called the "relationship maintaining" aspect of human systems and, like Ackoff and Banathy, recognized the goal-seeking nature of human activity systems.[20]

Drawing on the growing interest in the 1960s in action research as an interactive approach to organizational analysis and intervention, soft systems methodology provides a structured approach for engaging the whole *system* of an organization in a collaborative process of defining problem situations, exploring alternative solutions, and facilitating change. It is a seven-stage learning cycle, involving (1) the problem situation; (2) formulation of "rich pictures" of the situation; (3) defining six key dimensions of the situation, represented by the acronym CATWOE, standing for customers, actors, transformative processes, worldviews, owners, and environment; (4) developing conceptual models; (5) comparing models with "rich picture" descriptions of the problem situation; (6) reviewing change proposals according to desirability and feasibility; and (7) reaching accommodations between contrasting opinions and interests.[21] Flood further describes SSM as a reflective learning process, "working with people's cognitive processes in a purposeful way."[22]

It was in response to Checkland's approach that Michael Jackson and Robert Flood began to articulate the critical systems approach, which, like its predecessor, has been most influential in the UK. Drawing on the critical heuristics of Werner Ulrich, which addressed the political and coercive dimensions of social reality, CST shares the critique of hard systems approaches, and yet seeks to transcend what it perceives as the limitations of the soft systems paradigm, which Flood and Jackson describe in the introduction to their coedited volume as a "failure to question its own theoretical underpinnings and to be reflective about the social context in which it is employed."[23] They suggest that SSM is irrelevant and ineffectual in situations where there are inequalities of power and instead emphasize the importance of considerations of values and assumptions that enter into the process of systems inquiry and design. According to Flood, in addition to its commitment to critical awareness and human emancipation, CST recognizes a need for complementarity in theoretical and practical considerations, since various approaches each bring different perspectives and priorities to the process. It seeks to nurture the well being of all participants and to prevent any coercive exercise of power that might hinder open discussion of the issues.[24]

In parallel with the emergence of the soft systems approach, Eric Trist and Fred Emery developed an open systems approach—initially inspired by Bertalanffy—that eventually became known as sociotechnical systems. The Tavistock Institute for Human Relations was established in 1946 under the leadership of Trist and, like the Lancaster group, used action research to facilitate participatory approaches to organizational change and development in business and industry.[25] Action research can be traced to the earlier work of social psychologist Kurt Lewin, who was particularly influential in the development of the organization development field. According to Peter Reason and Hilary Bradbury,

> Action Research is a participatory process concerned with develop-ing practical knowing in the pursuit of worthwhile human purposes. It seeks to bring together action and reflection, theory and practice, in participation with others, in the pursuit of practical solutions to issues of pressing concern to people, and more generally the flourishing of individual persons and their communities.[26]

Echoing the orientation of West Churchman, although emerging relatively independently, action research is a form of systemic inquiry, with the explicit purpose of cultivating democratic capacities as well as improving the quality of working life.

Trist was inspired by a highly publicized series of group climate experi-ments conducted in 1939 by Lewin in collaboration with Ronald Lippitt and Ralph White. The study identified and examined the consequences of three fundamental group structures—autocracy, democracy, and laissez faire. While autocratic structures fostered hostility, quarreling, and scape-goating and tended to suppress creativity, initiative, and commitment to the task at hand, laissez faire environments suffered from lack of leader-ship and left participants feeling lost. Democratic structures, on the other hand, nurtured greater vitality, creativity, cooperation, and commitment. In 1951, Trist conducted a similar study of coal mining practices in England, in partnership with Ken Bamforth, that compared the relative efficacy of democratic and autocratic organizational structures.[27] The introduction of new technologies had undermined the earlier, more collaborative working relationships through the imposition of a scientific management approach, which in the spirit of Taylor allocated specific tasks to each individual and rigidly separated the roles of management and production. The study con-cluded that self-managing teams, with shared responsibility for the entire production process, were much more effective.[28]

Also in 1951, Fred Emery joined Trist for a one-year fellowship at Tavis-tock and in 1957 came to stay for twelve years before returning to his native Australia. Over the years, Trist and Emery worked closely with Ackoff; the similarities in their orientations are reflected in Emery and Ackoff, *On Pur-poseful Systems,* published in 1972. In her discussion of his work in this area, Emery's wife Merrelyn writes:

> The version of open systems theory developed by Fred Emery has two main purposes. The first is to promote and create change toward a world that is consciously designed by people and for people, living har-moniously within their ecological systems, both physical and social. The second purpose is to develop an internally consistent conceptual frame-work or social science, within which each component is operationally

defined and hypotheses are testable so that the knowledge required to support the first purpose is created.[29]

In an earlier work she describes the goal of the sociotechnical systems approach not only in terms of democratizing the workplace, but also in nurturing a truly participative democratic culture. Central to this orientation is an articulation of organizational design principles that facilitate the formation of self-managing groups. Further, she suggests that this approach requires fundamental structural change, noting that participatory management approaches do not in themselves achieve true democratization. Significantly, she points out that the United States, with its cultural emphasis on competition and individual achievement, has been slow to embrace such changes, which, like the critical systems approach, challenge fundamental power relationships.[30]

According to William Pasmore, who has nurtured the sociotechnical systems approach in the United States, the success of this approach is "attributable both to the theory of organizations upon which it is based and to the unique methods which have been developed to apply this theory to organizational redesign."[31] Further:

> The sociotechnical systems perspective considers every organization to be made up of people (the social system) using tools, techniques, and knowledge (the technical system) to produce goods and services valued by customers (who are part of the organization's external environment). How well the social and technical systems are designed *with respect to one another and with respect to the demands of the external environment* determines to a large extent how effective the organization will be.[32]

Thus, the sociotechnical systems approach seeks a kind of "joint optimization" in its dual concern with both the social and technical dimension of organizations and its careful attention to the complex interactions between the two, and in relation to both the social and environmental contexts.

UNDERSTANDING FEEDBACK: CYBERNETICS AND SYSTEM DYNAMICS

In conjunction with the approaches described above, which tend to be characterized by an orientation toward interactive and inclusive decision-making processes, another important evolutionary development in the emergence of systems thinking is the understanding of nonlinear or circular causality. Providing insights into the structural relationships of complex systems, feedback processes were first discovered in the biological sciences in connection with the homeostatic mechanisms in living organisms, which allowed them to maintain steady states in the midst of constantly changing conditions. Beginning in the 1940s, a series of conferences sponsored by the Macy Foundation brought together researchers from a broad range of disciplines, including biology, psychology, neurophysiology, anthropology, engineering, and the newly emerging information sciences to explore the significance of feedback processes in other fields. It was in the context of these conferences that the term "cybernetics" was coined to describe the phenomenon.[33]

Among those who participated in the Macy conferences, one of the most well known is Norbert Wiener, whose name is most commonly associated with the concept. Significantly, Kurt Lewin was also among the participants, as was Gregory Bateson, whose work was influential in the evolution of the concept of organizational learning. The title of Wiener's 1948 book, *Cybernetics: or Control and Communication in the Animal and the Machine,* which first introduced the concept to the larger public, fueled concerns that cybernetics, and systems approaches generally, were primarily oriented toward social control. However, as the field evolved, it expanded to encompass an appreciation of cognitive processes and the potential for self-reflexivity in human systems.

In the early years, the concept of feedback was focused primarily on what was described as *negative* feedback, or the process through which a system maintains itself in a steady state, by minimizing deviations from a desired state. In contrast, *positive* feedback is what is often described in terms of vicious circles, creating a self-reinforcing, *deviation maximizing* trend away from the desired state, which can potentially lead to the collapse of the system, a more widely oscillating state, or, in the best case, the emergence of a new stable state. In highlighting the dynamics of these circular processes, cybernetics helped to explain the operation of self-organization in human, technological, and natural systems. As the field evolved, it expanded beyond what became known as *first-order* cybernetics, which focused on the *observed* system, explaining processes of self-organization and self-regulation, to a *second-order* cybernetics of *observing* systems, highlighting self-referentiality and the phenomena of consciousness, cognition, meaning making, and learning.

Somewhat distinct from the tradition of cybernetics, although similarly concerned with feedback processes, is the field of system dynamics, which grew out of Jay Forrester's work at MIT and provided the framework for the Club of Rome report *Limits to Growth.*[34] Using complex mathematical equations to model feedback in the interactions among a number of variables such as population and technology, the report fueled growing concerns with environmental consideration. Cybernetics and system dynamics contributed in slightly different ways to the growing field of applied systems. George Richards provides an excellent analysis of the distinction between the two orientations.[35] System dynamics tends to focus on positive and negative feedback, as well as the flows of matter and energy through real-world systems, while cybernetics, particularly in the more recent emphasis on second-order cybernetics, is more focused on the flow of information in complex systems, as well as the cognitive processes involved in decision making in human systems.

ORGANIZATIONAL LEARNING

With his book *The Fifth Discipline: The Art and Practice of the Learning Organization,* Peter Senge has probably done more than any other contemporary author to popularize the concept of systems thinking.[36] In identifying five key principles involved in the cultivation of a learning organization, Senge describes systems thinking as the fifth. In *Rethinking the Fifth Discipline,* Flood points out that Senge's understanding of systems thinking is drawn primarily from the system dynamics tradition and neglects important dimensions of systems thinking developed in the context of other systems-oriented communities, including an explicitly ethical orientation and the deliberate cultivation of skills in inquiry, reflection, and surfacing assumptions. Further, he suggests that Senge's model emphasizes consensus, rather than accommodation, as in the soft systems approach, thus avoiding the issue of conflicting interests. Nevertheless, the five principles, as Senge outlines them, echo many of the same themes and orientations found in the soft systems, critical systems, and sociotechnical systems traditions:

(1) Team learning: a commitment to dialogue and cultivating meaningful relationships;
(2) Shared vision: an agreement on common purpose;
(3) Mental models: a clear articulation of assumptions, belief systems, values, etc.;
(4) Personal mastery: an emphasis on self-reflection and knowing oneself; and
(5) Systems thinking: an understanding of the relationship between part and whole.[37]

In their work on single- and double-loop learning, Chris Argyris and Donald Schön have also contributed substantially to the understanding of learning in organizations, drawing on insights from second-order cybernetics, specifically as elaborated in Gregory Bateson's work on levels of learning.[38] In Bateson's model, Learning 0 can be described as unquestioning and unreflective behavior, carrying out a task without the willingness or ability to reconsider basic procedures, much less the overall purpose of the activity. At the level of Learning I, which corresponds with what Argyris and Schon describe as single-loop learning, alternative approaches to achieving the desired ends may be explored, without examining the ends themselves.[39] Single-loop learning can be seen as simple problem solving, addressing superficial symptoms with the intention of improving a system as it exists.

Corresponding with what Bateson identified as Learning II, double-loop learning goes a step or two further, involving a more reflexive reexamination of existing goals, as well as the values, assumptions, belief systems, and worldviews underlying those goals. In addition, it implies a consideration of the consequences of one's action in the context of the larger environment. While a single-loop orientation reflects a more mechanistic or instrumental approach, double-loop learning implies the inclusion of ethical or normative considerations, as well as attention to the relational or interpersonal dynamics inherent in the situation.

Building on the concepts of single and double-loop learning, Argyris et al. identify two patterns of organizational behavior, which they describe as Model I and Model II.[40] Model I organizations are characterized by single-loop learning, and similar kinds of behavior—such as competitiveness, defensiveness, blaming others, and a lack of shared responsibility or concern for others—that Lewin et al. identified in autocratic environments.[41] In addition, information is easily distorted in these organizations as individuals seek to protect their own interests. Senge describes these kinds of dynamics in terms of what he calls organizational learning disabilities. Model II behavior, characterized by double loop learning, is really the essence of what Senge envisions as learning organizations. In these contexts, members of the organization are actively involved in decision-making processes, information is freely shared, and, echoing the sociotechnical approach, there is a collective ownership of tasks, where self-interest is understood as aligned with the interests of the whole system.[42]

ORGANIZATION DEVELOPMENT

Both Argyris et al. and Senge have had a significant impact on the evolution of the organization development field, although its earliest roots can be traced to Kurt Lewin's innovative and influential contributions in social psychology, specifically in action research and group dynamics. In fact, OD is often described as a series of footnotes to Lewin, whose work was also foundational in the evolution of the sociotechnical systems approach of the Tavistock Institute.[43] According to Marvin Weisbord, Eric Trist was so impressed with Lewin's ideas when they met in Cambridge, England in 1933 that he switched his major to psychology and "later became Lewin's leading exponent in Great Britain," and, in 1946, the two collaborated in founding the journal *Human Relations*.[44]

In their introduction to the comprehensive *SAGE Handbook of Action Research: Participative Inquiry and Practice*, Peter Reason and Hilary Bradbury describe action research as a series of cycles of action and reflection, citing Lewin's definition as foundational: "[action research] proceeds in a spiral of steps, each of which is composed of a circle of planning, action and fact finding about the results of the action."[45] They go on to note that Lewin emphasized the importance of "practical democracy and education in the practice of inquiry."[46] The spirit of action research clearly infuses the entire field of systems practice, providing a framework for the concept of learning organizations and for the distinction between single- and double-loop learning. In breaking away from the positivistic orientation of most research in the early twentieth century, Lewin laid the groundwork for more qualitative and interpretive approaches, as well as for a transformation in the relationship between knowledge and practice.

Growing out of this understanding, perhaps his most significant contribution to the evolution of the OD field is his work on group dynamics and the introduction of the T-group. The term "group dynamics" grew out of Lewin's work with Ronald Lippitt in connection with their 1939 group climate study. The T-group is a human relations skills-training methodology that might be compared to the encounter groups of the 1960s. The concept of the T-group emerged out of a 1946 project with the Connecticut State Inter-Racial Commission, intended to address racial and religious prejudice, which Weisbord describes as an "educational milestone."[47] In essence, it is a leaderless, self-reflexive process in which participants study their own behavior. Echoing insights from the coal mining studies of Trist and Bamford, Weisbord notes:

> Once members confronted their unrealistic dependency on the leaders, they made an interesting discovery: a leaderless group could rotate leadership based on relevant skills and knowledge. Where Taylor relied on external motivation and control, the T-group shifted control to its members.[48]

The T-group was nurtured in the context of the National Training Laboratories (NTL), which Lewin helped to found in 1947. NTL became and remains one of the leading centers of OD theory and practice. One of the many contributors to the evolution of this field is Douglas McGregor, who worked with Lewin at MIT and coined the terms "Theory X" and "Theory Y" to describe the assumptions behind the two approaches to organizational management structure identified by Trist in terms of autocracy and democracy. Theory X underlies Taylor's approach to management and assumes that people are "lazy, irresponsible, passive and dependent," requiring work to be closely supervised. In contrast, Theory Y suggests that "if given a chance, most people will take responsibility, care about their jobs, wish to grow and achieve, and do excellent work."[49]

CONCLUSION

In his overview of the organization development field, Weisbord describes a "learning curve" in the evolution of approaches to management from "experts solve problems" in the early twentieth century, to "everybody solves problems" beginning in the 1950s, to "experts improve whole systems" beginning in the mid-1960s, and ultimately to "everybody improves whole systems" beginning in the early twenty-first century.[50] As Bradbury et al. point out, however, "as much as collaboration is demanded, the average organizational member does not learn to develop collaboration or partnership skills along the course of the traditional Western education" and sadly, as a result, "our default social condition veers more easily toward autocracy than democracy."[51] Echoing the orientation of critical systems theory, Reason and Bradbury caution that "action research without its liberating and emancipatory dimension is a shadow of its full possibility and will be in danger of being co-opted by the status quo."[52] In addressing the challenge of overcoming this tendency, Weisbord cites a prophetic passage from Lewin:

> Today, more than ever before, democracy depends upon the development of efficient forms of democratic social management and upon the spreading of the skill in such management to the common man.[53]

This orientation is echoed in the sociotechnical tradition, which explicitly seeks to "revitalize people's confidence in their own abilities and potentials" and "revalue human potential and dignity."[54]

Clearly, the trajectory in this broad spectrum of applied systems approaches is toward the cultivation of greater self-reflective awareness and a capacity for informed self-organization in the economic and political affairs of humanity. Such capacity requires an understanding of the technical dimension of complex systems, in addition to the necessary skills in collaborative leadership; thus the concept of *sociotechnical* systems, which highlights the interdependent nature of the relationship between people and the rapidly evolving technological and organizational contexts of their lives. Technical approaches alone neglect the critical dimension of human experience, while a focus exclusively on interpersonal dynamics and collaborative decision making is insufficient in dealing with the challenges of the highly complex nature of the economic and technological environment within which individuals and organizations must learn not only how to survive but also how to thrive. Systems approaches, as evidenced in the communities of practice discussed above, provide some promising steps forward in this path.

NOTES

1. Ludwig von Bertalanffy, "General System Theory," *Main Currents in Modern Thought* 11 (1955): 75–83. See also his *General System Theory*, rev. ed. (New York: George Braziller, 1969), 49.

2. Ludwig von Bertalanffy, *Robots, Men and Minds: Psychology in the Modern World* (New York: George Braziller, 1967).
3. Kenneth Boulding, *The Organizational Revolution* (New York: Harper and Brothers, 1953). For a historical overview of the general systems community, see Debora Hammond, *The Science of Synthesis: Exploring the Social Implications of General Systems Theory* (Boulder, CO: University Press of Colorado, 2003).
4. See Gareth Morgan, *Images of Organization* (London: SAGE, 1986).
5. See Marvin R. Weisbord, *Productive Workplaces: Dignity, Meaning, and Community in the 21st Century,* 3rd ed. (San Francisco, CA: Jossey-Bass, 2012), 33–38.
6. Morgan, *Images of Organization,* 30; emphasis in original.
7. See C. West Churchman, Russell L. Ackoff, and E. Leonard Arnoff, *Introduction to Operations Research* (New York: John Wiley & Sons, 1957).
8. See C. West Churchman and Russell L. Ackoff, *Methods of Inquiry: An Introduction to Philosophy and Scientific Method* (St. Louis: Educational Publishers, 1950).
9. C. West Churchman, *The Systems Approach* (New York: Dell, 1968), 231.
10. See Debora Hammond, "Philosophical and Ethical Foundations of Systems Thinking," *tripleC: Cognition, Communication, Co-operation* 3 no. 2 (2005), accessed December 8, 2012, http://www.triple-c.at/index.php/tripleC/article/view/20.
11. See Robert L. Flood, *Rethinking the Fifth Discipline: Learning within the Unknowable* (London: Routledge, 1999), 61–68.
12. See Robert L. Flood and Michael C. Jackson, eds., *Critical Systems Thinking: Directed Readings* (New York: Wiley, 1991). See Churchman's *The Design of Inquiring Systems* (New York: Basic Books, 1971).
13. Gerald Midgley, "What Is This Thing Called Critical Systems Thinking?," in *Critical Issues in Systems Theory and Practice,* ed. Keith Ellis et al. (London: Plenum Press, 1995), 61; see below for a more comprehensive discussion of this field.
14. Russell L. Ackoff, *Redesigning the Future* (New York: Wiley, 1974); Maurice Kirby and Jonathan Rosenhead, "IFORS Operational Research Hall of Fame: Russell L. Ackoff," *International Transactions in Operational Research* 12 (2005): 129–34.
15. Ackoff, *Redesigning the Future,* 18; see also Russell Ackoff and Fred Emery, *On Purposeful Systems* (Chicago: Aldine-Atherton, 1972).
16. Ackoff, *Redesigning the Future,* 26; emphasis in original.
17. Bela H. Banathy, *Designing Social Systems in a Changing World* (New York: Plenum, 1996), 193.
18. See www.globalagoras.org; also Alexander Christakis and Kenneth C. Bausch, *Co-laboratories of Democracy: How People Harness Their Collective Wisdom to Create the Future* (Boston, MA: Information Age, 2006).
19. See isss.org.
20. See Peter Checkland, *Systems Thinking, Systems Practice* (New York: Wiley, 1981).
21. Flood, *Rethinking the Fifth Discipline,* 56.
22. Flood, *Rethinking the Fifth Discipline,* 51.
23. Flood and Jackson, *Critical Systems Thinking,* 2. For Werner Ulrich's influential work, see *Critical Heuristics of Social Planning: A New Approach to Practical Philosophy* (New York: Wiley, 1994).
24. See Flood, *Rethinking the Fifth Discipline.*
25. See www.tavistock.org.

26. Peter Reason and Hilary Bradbury, eds., *The SAGE Handbook of Action Research: Participative Inquiry and Practice* (London: SAGE, 2008), 4.
27. Merrelyn Emery, "Participative Design: Work and Community Life," in *Participative Design for Participative Democracy*, ed. Merrelyn Emery (Canberra: Australia National University, 1989); Weisbord, *Productive Workplaces.*
28. Eric L. Trist and Ken W. Bamforth, "Some Social and Psychological Consequences of the Longwall Method of Coal-Getting: An Examination of the Psychological Situation and Defences of a Work Group in Relation to the Social Structure and Technological Content of the Work System," *Human Relations* 4, no. 3 (1951): 1–37, http://hum.sagepub.com.
29. Merrelyn Emery, "The Current Version of Emery's Open Systems Theory," *Systemic Practice and Action Research* 13, no. 5 (2000): 623.
30. See Merrelyn Emery, *Participative Design.*
31. William A. Pasmore, *Designing Effective Organizations* (New York: John Wiley & Sons, 1988), 1.
32. Pasmore, *Designing Effective Organizations*, 1; emphasis in original.
33. See Steve Joshua Heims, *Constructing a Social Science for Postwar America: The Cybernetics Group, 1946–1953* (Cambridge, MA: MIT Press, 1991) for a comprehensive account of these meetings, which took place between 1946 and 1953. An in-depth summary of the meetings can also be found on the American Society for Cybernetics website: www.asc-cybernetics.org.
34. See Donella H. Meadows et al., *The Limits of Growth* (New York: Universe Books, 1972).
35. George Richardson, *Feedback Thought in Social Science and Systems Theory* (Philadelphia, PA: University of Pennsylvania Press, 1991).
36. Peter Senge, *The Fifth Discipline: The Art and Practice of the Learning Organization* (New York: Doubleday, 1990).
37. See Flood, *Rethinking the Fifth Discipline,* 1999.
38. See Gregory Bateson, *Steps to an Ecology of Mind* (New York, NY: Ballantine, 1972).
39. See Chris Argyris and Donald Schon, *Organizational Learning: A Theory of Action Perspective* (Reading, MA: Addison-Wesley, 1978).
40. See Chris Argyris, Robert Putnam, and Diana McLain Smith, *Action Science: Concepts, Methods, and Skills for Research and Intervention* (San Francisco, CA: Jossey-Bass, 1985).
41. See Kurt Lewin, Ronald Lippitt, and Ralph K. White, "Patterns of Aggressive Behavior in Experimentally Created Social Climates," *Journal of Social Psychology* 10, no. 2 (1939): 271–99.
42. A similar analysis of these ideas was developed for Hammond, "Reflections on the Role of Recursion in the Ecology of Ideas: A Non-linear Narrative on the Evolution of Learning," the plenary address at the 2012 annual conference of the American Society for Cybernetics, submitted for publication in *Kybernetes*, 2012.
43. Hilary Bradbury et al., "Action Research at Work: Creating the Future Following the Path from Lewin," in *The SAGE Handbook of Action Research: Participative Inquiry and Practice,* ed. Peter Reason and Hilary Bradbury (London: SAGE, 2008), 90.
44. Weisbord, *Productive Workplaces,* 89, 111.
45. See Kurt Lewin, "Action Research and Minority Problems," in *Resolving Social Conflicts,* ed. G. W. Lewin (New York: Harper and Row, 1946), 206.
46. Reason and Bradbury, *Handbook of Action Research,* 4.
47. Weisbord, *Productive Workplaces,* 106.

48. Weisbord, *Productive Workplaces,* 45.
49. Weisbord, *Productive Workplaces,* 18; see also Douglas McGregor, *The Human Side of Enterprise* (New York: McGraw-Hill, 1960).
50. Weisbord, *Productive Workplaces,* xxviii.
51. Bradbury et al., *Action Research at Work,* 89–90.
52. Reason and Bradbury, *Handbook of Action Research,* 5.
53. Kurt Lewin, "Frontiers in Group Dynamics," *Human Relations* 1 (1947), 153; in Weisbord, *Productive Workplaces,* 97.
54. Emery, *Participative Design,* 26.

REFERENCES

Ackoff, Russell, and Fred Emery. *On Purposeful Systems.* Chicago: Aldine-Atherton, 1972.

Ackoff, Russell L. *Redesigning the Future.* New York: Wiley, 1974.

Argyris, Chris, and Donald Schon. *Organizational Learning: A Theory of Action Perspective.* Reading, MA: Addison-Wesley, 1978.

Argyris, Chris, Robert Putnam, and Diana McLain Smith. *Action Science: Concepts, Methods, and Skills for Research and Intervention.* San Francisco, CA: Jossey-Bass, 1985.

Banathy, Bela H. *Designing Social Systems in a Changing World.* New York: Plenum, 1996.

Bateson, Gregory. *Steps to an Ecology of Mind.* New York, NY: Ballantine, 1972.

Bertalanffy, Ludwig von. "General System Theory." *Main Currents in Modern Thought* 11 (1955): 75–83.

———. *Robots, Men and Minds: Psychology in the Modern World.* New York: George Braziller, 1967.

Boulding, Kenneth. *The Organizational Revolution.* New York: Harper and Brothers, 1953.

Bradbury, Hilary, Phil Mirvis, Eric Neilsen, and William Passmore. "Action Research at Work: Creating the Future Following the Path from Lewin." In *The SAGE Handbook of Action Research: Participative Inquiry and Practice,* edited by Peter Reason and Hilary Bradbury, 77–92. London: SAGE, 2008.

Checkland, Peter. *Systems Thinking, Systems Practice.* New York: Wiley, 1981.

Christakis, Alexander, and Kenneth C. Bausch. *Co-Laboratories of Democracy: How People Harness Their Collective Wisdom to Create the Future.* Boston, MA: Information Age, 2006.

Churchman, C. West. *The Systems Approach.* New York: Dell, 1968.

———. *The Design of Inquiring Systems.* New York: Basic Books, 1971.

Churchman, C. West, and Russell L. Ackoff. *Methods of Inquiry: An Introduction to Philosophy and Scientific Method.* St. Louis: Educational Publishers, 1950.

———, and E. Leonard Arnoff. *Introduction to Operations Research.* New York: John Wiley & Sons, 1957.

Emery, Merrelyn. "Participative Design: Work and Community Life." In *Participative Design for Participative Democracy,* edited by Merrelyn Emery. Canberra: Australia National University, 1989.

———. "The Current Version of Emery's Open Systems Theory." *Systemic Practice and Action Research* 13, no. 5 (2000): 623–43.

Flood, Robert L. *Rethinking the Fifth Discipline: Learning within the Unknowable.* London: Routledge, 1999.

————, and Michael C. Jackson, eds. *Critical Systems Thinking: Directed Readings.* New York: Wiley, 1991.

Hammond, Debora. *The Science of Synthesis: Exploring the Social Implications of General Systems Theory.* Boulder, CO: University Press of Colorado, 2003.

————. "Philosophical and Ethical Foundations of Systems Thinking." *tripleC: Cognition, Communication, Co-operation* 3, no. 2 (2005). Accessed December 8, 2012. http://www.triple-c.at/index.php/tripleC/article/view/20.

————. "Reflections on the Role of Recursion in the Ecology of Ideas: A Non-Linear Narrative on the Evolution of Learning." Plenary address at the 2012 annual conference of the American Society for Cybernetics, submitted for publication in *Kybernetes*, 2012.

Heims, Steve Joshua. *Constructing a Social Science for Postwar America: The Cybernetics Group, 1946–1953.* Cambridge, MA: MIT Press, 1991.

Kirby, Maurice, and Jonathan Rosenhead. "IFORS Operational Research Hall of Fame: Russell L. Ackoff." *International Transactions in Operational Research* 12 (2005): 129–34.

Lewin, Kurt. "Action Research and Minority Problems." In *Resolving Social Conflicts*, edited by G. W. Lewin, 201–16. New York: Harper and Row, 1946.

————. 1947. "Frontiers in Group Dynamics." *Human Relations* 1 (1947): 143–53.

Lewin, Kurt, Ronald Lippitt, and Ralph K. White. "Patterns of Aggressive Behavior in Experimentally Created Social Climates." *Journal of Social Psychology* 10 (1939): 2, 271–99.

McGregor, Douglas. *The Human Side of Enterprise.* New York: McGraw-Hill, 1960.

Meadows, Donella H., and Dennis L. Meadows, Jorgen Randers, and William Behrens III. *The Limits of Growth.* New York: Universe Books, 1972.

Midgley, Gerald. "What Is This Thing Called Critical Systems Thinking?" In *Critical Issues in Systems Theory and Practice,* edited by Keith Ellis, Amanda Gregory, Bridget R. Mears Young, and Gillian Ragsdell, 61–71. London: Plenum Press, 1995.

Morgan, Gareth. *Images of Organization.* London: SAGE, 1986.

Pasmore, William A. *Designing Effective Organizations.* New York: John Wiley & Sons, 1988.

Reason, Peter, and Hilary Bradbury, eds. *The SAGE Handbook of Action Research: Participative Inquiry and Practice.* London: SAGE, 2008.

Richardson, George. *Feedback Thought in Social Science and Systems Theory.* Philadelphia, PA: University of Pennsylvania Press, 1991.

Senge, Peter. *The Fifth Discipline: The Art and Practice of the Learning Organization.* New York: Doubleday, 1990.

Trist, Eric L., and Ken W. Bamforth. "Some Social and Psychological Consequences of the Longwall Method of Coal-Getting: An Examination of the Psychological Situation and Defences of a Work Group in Relation to the Social Structure and Technological Content of the Work System." *Human Relations* 4, no. 3 (1951): 1–37, http://hum.sagepub.com.

Ulrich, Werner. *Critical Heuristics of Social Planning: A New Approach to Practical Philosophy.* New York: Wiley, 1994.

Wiener, Norbert. *Cybernetics: or Control and Communication in the Animal and the Machine.* Cambridge, MA: MIT Press, 1948.

Weisbord, Marvin R. *Productive Workplaces: Dignity, Meaning, and Community in the 21st Century.* 3rd Edition. San Francisco, CA: Jossey-Bass, 2012.

17 Systems, Tools, and Bateson's Cybernetics

A Joint Metalogue

Nora Bateson and Phillip Guddemi

INTRODUCTION

This paper is presented in the form of a metalogue, based on two (Skype) conversations between Nora Bateson and Phillip Guddemi about Gregory Bateson's participation with systems theory and cybernetics and the implications of his approach. Nora Bateson is best known for making the film *An Ecology of Mind*, which is a personal approach to the ideas of her father Gregory Bateson. Phillip Guddemi is an anthropologist who was Gregory Bateson's student as an undergraduate and who later did fieldwork in the province of Papua New Guinea where Gregory Bateson had worked; he is now president of the Bateson Idea Group, a nonprofit organization dedicated to Gregory Bateson's ideas and legacy.[1]

Why a conversation? This is an experiment toward exploring the foundations of a cybernetic way of knowing by trusting the notion that information in living complexity is a process that emerges through difference. Stepping outside a more standard form of language and presentation that is definitive and structured required a bit of faith. We would like to think there is something that the reader will find, not only in the words but also between them, that will be fodder for more conversations. The story isn't over yet. Cybernetics, so many decades after its foundation in the Macy Conferences in the 1940s and 1950s, has found traction in an academic voice among a few fearless travelers who have honed and cultivated it into a lovely art form. With that discipline in hand, we may be able now to take one more baby step into the fire, and we begin to play with the meta message, the meta story, the metalogue. What will happen if we risk everything? Predictability, formalism, professionalism, credibility . . . what will happen if we don't?

But there is one concern that we have to mention. Gregory Bateson is no longer with us, and we no longer have his voice available to let us know whether we got his ideas right. Therefore, these are our versions of what Gregory Bateson's ideas were about and their significance, from this point in our own lives and history. Our own understandings of his work are not what they were yesterday and they may change tomorrow. And this kind of understanding is also a very important part of what he taught.

CYBERNETICS AND TOOLS

Nora: I think that we should start with just a quick introduction and a date stamp, and then we can really begin. I'm Nora Bateson, and it is the 16th of May, 2013, and I'm here in London on Skype with Phillip Guddemi who is in Sacramento, California, and we are going to have a conversation to be transcribed that is about my father, Gregory Bateson, and his . . . his what, Phillip? His influences and the beginning of systems theory and cybernetics?

Phillip: I'd say that it's a bit of how his own particular epistemology and world view began, how it braided and interconnected with cybernetics, as it was emerging, and what it means—what cybernetics was about. And how that carried through in some of his later works, and also a little bit about what the community was that came together at this point—at the point of time of the Macy Conferences

Nora: What I'm thinking of right away is actually a very cybernetic sort of diagram much like what later came to be signature systems theory diagrams. Picture a Venn diagram with arrows to other Venn diagrams inside concentric circles. Illustrating the individual whose epistemology is inside the context of another framework with other people. In this case we are talking about the people who formed the Macy Conference participants— then zoom out to picture all of them inside the context of the time period and the social cultural structures they were in—all of that as if seen from right now in a timeline (that is clearly nonlinear), framing us here—whatever it is—sixty-something years later—

Phillip: Yeah.

Nora: It takes a cybernetic look at history to begin looking at the event of the Macy Conferences and the ideas that emerged. Remember we are making sense of them from here. Interestingly, that process, in and of itself—just of looking at it—calls a lot of cybernetic questions up right at the beginning. Questions surface of the shifting interpretations of the observer, and of the recursive adaptations of the information as it ping-pongs back and forth through time and people. Questions of knowing.

Phillip: Yes, very well stated. . . . So, really, Bateson's—or Gregory's own evolution in these things came out of his anthropological work and out of the ideas he applied to his anthropological work, except that he had different ideas to apply to his anthropological work because of his own background with his father and the particular type of way of thinking about biology, which was characteristic of his father, which was already dealing with, let's say, patterns rather than substance as its emphasis. So that when William Bateson was looking at genetics, he actually used the word "vibrations" to describe the kind of patterns that he was looking at, as opposed to what even he later on as a champion of Mendelian genetics put forward—this sort of gene-centric, substance-centric, thing-centric type of explanation of what made for change and continuity in a biological system. The original ideas that William Bateson had were moving away from that toward a more of a pattern way of thinking.

And I think that it's fair to say that even though Gregory moved from that field of study into anthropology going to New Guinea, and then with Margaret Mead, going to Bali, that something of that flavor of what made an explanation carried with him to the ways that he looked at, especially when he got his field notes home and started to put together what became *Naven*, which is a very interesting book, because it's a book that shows almost like a sedimentary process, almost like taking an archaeological dig; you can see the different layers of Bateson's thought about this New Guinea people that he studied.[2] And he thought and rethought and rethought it, so that you have this situation where you have various topical chapters, and then you have a first epilogue of 1936, and then you have a second epilogue in the 1950s after, in Gregory's mind, he had adopted and reframed everything in terms of cybernetics.

But the irony is that he was already anticipating a lot of the most important things in cybernetics, even in the earlier epilogue and his earlier work.

Nora: . . . I think we need to start over.
       [*laughter*]
Phillip: Why not?
Nora: Okay—all right, we have to try to work on having it be more of a dialogue.
Phillip: Okay. [*laughs*]
Nora: [*laughs*]
Phillip: All right. [*laughing*] Let's make it a dialogue.
Nora: [*laughs*]
Phillip: Yeah.
Nora: Okay. So, because all that you say is really true, but it needs to kind of come out as it comes out, not in a chunk, right?
Phillip: Yeah, not in a huge chunk like that, yeah.
Nora: Right. Okay. We're doing a little restart.
Phillip: Okay.
Nora: Given all that you've just said, even though we're doing a restart, let's open it up for that to come through by starting

with the notion that what is happening in the Bateson family is that there is a particular kind of observation that's being cultivated. And that observation on behalf of William Bateson and later Gregory and so on is an observation that is tested, not in terms of cultural viability, but in terms of its capacity to hold patterns and relationships.

I think that becomes something that certainly influences cybernetics, systems theory, and then later complexity—is this role of the observer. If we're going to talk about early cybernetics and Gregory's contributions, it's appropriate to start by looking at what sort of observer he was. The observations are what were driving the quest for seeing the world in another way.

Phillip: [*short pause*] It's a daunting thing to try to think about what kind of observer he was. Certainly, I have some great Macy Conference quotes and quotes from some of these early articles about how important in anthropology the personality of the observer is—how that is the instrument that you use, and how that has to be factored in to what is observed, to the science that results or to whatever type of work results.[3]

So I'd say that he was someone who did a lot of very close observation and then pulled back and looked at it in a very wide frame. So he would go from the extreme detail to very high-level ideas and sort of philosophical understandings. And that's kind of a dialectic process, or process of refocus. Would that be a way of looking at what kind of observer he was?

Nora: Yeah, I think so. And I think also, as I've been looking—observing his observations, one of the things that I'm noticing is that, really, what makes him unique is that he has a facility for seeing complexity or more systems within systems, or a greater level of cybernetic complexity than most people seem to have. We could ask—how and why did he have that? Because it was extremely valuable then and still is today to have the perspective of someone who is somehow able to see that. He opens up incredible vistas of dynamics that are not in a state of reveal for most people.

So, in a sense, a lot of the tenets of cybernetics and systems theory are the result of being able to actually see systems.

Phillip: Well, that's right. And people do it in different ways; people try to put these things together in different ways. There's a recent book by Andrew Pickering called *The Cybernetic Brain,*[4] which talks about how most—many of the other early cyberneticans, such as Ross Ashby, built machines, but they were building the machines primarily to "think about," and so they would construct them to enable them to think about what it means to be an adaptive system, what it means to keep certain aspects of your existence within certain numerical ranges, or else you would presumably die, and so on. They would invent these machines which then people look at now and either have the mistaken idea that they had a mechanistic idea of the world, or, you know, that they were just—I don't know, some of the negative ideas of what cybernetics means in terms of a mechanical world.

That wasn't what they were about. They were trying to do something different so that they could see different things. Now, with Gregory, it was a more naturalistic type of observation; he was trying to observe living systems, whether they were anthropological systems or ecological systems kind of as they are found—you know, as we find them—rather than an experimental point of view. Remember, in your film he says he didn't want to live his life in a lab. So he wanted to do this kind of naturalistic observation. And that was combined with an ability to see philosophical import without running it through experiment, which I think is extremely rare and kind of defines his gift.

Nora: Yeah, and he actually saw it everywhere. So he knew he didn't need a lab.

Phillip: Right.

Nora: Whether he was working with schizophrenic patients, dolphins, or Southeast Asian cultures, the first of level of motivation for him was to begin to see in a way that maintained complex fields of relations. But that's daunting for most people: there is a sense of, "Well, I can't see everything all at once and I can't see all the relationships, and where do you draw the boundaries, and it's just too much, I can't hold it in my head at once." For that reason, we simplify things, we reduce things into smaller bites and we try to make our observations hold water in those smaller containers.

Of course, the repercussions of that habit are visible all over the world now. And the disruption to the larger integrity of not only ecological, but social and psychological systems is tantamount to disaster and enormous destruction.

Phillip: Well, that's interesting, because a connection you're making, which is a connection I think he made, especially in his later life, is a connection between this very reductionist chopping up of the world analytically, in terms of science, and an equation of that to what happens when you then try to create an applied science out of it and then apply it to the world, or assume that you have a true model of the world and then use it to, I don't know, improve the stock market or something. I mean, many people would think that if you chopped the world into bits in order to just study it, in order to find scientific truths about it, that that really doesn't have any consequence in terms of how the world functions—in terms of how that becomes our daily lives. But in fact, it does, because we apply this same type of reductionist science.

Nora: I think that's painfully true. And it's interesting and important to note, because . . . well, you and I were in the Library of Congress not long ago, looking at Gregory and Margaret's early letters and early papers, their field notes, et cetera, that are in there, an incredible treasure trove of the sort of history of these ideas and these personalities of these people. And I have to tell you that I was deeply struck by what I perceived there as an absolutely impassioned dedication to stopping fascism. They were dedicated in every capacity, in everything that they were doing, to stopping the war and to stopping fascism. That passion then became part of a larger concern for the limitations and the sublimation, the objectification, and exploitation of everything from cultural difference to the life of the amoebas. It became, for Gregory, certainly, a scientific pursuit in the name of restoring our ability to perceive the integrity of life. This was actually a pacifist agenda.

I think it's an interesting contrast with our notions of what activism is, because I know that sometimes I go to systems sciences conferences and get involved with complexity theorists and theorists in cybernetics and feel this kind of undertone of "Let's use these ideas to save the world, these are the chosen ideas."

Phillip: Yes.

Nora: And then there's a kind of "Yeah, but what do we do with them—how do we make this into action, how do we take cybernetic action?" [*laughs*]

Phillip: That's right.

Nora: Or begin to take action in a way that holds in account our second-order roles as observers and participants while operating within the context, and how do we do this? In moments of frustration there is the audible sigh that says, "Why do we have these tools if we can't use them?"

When we were in the Library of Congress, we found a lot of interesting documents, and one of them both of us of homed in on. I just wanted to read you this last sentence of this paper that was written in 1946 on "Physical Thinking and Social Problems"—by Gregory—where he says: "In conclusion, it's worth stressing that the 'elimination of war as a means of settling international differences' is a project requiring basic and applied research, ranging from learning experiments on rats through comparative studies of simple communities up to analysis of the most complex phenomena of contact between contrasting cultures."[5]

Certainly you can see in the second part of that quote that he is bringing all manner of disciplines together. But the question of why and to what end is not to be underestimated. His pursuit of elimination of something as destructive as "war as a means of settling international differences," I think, is indicative of the very deep caring and the concern that actually drove Gregory's ability to perceive complexity.

Phillip: The context of this writing of Gregory's was a postwar environment in which most of American social science, including Margaret Mead, was very optimistic, and social scientists really felt that they were beginning to have a handle on child-rearing and education, that they could find new ways to do just about everything in personal and cultural life, new ways to deal with organization. Again, this sort of idea that you can design a world that people will want to live in—I think that was very much a part of the circle that Bateson—that Gregory was living in in the 1940s. And some of the sort of source books that I've been reading about the Macy Conference really talk about that period and about the circle of people that Gregory and that Margaret Mead were among at that time.[6] And just this sort of outpouring of trying to think of things differently and in a more hopeful way. Erik Erikson was part of that—a lot of people who had come as refugees from Nazi Germany, as well as a lot of very homegrown thinkers. The social sciences in this day were very much in this kind of reformist mode.

In a way Gregory got skeptical of that; his heart, I think, was always with it, but partly as a result of his war experience, where he got involved in all this sort of manipulative use of communication ideas abroad, I think that he did end up with a kind of skepticism about this reformist impulse. And in a certain sense, he wanted people to respect curiosity and interest and study of societies, of systems, of biological organisms, without knowing what you were going to do with it, without knowing where you were going with it. He said that curiosity was still—well, I'm not remembering the exact quote—but that it was still a kind of honorable motive.[7] So, it's a very complex picture.

Nora: But I don't think that he lost hope. I know that is a common story. But as I was in the Library of Congress and then doing some other work with his lectures and various parts of the world afterward, I'll tell you what I'm seeing again and again, because it absolutely fits into this question of the notion of systems theory and of cybernetics, and how what he saw this as was the possibility of a toolbox for using multiple perspectives and multiple versions of observation, multiple languages of description—multiple disciplines is really what I'm talking about—put towards something that was going to put Humpty Dumpty back together again.

Then in the questions that he was asking, whether he was working with the sort of fragmentation of the meaning-making process of somebody who was suffering from schizophrenia, or talking to the governor of California about the ethics of the research of arms control, there was always a similar thread. And that thread had to do with the fact that because systems function in such complex ways, with aggregates of variables, of all sorts of things interacting, from history to biology to culture to personal epistemology to language—all these things functioning together—that if you go at something with a notion of a linear approach toward a corrective, you are going to escalate the issues. When the thing that you want to correct is absolutely not functioning in a linear way, that effort to make that correction becomes not only misguided but more dangerous.

Phillip: Yes.

Nora: This is all part of that early business of causation, which is central to the pursuit of the study of cybernetics. Gregory had a really interesting and creative way of dealing with that, and I think ultimately that's where it was going—was to—enter the entanglement at multiple levels simultaneously. Here's an example: we see war as a way of settling international differences. Okay, now the result is that it will take everybody's version of how to undo this. This is an interesting application, actually, of systems and of cybernetic tools that I'm not sure ever really got put to use. What might happen if we started with the quest of what we want to tackle, and apply a multiple version, or description to the task of describing the problem, and to the task of interaction with it? The idea being to gather our multiple perspectives, diverse research, our knowledge, our observations, and begin to dialogue about how we're going to tackle this problem so that it doesn't get fragmented—and then have a conversation that is at a level that is one shelf higher than all the fragments.

Phillip: There are two sorts of caveats to that. One is that when you talk about a toolbox, one of the favorite things that Gregory would say whenever people would bring up the phrase "conceptual tools" had to do with a contrast that he thought existed between the Western mind and perhaps some ideas in the cultures of Japan and China and so on. And what he felt he learned from these Eastern cultures—for example, from *Zen in the Art of Archery* and similar things—was that our Western concept is that tools are ways that we—as ourselves—go out and change the world. But in the Eastern sense, these are also ways that change ourselves and that anything we try to use as a tool will also necessarily change ourselves, and that we have to be mindful of how it changes our selves, especially since the way we apply science definitely has a feedback on how we consider ourselves.

Nora: Absolutely—

Phillip: And if we consider ourselves as problem solvers, in *Steps to an Ecology of Mind,* in one of his articles on conscious purpose, he goes off on the medical profession as being divided by purpose. So you have a purpose of solving polio or solving cancer or solving schizophrenia, if you like, and then you develop a bag of tricks, and then you get something that seems to work, and then you go on to the next thing.

And what you sacrifice by this sort of bag-of-tricks way of looking at things, which is implicit in the way we fund and the way we organize charitable organizations and everything like that, but what you sacrifice is exactly the sense of the larger system. So in a way, the way that you work to tackle the problem is itself part of the problem. And I think that's really an important part of the lesson of how he began to look at conscious purpose in his later thinking about that. But actually it's implicit far back.

Nora: And . . . so, I think that's why his hopes for cybernetics were so high. Because he really wanted that tool to become part of a method of inquiry and a way of increasing our capacity to engage with that complexity—to see it and to see that context in all its many relationships.

Phillip: Well, yeah, I mean, cybernetics wasn't just one tool. There's a list in an article, "Gregory Bateson and the Mathematicians," of the concepts that Bateson was learning and dealing with in the Macy Conferences.[8] It's about eleven or twelve different major concepts, all of which he used very profoundly in his later work. But I think he used all of them in the interest, ultimately, of broadening the context, and broadening—I guess, what you are concerned with, both as an investigator and someone acting in life; not just with the narrow thing that you think you're about, but with a wider system. And there is his interest and contribution to systems, not only epistemologically, but ethically.

Nora: Mm hm.

Phillip: At the same time, you know, you have this business of never perceiving the thing as it is. Never being able to perceive the *Ding an sich*. And in order to see, you even have your nystagmus of your eye—your eye is always moving—it is always acting. So, in a sense—in a philosophical sense—Bateson would have to be ranked with the pragmatists. I think, if you look at recent philosophy that calls itself pragmatist, he's right in there. So that's the paradox.

Nora: Well, but I have to say that I disagree with you, Phillip, about your assessment of what is pragmatic, because I think the problem with being pragmatic or practical is that it has to do with doing something that is functional, but the problem is that doing something that is functional, that fits into a preexisting dysfunction only makes it worse. So, for example, it's practical to have standardized tests for kids in schools, because it gives us a practical way to measure them quantitatively, which makes sense in the cultural frame that we are perceiving. But it is enormously impractical at another level. If you want to find out what each child is thinking and how their minds work, and what they have to offer and what their thinking skills are, and develop that, it's enormously impractical.

So, I think that Gregory's issue with pragmatism wasn't so much about competition as it was about being practical at the level of reifying or affirming already existing errors. Because that would appear to be practical.

So the problem with what he called the—what did he call it?—the altar of pragmatism—the problem with the altar of pragmatism was that it served the wrong level. If there is a kind of practicality at the level of expanding the context of interfacing with the interrelationships, that's truly practical, because it hopefully creates less complications and destruction. But that would not require the same sort of—as we were saying—actions or interactions that being practical would in another sense . . .

And I think, you know, interestingly, this is one of the reasons why cybernetics and systems thinking itself has a hard time finding its footing: because people would like to be able to take these tools and just use them. But the problem with just using them is that the systems we're trying to use them within are incongruous.

But I want to go back to that example from that paper in '46, because I think there's a really valuable nugget there. And that is that in the process of asking the question and bringing people together from multiple perspectives to generate a conversation, what might look like problem-solving with a toolbox actually becomes something else. It seems to me that what it is, is not actually problem-solving, but a process of description from multiple perspectives, at the end of which the problem itself is very different. So it's not that it's solved, it's that it and the participants have been changed along the way. When you look at the way that he asks questions or works—really what he's dealing in is deep second-order patterning.

Phillip: Right.

Nora: And when you get into that business of describing from multiple situations and essentially sharing wisdom—

Phillip: Yes.

Nora: —the collective wisdom itself is a living, evolving process in the context and it changes the context, without ever having that lineal corrective . . .

Phillip: Right.

Nora: —action point put into play. So it's an interesting go-around to the notion of a problem-solving technique, because it isn't a problem-solving technique; it's a way of reorganizing the thinking around how we're interacting with a pattern.

Phillip: Well, and that makes it very difficult to chunk it and put it in the context of an elevator speech. I think that we're in an era dominated by the kind of questions that are asked increasingly of every college instructor. For example: What are the measurable outcomes? What is the take-away? What is the influence on the test scores, or what do we tell Congress as the result of our studies?

And that is the opposite: that thinking, in the way that Gregory thought, moves you away from that kind of evaluation, and towards something much more intangible, and I think that's very difficult for our present moment.

Nora: Well, it is difficult for our present moment. I think that that's one of the reasons that there was a lot of sadness at the end of Gregory's life. He felt that cybernetics was the most valuable contribution to the twentieth century. Now, when you mention it to people, they have some vague notion of a technological something or other, and if you talk about systems, people who are in the know about that are—systems sciences are very often separated from everything else. Interdisciplinary studies becomes a discipline.

There is a certain sense of lost-ness right now—of how do we begin to look at what that group actually found, because they found some treasures, they found some wonderful ideas. And their approaches were perceived, I think, at the time, as not having that take-away or those action points that you're talking about, even then.

However, when you look closely, they are there. They just look different, because when you're looking for a different kind of outcome, you have to go observing the situation in a different way. That was the mandate, if you will, then, and there's a possibility that we could be coming back to that, because goodness knows, the approach that we've been using isn't exactly working.

Phillip: Well, that's certainly my hope right now, is that there's this tremendous upsurge in interest in Gregory Bateson's work and to some extent in the Macy Conferences and in cybernetics. And I think that the time may be ripe again for us to think about these things again.

Nora: Mm hm.

Phillip: But I know that for decades we've been looking for simpler answers and more demonstrable conclusions, I suppose. And also these ideas of systems and cybernetics are alienating to a lot of people, based on some very superficial ideas I think they have about what they are about.

Nora: And, you know, I think they also got locked into a time-zone. I've had the experience of mentioning cybernetics to people and them saying, "Oh yeah, I remember that."

Phillip: Yes.

Nora: And, "Haven't we moved on from that now? Epistemology—didn't we do that already? Aren't we in post-modernism now?" And, you know, that it's sort of got a slot in the history of this kind of theoretical, academic on-to-the newest-thing habit. But what a loss, because I'm thinking of that group in Schio, Italy, near Venice . . .

Phillip: Yes.

Nora: Where there are these people today who are utilizing these ideas in ways that would be completely unexpected, and the metaphors and the methodologies are useful across multiple disciplines. This group in Schio that's doing rehabilitation of people who are in paralysis or terminal pain, and they have developed a collection of treatment exercises and practicing these activities that are physical—let's see, how to describe it?—physical illustrations of how the cybernetics of the body—so the muscular system, yes, and the vision system and the verbal capacity, and how that functions with cognition and memory, and utilizing all these things at once to restore the integrity of these people's bodily systems.

It's difficult to describe without looking at it, and I know I could hardly believe it myself. The idea is that they don't, for example, go after the paralyzed leg and give it exercises. The exercises that they're creating are largely verbal, they use hypotheses, and the concept is that they are integrating the entire body, of which the leg is obviously a part. So, with that entire integration, the leg is put essentially back into the complexity that it was somehow fragmented from. They're having incredible results; their work is inspirational as a model for systems theory as a medical tool.

Phillip: Yes. And it's interesting—I was just thinking of it in terms of both the way that grants work and also the way pedagogy works. It's a kind of paradox about the idea of anything new, which is that usually with a grant you're supposed to describe what you're going to find before you find it. And usually in putting together a lesson plan, you're supposed to put down what people are going to learn before they learn it. But if there's anything that is really new, then it's not going to be predictable in these ways, and you're not going to be able to tell before it happens what's going to happen. And I think this is very difficult for our systems of social and bureaucratic control. And maybe one of the reasons why Gregory's epistemology is so difficult for them.

Nora: Somehow technology got ahold of the terminology. Then, in the process of that happening, somehow the social sciences separated themselves from technology, and the idea that nature was separate from technology came into play. Every time something gets separated in that way, we get one step further from being able to see the way that they're functioning together.

I'm thinking of the example that Gregory used to use of the blind man walking with his stick, and the question of where does the man begin? Does the man begin at his hand? Or does the man begin at the end of the stick? Where does the information come from and how is it being read? Do the man and the stick—do they end there? Or does that system also include the sidewalk or the path they're walking on—and the environment that they're within?

What might change in the conversation about technology if the idea of excluding it from the dialogue of natural systems is seen as blurred, to the point of being a mistake? Also, excluding natural systems from the dialogue about technology might be a mistake.

Phillip: Well, this brings up the whole question of boundaries and this is kind of a technical question within cybernetics and systems theory that has big ramifications outside. There are a lot of people who are very concerned about what are the boundaries of the organism, what are the boundaries of a system, what does it mean that a social system or an ecosystem doesn't have the same kind of boundaries that you can observe in an organism.

And people who are concerned with this particular issue tend to look a little cockeyed at Gregory Bateson's work, because he really always defined boundary according to the problem that he was looking at, or according to just what it was that he was observing at that particular time. And he would see circuitries both inside and outside the skin.

So that made him different from a lot of the thinking even in second-order cybernetics as it developed, and certainly in systems theory, because you're not thinking of a system as something that is there, that interacts, but as a way of looking. And this goes back to his 1936 epilogue to *Naven*, where he learned that things like the economic system or the marriage system of this people in New Guinea—that these were not actually sort of in the model of physical objects that were interacting, but they were ways of looking, of himself and of the local people.[9]

Nora: Mm hm.

Phillip: And that was one of his main insights—or that was one of the great insights in the history of his thought.

Nora: Well, and I think that brings us right back to the beginning—

Phillip: Yes.

Nora: —that really what we're talking about is a way of observing, and observing not only the multiplicitous variables of any context, but also observing the multiplicitous variables of our own selves as we're observing them, and that—

Phillip: There's your second-order cybernetics.

Nora: Yeah, but that was always there.

Phillip: Yes.

Nora: It was always there. I think that William Bateson was employing that when he was rebuking the chromosome theory. There was some of that second-order going on there. But we won't get into that here.[10]

But just to bring it back around the circle, let's remember that there was hope in the dream that with a different way of observing, we might be able to see different patterns and to engage with those patterns in ways that we would not be able to predict now.

Phillip: Well, that's right. And how do you become sensitive to new patterns that you might see? How do you overcome the kind of previous learning that you had?

Nora: Right.

Phillip: Now this goes into another of Gregory's contributions, which was his concept of hierarchies of learning. All of us have this second-order learning, which is not just what it is that we learned about in going through life, but also the patterns of interaction—what we think life is about for us, or within our culture. These are patterns which become unconscious, which become habitual, and they're very hard to change. And they're very hard to step out of. Third-order learning would be the habit of being able to step out of them. But what are the ways *to* that? I think we should think about Noel Charlton a little bit, and think about art and aesthetics as something that—

Nora: Mm hm.

Phillip: Charlton showed also—now, I was aware that in Gregory's work near the end of his life—"Style, Grace and Information" in *Steps to an Ecology of Mind,* as an example, that Gregory was mentioning art as a way to overcome the blinders of conscious purpose in his later work.[11] But Charlton, in his book, shows that Gregory's engagement with the arts was there all along, that he was in dialogue with artists,[12] that he was—

Nora: Well, so was William Bateson. The place of art in the pursuit of what the Batesons called "unmuddled thinking" went way back. There's no question about it that William Bateson's work in genetics is inspired by Blake and the arts.

Phillip: So there are ways that we need to work to overcome some of the ways that we get channeled by our habitual ways of understanding, and the arts are one such way.

Nora: Mm hm.

Phillip: And that—again, the . . .

Nora: But Phillip, let's just be in the "you and me" for right now—for a quick second, okay?

Phillip: Okay?

Nora: Why do you think we see what we see? I mean, in moments in your personal life where you have missed something, or you have seen something that other people either saw or didn't see, what happened there? I mean, what's your personal experience with that?

Phillip: [*short pause*][*laughs*] Oh—something I'd like to explore some day when I'm not being recorded, but . . .

Nora: Well, I mean, maybe we just leave that as a question.

Phillip: Yeah.

Nora: Because I think . . . we are limited by the confines of our discourse.

Phillip: Yes.

Nora: We're limited by the confines of our language and education and experience.

Phillip: Mm hm, yes.

Nora: And I think, at a deeper level, we are limited by what you brought up earlier in one sense, but I think we need to open it at the back, as it were, is this notion of curiosity. Because it's easy to say, "Yeah, but all scientists are curious, science is filled with curiosity" . . . But there's a curiosity that has to do with . . . with caring very deeply. And when the stakes are high, the ethics of that curiosity and the dignity that's afforded whatever it is you're curious about, will include a much higher degree of complexity.

Phillip: Well, I just want to remark that I think curiosity is an indispensable part of empathy—that empathy is incomplete without curiosity, and that curiosity is an indispensable component of empathy, and that Gregory was bringing up the question of empathy. There are places where he's talking about it in the Macy Conferences.[13]

Nora: Mm hm.

Phillip: It goes back. So, to really be curious about—

Nora: So, I mean, I think that the first thing you have to say is this: the starting place of practice is to be able to see all of those otherwise invisible interrelationships and interdependencies—all those patterns—

Phillip: Mm hm.

Nora: —the first practice is one that requires such a level of caring that you don't want to oversimplify the problem. That's the first door into the curiosity of "How is this thing happening?"

Phillip: Mm hm.

Nora: That's not the same kind of curiosity as "How do I figure out the answer to this problem?"

Phillip: That's right.

Nora: It's a very different temperature, a very different version of what it means to be curious.

Phillip: I agree.

Nora: I'm thinking of a story. But you know what? I think we should wind this up.

Phillip: Okay.

Nora: Yeah. So, why don't we wind it up with—we could actually end it there.

Phillip: Yes, let's do that.

NOTES

1. We thank Kathy E. Jackson for transcription services.
2. Gregory Bateson, *Naven*, 2nd ed. (Stanford: Stanford University Press, 1958).
3. See, for example, Bateson's comment in the discussion following his own contribution to the 1952 conference, held March 20–21, 1952, in New York, "The Position of Humor in Human Communication," in *Cybernetics: Circular Causal and Feedback Mechanisms in Biological and Social Sciences: Transactions of the Ninth Conference,* eds. Heinz von Foerster, Margaret Mead, and Hans Leukas Teubner (New York: Josiah Macy, Jr. Foundation, 1952), 15:

The social scientist is not only in the sort of position that Ashby has suggested for his observer but, worse, he is investigating a dynamic system more or less in the dark with a flexible stick, his own personality, the characteristics of whose flexibility he does not fully know. There is, therefore, a set of unknowns in the observer, which are also subject to investigation. Every statement we make about the observed derives from premises about the self. I say this glass of water is there because I can touch it with my hands and feel it there with my eyes shut. In order to make this statement, 'It is there,' I have to know where my arm is, and, on the premise that my arm is out in that direction, I conclude that the glass is there. But the premise about myself is built into my conclusion. The whole gamut of projection phenomena follows. There are premises about one's self, in terms of which one understands something else. But the events in interaction between oneself and the something else may lead to a revision of premises about one's self. Then, suddenly, one sees the other thing in a new light. It is this sort of thing that leads to the paradoxes and to a great deal of humor, I would suspect.

4. Andrew Pickering, *The Cybernetic Brain: Sketches of Another Future* (Chicago: University of Chicago Press, 2010).
5. Gregory Bateson, "Physical Thinking and Social Problems," *Science* 103, no. 2686 (June 1946): 718.
6. See, for example, Steve J. Heims, *The Cybernetics Group* (Cambridge, MA: MIT Press, 1991).
7. "Let me then conclude with a warning that we social scientists would do well to hold back our eagerness to control that world which we so imperfectly understand. The fact of our imperfect understanding should not be allowed to feed our anxiety and so increase the need to control. Rather, our studies could be inspired by a more ancient, but today less honored, motive: a curiosity about the world of which we are part. The rewards of such work are not power but beauty." From Gregory Bateson, *Steps to an Ecology of Mind* (Chicago: University of Chicago Press, 2000), 269; first published as "Minimal Requirements for a Theory of Schizophrenia," in *A.M.A. Archives of General Psychiatry* 2 (1960): 477–91.
8. Steve P. Heims, "Gregory Bateson and the Mathematicians: From Interdisciplinary Interaction to Societal Functions," *Journal of the History of the Behavioral Sciences* 13 (1977): 145.

> On these two days of the conference Bateson witnessed expositions, by Wiener and von Neumann, of a whole collection of concepts originating in mathematics and engineering, on which he would draw heavily thenceforth: the difference between "analogical" and "digital" processes, coding, circuits, servomechanisms, positive and negative feedback, time series, measure of information and its relation to entropy, binary systems, Russell's Theory of Logical Types, "pathological" oscillations induced in a computer confronted with a Russellian paradox, the idea that the crucial concept to use in understanding communication systems is "information" and not "energy," etc. . . . During these two days, in effect Bateson was presented with a set of tools; he would make it his task to understand them as precisely as he could without mathematics, to examine them to see which of them would be useful to him for theory construction in the behavioral sciences, and he would learn to use them.

9. Bateson, *Naven*, 262: "labels for points of view adopted either by the scientist or by the natives." See also Phillip Guddemi, "Toward Batesonian

Sociocybernetics: from *Naven* to the Mind Beyond the Skin," *Kybernetes* 36 no. 7/8 (2007): 905–14.

10. For a recent treatment of William Bateson's work, see Alan Cock and Donald Forsdyke, *Treasure Your Exceptions: The Science and Life of William Bateson* (New York: Springer Science + Business Media, 2008).

11. Gregory Bateson, "Style, Grace, and Information in Primitive Art," in *Steps to an Ecology of Mind* (Chicago: University of Chicago Press, 2000), 128–52.

12. Noel Charlton, *Understanding Gregory Bateson: Mind, Beauty, and the Sacred Earth* (Albany, NY: State University of New York Press, 2008).

13. For example, "The Position of Humor in Human Communication," 23.

REFERENCES

Bateson, Gregory. "The Position of Humor in Human Communication." In *Cybernetics: Circular Causal and Feedback Mechanisms in Biological and Social Sciences: Transactions of the Ninth Conference*. Edited by Heinz von Foerster, Margaret Mead, and Hans Leukas Teubner, 1–47. New York: Josiah Macy Jr. Foundation, 1952.

———. *Naven*. 2nd ed. Stanford: Stanford University Press, 1958.

———. "Style, Grace, and Information in Primitive Art." In *Steps to an Ecology of Mind*. Chicago: University of Chicago Press, 2000.

———. "Physical Thinking and Social Problems." *Science* 103, no. 2686 (June 21, 1946): 717–18.

Charlton, Noel. *Understanding Gregory Bateson: Mind, Beauty, and the Sacred Earth*. Albany, NY: State University of New York Press, 2008.

Cock, Alan, and Donald Forsdyke. *Treasure Your Exceptions: The Science and Life of William Bateson*. New York: Springer Science + Business Media, 2008.

Guddemi, Phillip. "Toward Batesonian Sociocybernetics: From *Naven* to the Mind Beyond the Skin." *Kybernetes* 36, no. 7/8 (2007): 905–14.

Heims, Steve P. "Gregory Bateson and the Mathematicians: From Interdisciplinary Interaction to Societal Functions." *Journal of the History of the Behavioral Sciences* 13 (1977): 141–59.

———. *The Cybernetics Group*. Cambridge, MA: MIT Press, 1991.

Pickering, Andrew. *The Cybernetic Brain: Sketches of Another Future*. Chicago: University of Chicago Press, 2010.

Contributors

Nora Bateson is the writer, director, and producer of the award-winning documentary *An Ecology of Mind,* a portrait of her father, Gregory Bateson's, way of thinking. She has developed curricula for schools in Northern California and produced and directed award-winning multimedia projects on intercultural understanding. Nora leads seminars with international change-makers, ecologists, anthropologists, psychologists, designers, and IT professionals. Utilizing the film as a tool to introduce some of her father's thinking tools, Nora engages her audiences, providing a lens through which to see the world that affects not only the way we perceive our environment but also how we interact with it.

Dr. Nimrod Bar-Am is a senior lecturer and the head of the unit for the study of rhetoric and philosophy of communication at Sapir College, Israel. He published various papers on the history of logic. His book *Extensionalism: The Revolution in Logic* was published by Springer in 2008. He is currently working on the monograph *The Simple Introduction to the Philosophy of Communication.*

Dr. John Bruni teaches at Grand Valley State University. He has published a number of essays on systems theory, including most recently an essay on systems thermodynamics in *The Routledge Companion to Literature and Science.* His book, *Scientific Americans: The Making of Popular Science and Evolution in Early-Twentieth-Century U.S. Literature and Culture,* will be published by University of Wales Press in 2014.

Dr. Peter Finke is a professor emeritus of the theory of science at the Universität Bielefeld in Germany. He was honored with the first European chair for Evolutionary Cultural Ecology at the Private Universität Witten–Herdecke (Germany) and has held guest appointments at many European universities. He has been awarded an honorary doctorate by the University of Debrecen, Hungary. Among his publications are *Grundlagen einer linguistischen Theorie* (Vieweg), *Konstruktiver Funktionalismus* (Vieweg), and, more recently, *Die Ökologie des Wissens* (Karl Alber). Presently he is working on a book titled *Citizen Science.*

Dr. Phillip Guddemi is the president of the Bateson Idea Group, a non-profit group dedicated to Gregory Bateson's ideas and legacy. He is a cultural anthropologist and cybernetic thinker who has been grappling with Gregory Bateson's epistemology ever since studying with him as an undergraduate at the University of California, Santa Cruz in the 1970s. Phillip Guddemi is the managing editor of the journal *Cybernetics and Human Knowing*. He has done anthropological fieldwork in the Sepik region of Papua New Guinea, as well as in Macedonia. He has published academically broadly, recently on social cybernetics, the concept of power, and Bateson's legacy in anthropology.

Ranulph Glanville is the president of the American Society of Cybernetics. He is a professor of Innovation Design Engineering at the Royal College of Art in London, Luca-Arts at the Catholic University of Leuven, and Digital Futures at the Ontario College of Art and Design, Toronto, as well as an emeritus professor of architecture and cybernetics in the Bartlett at UCL, London. He has published more than 350 articles and books and edited numerous Festshrifts, conference proceedings, and journals, including issues on or for Heinz von Foerster, Ernst von Glasersfeld, Gordon Pask, and Gerard de Zeeuw. Three volumes of *The Black Box* are published by echaraum.

Dr. W. L. Goldfrank is a professor emeritus of sociology and Latin American & Latino/a studies at the University of California, Santa Cruz. He has published broadly on global political economy, especially the decline of hegemonic powers, social movements and revolutions, the social and environmental impacts of export agriculture, and historical sociology. His "Paradigm Regained? The Rules of Wallerstein's World-System Method" (*Journal of World System Research*) is an influential introduction to Wallerstein's thought. He has edited *Ecology and the World System* (Greenwood Press) and *World System of Capitalism* (Sage).

Dr. Joel Hagen is a professor and the chair of the department of biology at Radford University. His research areas include the history of ecology, systematics, and evolutionary biology, and he is one of the world's leading experts on the ecosystems thinking of Eugene Odum and Howard Odum. Among his writings are *An Entangled Bank: The Origins of Ecosystems Ecology* (Rutgers University Press) and articles on both Eugene Odum and Howard Odum in the *New Dictionary of Scientific Biography* (Charles Scribner's Sons).

Dr. Debora Hammond is a professor of interdisciplinary studies and director of the MA program in organization development at the Hutchins School of Liberal Studies of Sonoma State University, where she earlier served as provost. She is former president of the International Society for the Systems Sciences. Her volume *The Science of Synthesis: Exploring the Social Implications of General Systems Theory* (University Press of Colorado) focuses on the relevance of systems theory for social systems. She has written articles on the genealogy of systems theory, the theory's ethical and philosophical foundations, its relevance for environmental and social justice issues, and leading figures such as Kenneth Boulding and James Grier Miller.

Dr. **Bettina Mahlert** is a research associate in the department of sociology at RWTH Aachen University, Germany. She received her PhD in 2013 from the Universität Bielefeld, where she directed the Institute for World Society Studies (2007–2012). Her research fields include world society theory and globalization, social inequality, and sociological theory. Some relevant recent publications include "Soziale Ordnungsbildung durch Kollektivität? Luhmanns, Ebenenunterscheidung und die moderne Weltgesellschaft" in *Interaktion—Organisation—Gesellschaft* (Lucius) and "Familie und Nationalstaat: Zu den globalen Bezügen des Klassenbegriffs bei Talcott Parsons" in *Transnationalisierung Sozialer Ungleichheit* (VS-Verlag).

Dr. **Andrew McMurry** is an associate professor of English at the University of Waterloo, Ontario, where he teaches rhetorical theory, semiotics, and discourse studies. He has published widely on ecocriticism, and he is the author of *Environmental Renaissance: Emerson, Thoreau, and the System of Natures* (University of Georgia Press).

Dr. **Bob Mugerauer** is a professor and former dean of urban design and planning at the University of Washington's Center for Built Environments. His work focuses on theory and qualitative research methods, the impact of technology on built and natural environments, and the cultural and social factors in planning and architecture. Among his monographs are *Interpretations on Behalf of Space* (State University of New York Press), *Interpreting Environments: Tradition, Deconstruction, Hermeneutics* (University of Texas Press), *Environmental Dilemmas: Ethical Decision Making* (Lexington Books), and *Heidegger and Homecoming: The Leitmotif in the Later Writings* (University of Toronto Press).

Dr. **Dorothea Olkowski** is a professor of philosophy at the University of Colorado–Colorado Springs. Specializing in feminist theory, phenomenology and contemporary French philosophy, she has been a Fellow at the Australian National University in Canberra. A few of the many books she has written and edited include *Gilles Deleuze and the Ruin of Representation* (University of California Press), *Resistance, Flight, Creation,*

Feminist Enactments of French Philosophy (Cornell University Press), *Feminist Interpretations of Merleau-Ponty* (with Gail Weiss, Penn State University Press), *The Universal (In the Realm of the Sensible)* (Columbia University Press), and *Postmodern Philosophy and the Scientific Turn* (University of Indiana Press).

Dr. Bernhard Pörksen is a professor of media studies at the Eberhard Karls Universität Tübingen. He has published in this area and on cybernetics and constructivism. Among his works are interviews with Heinz von Foerster, *Understanding Systems: Conversations on Epistemology and Ethics* (Springer) and Humberto Maturana, *From Being to Doing* (Carl Auer International); both volumes have been translated into various languages.

Dr. David Pouvreau is a historian of science, a professor of mathematics, and a member of the Bertalanffy Center for the Study of Systems Science (B.C.S.S.S.), Vienna, Austria. Among his numerous publications on Ludwig von Bertalanffy are "On the History of Ludwig von Bertalanffy's General Systemology, and on Its Relationship to Cybernetics" with M. Drack (*International Journal of Systems Science*) and "On the Making of a System Theory of Life: Paul A. Weiss and Ludwig von Bertalanffy's Conceptual Connection" (*Quarterly Review of Biology*). He is also the author of *The Dialectic Tragedy of the Concept of Wholeness Wholeness—Ludvig von Bertalanffy's Biography Revisited: Exploring Unity Through Diversity* (ISCE Publishing).

Dr. Walter Reese-Schäfer is a professor of political theory and the history of ideas at the Georg-August-Universität Göttingen. He has written seventeen books and more than a hundred articles, covering a truly expansive range of thinkers and ideas. His books include a series of the most influential German-language introductions to important thinkers in the history of ideas and in present continental philosophy and sociology. The introductions are to Plato and to Aristotle (both with Nordhausen Verlag), as well as to Richard Rorty, Jürgen Habermas, Karl-Otto Apel, Amitai Etzioni, Lyotard, and Niklas Luhmann (all with Junius Verlag).

Dr. Raphael Sassower is professor of philosophy at the University of Colorado, Colorado Springs. He has authored more than a dozen books, including *Cultural Collusions: Postmodern Technoscience* (Routledge), *Confronting Disaster: An Existential Approach to Technoscience* (Roman & Littlefield), *Popper's Legacy: Rethinking Politics, Economics and Science* (McGill-Queens University Press), and *Digital Exposure: Postmodern Postcapitalism* (Palgrave).

Dr. Philipp Schweighauser is an associate professor of American and general literature at the Universität Basel. He has also held positions at the University of California–Irvine, University of Berne, and University of Göttingen. He is the author of *The Noises of American Literature, 1890–1985: Toward a History of Literary Acoustics* (University Press of Florida) and has published widely on eighteenth- to twentieth-century American literature and culture; literature and science; literary, cultural, and media theory; soundscape studies; life writing; and aesthetics.

Index